DATE			

Perceptual Development in Early Infancy: Problems and Issues

PERCEPTUAL DEVELOPMENT IN EARLY INFANCY: Problems and Issues

Edited by

BERYL E. MCKENZIE
La Trobe University

ROSS H. DAY
Monash University

LEA
1987
LAWRENCE ERLBAUM ASSOCIATES, PUBLISHERS
Hillsdale, New Jersey
London

603 63337

Lawrence Erlbaum Associates, Inc., Publishers
365 Broadway
Hillsdale, New Jersey 07642

Library of Congress Cataloging in Publication Data

Perceptual development in early infancy.

(Child psychology)
Includes bibliographies and indexes.
1. Perception in infants.   I. McKenzie, Beryl E.
II. Day, R. H. (Ross Henry), 1927–   . III. Series.
[DNLM: 1. Child Development.   2. Perception—in infancy &
childhood.   WS 105.5.D2 P428]
BF720.P47P47   1987   155.4'22   87-6811
ISBN 0-89859-943-1

Printed in the United States of America
10 9 8 7 6 5 4 3 2 1

iv

Contents

List of Contributors

Denis Burnham Department of Psychology, University of New South Wales, Kensington, New South Wales 2033, Australia.

Michael Cook Department of Psychology, Australian National University, Canberra, Australian Capital Territory 2600, Australia.

Boris Crassini Department of Psychology, University of Queensland, St. Lucia, Queensland 4067, Australia.

Ross Day Department of Psychology, Monash University, Clayton, Victoria 3168, Australia.

Lynda Earnshaw Department of Psychology, University of New South Wales, Kensington, New South Wales 2033, Australia.

Jeff Field Department of Psychology, The University of Auckland, Private Bag, Auckland, New Zealand.

David Finlay Department of Psychology, The University of Newcastle, Newcastle, New South Wales 2308, Australia.

Algis Ivinskis Department of Psychology, The University of Newcastle, Newcastle, New South Wales 2308, Australia.

Beryl McKenzie Department of Psychology, La Trobe University, Bundoora, Victoria 3083, Australia.

Ray Over Department of Psychology, La Trobe University, Bundoora, Victoria 3083, Australia.

Maria Quinn Department of Psychology, University of New South Wales, Kensington, New South Wales 2033, Australia.

Sharne Rolfe Zikman Institute of Early Childhood Education, Post Office Box 210, Kew, Victoria 3101, Australia.

Preface

This book is not intended to be either a comprehensive reference work or a systematic handbook on perception in infancy. Nor is it another published report of a recently held conference. It is a collection of "state-of-the-art" essays on perception during the first year or so of infant development. Rather than first choosing the topics and then finding experts to write about them we first chose the experts and invited them to write about those topics in which we know them to be interested and closely involved. The outcome of this approach is a collection of chapters in which the authors at the same time critically review earlier contributions to the topic, report their own work, identify numerous unresolved problems and key issues, and point out directions for future inquiry. Naturally the emphasis placed on these facets varies markedly with both topic and author. The result is a collection of commentaries that we believe to be comprehensive, informative, interesting, and provocative.

The twelve chapters encompass a broad range of problems. The first three are grouped under the heading of History and Methods and are concerned with a number of theoretical and methodological issues, the history and evolution of some current problems, and a detailed examination of particular indices for studying attention in infancy. The second group is devoted entirely to the problem of object perception considered in terms of visual size constancy, form perception and shape constancy, localization in the spatially extended environment, and the role of movement in perceiving objects. Given that perception at maturity commonly involves more than one sensory channel the question arises as to when and how information from different channels is combined. The three chapters in the third section are concerned with this problem. The fourth section is given over entirely to the perception of speech in early infancy, and the last section to a comment on some emergent themes.

For what readership is the book intended? We have mainly in mind that the work will be of greatest interest to those actively involved in research on infant perception, to those who are less involved but interested in being brought up to date on what the current research issues are, and graduate students who are at the beginning of, some way through, or nearly finished a program of research on perception in infancy.

It will be immediately obvious to the reader that all the contributors work or have worked until recently in Australia. This should not be interpreted as an attempt to bring work on early perceptual development in Australia before a wider readership. The explanation is that both the authors and their contributions are well known to and respected by the two editors. It is not so much a case of better the devils we know as better the angels we know.

Finally, Dr Algis Ivinskis died in the early stages of preparation of this work. Nevertheless his contribution to Chapter 3 was profound.

B. E. McKenzie
La Trobe University
R. H. Day
Monash University.

Perceptual Development in Early Infancy: Problems and Issues

HISTORY AND METHODS

1

Problems and Issues in the Study of Perceptual Development in Infancy

B. E. McKenzie
La Trobe University

R. H. Day
Monash University

Evidence of the rapid and extensive growth of knowledge of early development is provided in the *Handbook of Child Psychology* (Mussen, 1983) where the largest of the four volumes is devoted to the period of infancy (Haith & Campos, 1983). This intense interest derives from the general aim of investigators to outline the sequence of steps by which infants reach maturity and from the more circumscribed aim of specifying capacities and processes at the initial phase of development. It may also be, as Spelke (1983) argues, that by studying infants we can peel away the layers of specialized notions that are gradually acquired and so reveal more clearly the initial core conceptions about the nature of the world that guide our interactions throughout life.

The purpose of this chapter is to provide a background for the research described later. In the area of early perceptual development, no less than in other areas of psychological enquiry, models of reality influence research findings in terms of methods of investigation, question selection, and interpretation of data. Because the habituation paradigm is a pivotal method that is frequently used to examine the capacities of infants, one objective of this chapter is to explore its logic and evaluate the validity of inferences deriving from it. Particular attention is directed towards the multistimulus habituation procedure which involves presentation of several different items in an acquisition or habituation phase prior to examining responsiveness to novel items in the test phase of an experiment. An important issue arising from studies using this method is whether a distinction can be made between perceptual and cognitive processing, and if so, to examine the consequences of such a distinction. Changes in the nature of questions that are asked about perceptual development are next discussed. Whereas early studies were concerned mainly with the simple presence or absence of perceptual capacities, more recent studies direct attention to the processes that underlie them. The final section is concerned with the types of stimulus patterns and objects that might best serve to illustrate the nature of early perception.

METHODS FOR STUDYING INFANT PERCEPTION

The study of the development of perceptual systems has many facets with questions posed at several levels. The biological limitations of sensory systems throughout development place constraints on the information that may be processed. The methods of psychophysics and psychophysiology have been applied to define these limitations. Such findings have been described in detail elsewhere (e.g., Werner & Lipsitt, 1981) and are not considered further except to note that development in the visual modality has been studied in more detail than development in the other senses. The meticulous studies of Teller, Peeples, and Sekel (1978), for instance, indicate that infant color space is most likely different from that of trichromatic adults. The many studies of developmental changes in the contrast sensitivity function (e.g., Adams & Maurer, 1984; Atkinson & Braddick, 1981; Dobson & Teller, 1978) alert us to physiological restrictions that are relevant to the perception of form (Banks & Salapatek, 1981; Banks, Stephens, & Hartman, 1985; Gayl, Roberts, & Werner, 1983). How these changing capacities direct experience in each developmental period for sensory systems other than vision is less well known.

Questions concerning the phenomenological and feature-detection or descriptive (Marr, 1982) aspects of perception have been studied mainly by examining either differential spontaneous behavior or by the use of some method of training. Many studies indicate the selectivity of visual, auditory, haptic, and gustatory exploration in young infants (Gibson & Spelke, 1983; Werner & Lipsitt, 1981). Paired presentation of visual stimulus patterns may reveal a tendency to look at one rather than the other, some objects are mouthed more than others and some substances yield avoidance behavior when tasted or smelled while others do not. Differential behaviors in these circumstances index perceptual discrimination that is immediate. In this sense it is spontaneous and its demonstration is not based on training procedures. A productive variation of this approach exploits the tendency of infants to prefer matched to unmatched stimulus input. Thus in visual search studies Spelke (1979) has shown that, from an early age, infants will look towards one of two films that matches a nondirectional auditory input rather than at one that does not (see also Kuhl & Meltzoff, 1984).

Procedures that involve some form of training frequently rely on the infant's ability to detect change. After a period of exposure to one form of stimulation, behavior to familiar and novel stimulus input is compared. The typical finding is greater responsiveness to novel stimulation. However, the theoretical bases for this behavior are not well understood. Reference usually is made to stimulus-model comparator theories in which repeated or prolonged exposure is thought to produce some internal representation of external events. Orienting to stimulus change occurs because the external events no longer match the neuronal or cognitive model. Prediction of those stimulus changes that will elicit maximum orienting depends on theoretical position (e.g., Hunt, 1970; McCall & McGhee, 1977; Reznick & Kagan, 1983; Sokolov, 1963). Given the predominance of stimulus-model comparator theories and the general expectation of increased orienting to novel stimulation, it is disturbing that, with what appear to be basically similar procedures, increased attention to familiar stimulation sometimes occurs. For instance, Meltzoff and Borton (1979) found that infants at 4-weeks-of-age looked longer at an object that corresponded in shape to one that had been made haptically familiar by mouthing. That is to say, they oriented more to the familiar than the novel object. Theoretical clarification is needed concerning specification of the conditions under which greater responsiveness to novel or familiar, and matching or mismatching stimulation might be predicted. Some promising beginnings in this respect are emerging (e.g., Hunter, Ames, & Koopman, 1983; Reznick & Kagan, 1983; Rolfe-Zikman, Chapter 9). Whether novelty and, presumably, familiarity preference is exhibited depends intimately on the age of the subjects, the type of stimulus, procedural variables, and the response measure.

The Habituation-Discrimination Paradigm

A method that has been commonly used to specify the capacity of infants to distinguish between stimuli is that of habituation. The logic of this paradigm is similar to that of novelty preference but, rather than exposing the stimulus object or event for a fixed interval, stimulation is continued until a criterion of response decrement is attained. Following habituation to the one stimulus, generalization of habituation is predicted in the test phase to the same stimulus but not to another that is discriminably different. When response recovery to the latter occurs, it is concluded that the habituation stimulus is both recognized and distinguished from the comparison stimulus. In the absence of response recovery, however, it is not possible to conclude that the stimuli are not distinguished since memory for the habituation stimulus and preference for the comparison stimulus are confounded. As Sophian (1980) has observed, this confounding creates problems not only for the interpretation of null results, but also for the interpretation of age and condition comparisons even when reliable differences are obtained. If the experimental aim is simply to specify the presence of discrimination, this paradigm is relatively sensitive and flexible. However, specification of the aspects of the stimulus to which the infant is responding is more complex since it might involve the experimenter-defined stimulus, some particular aspect of it, or of the experimental situation as a whole. Nevertheless, it is clear that familiarization and habituation procedures reveal discrimination and recognition memory when spontaneous preferences are not evident.

Interpretation of visual habituation in terms of sensory adaptation can readily be discounted even for newborns. It has been observed that newborns habituated while viewing with one eye exhibit novelty preference when tested with the other (Slater, Morison, & Rose, 1983). Dannemiller and Banks (1983) suggest the possibility that visual habituation in infants less than about 4-months-of-age may be explained in terms not of retinal adaptation but of adaptation of feature-selective cortical neurons. This suggestion is not strongly supported. (For discussion of this argument see Slater & Morison, 1985; Dannemiller & Banks, 1986.) Further evidence against a sensory explanation of habituation derives from a variant of the paradigm—the multistimulus habituation procedure.

The Multistimulus Habituation Procedure

Infants are first made familiar with a range of stimuli from the same "conceptual" category before being tested with novel stimuli that either do or do not belong to it. The inference that infants perceive similarity between category members—an equivalence class—and recognize new instances of the category, is based on the demonstration of greater responsiveness to noncategory members and generalized habituation to new instances of the category. For this inference to be valid it needs to be established that the differences between stimuli are discriminable, i.e., that generalization is something other than sensory immaturity, and that the test stimuli, both category and noncategory members, have similar interest value for naive infants who have not undergone habituation. In this way it can be shown that infants have detected some similarity between different category members and differentiated these from stimulus items that do not share these properties.

Without an ability to apprehend equivalence in environmental stimulation, the task of abstracting object characteristics would be one of acquiring an infinite number of associations between sensory inputs. Although the human infant from birth (Little, Lipsitt, & Rovee-Collier, 1984) and possibly prior to birth (see Kolata, 1984) is well equipped to form such associations, it is clear that some properties of objects and events are recognized with minimal dependence on experience.

Using a multiple familiarization procedure, Bomba (1984) studied the formation and development of categorization of the orientation of grating patterns in infants aged from 2- to 4-months. When presented with a vertical (0°) and an oblique (45°) pattern following familiarization with patterns of intermediate slant, 4-month-old infants generalized habituation to the oblique but not to the vertical pattern. Greater attention to the vertical grating was found over a wide range of familiarization obliques, 14.5° to 45°, suggesting a process of categorization rather than stimulus generalization. In the absence of familiarization, there was no preference for vertical over oblique gratings. Thus oblique gratings were perceived as similar and different from vertical gratings well before acquisition of the linguistic terms that describe them. The perceptual boundary between them was at about 8°. Categorization could not be attributed to lack of discrimination because infants at this age were equally able to distinguish between- and within-category samples. Since, even at 2 months, novelty preferences were more reliable when vertical rather than oblique patterns were familiar, Bomba (1984) suggested the possibility that the human infant is born with a perceptual system that makes it easy to discriminate any variation from the vertical. Discriminations between obliques are more difficult and the development of an oblique category is more gradual. It is possible that the existence of a unique percept of ''vertical'' serves as a reference point around which the categories of orientation develop—a kind of natural category (Rosch, 1973). These findings have implications for theories of categorization and may represent an instance of one of the initial ''core conceptions'' that shape later development.

The multiple habituation technique has been used to examine categorization in such diverse areas as speech perception (Kuhl, 1983), face perception (Strauss, 1979), form perception (Bomba & Siqueland, 1983; Ruff, 1982), perception of hue (Bornstein, 1981), and perception of numerosity (Strauss & Curtis, 1984). These studies have demonstrated that infants at an early age abstract information about similarities of objects and events after exposure to a range of exemplars. The processes and abilities necessary for the formation of equivalence classes appear to be inherent aspects of the human information processing system.

It is of interest to establish the extent to which various types of information are categorized, to examine the timetable and sequence of categorization, and to compare the nature of the categories at different ages with that of adults. Bomba and Siqueland (1983) have begun a program of this kind to study two-dimensional form perception. Infants at 3- to 4-months-of-age, like adults, appear to recognize an unseen prototype of a category. When presented with various distortions of a triangular form, for instance, they recognize a regular triangle as the *best* example of the triangle category. This prototype effect, in infants as in adults, is increased both by delay procedures and by increasing the number of exemplars in the familiarization phase. These findings have interesting implications for memory as well as perceptual processing. Superior recognition of a prototype after delay may be produced by faster decay of the specific information pertaining to particular members than of general information that is relevant to the category as a whole.

Interpretation of multiple habituation data.   If we are to distinguish features of the environment to which infants exhibit a natural competence (e.g., orientation, number, color, speech sounds) it needs to be established that the ability is determined solely on the basis of the invariant feature and not on any other correlated attribute. For example, in studies of the perception of numerosity, factors such as configuration, brightness, density, and figural area need to be controlled. Strauss and Curtis (1984) conclude that the ability of infants from about the age of 5 months to detect the numerosity of small numbers of items in an array is well established, but that the process by which this is accomplished is as yet not clear. Is numerosity perceived in the same way as color or form? That infants generalize habituation to a novel instance of "twoness" and not to an instance of "threeness" and vice versa suggests discrimination of numerosity but does not mean that infants can count, that the abstract notion of "two" is immediately perceived, or that "three" is conceived as greater than "two." The early sensitivity to numerosity that is displayed in multiple habituation studies does not necessarily imply notions of ordinality, cardinality, counting, and other features that are associated with the mature number concept. In studies of this kind any given set of habituation events may be categorized in more than one way; it is important to recognize that the equivalence detected by the infant may not correspond to that defined by the experimenter.

Whether categorization is demonstrable at all depends on a complex set of factors including the characteristics of the infant, the stimulus set, and the experimental procedure. Procedural variables include the mode of stimulus presentation (paired or single), the number of trials in habituation, and the nature of the dependent variable (e.g., duration of looking, vacillation in looking between stimuli, heart rate). Stimulus-set variables include the size of the acquisition set in the habituation phase, the discriminability of the relevant dimension of the category, and the degree of discrepancy between the test and the acquisition set. Individual-difference variables have not yet been explored in any depth. There are however indications that the multistimuli habituation paradigm may be developed to serve a valuable clinical function. Caron and Caron (1981) have shown that the categorization of pre- and postmature infants may be distinguished from that of full-term infants of the same conceptional age. The substantial correlation between performance on tasks of this kind and later scores on standard tests of intellectual competence (Bornstein, 1985; Fagan & McGrath, 1981) suggests that such measures may be sensitive indices for use in early developmental assessment. This aspect of individual differences is discussed further in the final chapter.

CONCEPTUAL OR PERCEPTUAL PROCESSING?

Gibson and Spelke (1983) argue that perception is an active, purposive and meaningful process. Infants actively search for information about the invariant relationships between objects and their affordances, i.e., the possibilities for action that are offered by objects, events, and places. Rather than abstracting a rule that specifies the common attributes shared by members of a category, or judging the similarity of novel items to a prototype or ideal example, Gibson and Spelke suggest that no special act of categorization is required. What is required is the extraction of invariance over transforming events, as, for example, the detection of the size, shape, and rigidity of objects. It is argued that the end product is not "the construction of a category representation in the mind, but the perception of an affordance of the world" (Gibson & Spelke, 1983, p.57). Does the detection of shape, rigidity, verticality, or triangularity represent the formation of a concept or a percept? In opposition to information processing and traditional learning theories, Gibson and Spelke suggest that there is a continuity between perception and cognition and that meaningful groupings of objects and events reflect the order that exists in the real world. Through active and purposive experience the developing child detects the possibilities for action—the affordances—that different objects share without the need to perform a special act of categorization.

In an elegant study Warren (1984) has demonstrated how this Gibsonian concept of affordance may be operationalized and put to practical use. He examined the instance of stair climbing in adult subjects. The affordance of stairs for climbing was specified on the basis of a biomechanical model using the variables of step height and leg length. Subjects' perception of the boundary between climbable and unclimbable stairs correspond closely with the critical step height predicted by the model. As well, on the basis of visual information only, the preferred step height was similar to the height that involved minimal energy expenditure during climbing. Warren takes the view that perceptual categories (climbable/unclimbable) have a natural basis in animal-environment systems. There appears to be an intrinsic or body-scaled metric for the analysis of visual information relevant to the control of the activity of stairclimbing. Like Gibson and Spelke (1983), Warren also argues that it may not be necessary to appeal to mediating constructs such as mental categories or concepts since many boundaries may be perceptual in origin. The main contribution of this research is the independent specification of the affordance—the combination of environmental properties that support the activity of climbing stairs. While visual information seems sufficient for adult observers to perceive the critical and optimal points of affordances, it is of interest to ask what type of experience is necessary for the development of such perceptions. Does the child who has just achieved bipedal locomotion detect the environmental property that is energetically optimal? Does visual information provide an adequate basis for categorization of activities into those that are and those that are not supported by the nature of the environment?

The multistimuli habituation procedure has been used to study perceptual constancies such as size and shape. This work is described in detail in Part II of this volume (see Chapters 4 and 5). Infants have been shown to respond to the objective size and shape of objects by generalization of habituation to an object of the same size at a novel distance and to an object of the same shape in a novel orientation. In these instances objects sharing the *same* distal characteristics are perceived as similar despite variation in proximal stimulation and distinguished from objects that do not share these distal features. That is, a single object feature is recognized as being preserved across various transformations. This may be distinguished from categorization where objects and events are seen as separate and different but treated as equivalent according to some criterion. Individual identity, i.e., the perceived equivalence of variations of a single unit, may not involve the same kind of processing as the perceived equivalence of several units, i.e., category identity (Vurpillot, 1982). Categorization of faces, numerosity, and various intermodal equivalences such as matching the number and type of sounds to the number of visual items (Starkey & Cooper, 1980; Wagner, Winner, Cicchetti, & Gardner, 1981) may be more a conceptual process than categorization of the one sound across different voice qualities and pitch contours, or categorization of one object's shape or size across its various transformations. Whereas the latter instances involve properties that are attached to a single object or event, the former involve one property that is held in common by several objects or events. As Kuhl (1983) has observed, infants must solve the problem of categorization of speech sounds in order to produce speech. The suggestion that this phonetic categorization depends upon specialized speech processing mechanisms is weakened by the demonstration of similar categorization for non-speech sounds (Endman, 1984; see also Chapter 11).

Nevertheless the perception of some categories appears to be immediate and minimally dependent on experience (e.g., vertical-nonvertical) while others seem to require greater exposure to a range of exemplars before their similarity is detected (e.g., obliques). Specification of the various types of categories is a challenging task awaiting clarification.

The development of methods for examining the formation of equivalence classes—generalization of habituation, of familiarization and transfer of learned responses—permits examination of these issues. It is certainly clear that there is an early recognition of similarities and regularities in stimulation. This may be regarded as a foundation of cognitive and perceptual activity.

THE SELECTION OF PROBLEMS TO BE INVESTIGATED

It is perhaps not surprising that conceptualization of issues in perceptual development parallels changes that have occurred in methodology. The sophistication of a range of experimental paradigms specifically adapted to the preverbal, premobile infant allows examination of a wide variety of questions. Whereas early investigators were content to establish the existence of discriminative capacities (e.g., Can one form or color be distinguished from another?) or whether or not behavior was consistent with perception of constancy of size or form, attention is now directed towards specifying the kinds of abilities and processes that underlie these capacities and their limitations.

A striking example is provided by the work of Spelke and her colleagues (Kellman, Gleitman, & Spelke, unpublished; Kellman & Spelke, 1983) who are concerned with the infant's unlearned conceptions of the nature of the physical world and the relevance of these conceptions to adult modes of thinking. Spelke (1983) argues that the development of knowledge is a process of growth around a core of unchanging conceptions. Studies of infants' notions of the world can reveal "the conceptions that we hold most strongly, that we share with all other people, and that we may be bound to hold whatever our experience, as long as the world permits us to develop any conceptions at all" (p.29). This view is inconsistent with both Piagetian and Gestalt theory and more akin to the notions of Chomsky in the field of language acquisition. On the basis of studies dealing with the perception of objects that are partly occluded, that are adjacent to or behind other objects, that move or are stationary and that take part in possible or impossible events (created by manipulation of mirror images), Spelke concludes that core conceptions (at least at 5-months-of-age) include the notions that an object persists even when totally occluded, that its presence constrains the movement of other objects, and that it cannot disappear without moving on an uninterrupted path. These conclusions are certainly in marked contrast to those of the many studies in the Piagetian tradition that are concerned with the growth of the object concept. Like Spelke (1983), Bjork and Cummings (1984) also conclude that factors associated with the nature of the typical Piagetian search task may account for the seeming inconsistencies with regard to early conceptions of the nature of objects and events.

In studies concerned with the factors that determine whether infants perceive a partially hidden object as a single complete unit with a continuous boundary, Kellman and Spelke (1983), using an habituation paradigm, observed that infants at 4-months-of-age perceived a partially hidden object to be complete provided the object moved laterally behind a stationary occluder. On test trials without the occluder, dishabituation was much greater to an incomplete than to a complete object. Young infants, prior to extensive perceptual experience and self-induced movements, inferred the complete form of objects that were only partially visible. This ability was not evident when the object was stationary, when the object and occluder moved together or when the visible parts of the occluded object moved separately in a manner inconsistent with that of a single rigid object.

In a more recent study (Kellman et al., unpublished) the question was posed as to whether this perception of object unity depended on the actual motion of the partially hidden object or whether retinal motion by itself was sufficient. Behavior was compared when objects were stationary or moving and when infants were stationary or moving. The complete object was perceived only when the object itself moved, irrespective of movement of the observer. When the occluded object moved so as to maintain a constant relationship with the moving observer (i.e., there was no retinal displacement), discrimination of the complete from the incomplete object was equal to that resulting from a stationary observer and a moving object. Behavior was quite different when the observer was moved around the stationary display. This pattern of results implies that infants at 4-months-of-age can detect constancy of position of the object, considerably earlier than that described in the studies discussed in Chapter 7. This demonstration of the ability of infants to distinguish information resulting from self-movement from that provided by moving objects when they are stationary observers is an interesting confirmation of the capacity to detect invariance under conditions of optical change, in this case, the invariance of object position.

THE APPROPRIATENESS OF STIMULUS VARIABLES

While early studies of perceptual development in infancy used mainly two-dimensional static displays, there are now many that capitalize on the attention that is consequent upon stimulation provided by moving solid objects. The visual system has a remarkable capacity for detecting the three-dimensional form of moving objects even when they are unfamiliar. Of course, the young infant's commerce with the environment is mostly with objects, people, and events and not with two-dimensional representations. Slater, Rose, and Morison (1984) found that the differences between objects and their two-dimensional representations were more detectable than their similarities and they concluded that the potential for perceptual processing by newborns and possibly older infants could not be fully explored by using only two-dimensional stimulation.

Gibson (1966) and Johansson (1978) emphasize that the visual system uses continuous transformations in the optic array to abstract the critical relationships that specify the three-dimensional spatial characteristics of objects and surfaces. In a developmental study within this theoretical perspective Granrud, Yonas, Smith, Arterberry, Glicksman, and Sorkness (1984) found that 5- and 7-month-old infants reached for the apparently nearer of two surfaces on the basis of information provided by accretion and deletion of texture. Just as with adults, displays consisting of moving dots of lights were indicative of the presence of an edge and of the relative distances of two surfaces. Also in the Gibsonian tradition, Ruff (1982) found evidence that detection of some object features could better be demonstrated with moving than with stationary stimulus objects. These findings are discussed more fully in Chapter 7.

A further issue that merits consideration is the significance of stimuli for infant behavior. It may well be that some features of perceptual processing have evolved because of their relevance for human survival irrespective of cultural variation. Because human infants depend on caretaking by adults for a relatively long period, sensitivity to social signals is a major biological advantage. People play a very special role in the world of infants. Thus it is possible to elicit orienting to the sound of the human voice more readily than to white noise and the human face is more interesting to infants than simple geometric patterns (De

Casper & Fifer, 1980; Fantz, 1966). Johansson (1973) suggests that there may be innate decoding principles that determine the perception of a person from inherently ambiguous moving point light displays.

With regard to the problem of infant memory, it is important to consider its function for the organism. It seems paradoxical that most studies concerned with early memory have used a novelty detection paradigm where memory for a stimulus is inferred indirectly from the lack of attention given to it. It has been argued that novelty detection serves primarily as a vigilance function for organisms alerting them to changes in stimulation, whereas learned associations serve the function of predicting the relationship between responses and their consequences. Direct measures of retention are possible when conditioning procedures are employed. Rovee-Collier and her coworkers (Rovee-Collier, Sullivan, Enright, Lucas, & Fagen, 1980) used these to study the effect of reactivation—a brief exposure to the reinforcer 24 hours before retention testing—on retention in 3-month-old infants. They suggested that reactivation is a mechanism by which early experience may affect later behavior over long intervals. With a procedure analogous to that of cued recall they found that an encounter with the original training situation that, by itself, was not sufficient to establish new learning, alleviated forgetting over a 4-week interval. Moreover the response function after reactivation was similar to that after original training. These findings demonstrate that estimates of memory capacity may vary with the procedure that is used to index it. Where the behavior has functional significance for the organism and direct measurement of retention is possible, retention of learned associations over quite lengthy intervals is found. What appear to be memory deficits when using habituation or other procedures may better be considered as retrieval failures.

It seems evident that findings from habituation tasks that indicate recognition memory in infants need to be complemented by studies using other methods. Associative memory may be assessed by conditioning procedures, and recall rather than recognition memory may be demonstrated in deferred imitation when the subject recreates an absent event.

CONCLUSION

The astonishing advance in knowledge of perceptual processing in the infancy period is a consequence of increasing methodological and theoretical sophistication. There is at the same time an awareness of the limitations and ambiguities associated with various paradigms. The index of duration of fixation has carried a heavy burden with regard to the interpretation of much infant behavior. Duration of fixation, by itself, does not indicate what has been learned or how much has been learned and looks of equal duration do not necessarily imply lack of discrimination or similarity in what has been learned. Systematic manipulation of the stimulus conditions and experimental procedures leads to a more firmly founded knowledge base. Attention devoted to processes and to stimulus relevance is likely to result in a more complete understanding of early capacities and the possibility of greater theoretical integration.

Some emphasis in this review has been given to the search for core conceptions or universal aspects of early perception. In other sciences a distinction has been drawn between the degree of generalizability of a knowledge claim—a continuous concept—and universal versus specific knowledge claims (Van de Vijver & Poortinga, 1982). Because it seems reasonable to expect that most perceptual processes will be neither completely universal nor specific to particular conditions, the approach developed by Cronbach and his coworkers (Cronbach, Gleser, Nanda, & Rajaratnam, 1972) in which generalizability coefficients are estimated for different sources (e.g., particular stimulus variables, tasks, or subject groups) may well be fruitful. The definitional and methodological problems associated with the empirical demonstration of universal statements led to the development of generalizability theory. Application of this theory allows the degree of generalizability of statements to be approximated. We know of no studies of early perceptual processing that have applied this theory to evaluate cross-cultural or other subject group differences or similarities. Possible areas that could be examined in this way include cross-cultural studies of perception of hue (Bornstein, 1981), cross-cultural studies of babbling (de Boysson-Bardies, Sagart, & Durand, 1984), perception of speech sounds (Streeter, 1976) and of early cognitive processing (Kagan & Klein, 1973).

One of the most notable features that is painfully obvious to investigators of the infancy period is the degree of intersubject variability. These differences are frequently regarded as an impediment to the formulation of general principles. Rather than hindering the progress of knowledge of general principles of perceptual development, these differences may serve as pointers for the conditionalizing of knowledge claims. The explicit statement of the scope conditions under which a statement is thought to apply should serve to advance understanding in particular domains. For example, the statement that the degree of size constancy exhibited by children improves with age may be true for those subjects who are able to understand verbal instructions (see Chapter 4). It is possible to retain an agnostic position with regard to the relationship between degree of size constancy and age in preverbal subjects. Comparability of findings in different areas could be facilitated if investigators stated more explicitly the boundary conditions under which a predicted effect is thought to hold. The boundary conditions for expectation of novelty or familiarity preference or for imitation in newborns (see Chapter 10), for instance, are not yet clear.

As Cohen (1980) has observed, formulating scope conditions entails practical as well as scientific consequences. The general conclusion that early educational programs for the disadvantaged do not affect later scholastic achievement might have led to quite different consequences had the scope conditions under which the claim is and is not applicable been specified.

From this brief review it is evident that theoretical and methodological issues are closely related. We have attempted to show this interrelationship in terms of question selection, methods of investigation and interpretation of data. The issues of theoretical implications, emphasis on process rather than product, and individual differences are further discussed in our concluding commentary.

REFERENCES

Adams, R. J., & Maurer, D. (1984). Detection of contrast by the newborn and 2-month-old infant. *Infant Behavior and Development, 7*, 415–422.

Atkinson, J., & Braddick, O. (1981). Acuity, contrast sensitivity and accommodation in infancy. In R. N. Aslin, J. R. Alberts, & M. R. Petersen (Eds.), *Development of perception Vol. 2 The visual system*. Orlando, FL: Academic Press.

Banks, M. S., & Salapatek, P. (1981). Infant pattern vision: A new approach based on the contrast sensitivity function. *Journal of Experimental Child Psychology, 31*, 1–45.

Banks, M. S., Stephens, B. R., & Hartmann, E. E. (1985). The development of basic mechanisms of pattern vision: Spatial frequency channels. *Journal of Experimental Child Psychology, 40*, 501–527.

Bjork, E. S., & Cummings, E. M. (1984). Infant search errors: Stage of concept development or stage of memory development. *Memory and cognition, 12*, 1–19.

Bomba, P. C. (1984). The development of orientation categories between 2 and 4 months of age. *Journal of Experimental Child Psychology, 37*, 609–636.

Bomba, P. C., & Siqueland, E. R. (1983). The nature and structure of infant form categories. *Journal of Experimental Child Psychology, 35*, 294–328.

Bornstein, M. H. (1981). Psychological studies of color perception in human infants: Habituation, discrimination and categorization, recognition and conceptualization. In L. P. Lipsitt & C. K. Rovee-Collier (Eds.), *Advances in infancy research*. Norwood, NJ: Ablex.

Bornstein, M. H. (1985). Habituation of attention as a measure of visual information processing in human infants: Summary, systematization, and synthesis. In G. Gottlieb & N. A. Krasnegor (Eds.), *Measurement of audition and vision in the first year of post natal life: A methodological overview*. Norwood, NJ: Ablex.

Caron, A., & Caron, R. (1981). Processing of relational information as an index of infant risk. In S. L. Friedman & M. Sigman (Eds.), *Preterm birth and psychological development*. Orlando, FL: Academic Press.

Cohen, B. P. (1980). The conditional nature of scientific knowledge. In L. J. Freese (Ed.), *Theoretical methods in sociology*. Pennsylvania: University of Pittsburgh Press.

Cronbach, L. J., Gleser, G. C., Nanda, H., & Rajaratnam, N. (1972). *The dependability of behavioral measurements*. New York: Wiley.

Dannemiller, J. L., & Banks, M. S. (1983) Can selective adaptation account for early infant habituation? *Merrill Palmer Quarterly, 29*, 151–158.

Dannemiller, J. L., & Banks, M. S. (1986). Testing models of early infant habituation: A reply to Slater and Morison. *Merrill-Palmer Quarterly, 32*, 87–91.

de Boysson-Bardies, B., Sagart, L., & Durand, C. (1984). Discernible differences in the babbling of infants according to target language. *Journal of Child Language, 11*, 1–15.

De Casper, A. J., & Fifer, W. P. (1980). Of human bonding: Newborns prefer their mothers' voices. *Science, 208*, 1174–1176.

Dobson, V., & Teller, D. Y. (1978). Visual acuity in human infants: A review and comparison of behavioral and electrophysiological studies. *Vision Research, 18*, 1469–1483.

Endman, M. (1984, April). *Perceptual constancy for non-speech stimuli*. Paper presented at the International Conference on Infant Studies, New York.

Fagan, J. F., & McGrath, S. K. (1981). Infant recognition memory and later intelligence. *Intelligence, 5,* 121–130.

Fantz, R. L. (1966). Pattern discrimination and selective attention as determinants of perceptual development from birth. In A. H. Kidd & J. F. Rivoire (Eds.), *Perceptual development in children.* New York: International Universities Press.

Gayl, I. E., Roberts, J. O., & Werner, J. S. (1983). Linear systems analysis of infant visual pattern preferences. *Journal of Experimental Child Psychology, 35,* 30–45.

Gibson, E. J., & Spelke, E. S. (1983). The development of perception. In P. H. Mussen (Ed.), *Handbook of child psychology, Vol. 3.* J. H. Flavell & E. M. Markman (Eds.), Cognitive Development. New York: Wiley.

Gibson, J. J. (1966). *The senses considered as perceptual systems.* Boston: Houghton Mifflin.

Granrud, C. E., Yonas, A., Smith, I. M., Arterberry, M. E., Glicksman, M. L., & Sorkness, A. C. (1984). Infants' sensitivity to accretion and deletion of texture as information for depth at an edge. *Child Development, 55,* 1630–1636.

Haith, M., & Campos, J. (1983). Infancy and developmental psychobiology. In P. H. Mussen (Ed.), *Handbook of child psychology, Vol. 2.* New York: Wiley.

Hunt, J. McV. (1970). Attentional preference and experience: I. Introduction. *Journal of Genetic Psychology, 117,* 99–107.

Hunter, M. A., Ames, E. W., & Koopman, R. (1983). Effects of stimulus complexity and familiarization time on infant preferences for novel and familiar stimuli. *Developmental Psychology, 19,* 338–352.

Johansson, G. (1973). Visual perception of biological motion and a model for its analysis. *Perception and Psychophysics, 14,* 201–211.

Johansson, G. (1978). Visual event perception. In R. Held, H. W. Leibowitz, & H. L. Teuber (Eds.), *Handbook of Sensory Physiology, Vol. 8: Perception.* Berlin: Springer Verlag.

Kagan, J., & Klein, R. E. (1973). Cross-cultural perspectives on early development. *American Psychologist, 28,* 947–961.

Kellman, P. J., Gleitman, H., & Spelke, E. S. (unpublished). *Object and observer motion in the perception of objects by infants.*

Kellman, P. J., & Spelke, E. S. (1983). Perception of partly occluded objects in infancy. *Cognitive Psychology, 15,* 483–524.

Kolata, G. (1984). Studying learning in the womb. *Science, 225,* 302–303.

Kuhl, P. K. (1983). Perception of auditory equivalence classes for speech in early infancy. *Infant Behavior and Development, 6,* 263–286.

Kuhl, P. K., & Meltzoff, A. N. (1984). The intermodal representation of speech in infants. *Infant Behavior and Development, 7,* 361–381.

Little, A. H., Lipsitt, L. P., & Rovee-Collier, C. (1984). Classical conditioning and retention of the infant's eyelid response: Effects of age and interstimulus interval. *Journal of Experimental Child Psychology, 37,* 512–524.

Marr, D. (1982). *Vision: A computational investigation into the human representation and processing of visual information.* San Francisco: Freeman.

McCall, R. B., & McGhee, P. E. (1977). The discrepancy hypothesis of attention and affect in infants. In I. C. Uzgiris & F. Weizmann (Eds.), *The structuring of experience.* New York: Plenum Press.

Meltzoff, A. N., & Borton, R. W. (1979). Intermodal matching by human neonates. *Nature, 282,* 403–404.

Mussen, P.H. (Ed.). (1983). *Handbook of child psychology.* New York: Wiley.

Reznick, J. S., & Kagan, J. (1983). Category detection in infancy. In L. P. Lipsitt & C. K. Rovee-Collier (Eds.), *Advances in infancy research.* Norwood, NJ: Ablex.

Rosch, E. H. (1973). Natural categories. *Cognitive Psychology, 5,* 328–350.

Rovee-Collier, C., Sullivan, M. W., Enright, M., Lucas, D., & Fagen, J. W. (1980). Reactivation of infant memory. *Science, 208,* 1159–1161.

Ruff, H. (1982) Effect of object movement on infants' detection of object structure. *Developmental Psychology, 18,* 462–472.

Slater, A., & Morison, V. (1985). Selective adaptation cannot account for early infant habituation: A response to Dannemiller and Banks. *Merrill-Palmer Quarterly, 31,* 99–103.

Slater, A., Morison, V., & Rose, D. (1983). Locus of habituation in the human newborn. *Perception, 12,* 593–598.

Slater, A., Rose, D., & Morison, V. (1984). Newborn infants' perception of similarities and differences between two- and three-dimensional stimuli. *British Journal of Developmental Psychology, 2,* 287–294.

Sokolov, E. N. (1963). *Perception and the conditioned reflex.* New York: Macmillan.

Sophian, C. (1980). Habituation is not enough: Novelty preferences, search, and memory in infancy. *Merrill-Palmer Quarterly, 26,* 239–257.

Spelke, E. S. (1979). Perceiving bimodally specified events in infancy. *Developmental Psychology, 15,* 626–636.

Spelke, E. S. (1983). *Cognition in infancy.* Unpublished paper.

Starkey, P., & Cooper, R. S. (1980). Perception of numbers by human infants. *Science, 210,* 1033–1035.

Strauss, M. S. (1979). Abstraction of prototypical information by adults and 10-month-old infants. *Journal of Experimental Psychology: Human Learning and Memory, 5,* 618–632.

Strauss, M. S., & Curtis, L. E. (1984). Development of numerical concepts in infancy. In C. Sophian (Ed.), *The origins of cognitive skills.* Hillsdale, NJ: Lawrence Erlbaum Associates.

Streeter, L. A. (1976). Language perception of 2-month-old infants shows effects of both innate mechanisms and experience. *Nature, 259,* 39–41.

Teller, D. Y., Peeples, D. R., & Sekel, M. (1978). Discrimination of chromatic from white light by two-month-old human infants. *Vision Research, 18,* 41–48.

Van de Vijver, F. J. R., & Poortinga, Y. H. (1982). Cross-cultural generalization and universality. *Journal of Cross Cultural Psychology, 13,* 387–408.

Vurpillot, E. (1982). Perception and cognitive properties of the initial state. In J. Mehler, E. Walker, & M. Garrett (Eds.), *Perspectives in mental representation.* Hillsdale, NJ: Lawrence Erlbaum Associates.

Wagner, S., Winner, E., Cicchetti, D., & Gardner, H. (1981). 'Metaphorical' mapping in human infants. *Child Development, 52,* 728–731.

Warren, W. H. (1984). Perceiving affordances: Visual guidance of stair climbing. *Journal of Experimental Psychology: Human Perception and Performance, 10,* 683–703.

Werner, J. S., & Lipsitt, L. P. (1981). The infancy of human sensory systems. In E. S. Gollin (Ed.), *Developmental plasticity: Behavioral and biological aspects of variation in development.* Orlando, FL: Academic Press.

2
How to Know What Infants Know: Historical Notes on an Ever-Present Problem

Boris Crassini
University of Queensland

INTRODUCTION AND OVERVIEW

Intellectual curiosity by humans about how they perceive the world has a very long history. The origins of this interest in perception can be traced to the concern of the earliest philosophers with epistemological questions, i.e., questions about how humans acquire knowledge about the world (see Robinson, 1976). Throughout this long history, the most common conceptualization of perception has been one based on the proposition that perceiving the world is, in essence, a problem to be solved by the perceiver. This conceptualization endures in current discussions about the nature of perception (see Uttal, 1981), but is nowhere portrayed more graphically than in Plato's cave allegory used in *The Republic* (Bloom, 1968). Plato likened perceivers to prisoners bound by their necks and feet, and kept, since their early childhood, in a dimly lit cave. The prisoners had their backs to the cave entrance, and because of their bonds, were unable to turn around to look at the people and objects in the world outside the cave. Their only contact with the external world was an "indirect" contact; for example, through the shadows cast by the people and objects in the outside world onto the cave wall that the prisoners faced. The problem posed by Plato was how could the prisoners come to know about the world outside the cave.

The history of interest in perception has been characterized (e.g., by Uttal, 1981) as an ongoing debate between proponents of two contrasting answers to the problem of perception: Rationalism (in which stress is placed on the inadequate nature of sense data as a basis for perception), and empiricism (in which the assumption is made that sense data are the ultimate basis for perception). Plato's cave allegory was deliberately designed to emphasize the apparently

19

impoverished nature of sensory data available to the prisoners-perceivers (i.e., flickering shadows as visual sense data; reverberating sounds as auditory sense data). His rationalist solution to the problem of perception was to propose that sense data gave information only about the appearances of things, and that these appearances were fundamentally illusory. True knowledge required perceivers to use their powers of reason to supplement inadequate sense data.

Opposed to this rationalist, indirect account of perception is the empiricist account based on the proposition that sensory information is the sole and sufficient basis for knowing the world. Both accounts of perception are discussed more fully in the next section. However, it is within the framework of the ongoing argument between proponents of rationalism and empiricism that the investigation of perception in infancy has special relevance. The reason for this special relevance was expressed by John Locke in *An Essay Concerning Human Understanding* some 300 years ago:

> He that attentively considers the state of a child at his first coming into the world, will have little reason to think him stored with plenty of ideas that are to be the matter of his future knowledge. It is by degrees he comes to be furnished with them: . . . and, if it were worthwhile, no doubt a child might be so ordered as to have but a very few even of the ordinary ideas till he were grown up to a man . . . if a child were kept in a place where he never saw any other but black and white till he were a man, he would have no more ideas of scarlet or green than he from his childhood never tasted an oyster or a pineapple has of those particular relishes (Locke, 1690; cited in Burtt, 1939, p. 250).

If knowing the world involves a process of reason to supplement sense data (the rationalist position), it follows that this process must be available to the perceiver *prior* to sensory experience. That is, rationalist accounts of perception are necessarily nativist in nature. Conversely, if knowledge of the world is based solely on sensory experience, it follows that in the absence of such experience, knowledge of the world must be absent. It was on the basis of this argument that Locke made his two claims; first, that the investigation of the state of neonates, and second, that the investigation of the effects of sensory deprivation would, in both cases, provide clear support for his empiricist theory.

Although Locke's *Essay* was published in 1690, his suggestion, in effect, to begin an experimental developmental psychology did not prompt a flurry of studies of infancy or sensory deprivation. It took almost 40 years before William Cheselden (1728) published his report of the "restoration" of vision to a child born blind; almost 100 years before Dietrich Tiedemann (1787) published a diary of his son's early development; and almost 200 years before William Preyer (1882) published *The Mind of the Child* (taken by some historians of developmental psychology, e.g., Cairns, 1983, to mark the beginning of modern developmental psychology). Despite the long period of time between Locke's initial informal suggestion and the beginning of a formal developmental psychology, the rationale expressed by Locke for the study of human development was central to the first developmental investigations. Consider, for example, Sully's words in the Introduction to his *Studies of Childhood* (1896).

If, reflects the psychologist, he can only get at this baby's consciousness so as to understand what is passing there, he will be in an infinitely better position to find his way through the intricacies of the adult consciousness. . . . In this genetic tracing back of the complexities of man's mental life to their primitive elements in the child's consciousness, questions of peculiar interest will arise. A problem, which although having a venerable antiquity is still full of meaning, concerns the precise relation of the higher forms of intelligence and of sentiment to the elementary facts of the individual's life-experience. Are we to regard all our ideas, even those of God, as woven by the mind out of its experiences, as Locke thought, or have we certain "innate ideas" from the first? Locke thought he could settle this point by observing children. (pp. 7–8)

The influence of Locke's ideas was apparent also in the early studies of the effects of sensory deprivation on perceptual and other aspects of mental development. In 1728, for example, William Cheselden published his report describing the effects on a child's behavior of living for 14 years in the absence of normal visual experience and then having sight restored. Cheselden's description (discussed more fully later in this chapter) was couched in terms of the nativist-empiricist argument set out by Locke in his *Essay*. Locke's theoretical framework was reflected also in many of the other early descriptions of "restored vision" (see Preyer, 1889, for a review). In addition, this theoretical argument was apparent in the early reports of the so-called feral children (i.e., children abandoned in infancy and reared in the wild without human contact; see Zingg, 1940 for a review). Itard (1801, 1806), for example, is quite explicit in claiming that the case of the feral child known as the Wild Boy of Aveyron is an ideal test of the nativist-empiricist argument set out by Locke.

In the remainder of this chapter I want to discuss Locke's claim about the usefulness of studying the state of newborn infants, and the effects of sensory deprivation, in differentiating between empiricism and rationalism-nativism. My discussion focuses on some fundamental problems inherent in his claim, and in the investigation of infant development in general. It is based on studies of normal and abnormal human development published in the 18th and 19th centuries. My decision to discuss historical developmental literature should not be taken to suggest that these pioneering investigations of normal and abnormal development are curiosities reflecting the unsophisticated nature of early psychological studies. My purpose in discussing research material published in the 18th and 19th centuries is twofold: First, I want to provide an historical background (albeit a sketchy background) to current studies of infancy as represented in the experiments presented in subsequent chapters; second, I want to provide illustrations of the problems arising from Locke's claim (and the study of infants in general) to which I have alluded, and the early developmental research literature provides good illustrations of these problems. In addition, I want to suggest that these same problems have significant bearing on some of the current controversies in the developmental literature as addressed in the subsequent chapters.

What then is the nature of the problems raised by Locke's claims concerning the value of studying normal and abnormal human development? In essence, their nature lies in the very limited communication that is available between infant (as experimental subject) and investigator. Communication between subject and investigator facilitates the understanding of *both* parties (ideally, at least) about what is *expected* during the process of experimental investigation. Such communication was the cornerstone of Wundt's method of analytic introspection in the experimental study of human mind (e.g., see Wundt, 1907). In Wundt's method, subjects *observed* their own mental processes and communicated these observations to the investigator. Similar self-report plays an important role in modern cognitive psychology (Lachman, Lachman, & Butterfield, 1979). With infants, of course, such communication is absent, and alternative methods must be adopted to get access to "this baby's consciousness so as to understand what is passing there," as Sully (1896, p. 7) described the rationale of infant research. One alternative method is to observe the behavior of infants and draw inferences about neonatal mental abilities on the basis of the behavioral observations. This, in fact, was Locke's argument: The nature of human mind in the absence of experience could be inferred from the "attentive consideration" of the state of neonates.

However, given the inability of investigators of infants to instruct their subjects in specific procedures, tasks, etc., the limitations of this alternative method are clear. If the full behavioral repertoire of neonates is not sampled by the investigator, then any interpretations of, for example, the state of a child at its first coming into the world (to paraphrase Locke) must be biassed and inadequate. The inadequacy of interpretations of infant behavior in this situation is apparent even if the investigator adopts a purely inductivist approach to research (i.e., having no preconceived theories to guide data gathering). However, researchers seldom carry out research in this fashion (see Chalmers, 1982, for an informative tutorial in current issues in the philosophy of science). Research, in most cases, is guided by theories about what phenomena are likely to occur in particular settings. It was this *guiding* function of preconceived theory in research that was the basis of Wundt's complete rejection of the possibility of a science of the development of mind. He argued that since infants were unable to communicate the outcomes of their observations of their own mental processes (as adults and older children were able), inferences about neonatal mental abilities derived by scientists from observations of infant behaviour were, in fact, nonscientific. They were nonscientific because they were subjective, depending on the theoretical assumptions and biasses of the investigator making the observations and inferences. On this basis, Wundt (1907) concluded:

> During the early periods of the child's life experimental methods are hardly applicable at all. The results of experiments which have been tried on very young children must be regarded as purely chance results. (p. 336)

The flourishing growth of experimental developmental psychology over the last hundred years is clear indication that Wundt's proscription had little effect (see Borstlemann, 1983; Cairns, 1983). However, the fundamental basis for Wundt's rejection of an experimental developmental psychology cannot be ignored. This becomes clear when consideration is given to the processes by which theories of human development are *converted* into predictions about the behaviors and abilities of infants. Within the terms of Locke's empiricist vs. rationalist-nativist debate, difficulties arise when attempts are made to specify exactly what behaviors/abilities would be expected of "empiricist" newborns and "rationalist-nativist" newborns; or "empiricist" children reared in the absence of particular sensory experiences and "rationalist-nativist" children reared likewise. In the next section these difficulties are illustrated through descriptions of how the theoretical assumptions held by the earliest investigators of infancy were manifested in their interpretations of the infant behavior they observed. Before discussing these examples, however, it is necessary to outline the basic assumptions of rationalist-nativist and empiricist accounts of how knowledge of the world is acquired.

RATIONALISM-NATIVISM AND EMPIRICISM: IMPLICATIONS FOR THE STUDY OF NEONATES

The rationalist solution to the perceptual problem faced by Plato's prisoners in their cave is to posit an intermediate stage between the incoming sense data and the *emergence* of perception. In Plato's theory, this intermediate stage involved the intervention of ideal Forms that were entities existing eternally, and independently of any real form or any perceiver. The minds of all perceivers were said, by Plato, to be furnished innately with these ideal Forms, and knowledge was acquired through recollection of the Forms (see Cornford, 1935). The explicit dualism of Plato's theory (i.e., his belief in the separate existence of ideal Forms and real forms) is somewhat modified in more modern rationalist accounts of perception. Also somewhat modified in modern rationalist theories is the rather specific nature of innate knowledge in Plato's theory (e.g., his demonstration that a slave, despite lacking a formal education nevertheless, "knew" laws of geometry; see Plato's *Meno,* Jowett, 1953). However, "neorationalism" (as

Uttal, 1981, terms such accounts) is firmly based on the proposition so compellingly represented by Plato's cave allegory; namely that sense data are an inadequate bases for perception. Consider, for example, the visual sense data (proximal visual stimuli to use Hochberg's 1978 terminology) produced as an observer approaches an object. The size of the images of the object on the observer's retinae increases in an inverse ratio to the distance between object and perceiver, yet the object is commonly perceived as remaining constant in size. That is, there is a mismatch between the available sense data and perception, and this mismatch is resolved in neorationalist accounts because:

> Perception must be considered to be a process in which a mental representation of the external world is constructed, not solely as a direct and deterministic result of a simple aspect of an incoming stimulus, but rather as a result of complex symbolic interpretations, inferences, and integrations of a wide variety of currently arriving and previously stored patterns of information (Uttal, 1981, p. 5)

The "complex symbolic interpretations, inferences, and integrations" supplement the ambiguous proximal stimuli (e.g., the increasing size of the retinal image of an approaching object) enabling accurate perception to occur (i.e., the object, in the example above, is perceived as remaining a constant size).

The contrast between rationalist and empiricist approaches to perception is clear. The basic assumption of empiricism is that all knowledge about the world is derived *in the first place* from sensory experience. However, the assumption that sensory experience is the basis of perception does not imply that perception is *immediately* given by the senses. Locke, for example, proposed that activation of the separate sensory modalities produced modality-specific, simple ideas in the mind of the perceiver. Furthermore, simple ideas could be stored as memories, and could be formed into complex ideas through processes Locke termed reflection and association. The formation of these complex ideas took time and was contingent on the perceiver interacting with complex objects and events in the external environment. However, although reflection and association gave rise to complex ideas, these processes did not add to the information provided by the senses. This point is made nicely by Robinson (1976):

> Locke argues . . . the ideas resulting from perception are initially simple but, through associated experiences and memory, the simple ideas are combined to form complex ones. However, no matter how complex our ideas become, they remain rooted to the soil of experience and nurtured by the reflective faculty. (p. 211)

There is some debate in the philosophical literature about Locke's use of the term "idea." It has been suggested, for example, that Locke's concept of "idea" is little different from the concept of "mental representation of the external world" that is central to neorationalist accounts of perception (Uttal, 1981). In these terms, Locke's account is dualist in nature since he is said to assume the separate existence of the external world, and the ideas of that world in the mind of the perceiver. However, although Locke's explicitly stated concern was with human mind and its contents (i.e., ideas), he did not propose the existence of a special sort of substance, existing separately from the world, necessary for the genesis of ideas. For example, writing in the Introduction to his *Essay*, Locke stated:

> This, therefore, being my purpose, to inquire into the original, certainty, and extent of *human knowledge*, together with the grounds and degrees of *belief, opinion,* and *assent,* I shall not at present meddle with the physical consideration of the mind, or trouble myself to examine wherein its essence consists or by what motions of our spirits, or alterations of our bodies, we come to have any sensation by our organs, or any *ideas* in our understandings; and whether those ideas do, in their formation, any or all of them, depend on matter or not. (Locke, 1690; cited in Burtt, 1939, p. 244)

Locke's words suggest that while he discussed the contents of mind as though these contents were entities, he was agnostic with respect to the relationship between mind and body. In this respect, Locke's position regarding the mind-body issue may be characterized as the intellectual forerunner to the approach adopted by many modern cognitive psychologists, in particular those who use the functioning of computers as a metaphor for human cognitive functioning. Consider, for example, the similarity between Locke's statement about the physiological basis of mind and the argument of Pylyshyn (1980). Pylyshyn claims it is possible and appropriate to investigate human "software" (mental processes) to determine lawful relationships therein, independently of investigating human "hardware" (the nervous system), and to do this without assuming a form of dualism.

Resolution of arguments about Locke's use of the concept of "idea" is beyond the scope of this chapter. The issue is discussed in more detail in a collection of essays edited by Tipton (1977). However, irrespective of the ontological status given to Locke's "ideas," there is little doubt that Locke wrote, in his *Essay,* as if ideas were entities existing in a person's own mind and in the minds of other persons.

> I presume it will be easily granted me, that there are such *ideas* in men's minds. Everyone is conscious of them in himself; *and men's words and actions* (my italics) will satisfy him that they are in others." (Locke, 1690; cited in Burtt, 1939, p. 247)

Thus while Locke was not prepared to discuss the nature of the relationship between physiological activity and ideas, he nevertheless argued that the existence of ideas could be inferred from physiological activity of a sort (i.e., "men's words and actions"). In this sense, Locke adopted what Pylyshyn (1980) has termed the common-sense or folk-psychology approach of attributing human behavior to mental states, and consequently being able to infer mental states from observations of human behavior. It was on the basis of this assumption that Locke asserted:

> He that attentively considers the state of a child at his first coming into the world, will have little reason to think him stored with plenty of ideas that are to be the matter of his future knowledge. (Locke, 1690; cited in Burtt, 1939, p. 250)

I have already alluded to the problems inherent in Locke's claim. However, assuming for the present that it is appropriate to infer mental states from observations of "the state of a child at his first coming into the world," the question remains: Just what aspects of the infant's behavioral state (given that these are the only things that can be attentively observed) are to be used to infer the infant's mental state? Locke's assertion about the state of newborn humans did not relate to particular behaviors/ideas. Rather his assertion was based on the self-evident proposition that newborn humans are helpless and primitive organisms. Consider, for example, this rather poetic description of the helpless human neonate:

> What a difference there is between the little animal which walks as soon as it is born, knows how to find its mother, to run after its food, and to get itself out of trouble, and the poor little human being who can not do anything by himself, and would surely perish if its parents did not come to his aid! (Compayré, 1896, p. 51)

Not only were human neonates incapable of speech, they were incapable of many (all?) purposive behaviors (walking; finding their mother; running after food; etc.) performed by the young of other species. The absence of, or, at best, the extremely primitive nature of "words and actions" in human neonates was taken by Locke to be self-evident proof of empiricist philosophy.

I use the term "self-evident" deliberately since Locke did not present any formally collected data to support his assertion. As I indicated earlier, one of the first published reports of observations of infant behavior and development was that of Tiedemann (1787). Tiedemann's report was based on observations of, and experiments performed on, his son, over a period of about 3 years beginning from the time of his son's birth. Tiedemann's description was very comprehensive: In the introduction to his reprint of Tiedemann's report, Dennis (1972) says "Many aspects of child behaviour mentioned by Tiedemann have become areas of research for present-day workers. If one translates Tiedemann into current psychologese, he sounds most modern" (p. 11). However, of particular relevance to the present discussion are Tiedemann's generalizations about what may be termed the visual behavior of neonates, as well as his description of the visual behavior of his son.

> *It is a matter of common knowledge* (my italics) that children immediately after birth, and thereafter always upon waking, turn their eyes to the light, proof that

light makes upon them a pleasing impression (Tiedemann, 1787; cited in Dennis, 1972, p. 13). The eyes of my son were now moved in all directions, not unsteadily, but from the first *as though they were in search of objects,* (my italics) and they rested first upon moving objects. And indeed all moving objects, because they produce in us constant variation and modification, attract our senses, so that *merely sensuous persons* (my italics) find therein the greatest entertainment. (Tiedemann, 1787; cited in Dennis, 1972, p. 14)

According to Tiedemann, infants are able ''from the first'' to look at particular objects (i.e., lights; things in motion) in preference to other objects. This rather flattering characterization of the visual abilities of infants seems inconsistent with an empiricist theory of perception in that infants are described as being innately able to demonstrate visual preferences. Yet Tiedemann did not hold a rationalist-nativist philosophy as he makes explicit in the opening words of his report:

The fact that experience and practice teach us to use our senses and perceive correctly has been proved by Cheselden's blind man: observations on persons who were found in forests, speechless, reared by animals, have shown that the mental faculties develop slowly, successively, and confusedly (Tiedemann, 1787; cited in Dennis, 1972, p. 13).

Further evidence of Tiedemann's empiricism is found in his description of the development of infants' ability to perceive stationary (as distinct from moving) objects (indeed the words could have been written by Locke):

Before reflection and contemplation, through inward autonomous motion, have found occupation also with inert objects, these are little observed; therefore such things as are in motion must primarily attract the childish mind (Tiedemann, 1787; cited in Dennis, 1972, p. 14).

Although Tiedemann began with the premise that ''experience and practice teach us to use our senses and perceive correctly,'' he nevertheless described newborn infants as being capable of demonstrating visual attention to particular classes of stimuli, and capable also of demonstrating visual preferences. Before discussing this apparent contradiction I want to present a further example of an apparent contradiction between the theory of human development held by an investigator of infancy and his observations of infant behavior. The example is drawn from the work of William Preyer. Preyer was a physiologist who was interested initially in the course of development of the human embryo (see Cairns, 1983). He became interested in the development of mental abilities, and he published his classic developmental text (*The Mind of the Child*) in 1882. Much of the material presented in *The Mind of the Child* was based on observations of his son's development. In addition Preyer performed a number of psychophysical experiments using his son as subject. Preyer makes a revealing allusion to his data-gathering procedures in his preface to the first English edition of his book:

> Occupying myself with the child at least three times a day—at morning, noon, and evening—and almost every day, with two trifling interruptions, *and guarding him, as far as possible, against such training as children usually receive* (my italics) I found nearly every day some fact of mental genesis to record. (Preyer, 1888, p. x)

The theoretical implication of Preyer's words is clear, namely that mental development ("some fact of mental genesis") occurs with minimal experience (without "such training as children usually receive"). Before discussing this point further it is instructive to consider Preyer's description of the abilities of newborns in whom this mental genesis was taking place. Preyer was concerned that those charged with the care of infants should have access to the material related to psychogenesis (Preyer's term for mental development) published in *The Mind of the Child*. To this end he published *Mental Development in the Child* in 1893 in which a summary of his developmental work was presented "with special reference to practical use and application" (Preyer, 1893, p. xvii). The description of neonatal abilities given in *Mental Development in the Child* by Preyer stands in marked contrast to Tiedemann's rather flattering description of the perceptual behaviour of neonates (e.g., their ability "from the first" to attending visually to particular stimuli and to demonstrate visual preferences).

> Every child when just born is completely deaf, and sometimes several days elapse before the tympanium, with the auditory ossicle, is capable of conducting external impressions of sound properly to the brain, which is as yet by no means sufficiently developed for hearing. (p. 5)

> Although the child does not, like puppies and kittens, come into the world with the eyelids tightly closed, and cannot be called blind in the strict meaning of the word, yet he is quite incapable of seeing (p. 7). It is idle, therefore, to dispute whether the newborn infant sees an object single, not double, with his two eyes; or whether he sees it upright, or upside down; or whether he confounds right and left in the field of vision. In reality he sees no objects at all yet. (p. 8)

On first reading, Preyer's description of neonates seems to be the protypical characterization of the "empiricist" infant born with a mind empty of ideas, and capable only of the most primitive behavior. However, Preyer was not an empiricist, and stated this explicitly in his preface to the first edition of *The Mind of the Child*

> The mind of the new-born child, then, does not resemble a *tabula rasa,* upon which the senses first write their impressions, so that out of these the sum-total of our

mental life arises through manifold reciprocal action, *but the tablet is already written upon before birth,* (my italics) with many illegible, nay, unrecognizable and invisible, marks, the traces of the imprint of countless sensuous impressions of long-gone generations. So blurred and indistinct are these remains, that we might, indeed, suppose the tablet to be blank, so long as we did not examine the changes it undergoes in earliest youth. But the more attentively the child is observed, the more easily legible becomes the writing . . . then we perceive what a capital each individual has inherited from his ancestors—how much there is that is not produced by sense-impressions, and how false is the supposition that man learns to feel, to will, and to think, only through his senses. Heredity is just as important as individual activity in the genesis of mind. (Preyer, 1888, p. xiv)

Clearly, then, Preyer believed that humans acquired knowledge not only through sensory experience, but through the unfolding of innate abilities "inherited from [their] ancestors." These abilities are not manifested at birth (Preyer described the innate abilities as "illegible," "unrecognizable and invisible," "blurred," and "indistinct" marks on the "tablet" of infant mind). However they are there in potential and emerge as the infant matures. Furthermore, there is the suggestion in the description by Preyer of his data-gathering procedures that experience (in the form of the training that children "usually receive") is not necessary for these potential abilities to emerge.

Preyer's form of nativism is similar, in some respects, to that proposed by Aristotle in response to the problem in Plato's theory of ideal Forms. These problems were: First, the observation of obvious differences in the mental abilities of very young, adult, and very old humans suggesting that experience and the passage of time have some influence on a person's knowledge of the world; and second, the observation that perceivers did not seem aware of the mismatch between their ideal Forms and the real forms of the world.

Now it is strange if we possess them (ideal Forms) from birth for it means that we possess apprehensions more accurate than demonstration and fail to notice them. If on the other hand we acquire them and do not previously possess them, how could we apprehend and learn without a basis of pre-existent knowledge? (Aristotle; cited in Robinson, 1976, p. 88)

Aristotle's answer to the issue of how "we apprehend and learn without a basis of pre-existent knowledge" was to propose, first, that humans have an innate potential to know; and second, that maturation is accompanied by the unfolding or realization of this innate potential.

The problem with such propositions is that they seem merely to be a post-hoc attempt to incorporate into a nativist theory some problem data (e.g., the primitive state of human neonates). One answer to this criticism is to attempt to supply a mechanism for the emergence of the innate potential. Preyer's solution was to link the emerging mental abilities of the developing child to maturational changes in the child's brain:

The older child, *or rather his growing brain* (my italics), enlarges his clear ideas, ordering his original, aimless often ill-adapted, inborn, impulsive movements. (Preyer, 1893, p. 159)

Preyer's explicit linking of mental development to physiological maturation of the brain accounted for the problem (for nativist theories) of the supposedly primitive state of human neonates.

My use of the word "supposedly" is deliberate because of the very different descriptions of infant behavior and abilities given by Tiedemann and Preyer. At one level these differences may be explained in terms of differences in the quality of the data-gathering of Tiedemann and Preyer. However, it seems to me that this level of explanation does not reflect the more fundamental and less tractable differences between the two investigators of infancy. These less tractable differences involve assumptions about the relationship between mental activity, behavior, and neural activity, one of the most difficult and enduring philosophical problems (see Armstrong, 1980; Hebb, 1980; Robinson, 1976). If it is assumed that mental activity ("wanting to") is the final "cause" of behavior, then complex behavior must be taken to indicate the presence of complex mental activity. In these terms, descriptions of complex behavior in newborns must be interpreted as supporting a nativist philosophy, or so it would seem. However, it is obvious from the contradictions between the theoretical assumptions and behavioral observations of Tiedemann and Preyer that this (simple) argument does not hold: complex neonatal abilities are incorporated into an empiricist theory by Tiedemann and primitive neonatal abilities are incorporated into a nativist theory by Preyer. As I have suggested, these contradictions can be understood in terms of different assumptions about the relationship between mental activity, behavior, and the state of maturation of the nervous system held by Tiedemann and Preyer. However, before discussing this point in further detail I want to provide further examples of paradoxes involving apparent contradictions between theory and data. These examples are taken from the pioneering studies of the influence of sensory deprivation on human development.

RATIONALISM-NATIVISM AND EMPIRICISM: IMPLICATIONS FOR THE STUDY OF SENSORY DEPRIVATION

In the extract from Locke's *Essay* cited in the *Introduction and Overview* to this chapter, Locke's predictions concerning the debilitating outcomes of sensory deprivation are stated explicitly (e.g., a child reared in a world devoid of color would have no idea of "scarlet or green"). A more dramatic description of the supposed consequences of sensory deprivation is given by Rousseau in *Emile* (first published in 1762):

We are born capable of learning, but knowing nothing, perceiving nothing. The mind, bound up within imperfect and half grown organs, is not even aware of its own existence. The movements and cries of the newborn are purely reflex, without knowledge or will. Suppose a child born with the size and strength of manhood, . . . he would see and hear nothing, he would recognize no one, he could not turn his eyes towards what he wanted to see; not only would he perceive no external object, he would not even be aware of sensation through the several sense-organs . . . all his sensations would be united in one place, they would exist only in the common "sensorium", he would have only one idea, that of self, to which he would refer all his sensations; and this idea, or rather this feeling, would be the only thing in which he excelled an ordinary child''. (Rousseau, 1911, p. 28)

The obvious test of such empiricist predictions about the role of sensory experience on the acquisition of knowledge about the world would be to rear children from birth in conditions of sensory deprivation, and monitor the consequences. Such a proposal is, of course, outside the scope of an ethical experimental developmental psychology, and was suggested by Locke in a rhetorical fashion. However, cases of sensory deprivation do occur outside the psychological laboratory: For example, children abandoned as infants and surviving in the absence of human contact (the so-called feral children; Zingg, 1940); children raised by parents or other care-givers in situations of minimum human contact (e.g., Curtiss, 1977); and children born with some sensory disability (commonly blindness and/or deafness). The occurrence of these cases of what may be termed natural sensory-deprivation experiments was recognized by the earliest investigators of human development as important tests of empiricism of the type hypothesized by Locke. Itard (1801), for example, in his report of the feral boy Victor (the Wild Boy of Aveyron) wrote:

If it were proposed to solve the following problem of metaphysics: *to determine what would be the degree of intelligence and the nature of the ideas of an adolescent, who, deprived from his childhood of all education, had lived entirely* separated from individuals of his own species, unless I am greatly mistaken the solution of the problem would be found as follows. There should first be assigned to that individual nothing but an intelligence relative to the small number of his needs and one which was deprived, by abstraction, of all the simple and complex ideas we receive by education, which combine in our mind in so many ways solely by means of our knowledge of signs, or reading. Well, the mental picture of this adolescent would be that of the Wild Boy of Aveyron. (Itard, 1801; cited in Dennis, 1972, p. 35)

The Wild Boy of Aveyron was one of the best-documented cases of feral children. Victor was captured in 1799 in woods near Aveyron and was thought to be about 12-years-old when taken into custody. Little was known about Victor's origins but Itard estimated that he had been abandoned at least 7 years earlier.

The results of this time spent living in the wild were described graphically by Itard:

> his senses were reduced to such a state of inertia that the unfortunate creature was . . . quite inferior to some of our domestic animals. His eyes were unsteady, expressionless, wandering vaguely from one object to another without resting on anybody; they were so little experienced in other ways and so little trained by sense of touch, that they never distinguished an object in relief from one in a picture. (Itard, 1801; cited in Dennis, 1972, p. 35)

Itard was aware of, but dismissed, the possibility that Victor's perceptual deficiencies were due to mental retardation; that is, that Victor was a "poor imbecile whom his parents in disgust had recently abandoned at the entrance to some woods" (Itard, 1801; cited in Dennis, 1972, p. 35). Instead, Itard interpreted the primitive state of Victor as strong support for empiricism. However, there are a number of reasons why caution needs to be taken in the interpretation of data provided by cases of feral children. One of these is based on the quality of the observations made of the abilities of the feral children. Itard, for example, describes Victor's senses as being inferior to those of domestic animals. This implies that wild animals (presumably reared in similar conditions to those of Victor) have senses that are inferior to those of domestic animals. Intuitively the opposite would seem more likely. Descriptions of the sensory abilities of other feral children (Zingg, 1940) indicate that some of these children had superior sensory abilities (e.g., seeing at night; smelling food) compared to normal children. However, a more important reason for caution when discussing cases of feral children and natural experiments, in general, is the lack of control such cases exhibit in comparison to properly-conducted laboratory or field studies (see Dennis, 1941, and the reply by Zingg, 1941). Less caution is necessary in the other class of natural experiment taken to be relevant to the rationalism-nativism vs. empiricism argument. I refer to the cases of children born blind, living for many years in the absence of normal visual experience, and then having their vision "restored."

The earliest of these cases of restored vision were reported by physicians involved in the diagnosis and treatment of infants born with sensory impairments. Case histories, of a sort, were therefore available, and these provided some information about the age of onset of the sensory loss, its extent, and the results of tests performed to assess function following treatment by the physician. Of particular interest in terms of the present discussion are the cases involving infants with congenital cataracts. The opaque lenses in the eyes of these infants may allow some light to enter the eye so that night may be distinguished from day, but the ability to see shapes, sizes, colors, etc., is absent. Prior to the early 1700s such infants, if they survived childhood, lived the life of a blind person. However, in the early part of the 18th century surgical treatment of cataracts was developed involving either the removal of the opaque lens, or the physical displacement of the lens in the eyeball away from the pupil. The surgical treatment must have been a terrible ordeal for the patients. There was no anaesthetic, and Wardrop (1813) provides a chilling description of a wooden, coffin-like, restraining device needed to immobilize one patient during cataract surgery. However, the result (when surgery was successful) was that the possibility for vision was restored in that the barrier to light entering the eye was removed. The question of philosophical interest was what was the outcome, in terms of the patient's experience of the world, of such surgery.

This question had been, in fact, discussed by Locke in his *Essay* in response to a specific request made by his colleague, William Molyneaux. It is instructive to read Locke's account of Molyneaux's question as well as Locke's answer because (as Morgan, 1977, points out) both Molyneaux's question and Locke's answer have become somewhat distorted in secondary sources over the years. Locke wrote:

> Suppose a man born blind, and now adult, and taught by his touch to distinguish between a cube and a sphere of the same metal, and nighly of the same bigness, so as to tell, when he felt one and the other, which is the cube, which the sphere. Suppose then the cube and sphere placed on a table, and the blind man to be made to see: quaere, whether by his sight, before he touched them, he could now distinguish and tell which is the globe, which the cube? To which the acute and judicious proposer answers: Not. For though he has obtained the experience of how a globe, how a cube, affects his touch; yet he has not yet obtained the experience, that what affects his touch so or so, must affect his sight so or so; or that a protuberant angle in the cube, that pressed his hand unequally, shall appear to his eye as it does in the cube. I agree with this thinking gentleman, whom I am proud to call my friend, in his answer to this his problem; and am of opinion that the blind man, at first sight, would not be able with certainty to say which was the globe, which the cube, whilst he only saw them; though he could unerringly name them by his touch and certainly distinguish them by the difference of their figures felt (Locke, 1690; cited in Burtt, 1939, p. 274).

The conventional portrayal of Molyneaux's question is as follows: If a man is born blind and is then made to see, and if he were shown a cube and a sphere, could he see them? It is clear from Locke's words that this was not his interpretation of Molyneaux's question. In Locke's terms, the issue is whether the previously blind man "could now *distinguish and tell* (my italics) which is the globe, which the cube." Locke's answer was that the previously blind person would be able to *see* the globe and the cube following restoration of vision, but he would be unable to name the two objects.

The basis of Locke's answer lies in his theory of the formation of complex ideas. According to Locke, normal experience with, for example, a wooden cube gives rise initially in the mind of the perceiver of separate simple visual, tactile, kinesthetic, etc., ideas. Reflection on, and association between, these simple ideas produces the complex idea of cube. Furthermore, the word "cube," when used by this normal perceiver, signifies "nothing but the ideas in the mind of him that uses [it]" (Kretzmann, 1968; cited in Tipton, 1977, p. 126). Since simple and complex ideas in Locke's theory are "rooted to the soil of experience," any interference in the sensory systems that mediate experience must interfere with the formation of ideas held by the perceiver suffering sensory deprivation. A blind person, therefore, would lack visual ideas, and this person's complex idea of the wooden cube used in the example above would lack a "visual" component.

In these terms, what are the consequences of restoring the function of the deficient sensory system? It is important to differentiate between two separate, though related, consequences: first, restoration of the missing sensory function *would not result* in immediate restoration of the missing ideas; second, restoration of the missing sensory function *would result* in immediate restoration of the ability to form ideas based on the activity of the newly functioning sensory system. A period of time allowing sensory experience with the restored sensory system would be needed to incorporate the newly available ideas into the perceiver's existing ideas. In the situation described by Molyneaux, the previously blind person would now (with vision restored) be able to have visual ideas of the cube and sphere (i.e., he could *see* them), but these new visual ideas would not form part of the *preexisting* (i.e., prior to restoration of vision), and separate, complex ideas of cube and sphere. Since the words cube and sphere signify for the previously blind person, these *preexisting* ideas she or he would be unable to use them in relation to visual experience.

In general, the results of the cases of restored vision reported in the 18th and 19th centuries were consistent with Locke's expectations (e.g., Cheselden, 1728; Wardrop, 1813; see Preyer, 1889 for a discussion of several such cases). For example, Cheselden's (1728) patient could *see* objects immediately following removal of a cataract from one eye, although his depth perception was deficient (understandable perhaps as his viewing was monocular). Furthermore, he was able to indicate which objects were visually more "agreeable" to him. However, although he could visually differentiate between objects and even make aesthetic judgments about them, he was unable to make a "judgment of their shape, or guess what it was any object that was pleasing to him" (Cheselden, 1728; cited in Dennis, 1972, p. 3).

While such cases of restored vision are consistent with Locke's hypotheses, they also highlight the significant nativist component of Locke's theory. Absence of sensory experience (e.g., visual experience) results in the absence of ideas (e.g., visual ideas) in the mind of a person. However when the sensory system is made functional, acquisition of ideas is immediately possible, as is the behavior thought to be contingent on these new ideas (e.g., Cheselden's patient being able to make visual aesthetic choices immediately vision was restored). Such apparently innate abilities are not inconsistent with Locke's empiricism according to Harris (1974):

We should perhaps add something that Locke thought too obvious to mention explicitly in the *Essay;* that he nowhere denies the existence of *natural faculties* (my italics) such as perception, understanding and memory, and *innate mental powers* (my italics) like those of abstraction, comparison and discernment. The ''white paper'' metaphor is meant to indicate that the understanding (and hence the mind) is originally empty of *objects* of thought like ideas; but it has whatever apparatus is necessary *to acquire them through experience* (my italics) and then to derive knowledge by comparing and contrasting them with each other.'' (Harris, 1974; cited in Tipton, 1977, p. 27)

There seems little difference with respect to the expected abilities of newborn infants between Harris' version of Locke's empiricism, and the version of nativism proposed initially by Aristotle and then by Preyer (see p. xxx). In Harris' terms, Locke's theory predicts that infants are born with few, if any, ''*objects* of thought like ideas''; but it does predict that infants are born with ''natural faculties,'' ''innate mental powers'', and ''whatever apparatus is necessary to acquire them [i.e., ideas] through experience.'' In other words, infants are born with the potential to know. Harris' interpretation of Locke's expectations about innate abilities, as well as Locke's predictions about, and the experimental results of, restoration of vision lend further support to the argument made at the conclusion of the previous section. That is, that Locke's claim about the usefulness of investigating the state of newborn infants with respect to differentiating rationalism-nativism and empiricism cannot be sustained. Earlier, I discussed a version of nativist theory in which few abilities were expected of neonates, and, on closer inspection, it seems that in Locke's empiricist theory some innate abilities are expected of neonates. To be added to this already-complex situation are the conflicting descriptions of the abilities of neonates given by, for example, Tiedemann and Preyer. I want to argue, in the final section, that a possible solution to the complex amalgam of conflicting theory and observation lies in the understanding of the role that theories of the relationship between mind and body play in investigations of human development.

Before doing so it should be said that Locke's second claim (i.e., regarding the role of studies of sensory deprivation in differentiating between rationalism-nativism and empiricism) may be less contentious than his first. For example, a strong form of rationalism-nativism would predict that ideas (knowledge of the world) should arise in the mind of the perceiver in the absence of sensory experience. Although such a strong prediction may be criticized as a caricature of the nativist position, it was implicit in Preyer's claim that his son showed daily signs of ''mental genesis'' in the absence of (or at least with minimal) ''training as children usually receive.'' In contrast to this, empiricst theory would lead to the prediction that atypical rearing (i.e., the absence of particular sensory experiences) would result in the absence of particular ideas in the mind of the deprived perceiver. However, while it may seem as though the study of the effects of atypical rearing provides a means of testing between rationalism-nativism and empiricism, this procedure is not without difficulty. There are, for example, the ethical issues involved in the deliberate manipulation of sensory experience, in particular, depriving humans (and indeed other species) of sensory experience. Although naturally occurring cases of sensory deprivation may be investigated, they are replete with methodological difficulties. Some of these difficulties may be overcome by using nonhuman subjects in atypical rearing studies; however, this raises the further question of generalization of results from nonhuman to human species. Morgan (1977) provides a more detailed discussion of the relevance of atypical rearing studies to the rationalism-nativism vs. empiricism issue with respect to the relationship between vision and touch. In conclusion, then, although the study of the effects of sensory deprivation on mental development appears to provide a test between rationalism-nativism and empiricism, such a test is critically dependent on the assumed relationship between ideas (i.e., mental activity) and observed behavior.

INTERPRETATIONS OF NEONATAL BEHAVIOR: THE NOTION OF REFLEX

In the two preceding sections the related issues of (i) precise specification of the behaviors expected of neonates (and experientially naive children) within rationalist-nativist theoretical frameworks, and (ii) the subjective nature of the interpretations of observed behaviors that form the basis of experimental developmental psychology were considered. These issues were illustrated, first through discussion of the basic assumptions of Locke's empiricist theory, and Preyer's (Aristotle's) variation of rationalist-nativist theory; and second, through presentation of apparently conflicting descriptions and interpretations of neonatal behaviors and abilities. However, it would be wrong to conclude that since these examples of apparent conflict between theory and observation were drawn from the developmental literature published in the 18th and 19th centuries, the investigators of infancy working then were unaware of the problems associated with neonatal research. I have already mentioned Wundt's assertion that an experimental child psychology was not possible. Sully (1896) was less pessimistic, yet was aware of the basis for Wundt's concern:

> The awakening in the modern mind of this keen and varied interest in childhood has led, and is destined to lead still more, to the observation of infantile ways. This observation will, of course, be of very different value according as it subserves the contemplation of the humorous or other aesthetically valued aspects of child-nature, or as it is directed towards a specific understanding of this. Pretty anecdotes of children which tickle the emotions may or may not add to our insight into the peculiar mechanisms of children's minds . . . The phenomena of a child's mental life, even on its physical and visible side, are of so subtle and fugitive a character that only a fine and quick observation is able to cope with them. *But observation of*

children is never merely seeing (my italics). Even the smile has to be interpreted as a smile by a process of imaginative inference. Many careless onlookers would say that a baby smiles in the first days from very happiness, when another and simpler explanation of the movement is forthcoming. Similarly, it wants must fine judgment to say whether an infant is merely stumbling accidentally on an articulate sound, or is imitating your sound." (Sully, 1896, pp. 10–11)

It is this "process of imaginative inference," together with the application of "another and simpler explanation of the movement" (i.e., simpler than attributing the movement, e.g., a smile, to a mental state, e.g., happiness), that allows the apparent conflict between Tiedemann and Preyer to be resolved. By "another and simpler explanation of the movement" I refer to the use of the reflex concept to account for the complex and apparently purposive behaviors of neonates (e.g., looking at lights and moving objects, as described by Tiedemann; sucking when stimulated on some parts of the mouth, but not others, as described by Preyer).

The use of the reflex concept in explaining human behavior was associated with the rise of materialist philosophies of mind in the 17th and 18th centuries (Boring, 1950; Fearing, 1964; Robinson, 1976). This took place in association with significant advances in knowledge in the disciplines of physics and physiology during this period of history. As more became known about the anatomical structures involved in the processing of sensory stimuli and in the execution of movements, a physiological model of the reflex was proposed to replace the hydraulic model originally suggested by Descartes (Fearing, 1964). There were similarities between the two models: both included pathways between receptor organs and effector organs that served to connect receptors and effectors into functional units. Stimulation of the receptors could produce appropriate (i.e., purposeful) behavior in the absence of learning or experience. This was because in both models, the pathways linking receptors and effectors (i.e., the bases of purposeful action) were taken to be part of the biological inheritance of the person, and consequently were taken to be operational prior to experience. In these terms, the occurrence of innate purposeful behavior in infants (e.g., of the type described by Tiedemann and Preyer) did not necessarily indicate the presence of innate ideas; innate behavior merely indicated the presence of an intact and functional nervous system (at least that part connecting the receptors and effectors involved in the "purposeful" behaviors in question).

The idea that complex neural units (i.e., reflex pathways) and consequently the behaviors mediated by these pathways could be inherited by a newborn infant from its ancestors received impetus from publication of Darwin's *The Origin of Species* in 1859. Darwin proposed that the complex anatomical structures (and the concomitant complex behaviors) that characterized modern species had developed over time from the more simple structures of older species. Members of a species varied in their structure and their behavior, and those that were better equipped to adapt to their environment were more likely to survive. The "fittest" members of the species were therefore more likely to propagate and ensure the continuation of the species. As the environment changed, so did the requirements for survival. Over millions of years processes of successful adaptation to, and propagation in, changing environments resulted in the evolution of the complex modern species. Although Darwin did not propose explicit mechanisms to explain either the variation of characteristics within a species, or the transmission of characteristics from parents to offspring, this did not inhibit the inclusion of Darwinian ideas into theories of human physiological and mental development. For example, Robinson (1976) cites Ernst Haeckel's "biogenic law"

according to which ontogeny recapitulates phylogeny. (Robinson, 1976, p. 323)

Such a law could "explain" how an infant born with primitive mental abilities could develop (evolve?) into an adult with the mental abilities of adulthood. This explanation is based on the assumption of psychophysical parallelism (Boring, 1950) in which an intimate relationship (in the extreme case, an identity) is said to exist between a person's nervous system and mental ability. In the case of the newborn infant, mental abilities are primitive because of the still primitive state of development of the neonatal nervous system. Rousseau expressed such a point of view eloquently when he described the neonatal mind as "bound up within imperfect and half grown organs" (Rousseau, 1911, p. 28). Preyer also held this view, and attributed the mental development of infants to their "growing brains." Within this framework, processes (whatever their precise nature) of the type that enabled simple species to evolve into complex species could underlie the "evolution" of the human from the primitive physiological and mental state of infancy to the complexity of adulthood.

I indicated earlier that Locke had taken as a basic premise to his argument that men's "words and actions" could be taken to signify the presence of ideas. Within Locke's empiricist theory, however, the occurrence of complex purposeful actions in neonates was problematic as it suggested the presence of innate ideas. However, the reflex concept provided a means of resolving the paradox of "empiricist" infants displaying complex purposeful actions from birth since these actions could be categorized as automatic, mechanistic, involuntary in nature. In this way an "empiricist" investigator of infant development could describe complex purposeful behavior in the newborn infant without seeming to contradict his empiricist philosophy. This was the approach adopted by Tiedemann. Consider his description of his son's first grasping movements:

He had no idea as yet of purposely grasping anything; grasping occurred only by instinctive reflex, by which the fingers, like the leaves or flowers of certain sensitive plants, contract when their inner surfaces are touched by a foreign object. (Tiedemann, 1787; cited in Dennis, 1972, p. 15)

A similar explanation of innate purposive behavior was proposed by Darwin in the report of his son's development.

During the first seven days various reflex actions, namely sneezing, hiccuping, yawning, stretching, and of course sucking and screaming, were well performed by my infant . . . The perfection of these reflex movements shows that the extreme imperfections of the voluntary ones is not due to the state of the muscles or of the coordinating centres, but to that of the seat of the will. (Darwin, 1877, p. 285)

The innate activities explained away by Tiedemann and Darwin consisted not only of grasping, and sneezing, hiccuping, yawning, etc., but also more complex behaviors. For example, I have already presented Tiedemann's description of infant's purposeful looking behavior "from the first." Consider, as a further example, Darwin's interpretation of his son Doddy's behavior during breastfeeding:

At the age of 32 days he perceived his mother's bosom when three or four inches from it, as was shown by the protrusion of his lips and his eyes becoming fixed; *but I much doubt whether this had any connection with vision* (my italics); he certainly had not touched the bosom. Whether he was guided through smell or the sensation of warmth or through association with the position in which he was held, I do not at all know. (Darwin, 1877, p. 286)

Darwin's use of the phrase "perceived his mother's bosom" is somewhat idiosyncratic in that Darwin was convinced that Doddy could not "see" (perceive) as adults do: Doddy's actions (protrusion of his lips, his eyes becoming fixed) were due as far as Darwin was concerned to other, nonvisual factors (e.g., smell, warmth, kinesthetic cues).

Although both Tiedemann and Darwin presented a more flattering description of the abilities of newborn infants than that provided by Preyer, these abilities were not interpreted by Tiedemann or Preyer as indicative of innate mental functioning. Indeed, both Tiedemann and Darwin were less than flattering in their characterizations of the mental abilities of neonates. Tiedemann, for example, referred to newborn infants as being like "merely sensuous persons," and compared his son's actions to that of "sensitive plants"; Darwin described Doddy at birth as possessing "extreme imperfection of the seat of the will [i.e., mind]." As far as Tiedemann and Darwin were concerned it was only after a period of time that mind began to emerge in the growing child and manifest itself in behavior. *More correctly, it was only after a period of time that particular behaviors emitted by growing children were interpreted as voluntary (i.e., due to ideas in the infant's mind) rather than reflexive.* Indeed Darwin provides an exact date for the emergence of Doddy's mind:

After grasping my finger and drawing it to his mouth, his own hand prevented him from sucking it; but on the 114th day, after acting in this manner, he slipped his own hand down so that he could get the end of my finger into his mouth. This action was repeated several times, and evidently was not a chance but a rational one. (Darwin, 1877, p.287)

The use of the reflex concept to explain innate purposive behavior within an empiricist framework resolves the apparent conflict between theory and observation in, for example, Tiedemann's report. However this resolution is itself problematic in that it blurs even further the distinction between empiricism and rationalism-nativism with respect to predictions about the behavior of newborns. That is, there are no differences, as far as I can determine, between the behaviors expected of infants based on the following propositions: (i) any abilities manifested by infants at birth or soon after are due to neural structures inherited from their ancestors; (ii) any abilities manifested by infants at birth or soon after are due to innate ideas held by infants. The situation is complicated even further by reports such as those of Preyer that attribute only the most primitive abilities to neonates yet maintain a nativist philosophy by explaining these primitive abilities in terms of the immature state of the neonatal nervous system.

Given the fuzziness of the boundary between empiricism and rationalism-nativism, what are the consequences for Locke's claims about the theoretical importance of developmental psychology? My argument is that Locke's claims about observations of infants immediately after birth, and observations of the outcomes of sensory deprivation need to be separated. As I suggested earlier, distinct predictions about the consequences of what is termed abnormal rearing on the perceptual abilities of children can be made within empiricist and rationalist-nativist frameworks. In this respect, then, the second of Locke's claims can be sustained. However, the sorts of crucial experiments that would enable the testing of these distinct predictions cannot be performed due to ethical considerations. Furthermore, the occurrence of natural experiments approximating these unable-to-be-performed studies are suspect because of methodological problems. Locke's claim therefore remains as it was intended, a rhetorical device designed to demonstrate the self-evident nature of his empiricist claims.

What of Locke's first claim concerning the ''attentive consideration'' of neonates. As I have already indicated, this claim was also a rheotrical device based on the common-sense notion that human infants were helpless creatures. However, ''attentive consideration'' of infants as long ago as 1787 revealed them to be capable of complex, apparently purposive behavior, an observation that would seem to be fatal for an empiricist philosophy. It is clear, however, that investigation of infant behavior is less about empiricism vs. rationalism-nativism, and more about the assumed causes of particular behaviors. For example, neither Teidemann nor Darwin were willing to classify the complex visual search behaviors of their sons as intentional. Both Tiedemann and Darwin assumed that newborn infants did not possess the mental ability necessary for voluntary purposive actions and therefore attributed their sons' complex behavior to reflexes. An equally plausible explanation, of course, is that Tiedemann's and Darwin's offspring were born with innate ideas about the properties of the external world and that these ideas gave rise to the behaviors observed by Tiedemann and Darwin. There is no definitive test that I know to determine which of these alternative hypotheses is correct. This is the flaw in Locke's claim about the theoretical value of "attentive consideration" of infants. Because infants cannot report on their own mental processes, and because investigators are unable to access directly the mental processes of others (human adults as well as infants)

> the mistake [is made] of not interpreting observations objectively. The observations [of infant behavior] are filled out with subjective reflections. (Wundt, 1907, p.335)

As far as Wundt was concerned, such "subjective reflections" (or "imaginative inferences" as Sully termed them) meant that mental development was not amenable to experimentation, and that developmental psychology was not scientific. It is clear that Wundt's views did little to stop the growth of experimental investigation of infant behavior and development. However, I want to suggest that the basis of Wundt's qualms about experimental developmental psychology (i.e., the influence of the investigator's theoretical presuppositions on interpretations of observations of infants and children) needs to be kept in mind by those engaged in infant research, and those reading the results of this research. This is particularly the case given the fuzzy boundary between some empiricist and rationalist-nativist conceptualizations about the abilities of neonates.

To reinforce this suggestion I will describe briefly two experiments. The first was performed by Darwin on Doddy when the latter was a little over 4-months-of-age. Darwin walked towards Doddy *backwards* until he was quite close to Doddy, at which point he stood still.

> [Doddy] looked very grave and much surprized, and would soon have cried, had I not turned round; then his face instantly relaxed into a smile. (Darwin, 1877, p.288)

I should point out that Darwin does not explain how he was able to observe Doddy while facing the other way. However, the description of Doddy's reaction was made in a subsection of Darwin's (1877) report titled *Fear*. Darwin stated that the feeling of fear

> is one of the earliest which is experienced by infants . . . May we not suspect that the vague but very real fears of children, which are quite independent of experience, are the inherited effects of real dangers and abject superstitions during ancient savage times? (Darwin, 1877, p.288)

More than 100 years later, I and my colleagues (Broerse, Peltola, & Crassini, 1983) presented 3-month-old infants with experimental displays we termed "perceptual paradoxes" that were similar, in some respects, to that used by Darwin. They consisted of the infant subjects in our study being exposed to (i) their mothers' "disembodied" voices (the mothers were rendered invisible to the infants by the use of special lighting), and (ii) their mothers' "voiceless" faces (the mothers spoke to the infants so their lips etc. moved but the mothers were rendered inaudible to the infants by a special sound apparatus). Our infant subjects were judged by impartial observers to have "looked very grave and much surprized, and would soon have cried" (indeed some did!) in comparison to their responses to a control condition in which they could both see and hear their mothers. Despite the similarity in behavior emitted by our subjects and Darwin's son, our interpretation ("imaginative inference"/"subjective reflection") was very different from that of Darwin. We argued that our data supported the Gibsonian proposition (E. J. Gibson, 1969; J. J. Gibson, 1966, 1979) that the infant's perceptual world is integrated from birth. Any deviation from this integration (i.e., situations of perceptual paradox) produce in infants the sorts of negative affective responses that we (and Darwin) observed.

Which interpretation is correct? Darwin's interpretation may be described as being "closer" to the data in that he attributed Doddy's behavior to innate fear of the strange, where fear was taken to be a "feeling" in a person manifested by the person exhibiting reactions of the type made by Doddy. My colleagues and I went beyond the data in our interpretation in that we took the negative affective responses of our infants to be the outcome of a further, unobservable process. This private process involved a mismatch between the array of stimulation received by our infants and their perceptual "expectations." I put the word "expectations" deliberately in quotation marks because in our report we (like Locke in his *Essay*) did not discuss the exact nature of these neonatal expectations. The rationale of our report was that our study addressed the question of whether perceptual integration is innate or is acquired through experience. In terms of the argument I have made in this chapter this rationale was incorrect. With respect to our data, one possible explanation is that infants are born with expectations in the form of innate ideas about the proportions of the external world. In these terms, situations of perceptual paradox produce a mismatch between the innate ideas and the ideas generated by the sensory input resulting in the negative responses that we observed. An alternative possibility is that the responses of infants to situations of perceptual paradox are reflexive, and are triggered by the inappropriate stimulation of sensory systems that have evolved, in Gibson's terms, to "pick up" information from the external world. Both possibilities described above are consistent with the data. However, accepting either possibility involves making very different assumptions about the nature of mental activity and its development, and the relationship between mental activity, physiological activity, and behavior. A criticism of our report, and many of the current investigations of infant behavior is that these assumptions are not discussed sufficiently, if at all. I want to suggest that this lack needs to be remedied.

In this chapter I have argued that the differences between empiricist and rationalist-nativist philosophies are less obvious than have been assumed by investigators of infant behavior and development over the past 200 years. In making this argument I have proposed that studies ostensibly designed to test empiricist vs. rationalist-nativist predictions are more tests of mind-body assumptions than nature-nurture assumptions. I offer no simple resolution of this problem, and indeed there can be none given the nature of the philosophical assumptions involved. However, it is my view that a number of the conflicts that characterize the developmental literature (and that are addressed in subsequent chapters) could be, if not resolved, at least better understood if investigators of infancy made explicit their assumptions about (i), the nature of mental activity, and (ii), the relationship between mental development, maturation of the nervous system, and observable behavior.

ACKNOWLEDGMENT

My involvement in infant research was initiated by the births of Emma and Kyle, and was made possible by grants from the Australian Research Grants Scheme. I thank Jack Broerse and Di Catherwood for their comments on earlier versions of this chapter, and Edna for her support when it was most needed.

REFERENCES

Armstrong, D. M. (1980). *The nature of mind and other essays.* St. Lucia, Queensland: University of Queensland Press.

Bloom, A. (1968). *The Republic of Plato.* New York: Basic Books.

Boring, E. G. (1950). *A history of experimental psychology (2nd edition).* Englewood Cliffs, NJ: Prentice-Hall.

Borstelmann, L. J. (1983). Children before psychology: Ideas about children from antiquity to the late 1800s. In W. Kessen (Ed.), *Handbook of child psychology, Volume 1: History, theory, and methods.* New York: Wiley.

Broerse, J., Peltola, C., & Crassini, B. (1983). Infants' reactions to perceptual paradox during mother-infant interaction. *Developmental Psychology, 19,* 310–316.

Burtt, E. A. (Ed.). (1939). *The English philosophers from Bacon to Mill.* New York: Random House.

Cairns, R. B. (1983). The emergence of developmental psychology. In W. Kessen (Ed.), *Handbook of child psychology, Volume 1: History, theory, and methods.* New York: Wiley.

Chalmers, A. F. (1982). *What is this thing called science? An assessment of the nature and status of science and its methods (2nd edition).* St. Lucia, Queensland: University of Queensland Press.

Cheselden, W. (1728). An account of some observations made by a young gentleman, who was born blind, or lost his sight so early, that he had no remembrance of ever having seen, and was couched between 13 and 14 years of age. In W. Dennis (Ed.), *Historical readings in developmental psychology.* New York: Appleton-Century-Crofts.

Compayrè, G. (1896). *The intellectual and moral development of the child. Part 1: Containing the chapters on perception, emotion, memory, imagination, and consciousness.* New York: D. Appleton and Company.

Cornford, F. M. (1935). *Plato's theory of knowledge.* London: Routledge & Kegan Paul.

Curtiss, S. (1977). *Genie: A psycholinguistic study of a modern-day "wild child".* Orlando, FL: Academic Press.

Darwin, C. (1859/1979). *The origin of species by means of natural selection.* New York: Avenel Books.

Darwin, C. (1877). A biographical sketch of an infant. *Mind, 7,* 285–294.

Dennis, W. (1941). The significance of feral man. *The American Journal of Psychology, 54,* 425–432.

Dennis, W. (1972). *Historical readings in develpomental psychology.* New York: Appleton-Century-Crofts.

Fearing, F. (1964). *Reflex action: A study in the history of physiological psychology.* New York: Hafner Publishing Company.

Gibson, E. J. (1969). *Principles of perceptual learning and development.* New York: Appleton-Century-Crofts.

Gibson, J. J. (1966). *The senses considered as perceptual systems.* Boston: Houghton Mifflin.

Gibson, J. J. (1979). *The ecological approach to visual perception.* Boston: Houghton Mifflin.

Harris, J. (1974). Leibniz and Locke on innate ideas. In I. C. Tipton (Ed.) (1977), *Locke on human understanding.* Oxford: Oxford University Press.

Hebb, D. O. (1980). *Essay on mind.* Hillsdale, NJ: Lawrence Erlbaum Associates.

Hochberg, J. E. (1978). *Perception (2nd Edition).* Englewood Cliffs, NJ: Prentice-Hall.

Itard, J. M. S. (1801). First developments of the young savage of Aveyron. In W. Dennis (Ed.) (1972), *Historical readings in developmental psychology.* New York: Appleton-Century-Crofts.

Itard, J. M. S. (1806). A report made to his Excellency, the Minister of Interior. In W. Dennis (Ed.) (1972), *Historical readings in developmental psychology.* New York: Appleton-Century-Crofts.

Jowett, B. (1953). *The dialogues of Plato: Volume 1 (4th ed.).* London: Oxford University Press.

Kretzmann, N. (1968). The main thesis of Locke's semantic theory. In I. C. Tipton (Ed.) (1977), *Locke on human understanding.* Oxford: Oxford University Press.

Lachman, R., Lachman, J. L., & Butterfield, E. C. (1979). *Cognitive psychology and information processing: An introduction.* Hillsdale, NJ: Lawrence Erlbaum Associates.

Locke, J. (1690). An essay concerning human understanding. In E. A. Burtt (Ed.) (1939), *The English philosophers from Bacon to Mill.* New York: Modern Library.

Morgan, M. J. (1977). *Molyneaux's question: Vision, touch, and the philosophy of perception.* Cambridge: Cambridge University Press.

Preyer, W. (1882/1888). *The mind of the child, Part I: The senses and the will.* New York: D. Appleton and Company.

Preyer, W. (1889). *The mind of the child, Part II: The development of the intellect.* New York: D. Appleton and Company.

Preyer, W. (1893). *Mental development in the child.* New York: D. Appleton and Company.

Pylyshyn, Z. W. (1980). Computation and cognition: Issues in the foundations of cognitive science. *The Behavioural and Brain Sciences, 3,* 111–169.

Robinson, D. N. (1976). *An intellectual history of psychology.* New York: Macmillan.

Rousseau, J. J. (1780–1911). *Emile.* London: J. M. Dent & Sons Ltd.

Sully, J. (1896). *Studies of childhood.* London: Longmans Green.

Tiedemann, D. (1787). Observations on the mental development of a child. In W. Dennis (Ed.) (1972), *Historical readings in developmental psychology.* New York: Appleton-Century-Crofts.

Tipton, E. C. (1977). *Locke on human understanding.* Oxford: Oxford University Press.

Uttal, W. R. (1981). *A taxonomy of visual process.* Hillsdale, NJ: Lawrence Erlbaum Associates.

Wardrop, J. (1813). History of James Mitchell, a boy born blind and deaf with the account of an operation performed for recovery of his sight. In W. Dennis (Ed.) (1972), *Historical readings in developmental psychology.* New York: Appleton-Century-Crofts.

Wundt, N. (1907). *Outlines of psychology.* Leipzig: Wilhelm Engelmann.

Zingg, R. M. (1940). Feral man and extreme cases of isolation. *The American Journal of Psychology, 53,* 487–517.

Zingg, R. M. (1941). A reply to Professor Dennis. *The American Journal of Psychology, 54,* 432–435.

3 Cardiac Change Responses and Attentional Mechanisms in Infants

David Finlay
Algis Ivinskis (deceased)
The University of Newcastle

INTRODUCTION

The responsiveness of infants to external events includes orientation toward stimuli, preference for particular stimuli, internal bodily adjustments such as heart rate changes, and changes in overt bodily activity. This chapter explores the ways in which these responses index aspects of infant attention.

In the extensive literature dealing with adult attention a wide range of topics such as vigilance, limited channel capacity, selective attention, sustained attention and arousal are included. Many of these topics were foreshadowed by Woodworth (1927) when he stated: "Attention is preparatory, selective, mobile, highly conscious . . . Primitive attention amounts to the same as the instinct of exploration" (p. 244).

Any attempt to propose a model of developmental continuity in attentional mechanisms runs into difficulties, not least being the many uses of the term bound to specific experimental paradigms, not all of which are readily translatable for use with infants. The term attention is used to describe those behaviors that are directly ascribable to an infant's orientation toward, detection, and prolonged fixation of environmental stimuli. These behaviors include orientation of head and eyes toward a stimulus, habituation of head turning and visual fixation, together with changes in autonomic activity. In particular, cardiac activity and its changes in various situations are emphasized.

Traditionally there has been a separation of interests between models based on overt behaviors such as fixation duration and on autonomic measures, although both are supposedly measures of attention. Different insights may be gained from one set but not from the other (Clifton & Nelson, 1976). For example, it may be possible to record cardiac change to auditory stimuli when no overt response is apparent.

At least four attentional mechanisms are proposed: (a) an alerting mechanism, (b) a directing mechanism, (c) a detecting mechanism, and (d) a mechanism underlying prolonged visual fixation. Posner and Rothbart (1980) also propose a 4-point structure and some of their ideas will be adopted here.

The alerting mechanism is related to the infants' state and to some extent determines it. As well, alertness is related to stimulus change. Stimulus change picked up by the organism can affect the alerting mechanism which can in turn alter the state of the child. Conversely, the state of the infant can depress the likelihood of the involvement of the alerting mechanism (Posner & Rothbart, 1981).

The directing mechanism refers to covert or overt directing of attention. Covert directing involves the shifting of attention without eye-movements whereas overt directing involves eye and/or head movements. According to Posner and Rothbart (1981) directing, or, in their terms orienting, is a property of a central mechanism and there is a great deal of independence between this mechanism and the eye-movement system.

We wish to make the further distinction between detection and prolonged fixation. Detection involves the acknowledgment that some event has occurred and to some extent will be affected by the stimulus properties of the event whereas prolonged fixation involves the ongoing inspection of the stimulus event.

Each of these mechanisms characterizes aspects of attention. In what follows we propose to examine whether cardiac responses can provide evidence for these different aspects. For several reasons we will concentrate on infants 3- to 4-months-of-age. First, there is some agreement that the nature of attentional behaviors change around 2-months-of-age (Haith, 1978). Second, although there are data showing systematic cardiac responses in very young infants, it seems clear that the system is less predictable with this group.

The cardiac data is initially presented in terms of an orienting reflex (OR) response (Graham, 1979; Sokolov, 1963). The framework described earlier permits an exploration of the usefulness of cardiac data with regard to each of the mechanisms—alerting, directing, detecting, and prolonged fixating, rather than simply within the broader, less defined, context of an orienting reflex.

ORIENTING RESPONSES AS A MEASURE
OF INFANT ATTENTION

Sokolov (1963) proposed that there are two generalized systems which produce opposite effects on sensitivity to incoming stimulation—the orienting reflex (OR), which is said to prepare the organism for stimulus receptivity and learning, and the defence reflex (DR), which prepares the organism for activity but inhibits stimulus receptivity. According to Sokolov, the OR depends heavily on the cerebral cortex for its habituation. As the incoming stimuli impinge on the organism, this information is compared with a neuronal model which has been acquired through previous experience. If no match can be found between the new information and the neuronal model, an OR occurs resulting in behavioral and physiological changes. However, if a match is found the OR is inhibited. Any new, discrepant stimulus, or any change in a stimulus of moderate intensity will evoke an OR response. Painful or intense stimuli tend to evoke a DR response.

Sokolov's formulations were based on adult data and for this reason they may not be directly applicable to the behavior of infants (Graham, 1979). It might be expected that the younger the infant the less complex would be the model, as presumably the acquisition and storage of external events depends on neural maturation.

Graham (1979) has specified four features which differentiate an OR and a DR. These are: (1) Offset of a stimulus should elicit an OR and not a DR; (2) High and low intensities of stimulation should evoke different reflexes; (3) Rates of habituation of an OR and a DR should differ, and (4) An habituated OR but not a DR should recover with a stimulus change that does not increase stimulus intensity.

In addition to these two reflexes Graham also discusses the startle reflex (SR). She suggests that the SR serves the function of protecting the organism. This reflex occurs in situations where the stimuli are sudden and intense and have an interrupting function on ongoing activities. The distinction between a DR and SR is that in the former responses tend to increase with stimulus repetition while in the latter the responses tend to habituate.

Heart Rate (HR) as a Component of OR

Heart rate (HR) deceleration as a component of OR has been investigated by, *inter alia,* Graham (1979), Graham and Clifton (1966), Graham and Jackson (1970), Lacey and Lacey (1958) and Lynn (1966). Several studies have shown that cardiac changes can provide a sensitive and reliable index of infant attention (e.g., Clifton & Nelson, 1976, Kagan, Henker, Hen-Tov, Levine, & Lewis, 1966; McCall & Kagan, 1967; McCall & Nelson, 1970). One of the most consistent findings is that, given appropriate conditions, infants respond to visual and auditory stimuli with HR deceleration (De Loache, 1976; Kagan & Lewis, 1965; Kagan, 1971, McCall & Kagan, 1967; Berg, Berg, & Graham, 1971; Brown, Leavitt, & Graham, 1977; Lewis, 1971). It has been suggested (Brown, Leavitt, & Graham, 1977) that age, state of the child, sensory modality, and the type of stimulus are all relevant variables. Clifton and Nelson (1976) and Von Bargen (1983) provide excellent reviews. At least two criteria seem relevant when assessing the usefulness of cardiac data. They should provide reliable and repeatable measures of the occurrence of stimulus events. In addition, they should discriminate between various stimulus events.

Our aim in the studies reported here was to examine a number of different stimulus parameters of auditory and visual stimuli in order to establish whether cardiac responses reflect changes in attention. There are few systematic findings in this area.

According to some (Fantz & Fagan, 1975; Karmel, 1969; Lewkowitz & Turkewitz, 1980) infant behavior is largely influenced by the quantitative aspects of a stimulus rather than its quality. Such stimulus characteristics as rate of change, size, contour density, and variations in sound intensity are important components that determine attentional responses. The effects produced by these quantitative aspects of stimuli may be explained in terms of the alerting mechanism of attention. For more selective or qualitative aspects the other mechanisms of directing, detecting, or prolonged fixation may be invoked.

Cardiac Change and the Alerting Mechanism of the Orienting Reflex

HR Change to Visual and Auditory Stimuli

In the five studies that follow, we used 3- to 4-month-old infants. Their state was controlled by only including those who were awake and alert throughout the testing session. In Study 1 we tested the reaction of 4-month-old infants to stimulus change using moving visual stimuli and HR changes as the measure of their attention. Visual patterns moving at different velocities were chosen since several studies have indicated that motion is a potent variable in capturing infant attention (e.g., McKenzie and Day, 1976; Volkmann & Dobson, 1976). McKenzie and Day (1976) report that moving objects are fixated longer than stationary ones over a range of distances. Volkmann and Dobson (1976) noted that faster stimuli were more effective in eliciting first fixations.

Infants were presented with a 7 cm black square which moved along a horizontal path at slow (3.6 cm/sec), medium (31 cm/sec), or fast (41 cm/sec) speeds at a distance of 75 cm from the infant. Each of 7 infants was presented with the stimulus at one speed for 8 trials. Trials were of 10-sec duration with 15-sec intertrial intervals. The stimuli were displayed on a TV monitor. All infants responded with heart rate deceleration during the period of stimulus exposure and the magnitude of the responses differed according to stimulus velocity. The average HR changes over the 10-sec stimulus period were 9.9, 3.6, and 2.8 beats per min for the fast, medium, and slow speed groups respectively. For the medium and slow group the HR changes returned to the prestimulus baseline value during the 10-sec period. In the fast group the baseline value was not restored until well into the interstimulus interval. The maximum HR change for the medium and fast groups was reached, on average, between 4 and 5 sec after stimulus onset. For the slow group the maximum HR deceleration occurred 7 sec after stimulus onset. These results are shown in Fig. 3.1. As indicated by the

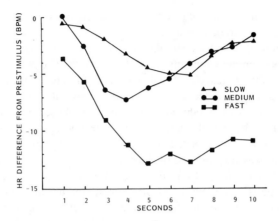

FIGURE 3.1.   Heart rate changes in response to a moving rectangle which was presented at three different speeds—slow, medium, fast.

magnitude of cardiac deceleration and rate at which HR returned to baseline, the fastest speed produced the greatest change. There was a functional relationship between the velocity of the stimulus and the amount of attention it attracted as indicated by the HR responses.

In Study 2 the manner in which stimulus duration affected the attentional behaviour of infants was examined. A sample of 4-month-old infants was presented with a black rectangle which moved at constant velocity in a vertical direction for a 1-, 5- or 10-sec period. The results are presented in Fig. 3.2.

Marked differences between the three experimental conditions are apparent. In the 5- and 10-sec periods infants showed similar maximum HR deceleration but differed in the rate at which HR returned to baseline. There was no strong trend indicating HR deceleration to the offset of the stimulus. Because of the

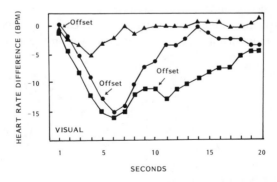

FIGURE 3.2.   Heart rate changes in response to a moving rectangle which was exposed at three different durations. (▲-▲, 1 sec; ●-●, 5 sec ■-■ 10 sec)

latency of the onset response, it is not possible to separate onset and offset effects in the 1- and 5-sec duration groups.

In a variation of this study an auditory stimulus, a 500 Hz pure tone, was presented to three groups of infants at 60, 75, or 85 db. The same procedure was used as before. Infants responded with HR decelerations to all three intensities with the most pronounced deceleration for the highest intensity, i.e., 85 db. On average the responses were reduced in comparison to those for visual stimuli but for each intensity large and consistent offset responses were obtained. Two points merit consideration. First, although a sudden stimulus onset was used in this study there was no evidence of the startle responses which have been reported in other studies (e.g., Berg, Berg, & Graham, 1971). Second, the infants responded to the stimulus onset and offset with similar amplitudes of HR deceleration. Whereas HR deceleration at stimulus offset has been reported in other studies (e.g., Berg, 1972; Bohlin, Lindhagen, & Hagekull, 1981) such an effect has usually been small.

In another experiment a 1,000 Hz pure tone was presented at 75 db for 1-, 5- or 10-sec periods. The results are shown in Fig. 3.3. The pattern of HR deceleration was quite different from that obtained in the visual mode. The amplitude of HR responses was smaller, the maximum response occurred earlier (after 2 and 3 sec compared to 5 and 6 sec), and the infants responded with cardiac deceleration to both stimulus onset and offset. For the 1-sec duration stimulus it is not possible to separate effects of onset and offset. Although stimuli were presented with sudden onset there was no evidence of a startle response; i.e., there was no evidence of cardiac acceleration.

Another sample of 4-month-old infants was exposed to 270, 500, 1,000 or 1,500 Hz pure tones at 75 db. The tones had sudden onset and were presented for 10 sec followed by a 15-sec offset period. Eight trials were given. All frequencies produced consistent and large HR deceleration during the stimulus onset and offset periods. It is quite clear that the frequencies used in this study produced the typical cardiac deceleration behavior in infants.

In these experiments the cardiac change produced in a variety of situations was both regular, in that it varied systematically over time, and was repeatable.

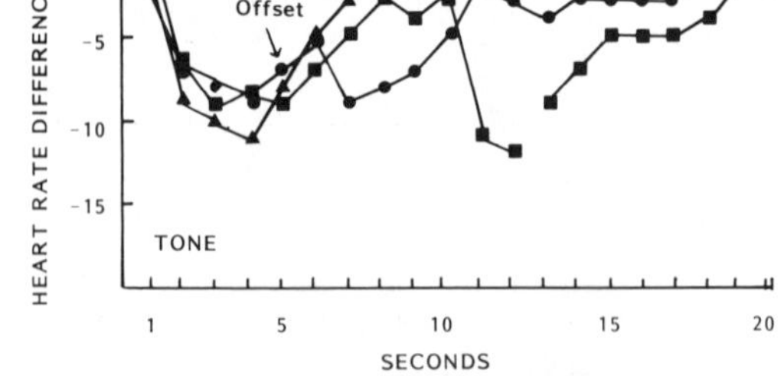

FIGURE 3.3. Heart rate changes as a function of a 1,000 Hz-tone presented at three different durations. (▲-▲, 1 sec; ●-●, 5 sec; ■-■, 10 sec)

The responses elicited varied in their magnitude with changes in the stimuli such as duration, intensity, and speed of movement. Although no attempt was made to equate stimuli from different sensory modalities, these results suggest that there are differences in the cardiac response when visual and auditory sensory modalities are compared. The OR responses are less rapid, of greater magnitude, and relatively more enduring when the stimuli are presented in the visual rather than the auditory sensory modality. None of our studies revealed evidence of a startle reflex, even in cases where sudden stimulus onset was used.

When duration, intensity, or speed was varied systematic changes in HR occurred, but when frequency was varied at constant intensity the HR changes were the same for all conditions. This detection of change in quantitative rather than qualitative aspects of stimuli is proposed to be a function of the alerting mechanism. Posner and Rothbart (1981) argue that behavior after repeated presentations of a stimulus may be an habituation of this alerting capacity and not a reflection of the formation of some stimulus specific internal code. It may not be necessary to propose a cortically located neuronal code as Sokolov (1963) has proposed.

Cardiac Change and the Directing and Detecting Aspects of the Orienting Reflex

Sokolov (1963) described in adults a collection of behaviors associated with the OR, which was preparatory to the organism being receptive to stimulation. Several findings suggest that cardiac data can reflect both a directing towards stimuli and a detection of them.

In two separate experiments (Finlay, Quinn, & Ivinskis, 1982) cardiac change for infants was measured while they oriented away from a central fixation stimulus to a brief, peripheral, moving pattern. In one experiment, viewing was monocular with stimuli appearing in either the nasal or temporal visual field, whereas in the other, viewing was binocular and stimuli were presented either to the right or left. The results were essentially the same in both experiments. The main features of the results were the small cardiac change and the fact that the amount of change was similar whether the stimuli were presented at 20° or at 75° in the periphery. It seems from these results that the physical act of directing attention does not have a large effect on cardiac change.

In another experiment (Finlay & Ivinskis, 1982) the position of the stimulus was kept constant but both the speed of the peripheral stimulus and its duration were varied. Five trial types were used to separate out the effects of directing and detection on cardiac change. Two conditions were considered—brief and prolonged fixation. The first trial type was a brief, 2-sec presentation directly in front of the infant. This was included to ascertain the effect of centering the infant so that the peripheral angle could be defined. In the second trial type the central presentation was followed by a 2-sec presentation at 25° in the periphery of a slow, or fast (trial type 3) moving stimulus. On the final two trial types the central presentation was followed by a 10-sec presentation at 25° of either the slow, or fast moving stimulus.

For the central stimulus alone and the central stimulus plus the brief, slow peripheral stimulus, cardiac changes were small and essentially the same. This finding reinforces those outlined earlier,indicating that the physical aspects of directing attention have little effect on the HR. However, when the central stimulus was followed by a brief, fast stimulus, larger cardiac changes were produced. These results suggest that the detection of peripheral stimuli are reflected in HR changes as a function of the magnitude of the stimulus used over and above the small changes produced by the directing of attention to that stimulus.

The directing and detecting aspects can be distinguished in their effect on cardiac change. There were differences between those trials in which the peripheral stimulus was presented for 2 sec and those where the presentation was for 10 sec. The difference was not in the magnitude of the cardiac change but rather in the time taken to return to baseline, it being longer for the prolonged viewing trial type. The effects of prolonged viewing is taken up later when fixation is considered.

In summary, the addition of a peripheral stimulus produced an increase in the magnitude of the HR change over that obtained with a single central stimulus. The extent of the change varied with the speed of the peripheral stimulus. Further, prolonging the peripheral stimulus tended to delay the return to baseline instead of further increasing the HR change over the levels obtained with the brief peripheral stimulus. An obvious suggestion is that the greater cardiac response obtained with the fast peripheral stimulus may simply result from a shorter latency of head and eye movements. Although we have demonstrated that the magnitude of the directing movement produces no differential HR responses it is possible that the speed of these directing movements will produce such cardiac changes. This possibility was not supported as the latency of eye movements did not differ between the two stimulus speed combinations.

In this experiment we have demonstrated that the physical allocation of attention, i.e., the directing of attention, together with the mechanisms that direct this process, are separable from the detection process. The distinction being made is between an event having occurred at a point in the field and eyes (and head) directed to that point, and knowledge of what that event is. The prolonged inspection of that event needs to be considered separately as we do in the next section. Before doing that, however, we wish to discuss an experiment in which there is evidence of directing and detection without eye movements.

Cardiac measures taken in experimental situations which produce a conflict between a central fixation stimulus and a peripheral target stimulus produce interesting results. If infants are presented with a peripheral stimulus while they are fixating another stimulus, overt directing toward the peripheral stimulus is reduced (Harris & MacFarlane, 1974). Tronick (1972) referred to the effect as a narrowing of the "effective visual field"; a seemingly related effect in adult vision is known as "foveal load" (Ikeda & Takeuchi, 1975).

Finlay and Ivinskis (1984) studied two groups of infants receiving simultaneous presentations of central and peripheral stimuli. One group was presented with a combination of a slow-speed central stimulus and a faster speed peripheral stimulus. The other group received the combination of a medium-speed central stimulus and a medium-speed peripheral stimulus. Expressed in terms of numbers of eye movements to the peripheral stimulus the results were 75% for the first group and 40% for the second. Narrowing of the effective visual field was dependent upon the speed of the central stimulus. These findings replicate and extend the studies already described. Cardiac change was also examined. On trials with peripheral stimulus presentation but without overt directing, a cardiac change was obtained that was greater in magnitude than that produced to the central stimulus alone but smaller than that produced when an actual directing and detection occurred. These results may be interpreted as providing evidence that the peripheral stimulus is being detected without overt direction of attention towards it.

Taken together these findings point to the following attentional mechanisms:

1. An alerting function.

2. A behavioral or overt directing (or alignment) of attention.

3. A detection function that varies with the stimulus dimension and its magnitude.

4. A covert directing.

5. A decision process for the allocation of attention which is based upon stimulus values. For a single stimulus the process is probably automatic or reflexive whereas for two or more stimuli in competition the allocation of attention is not so automatic but based in part upon the magnitude of the stimuli.

6. Some indication of stimulus processing under conditions of prolonged fixation.

A point that Posner and Rothbart (1980) make forcibly is relevant; the OR fails to distinguish between the processes occurring prior to detection and those occurring subsequently. The procedures described above go some way towards distinguishing between these and show that their effects on HR can be separated.

Cardiac Change and the Prolonged Fixation Aspect of the Orienting Reflex

Most theories of attentional behavior in infants have concentrated on the fixation aspect of the attention—why babies look longer at some patterns. The explanations are usually couched in terms of novelty, discrepancy, complexity, or contour density. As Haith and Campos (1977) point out, each of these classes of explanation has its difficulties. Many argue for an internal representation of the stimulus on the basis of habituation data and some rely heavily on measures such as duration of looking to infer properties of the information processing system. A central problem is the definition of the stimulus and its coding by the infant visual system. Interrelated with this problem of stimulus definition and possible coding strategies is the general growth and development in a wide variety of visual functions over the first year of life. This development raises interesting questions regarding the limitations imposed upon an infant's visual processing at any point in the developmental sequence and has implications for the ongoing cognitive growth of the child. Aspects of particular relevance here are the development of acuity, accommodation, contrast sensitivity, and binocular function.

The development of acuity in infants has been reviewed by Atkinson and Braddick (1981) and Dobson and Teller (1978). Using a variety of measures, increases in acuity have been reported to occur over the first half year. There is now an extensive literature on the development of ocular accommodation (Banks, 1980; Braddick, Atkinson, French, & Howland, 1979; White, 1971) which indicates a dramatic change in accommodative ability over the first months of life.

It has been argued (Braddick, 1981) that because it is measured over a range of spatial frequencies, the contrast sensitivity function provides a more general assessment of vision. Reviews by Banks and Salapatek (1978) and Atkinson and Braddick (1981) indicate that contrast sensitivity increases over the first 6 months but is still considerably less than that found in adults in terms both of the range of spatial frequencies involved and the contrast sensitivity of any particular spatial frequency. Not only is the high-frequency cut-off considerably less than in adults, but, at least until 3 months, the low-frequency end of the function is of a different shape to that found in adults.

As with acuity, accommodation, and contrast sensitivity, different aspects of binocular functioning have been shown to develop over the first 12 months-of-life. As well as development in bifoveal fixation, fusion, and stereopsis (see Aslin & Dumais, 1980) visual field characteristics seem to develop too. For adults the horizontal field of view is somewhat greater than 180° due to the refractive qualities of the cornea. The visual field in infants seems to be somewhat less than this value.

Lewis (1979) found that infants 1-month-old were able to detect stimuli placed 30° in the temporal visual field but not beyond 10° in the nasal visual field when viewing monocularly. These figures suggest a visual field width of 60° incorporating a 20° region of binocular overlap. The corresponding field sizes in adults are 210° for the field width and 100°–120° for the size of the region of binocular overlap.

By 2 months, Lewis (1979) found monocular detection of stimuli at 20° in the nasal field. Harris and MacFarlane (1974) also provide evidence that the visual field increases with age. Using a monocular patching technique Finlay, Quinn, and Ivinskis (1982) demonstrated that the binocular field of 4-month-old infants was greater than 140° and the binocular overlap field was at least 80°. For the 3-month-old infants tested in the same experiment the binocular overlap field width did not extend much beyond 60°.

IMPLICATIONS FOR INFANT VISION AND THE PROLONGED FIXATION ASPECT OF THE OR

It is clear that these developing visual functions have implications for theories concerning the fixation aspect of attention. As Banks and Salapatek (1981) point out, the amount of pattern information available to the infant's visual system is just a small fraction of that available to the adult. Any theories that propose the construction of internal representations, or schema, to account for fixation behavior and for habituation should be mindful of this. Atkinson and Braddick (1981) and Banks and Salapatek (1981) propose that the infant's visual world is limited to objects within several feet of their bodies at which distance they are capable of resolving gross detail such as facial features. With development the infant will increasingly be able to see objects at greater distances and with more detail in near objects. Linear Systems Theory having as its basis the contrast sensitivity function seems well suited to modeling some of these changes. Gibson's theory also seems to offer the scope to accommodate the developmental changes provided at least some rudimentary ability to respond to transformations and invariant properties under these transformations exist.

Linear Systems Theory

Linear systems analysis provides a potentially powerful approach for understanding vision in infants. In essence, this view holds that the output of a system can be predicted from a knowledge of both the dimensions of the input signal and the transfer characteristics of that system (i.e., the modulation transfer function, or, contrast sensitivity function, CSF). Using Fourier analysis, any two-dimensional visual pattern (the input signal) can be decomposed into a combination of sine-wave components that vary in their spatial frequency, their phase relationships, amplitude (contrast), and orientation.

The contrast sensitivity function (CSF) reflects the transfer characteristics of the human visual system for the spatial frequency dimension (Braddick, 1981; Braddick, Campbell, & Atkinson, 1978; Salapatek, Bechtold, & Bushnell, 1976) if certain conditions are satisfied. The conditions necessary for a system to be considered linear are isotropy, state-invariance, linearity, and homogeneity (Cornsweet, 1970). In practical terms, these involve the use of stimuli with (a) contrasts not significantly above threshold, (b) fixed space average luminance, and (c) central visual field presentation (Banks & Salapatek, 1981). The response of the visual system to phase and orientation information needs to be considered separately.

It has been shown that the contrast sensitivity functions of infants of less than 6-months-of-age are characterized by a relatively high contrast threshold and poor resolution of high spatial frequencies (i.e., >10 cycles/degree).

Banks and Salapatek (1981) and Allik and Valsiner (1980) have explored the advantages and limitations of the linear systems approach as applied to infant vision. When the above conditions were met the power of the technique was clearly demonstrated. However, Banks and Salapatek (1981) state that "we do not believe that the CSF approach can at present provide any general account of the pattern discrimination capabilities of young infants" (p.38). They proposed that pattern discrimination in infants is governed by pattern information available to "CNS" decision centers and that the CSF determines in part what the information conveyed to these centers will be. They suggested three rules that may be relevant to the decision center. First, preferences are determined by the "patterned stimulus which possesses the spatial frequency component of highest amplitude" (p.39). Using this rule, they were able to predict preferences for element size within checkerboards shown by infants of various ages on the basis of their CSFs. Second, the preference will be modulated by the total energy in the amplitude spectrum and, third, infants will show preference (fixate longer) for those stimuli possessing the greatest contour density.

Finlay and Ivinskis (1982) have reported data from an experiment using 2-dimensional checkerboard patterns that had been variously band-pass filtered, i.e., had regions of the spatial frequency spectrum removed. The original checkerboard pattern was converted, by computer, into digital form and then Fourier analyzed by an FFT (fast Fourier transform) routine and while in the Fourier domain was variously band-pass filtered to produce stimuli having spatial frequencies confined to fairly narrow bands as shown in Table 3.1.

In terms of CSF data for 3-month-old infants (that is, at threshold measurement) responsiveness is largely confined to spatial frequencies between .10 and 2.00 cycles/degree (Banks & Salapatek, 1978) peaking at about .50 cycles/degree. The stimuli were selected to cover this range (.00–2.90), to vary spatial frequency content within this range (0.00–1.00 and 1.00–2.90), as well as

TABLE 3.1
The Spatial Frequency Composition of the Stimulus
in Cycles/Degree Visual Cycle

	Spatial Frequency Range (Cycles/Degree)
1	0.00 – 1.00
2	0.00 – 2.90
3	0.00 – 1.00 and 2.90 – 11.60
4	1.00 – 2.90
5	1.00 – 11.60
6	2.90 – 11.60

including spatial frequencies well outside this range (e.g., 2.90–11.60). The remaining stimuli in Table 3.1 complete the design. On this basis, an ordering of preference might be predicted: 2,1,3 > 4,5,6. As well as the spatial frequency composition, the stimuli varied in a measure of the amplitude spectrum energy. If infants responded to the stimuli with the greatest energy, an ordering of 5>3>6>2>4>1 would be expected.

The infant was seated on a research assistant's lap 75 cm from a semicircular, grey screen which housed two video monitors positioned at eye level for the infant. Two sets of the six stimuli were made, one set having a contrast of .6 and the other .3 for presentation on the video screens. One group of seven infants received the high contrast stimuli and a second group of seven the low contrast.

The experimental procedure began with a 10-sec pretrial period which was followed by a 2-sec presentation of a blank illuminated screen directly in front of the infant. Immediately after the 2-sec central stimulus, a 15-sec stimulus (one of the filtered checkerboard patterns) appeared at 15° in the infant's periphery. Following a 10-sec intertrial period, the sequence was repeated for 12 trials for each infant. The purpose of the central blank field was to provide a means of measuring fixation latency of orientation towards the peripheral stimulus. Each infant received each of the six stimuli twice in a different random ordering.

Latency to fixation indicated significant effects for both pattern and contrast. Fixations to the higher contrast were made more quickly than to the lower. Response latencies to the 0.00–0.290 Hz pattern were faster than to the 1.00–2.90 Hz pattern but no other comparisons were significant. Duration of looking did not indicate any significant effects of either contrast or pattern type. Cardiac data collected during the experiment showed significant change during those periods when the infant was fixating. The lower contrast stimuli produced smaller changes than the higher. The visual latency data, with partial support from the cardiac data, indicated that the contrast level had an effect on the speed with which infants oriented towards a stimulus. Infants' directing behavior was also affected by the spatial frequency composition of the stimuli.

It was to be expected on the basis of the decision rules proposed by Banks and Salapatek (1981) that there would be strong orderings in the duration of fixation. This was not the case. Fixation duration was not simply determined by the spatial frequency composition of the stimuli although there was some indication that this had an effect on the directing aspect. The other factor considered, the energy in the filtered amplitude spectrum as a percentage of the energy of the unfiltered vision, did not adequately account for the results either.

It is possible that Linear Systems Theory will provide a useful approach to modeling visual perception and its development in the infant as Banks and Salapatek (1981) have so cogently argued. However, the data presented here indicate that its application is by no means straightforward.

The main aim of this study was to examine HR changes in situations where the infant fixated the stimulus pattern for a prolonged period. The data paralleled those obtained from visual fixation measures in two ways; first, cardiac decelera-tion was evident during stimulus exposure periods confirming that the infants were aware of the stimuli and, second, greater cardiac deceleration was obtained for the higher contrast stimuli. As we have argued in earlier sections, these changes can be explained in terms of alerting, directing, or detecting mecha-nisms without recourse to special mechanisms operating during prolonged fixation.

Gibson's Theory

Gibson's theoretical writings (Gibson, 1979) also provide a potentially powerful approach to understanding the development of perception in infants. The two aspects of Gibson's theory that are important here are first that the structure of the ambient optic array contains a very rich source of information at least some of which the human visual system can respond to directly, and second, that trans-formations of this structure lead to the concepts of variants and invariants within the transforming display. Generally it is the ability to detect invariants under transformation that permits knowledge of the environment and one's position and motion within it, and, more specifically, form perception.

With the infant's visual system in a state of continual development Gibson's position is still relevant. If we propose that the newborn has some ability to detect invariants under transformation then this ability can be elaborated over time as the visual system develops. Tests of the theory would include demonstra-tions that infants can respond to transformations, per se, and that they can respond differentially to variant and invariant structures within these transforma-tions.

There are many studies that could be interpreted as support for the notion that infants can respond to transformations (e.g., Day & McKenzie, 1973) but few that have attempted specific tests of the theory. Some that have are the visual cliff, "looming" stimuli (see Yonas, 1981, for a review), and the perception of invariants (Gibson, Owsley, & Johnston, 1978; Gibson, Owlsey, Walker, & Megaw-Nyce, 1979).

Some investigators have attempted to show that infants are able to respond to invariant structures within transforming displays. For example, using an habitua-tion and dishabituation paradigm Gibson et al. (1978) argued that substance and shape can be detected as invariant properties in transforming displays. Finlay, Sacchetti, and Ivinskis (1982) suggest, however, that these findings were not conclusive in demonstrating that the infants were responding to the transforma-tion but rather could be more simply described in terms of "change detection," that is, in terms of an infant's response to an aspect of the display rather than to the transformations as a whole. Finlay et al. (1982) carried out a study in which infants between 3- and 4-months-of-age habituated either to repeated presenta-tions of a shape successively undergoing one of two rigid motions, or to repeated presentations of a single rigid motion while two shapes were varied successively.

To support the transformation theory the evidence must show that the infant can abstract the invariant aspect of the stimulus presentation, in this case stimulus shape. If this were to occur there would be little or no change across habituation/dishabituation trials when shape remains constant but the transformation is altered. To test this there were four groups: the first was presented with the same motion transformations but shape was changed in the dishabituation trials; in the second, shape was constant but the motion transformation was changed, and in the other two both shape and their transformations were changed. There was no support for the prediction of differential dishabituation in either the visual or cardiac data. These results suggest that infants are unable to dissociate the shape from the transformation. Infants were presumably detecting change whether it was of shape, motion transformation, or both. In terms of the scheme used here these results could be explained in terms of the alerting, directing, or detecting mechanisms without recourse to other mechanisms.

It is interesting to compare the two measures used in this experiment— fixation duration and cardiac change using interbeat-interval (IBI). The mean fixation duration for the two prehabituation trials, the 10 habituation trials, and the posthabituation trials is shown in Fig. 3.4.

The cardiac change for the habituation trials only are shown as mean IBI change from a prestimulus baseline value for each second within a trial. It is important to note that cardiac change is represented as a change in IBI—not cardiac rate units, beats per min. Results for each successive pair of trials were collapsed to give the five blocks of trials shown in Fig. 3.5. Habituation and dishabituation were evident in both response measures, although not shown in Fig. 3.5.

Habituation of visual fixation is often interpreted as reflecting the building up of an internal representation of the repeated stimulus. Our results would seem to indicate that cardiac change can also be a reflection of the same process. An alternative explanation can be made consistent with the terms of Gibson's theory.

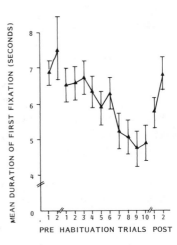

FIGURE 3.4. The mean duration of the first fixation in seconds is shown averaged across the four experimental groups for the prehabituation, the habituation and posthabituation trials.

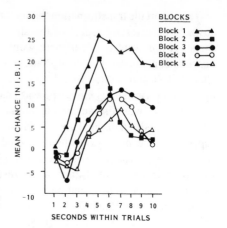

FIGURE 3.5. The mean IBI change from a prestimulus baseline value, for each second during an habituation trial. The data are presented in blocks of two trials.

If there are processes that respond directly to the variant and invariant structures within temporally transforming displays it could indeed be these that habituate over time. The appearance of dishabituation could reflect stimulation of different aspects of the structure. This implies that other experimental designs are needed to tease out, first, whether infants can respond to transformations per se and, second, whether they can detect invariant structures within these transformations.

We have made preliminary examinations of two theoretical positions, Linear Systems Theory and Gibson's Theory of Direct Perception, that may help to explain the processes behind infants' fixation behavior. Potentially both approaches are able to accommodate the many and rapid changes that are taking place in the visual system at this stage of development. Unfortunately neither position received unequivocal support and the fixation results obtained in each experiment can be explained in terms of the other aspects of attention:alerting, directing, or detecting.

SUMMARY

Most discussions of attentional behavior that use cardiac measures make reference to the orienting reflex. We have attempted to dissect this collection of behaviors in order to look at various aspects of attention. We have considered the alerting, directing, and detecting aspects of attention and have provided some discussion of fixation behavior. The central issue has been the relationship between cardiac change and other measures of attention.

It is clear that cardiac measures can reliably be used as indicators of an infant's ability to differentiate along a variety of stimulus dimensions as can other more overt measures. We have attempted to account for these data in terms of the alerting aspects of the attention process. Differentiation was clearly shown when a dimension was varied quantitatively and did not occur when qualitative changes in the frequency of pure tones were made. This general finding was used to differentiate between directing and detection aspects of the attention. Directing of attention involving eye movements produces small changes in cardiac response whereas detection, whether accompanied by overt directing or a covert allocation of attention, produces cardiac change which varies with the stimulus situation.

Another aspect that was investigated was the effect of fixation on cardiac behavior. Prolonged fixation is reflected in some situations by the time the cardiac change activity takes to return to prestimulus baseline values. Using this observation we examined predictions that may be made from two current theories—Linear Systems Theory and Gibson's Theory—concerning fixation behavior. Neither the cardiac nor the fixation data confirmed predictions from the two theories although the cardiac data did show clear and consistent changes. We were unable to demonstrate specific effects of fixation, and the processes that may underlie those behaviors, on cardiac behavior. There are many difficulties in current theories of fixation behavior in infants (Haith & Campos, 1977) and we have attempted to disentangle some of the complexity in this behavior so that models may provide the grammars whereby such notions as internal representations can be more systematically investigated.

ACKNOWLEDGMENT

The research reported in this chapter was supported by an ARGS grant.

REFERENCES

Allik, J., & Valsiner, J. (1980). Visual development in ontogenesis: Some reevaluations. In H. W. Reese & L. P. Lipsitt (Eds.), *Advances in child development and behaviour.* Orlando, FL: Academic Press.

Aslin, R. N., & Dumais, S. T. (1980). Binocular vision in infants: A review of a theoretical framework. *Advances in Child Development and Behaviour, 81,* 53–94.

Atkinson, J., & Braddick, O. (1981). Acuity, contrast sensitivity, and accommodation in infancy. In R. N. Aslin, J. R. Alberts, & M. R. Peterson (Eds.), *Development of perception: Psychobiological perspectives.* Orlando, FL: Academic Press.

Banks, M. S. (1980). The development of visual accommodation during early infancy. *Child Development, 51,* 646–666.

Banks, M. S., & Salapatek, P. (1978). Acuity and contrast sensitivity in 1-, 2- and 3-month-old human infants. *Investigative Ophthalmology and Visual Science, 17,* 361–365.

Banks, M. S., & Salapatek, P. (1981). Infant pattern vision: A new approach based on contrast sensitivity function. *Journal of Experimental Child Psychology, 31,* 1–45.

Berg, W. K. (1972). Habituation and dishabituation of cardiac responses in four-month-old awake infants. *Journal of Experimental Child Psychology, 14,* 92–107.

Berg, K. M., Berg, W. K., & Graham, F. K. (1971). Infant heart rate response as a function of stimulus and state. *Psychophysiology, 8,* 30–44.

Bohlin, G., Lindhagen, K., & Hagekull, B. (1981). Cardiac orienting to pulsed and continuous auditory stimulation: A developmental study. *Psychophysiology, 18,* 440–446.

Braddick, O. (1981). Spatial frequency analysis in vision. *Nature, 291,* 9–11.

Braddick, O., Atkinson, J., French, J., & Howland, H. C. (1979). A photo refractive study of infant accommodation. *Vision Research, 19,* 1319–1330.

Braddick, O., Campbell, F. W., & Atkinson, J. (1978). Channels in vision: Basic aspects. In R. Held, H. Leibowitz, & H. L. Teuber (Eds.), *Handbook of Sensory Physiology, Vol. III, Perception.* Heidelberg: Springer.

Brown, J. W., Leavitt, L. A., & Graham, F. K. (1977). Response to auditory stimuli in 6- and 9-week-old human infants. *Developmental Psychobiology, 10,* 255–266.

Clifton, R. K., & Nelson, M. N. (1976). Developmental study of habituation in infants: The importance of paradigm, response system and state. In T. J. Tighe & R. N. Leaton (Eds.), *Habituation: Perspectives from child development, animal behaviour and neurophysiology.* Hillsdale, NJ: Lawrence Erlbaum Associates.

Cornsweet, T. N. (1970). *Visual perception.* Orlando, FL: Academic Press.

Day, R. H., & McKenzie, B. E. (1973). Perceptual shape constancy in early infancy. *Perception, 2,* 315–320.

De Loache, J. (1976). Rate of habituation and visual memory in infants. *Child Development, 47,* 145–54.

Dobson, V., & Teller, D. Y. (1978). Visual acuity in human infants: A review and comparison of behavioral and electrophysiological studies. *Vision Research, 18,* 1469–1485.

Fantz, R. L., & Fagan, J. F. (1975). Visual attention to size and number of pattern details by term and preterm infants during the first six months. *Child Development, 46,* 3–18.

Finlay, D. C., & Ivinskis, A. (1982). Cardiac and visual responses to stimuli presented foveally and peripherally as a function of speed of moving stimuli. *Developmental Psychology, 18,* 692–698.

Finlay, D. C., & Ivinskis, A. (1982, August). Visual and cardiac responses to variously filtered 2-D stimuli in three-month-old infants. *Proceedings of the IECD Conference,* Melbourne.

Finlay, D. C., & Ivinskis, A. (1984). Cardiac and visual responses to moving stimuli presented either successively or simultaneously to the central and peripheral visual fields in four-month-old infants. *Developmental Psychology, 20,* 29–36.

Finlay, D., Quinn, K., & Ivinskis, A. (1982). Detection of moving stimuli in the binocular and nasal fields by infants three and four months old. *Perception, 11,* 685–690.

Finlay, D., Sacchetti, A., & Ivinskis, A. (1982). Perception of invariants, or "change", across transformations of shape and substance? *Australian Journal of Psychology, 34,* 281–288.

Gibson, J. J. (1979). *The ecological approach to visual perception.* Boston: Houghton Mifflin.

Gibson, E. J., Owsley, C. J., & Johnston, J. (1978). Perception of invariants by five-month-old infants' differentiation of two types of motion. *Developmental Psychology, 14,* 407–415.

Gibson, E. J., Owsley, C. J., Walker, A., & Megaw-Nyce, J. (1979). Development of the perception of invariants: Substance and shape. *Perception, 8,* 609–619.

Graham, F. K. (1979). Distinguishing among orienting, defense and startle reflexes. In M. D. Kimmel, E. H. Van Olst, & J. F. Orlebeke (Eds.), *The orienting reflex in humans.* Hillsdale, NJ: Lawrence Erlbaum Associates.

Graham, F. K., & Clifton, R. K. (1966). Heart rate change as a component of the orienting response. *Psychological Bulletin, 65,* 305–320.

Graham, F. K., & Jackson, J. C. (1970). Arousal systems and infant heart rate responses. In H. W. Reese & L. P. Lipsitt (Eds.), *Advances in child development and behavior.* Orlando, FL: Academic Press.

Haith, M. M. (1978). Visual competence in early infancy. In R. Held, H. Leibowitz, & H. L. Teuber (Eds.), *Handbook of sensory physiology: Vol. VIII.* Berlin: Springer-Verlag.

Haith, M. M., & Campos, J. J. (1977). Human infancy. *Annual Review of Psychology, 28,* 251–293.

Harris, P., & MacFarlane, A. (1974). The growth of the effective visual field from birth to seven weeks. *Journal of Experimental Child Psychology, 18,* 340–348.

Ikeda, M., & Takeuchi, T. (1975). Influence of foveal load on the functional visual field. *Perception and Psychophysics, 18,* 255–260.

Kagan, J., Henker, B. A., Hen-Tov, A., Levine, J., & Lewis, M. (1966). Infants' differential reactions to familiar and distorted faces. *Child Development, 37,* 519–532.

Kagan, J., & Lewis, M. (1965). Studies of attention in the human infant. *Merill-Palmer Quarterly, 11,* 95–127.

Karmel, B. Z. (1969). The effect of age, complexity and amount of contour on pattern preferences in human infants. *Journal of Experimental Child Psychology, 7,* 339–354.

Lacey, J. I., & Lacey, B. C. (1958). The relationship of resting autonomic activity to motor impulsivity. *The brain and human behavior* (pp. 144–209). Baltimore: Williams and Wilkins.

Lewis, M. (1971). Individual differences in the measurement of early cognitive growth. In J. Hellmuth (Ed.), *Exceptional infant studies in abnormalities.* New York: Bruner Mazel.

Lewis, T. L. (1979). *The development of nasal field detection in young infants.* Unpublished doctoral thesis, McMaster University.

Lewkowitz, D. J., & Turkewitz, G. (1980). Cross-model equivalence in early infancy: Auditory-visual intensity matching. *Developmental Psychology, 16,* 597–607.

Lynn, R. (1966). *Attention, arousal and the orienting reaction.* New York: Macmillan.

McCall, R. B., & Kagan, J. (1967). Stimulus-scheme discrepancy and attention in the infant. *Journal of Experimental Child Psychology, 5,* 381–390.

McCall, R. B., & Nelson, W. H. (1970). Complexity contour and area as determinants of attention in infants. *Developmental Psychology, 3,* 343–349.

McKenzie, B., & Day, R. H. (1976). Infants' attention to stationary and moving objects at different distances. *Australian Journal of Psychology, 28,* 45–47.

Posner, M. I., & Rothbart, M. K. (1980). The development of attentional mechanisms. In H. E. Howe (Ed.), *Nebraska Symposium on Motivation.* Lincoln/London: University of Nebraska Press.

Salapatek, P., Bechtold, A. G., & Bushnell, E. W. (1976). Infant visual acuity as a function of viewing distance. *Child Development, 47,* 860–863.

Sokolov, Y. N. (1963). *Perception and the conditioned reflex.* Oxford: Pergamon.

Tronick, E. (1972). Stimulus control and the growth of the infant's effective visual field. *Perception and Psychophysics, 11,* 373–376.

Volkmann, F. C., & Dobson, M. V. (1976). Infant responses to ocular fixation to moving visual stimuli. *Journal of Experimental Child Psychology, 22,* 86–99.

Von Bargen, D. (1983). Infant heart rate: A review of research and methodology. *Merrill Palmer Quarterly, 29,* 115–149.

White, B. L. (1971). *Human infants: Experience and psychological development.* Englewood Cliffs, NJ: Prentice-Hall.

Woodworth, R. S. (1927). *Psychology: A study of mental life.* London: Methuen.

Yonas, A. (1981). Infants' responses to optical information for collision. In R. N. Aslin, J. R. Alberts, & M. R. Peterson (Eds.), *Development of perception: Psychobiological perpectives.* Orlando, FL: Academic Press.

PERCEPTION
OF OBJECTS

4 Visual Size Constancy in Infancy

R. H. Day
Monash University

INTRODUCTION

For the adult observer the visually perceived environment is by and large a stable place. Objects remain more or less the same in their "intrinsic" properties of size, shape, color, and brightness and in their orientation, position, and state of movement (including their stationariness) as the observer moves about the environment and ambient light changes in its composition and intensity. But there is a paradox in all this. The representation of intrinsic and relational characteristics at the eyes is far from stable. The size and shape of the retinal images vary with the distance and bearing of the observer from the object. Furthermore their colors and luminances change with the wavelength composition and intensity of light. Likewise, the representation of orientation, position, and motion varies as the observer changes posture and position and scans the environment with eye and head movements.

Such apparent stability in the face of unstable representation at the sense organs is called perceptual constancy. It is a ubiquitous perceptual phenomenon by no means restricted to vision. It occurs also in the auditory (Day, 1968; Mohrmann, 1939) and proprioceptive (Izzet, 1934) modes.

Perceptual constancy is regarded as complete or "perfect" when the perceived properties of objects remain unchanged although their sensory representations vary. For example, visual size constancy is regarded as complete when apparent size is unchanged with changes in object-observer distance and consequently, in the size of the retinal image. Incomplete constancy or "underconstancy" refers to a tendency for the perceived state of affairs to shift in the direction of its sensory representation and "overconstancy" to the opposite

67

tendency, i.e., an "overcompensation" for the change. In terms of apparent size, underconstancy is a tendency for the object to appear progressively smaller with increases in its distance from the observer and overconstancy a tendency for it to appear progressively larger. Both effects occur under specified conditions of information from environmental cues and instructions.

At the beginning of their review of perception in human infancy Banks and Salapatek (1983) raised the question of the purposes of vision and outlined the answers proposed by Gibson (1968) and Marr (1982). The former emphasizes the part played by vision in extracting information from the environment, a role which, of course, vision shares with other perceptual systems. Marr saw the main purpose as that of recognizing and identifying objects and determining their spatial properties and layout. Thus in Marr's terms the perceptual constancies can be regarded as the outcomes of recognition and identification processes with frequently changing sensory representations. If we agree that among the main functions of vision is the perception of objects in space, and we bear in mind that object representations are highly variable, the issue arises concerning whether perceptual stability with variable representation is at all evident in the first year of life. It is with this issue that we are mainly concerned. Three questions can be asked. First, can size constancy be demonstrated in the first year? Second, if so, how early can it be detected? Third, if constancy is evident, how complete is it? As it will be seen, the first and second questions can now be answered; the third can not.

It can be presumed that size constancy in infancy is continuous with that occurring later in life. It is therefore relevant to consider here the character and determinants of size constancy in both childhood and adulthood. In this connection it can be noted that it appears to be complete by about 11–12 years-of-age. However, as is noted below, the instructions given to subjects in an experiment play a major role in determining whether objects are responded to in terms of their "projective" (retinal) or "real" size. This observation indicates a measure of cognitive control over the perceptual processes involved in size constancy. It is therefore probable that the development of size constancy reflects in some part the emergence of the cognitive capacity to follow instructions and of cognitively based strategies as well as the basic perceptual processes that give rise to size constancy. However, it is to be noted that the contribution of basic perceptual processes and higher-order cognitive processes to size constancy and their mode of interaction in determining size constancy are far from clear. Until this issue is clarified it is not possible to give a "process-oriented" account of visual size constancy for either infants or older subjects.

It is helpful first to consider briefly the history of the study of size constancy and the situations in which it was first studied. Since size constancy in infancy must necessarily involve a capacity to discriminate object size, evidence for this capacity will also be considered before turning to size constancy itself. Distance discrimination, which is also involved in size constancy is discussed later in the paper.

VISUAL SIZE CONSTANCY

The relative constancy of visually perceived size with variation in the size of the retinal projection due to changes in distance was the first of the perceptual constancies to be recognized and to receive serious scientific attention. Berkeley (1969) mentioned it in his *A New Theory of Vision* in 1734 and attributed it to simultaneous perception of object distance, a view which still has currency (see Boring, 1942). Fechner in 1860 quantified the effect in the near field of vision by matching the apparent separation between one pair of compass points at one distance with the apparent separation between a second pair at another distance. Early systematic studies of size constancy were conducted by Martius (1889) using vertical rods placed at different distances and by Hillebrand (1902) using frontoparallel extents between a "corridor" of hanging threads, an arrangement that came to be called the vista or alley effect. Later, Thouless (1931) and Brunswik (1933) recognized visual size constancy as one of a class of effects which they investigated and compared by means of an appropriate common index. Thouless (1931) referred to perceptual constancy as "phenomenal regression to the real object" thus characterizing it as a shift of the perceived property away from its retinal representation towards the physical or "real" state of affairs.

VISUAL SIZE CONSTANCY IN ADULTHOOD

For an adult observer viewing under "normal" conditions—binocular vision with unrestricted eye and head movements in a setting rich in texture, pattern and objects—overconstancy of size is usual (Gilinsky, 1955; Holway & Boring, 1941; Wohlwill, 1963a, 1963b). This "overshoot" effect occurs for objects as far away as about 1200 m (Gilinsky, 1955). The degree of overconstancy varies according to the instructions to the observer, the availability of information or "cues" to distance, and experimental procedures. Carlson (1960, 1962) found that when observers were asked to make "objective" judgments, i.e., to judge the object in terms of its physical size, overconstancy occurred. If they were instructed to judge in terms of how the object appeared, i.e., to adopt a "phenomenal attitude" the judgments accorded closely with the object's true size, i.e., size constancy was virtually complete.

With reduction in the availability of distance information as occurs with monocular vision, restriction of the visual field, and reduced illumination there is a shift from overconstancy to underconstancy of size (Holway & Boring, 1941). With elimination of distance cues there is a close accord with visual angle expectations (Hastorf, & Way, 1952; Holway & Boring, 1941; Tada, 1956). Wohlwill (1963a) has made the point that failure to find overconstancy in perception, including overconstancy of shape and brightness, is generally attributable to impoverished conditions of viewing.

Departure from the usual overconstancy of apparent size also occurs in consequence of certain arrangements of the standard and variable stimulus objects. There is a consistent bias towards overestimation of the standard. Thus when the standard object is far and the variable near the level of size constancy is greater than for the reversed arrangement. This is because the standard is not only constant in size but is overestimated (Akishige, 1937; Chalmers, 1952; Piaget & Lambercier, 1943). When the standard is near it is still overestimated but the measured level of size constancy is smaller. This variation due to the relative position of the standard object means that it must be located both near and far relative to the variable in order to obtain a valid measure of the level of size constancy.

In summary, as a rule overconstancy of apparent size obtains for adults observing under normal viewing conditions. However, the degree of overconstancy varies according to instructions, information for distance, and the relative position of standard and variable objects. As is shown in the next section, overconstancy has not been found to occur with children younger than about 7 years.

VISUAL SIZE CONSTANCY IN CHILDHOOD

That size constancy varies as a function of age, appearing to achieve adult levels by about 10–11 years, was claimed by Beyrl on the basis of his careful experiment reported in 1926. Beyrl used the method of constant stimuli and, not surprisingly, some doubt has been expressed concerning whether, with this method requiring repeated comparisons, data for the younger subjects aged 2 and 3 years are reliable (Vurpillot, 1976). This criticism notwithstanding, the finding of an increase from marked underconstancy to complete constancy by 10 years has been sustained in more recent studies (Denis-Prinzhorn, 1961; Lambercier, 1946; Piaget & Lambercier, 1943; Zeigler & Leibowitz, 1957). The literature has been critically reviewed by Vurpillot (1976) and Wohlwill (1963b). Before commenting on the processes that might be reflected by this trend, it is as well to describe Beyrl's experiment in more detail.

A total of 75 children between the ages of 2 and 10 years together with 5 adults were tested. The task was to compare the size of a standard object, a cube or a disc, placed at 1 m with a similar object placed at various distances between 2 and 11 m. A fairly regular trend of increasing size constancy was found from the youngest to the oldest children. Size constancy appeared to be virtually complete at all distances for the 10-year-old children and indistinguishable from that for adults. Underconstancy was evident for younger children and increased with distance. Thus, while at 9 years constancy seemed complete at between about 2 and 7 m, underconstancy occurred at 9 and 11 m. At 3 years slight underconstancy was apparent even at 2 m and was marked at 11 m. At 2 m an 11-

cm object was matched to the 10-cm standard whereas at 11 m a 16-cm object was necessary to achieve a match.

Although the results from Beyrl's (1926) study seem clear they must be considered in the light of more recent data concerning the relative positions of standard and variable stimulus object and the instructions to subjects. The effect of relative positions of standard and variable has been investigated by Piaget and Lambercier (1951, 1956) and the effect of instructions by Rapoport (1967).

In comparing a number of studies involving young children Wohlwill (1963) showed that, as with adults when the variable is near and the standard far, there is generally a strong tendency for overconstancy to obtain. This proved to be so from as early as 5–6 years (Piaget & Lambercier, 1951, 1956). For the reverse arrangement there was a progressive increase from marked underconstancy at 5 years to either a reduced level of underconstancy or near-complete constancy by about 10 years. These data indicate that the "error of the standard," i.e., a tendency to overestimate the size of the standard object, interacts with size constancy to affect the outcome differentially according as the standard is near or far. The effect of instructions was demonstrated by Rapoport (1967). She found that from about 9 years-of-age size constancy was greater when the child was asked to judge in terms of the physical size of the object than when asked to judge apparent size. This difference between "objective" and "phenomenal" instructions did not occur with children aged between 5- and 7-years. It is conceivable, of course, that with children in this lower age range the absence of a difference between the two forms of instruction was due to a failure fully to grasp their meaning. As far as is known this possibility has not been investigated. This is to be regretted. An effect of instructions on size constancy serves to indicate that the processes involved can be brought to some degree under cognitive control. As matters stand such control seems to occur from about 9 years. It is conceivable that appropriately phrased instructions could demonstrate the occurrence of cognitive involvement earlier in development.

Two further claims have been made about size constancy in childhood. First, Edgren (1953) and Lambercier (1946) found that the structure of the visual field, i.e., the number of visible objects in the field, has little or no effect on the degree of constancy. Second, Wohlwill (1963a) reported that judgments of *distance* show a trend from underconstancy to overconstancy in childhood. Wohlwill required subjects aged from about 7- to 17-years-of-age to bisect an extent of about 1 m in the median axis. The near point of this extent was located about .5 m from the eye. A progressive change from underconstancy at about 7 years to marked overconstancy at 17 years was found. Overconstancy occurred from about 11 years. Two points can be raised about these findings. First, given that size constancy is dependent on stimulus information for distance (Holway & Boring, 1941) and this information derives in some part from environmental objects and features, the finding that the number of objects in the field had no effect is unexpected. Of course, it is possible that information for distance from retinal disparity and parallax from only a few objects was sufficient to provide the necessary information for distance. Second, progression from under- to over-constancy between 7- and 17-years could, as pointed out earlier, be due partly or even wholly to increasing ability to understand instructions and so more adequately to execute the task. Because adult subjects can switch under instructions from the "projective" to the "objective" mode (see Carlson, 1977) it is quite conceivable that with improving capacity to follow instructions higher levels of size constancy would be achieved.

In regard to the data on distance constancy in childhood, it is to be noted that the apparent extent of relatively short distances along the ground in the median axis is no different in principle from apparent size (i.e., extent) in the vertical or horizontal planes. The different extents simply lie in different planes of space. In these terms it is perhaps not surprising that allowing for the different tasks, bisection of median extents and comparisons of the size of near and far objects, there is close similarity between the trends for distance and size constancy.

SIZE DISCRIMINATION IN INFANCY

Experiments on size constancy rest, of course, on the assumption that the subjects can discriminate differences in object size and object distance. Although these abilities can reasonably be taken for granted with adults and older children who are able to verbalize sameness or difference, it cannot be assumed with younger children and infants. With preverbal subjects, independent indexing of the capacity to discriminate size and distance is an essential preliminary to the investigation of size constancy. Data on size discrimination are reviewed here and those on distance discrimination in a later section.

Day and McKenzie (1977) have already reviewed the (then) relatively sparse data on size perception. Some experiments proved to be badly flawed so that the data could not be accepted as reliable indicators of size discrimination. The situation is now clearer.

Bower (1972) presented infants between 1- and 2-weeks-of-age with rods and balls of different diameters and recorded finger-thumb separations for one-handed contacts and interhand separations for two-handed contacts. The dependent variables were these two types of responses just prior to contact with the object. Both indexes increased steadily with size. Day and McKenzie (1977) pointed out that Bower's method of single-camera recording of finger-thumb and interhand separations could not yield an unambiguous measure because only two-dimensional records of movement in three dimensions were collected. More recently Lockman and Ashmead (1983) have argued that it is possible that the infant's hands were closed until the object was actually contacted. Since they would have contacted the larger object *sooner* both types of separation would have been greater in response to it. On both grounds Bower's (1972) data are far from satisfactory.

In an experiment reported by Bruner and Koslowski (1972), 10 infants were presented every 2 weeks from 8- to 21-weeks with a small- (1.5 in) and large- (10 in) diameter ball. It was noted that before contact with the ball was achieved, both arm and hand movements were differentiated with respect to the two sizes. For the small ball there were more forward arm movements towards the midline and increased hand activity. Lockman and Ashmead (1983) have also criticized the interpretation of these data in suggesting that the infants might have been responding to location rather than to size; since the larger ball would have extended farther from the midline of the body more side reaching might have occurred. Thus, side reaching for the large, ungraspable object might have been as appropriate as midline reaching was for the smaller, graspable object. Nevertheless, these different directions of response would seem to have indicated discrimination of relative size prior to contact.

More convincing evidence in favor of size discrimination in the first year derives from experiments in which the index was either visual preference or habituation of looking.

Fantz and Nevis (1967a, 1967b) found that, up to about 8-weeks-of-age, infants look longer at large objects compared with small ones. This preference disappeared after 8 weeks. With newborns Miranda and Fantz (1971) reported that patterns with large elements and those with more numerous elements were preferred over those with small elements and less numerous elements. Later, Fantz and Fagan (1975)—see also Fantz, Fagan, and Miranda (1975)—varied the size and number of elements in an array in such a way that the effectiveness of both these features could be evaluated separately and together. Their results show that infants between about 5 and 25 weeks have a preference for patterns with larger and more numerous elements. However, the relative effectiveness of element size diminished with age. Given that Fantz and Nevis (1967a, 1967b) used different stimulus patterns to those used by Miranda and Fantz (1971) and Fantz and Fagan (1975), the disappearance of the size preference after 8-weeks-of-age in the first of these studies is not necessarily inconsistent with the continuation of the preference to a later stage in the third. The main point to be noted is that all three studies suggest that capacity to discriminate size is apparent from early in the first year.

Day and McKenzie (1977) referred to McKenzie's (1972) earlier experiment in which 40 infants aged between 7 and 19 weeks were presented with large and small unpatterned 2- and 3-dimensional objects. After habituation to an object of one size that of another size was presented and recovery from habituation (dishabituation) recorded. Whereas response recovery occurred with the three-dimensional objects it did not do so with the two-dimensional ones. This suggested that motion parallax is implicated in discriminating the size of unpatterned, solid objects. The involvement of motion parallax in depth perception by infants in this age range was also claimed by Bower (1965) in his experiments on size discrimination of two- and three-dimensional objects (see below).

Ruff and Turkewitz (1979) used visual fixation times to index preference for one of two simultaneously or successively presented patterns, concentric rings, and parallel bars. Both were two dimensional. They were concerned with the effects of size and luminance, alone and in combination. There were three age groups, 6, 8, and 24 weeks, with 12 infants in each group. The results from three experiments showed that both larger and brighter patterns were preferred to smaller and dimmer ones at all ages with the preferences declining with age. The effects of size and brightness were additive, thus implicating the prominence or "salience" of the stimulus as a determinant of visual attention. Of significance for size constancy was the observation that with these highly patterned, two-dimensional stimuli size differences could be discriminated between 6 and 24 weeks.

Recently Lawson and Ruff (1984) demonstrated by means of visual following that the size of moving three-dimensional objects can be discriminated by infants aged 4 and 8 weeks. This ability was general for various objects at 4 weeks but limited to models of heads at 8 weeks.

Taken together, the evidence from early and recent experiments indicates that for young infants size is a discriminable object property. However, whether or not size discrimination is manifested in a particular experiment depends in large part on the indexing response and on the properties of the objects themselves, including whether they are plain or patterned or two- or three-dimensional. The interplay between the indexing response and various object properties has yet to be unravelled. In this regard it can be noted that Dannemillar and Banks (1983) after considering the data on habituation in infancy have arrived at the view that there may be a shift between early and later infancy in the mechanisms that underly habituation. They propose that in early infancy habituation may reflect the adaptation of cortical feature analyzers and in later infancy more cognitive-like processes. This point is worth consideration here since the abrupt shifts in the capacity of infants to discriminate size (Fantz & Nevis, 1967a, 1967b) could conceivably reflect a change in the processes associated with size discrimination.

At the end of a detailed review of perception in infancy, Allik and Valsiner (1980) arrived at the view that a complete set of "global" visual abilities are present at or soon after birth. These enable the infant to analyze the most significant properties of the visual environment, which include pattern, movement, color, and depth. Allik and Valsiner also contended that the infant processes these features of the stimulus array in a manner qualitatively similar to that of an adult. The outcomes of the experiments discussed in this section suggest that it would not be unreasonable tentatively to add size discrimination to Allik and Valsiner's list of global visual abilities.

EARLY STUDIES OF SIZE CONSTANCY IN INFANCY

The earliest-reported investigations of size constancy in infancy are those of Cruikshank (1938, 1941) and Misumi (1951). As already pointed out (Day & McKenzie, 1977) these experiments were badly flawed in their design and procedure with the result that their outcomes are inconclusive. Nevertheless, since both raise significant methodological issues they warrant some discussion here.

In Cruikshank's (1941) experiment 73 children aged between about 10 and 50 weeks were presented with a rattle 19 cm long at a distance of 25 cm (condition A), the same rattle at 75 cm (condition B), and a rattle 57 cm long at 75 cm (condition C). Thus in A and B the same object was presented at different distances and therefore subtended different visual angles. In C a larger object was presented at the greater distance and subtended the same visual angle as the smaller object when nearer (condition A). The objects were presented separately for 30 sec and the infant's reaching in response to them observed and recorded. The logic of the experiment was that if the response in A, B, and C were similar, no differences in discrimination of the objects in the stimulus array could be assumed. If responses in B and C were similar but different from A distance would be strongly implicated, and if responses to A and B were similar but different from C real size would be implicated thereby suggesting the operation of size constancy.

In point of fact, whatever the outcomes of this experiment the data would be inconclusive. If distance perception were assumed, the subjects could perceive that the object was the same size at the two distances (A and B) yet reach more frequently for the nearer. In addition, since there was no condition in which the two objects were at the same distance, no conclusions could be drawn about differences in reaching when the two objects were at different distances. More frequent reaching for, say, the larger object when the two were equidistant would determine the interpretation put on more frequent reaching for that object when it was at a different distance from the smaller.

In a series of eight experiments involving a total of 457 infants aged between 12 and 59 weeks Misumi (1951) recognized this inadequacy in Cruikshank's experiment and presented pairs of objects at the same and different distances. In the first three experiments the objects were toy goldfish 10 and 17.5 cm long. In the four experiments that followed small balls .25 and either .33 or .45 cm in diameter, were used. In the last experiment the stimulus objects were two series of cubes between 1 and 15 cm along an edge. The very small objects were used after it was shown that the frequency of reaching, which was the dependent variable throughout, was markedly greater for small than for large objects. In six of the eight experiments the two objects were at the same distance and in two (Experiments 2 and 6) at different distances. Because of the low frequency of responding the data from the experiments with the large objects were inconclusive.

The data for the .25- and .45-cm balls located respectively at 17.5 and 23.8 cm indicated that a greater frequency of reaching for the larger object persisted when it subtended the smaller visual angle. Of the total of 375 responses for subjects of about 26 weeks and older (younger subjects hardly responded at all), 301 (82%) were to the larger, further object. When the two objects were at the same distance (Experiment 5) 474 (88%) of a total of 558 responses were made to the larger ball.

Three issues from Misumi's experiment warrant comment. First, he found, as did Bruner and Koslowski (1972) later, that objects too large for manipulation are of little interest, as indexed by reaching, to young infants. Such objects are therefore quite unsuitable for use in experiments in which frequency of reaching serves as an index. Misumi's last experiment (Experiment 8) is especially informative in this regard. Subjects reached much more frequently for small red cubes measuring between .5–7.5 cm along an edge than for large ones measuring between 15 and 20 cm. Second, and more critically, Misumi did not describe how the very small (.25- and .45-cm) objects in his main experiments were presented to his subjects. If they were held by the experimenter they could easily have been partly occluded by the fingers. Third, Misumi did not describe the criteria for treating a response as reaching towards one object rather than the other. Since the two objects were laterally separated by only 5 cm, particularly careful attention by the experimenter to the direction of reaching would have been essential.

These criticisms notwithstanding, Misumi's experiments were the first to adduce some evidence for the operation of visual size constancy during the first year. As far as is known, they were also the first to show that whether or not reaching responses are elicited is determined in large part by the size of the stimulus objects.

BOWER'S SIZE-CONSTANCY EXPERIMENTS

Bower's (1964, 1965) experiments differed markedly from those of Cruikshank (1941) and Misumi (1951) in terms of both the responses by means of which perceptual discrimination was indexed and the size and distance of the stimulus objects. Discrimination was indexed by conditioned head turning and the objects were 12- and 36-in cubes located at either 36 or 108 in (Bower, 1964) and 30- and 90-cm cubes at either 100 or 300 cm (Bower, 1965).

The first experiment was concerned primarily with the discrimination of distance by young infants and only incidentally with size constancy. The issue was with whether, if prior action in space is necessary for distance discrimination as argued by Drever (1960) and Held (1961), premotor infants can discriminate distance. Prior action referred to ''. . . the action enabling the organism to use the information available in light, information which was previously meaningless for the ordering of objects in space'' (Bower, 1964, p. 368). Bower contended that this theory implies premotor infants who have not yet crawled or walked should not be capable of discriminating changes in the position of objects except in terms of variation in the size of their retinal images. To examine whether this is so, the leftward head turns of nine infants aged between 10 and 12 weeks were reinforced in the presence of a 12-in cube, the conditioned stimulus, situated at 36 in from the subject. ''Peek-a-boos'' made by an experimenter served as reinforcements. After training, the generalization of head turns was observed with (1) the 12-in cube at 36 in (the training situation), (2) the 12-in cube at 108 in, (3) the 36-in cube at 36 in, and (4) the 36-in cube at 108 in, each presented for 30 sec. The mean numbers of responses for these four conditions were respectively 102.7, 66.0, 54.1, and 22.9.

The number of responses in conditions (1) and (4) in which the size of the retinal image was the same were maximally different. Thus, the argument that for premotor infants the only basis for the discrimination of distance is in the size of the image was not supported. The smallest reduction in the number of responses relative to the training condition was in condition (2), the 12-in cube at 108 in. This suggested to Bower that size-at-a-distance is specified and size constancy is operative at 10-weeks-of-age. The relatively large number of responses in condition (3) compared with condition (4) suggested that distance was also discriminated.

The primary aim of Bower's (1965) second experiment was to investigate the role of motion parallax which had earlier been implicated in the discrimination of distance in infancy (Walk & Gibson, 1961). The procedure and stimulus arrangements were essentially the same as in the first experiment. There were 3 groups of 9 infants aged between about 6 and 9 weeks. The stimulus object during training for the first group (A) was a 30-cm cube at 100 cm viewed binocularly, for the second group (B) the same cube at the same distance viewed monocularly, and for the third group (C) a 30-cm square of light of about the same luminance as the cube viewed binocularly. The test conditions for groups A and B were (1) the 30-cm cube at 100 cm (the training condition), (2) the 30-cm cube at 300 cm, (3) a 90-cm cube at 100 cm, and (4) the 90-cm cube at 300 cm. The test conditions for group C were the same with 30- and 90-cm squares replacing the cubes.

The mean number of head turns for the three groups under the four conditions were:

A-(1) 98.7, (2) 58.1, (3) 54.2, and (4) 22.1;
B-(1) 101.0, (2) 60.9, (3) 53.6, and (4) 22.9;
C-(1) 94.8, (2) 52.0, (3) 44.1, and (4) 96.0.

The pattern of results for A and B are similar to those of Bower's earlier experiment with the response frequencies for conditions 2 and 3 less than for 1 but greater than for 4. The pattern of responses for C differs from that of A and B in condition 4, for which the response frequency is about the same as that for condition 1.

The data were interpreted by Bower to mean that between 6- and 10-weeks-of-age infants can discriminate size and distance and that size constancy is sustained when the distance of the object is changed. The mean response frequency in condition 4 (90-cm cube at 300 cm) for C with two-dimensional squares compared with the frequencies in A and B with three-dimensional cubes was interpreted as showing that motion parallax serves to specify distance with three-dimensional objects but not with two-dimensional ones. Of course, this interpretation implies that the close similarity between the results for groups A, B and C for conditions 2 and 3 must be attributed to information for distance other than that of motion parallax. Bower (1965) suggested that this information could have been the size of the retinal image. While this is plausible it seems somewhat unparsimonious to attribute specification of distance for groups A and B in condition 2, the 30-cm cube at 300 cm, to retinal size and in condition 4, the 90-cm cube at 300 cm, to motion parallax.

It could reasonably be assumed that the consistent outcomes of Bower's (1964, 1965) experiments would be sustained using alternative methods. McKenzie and Day (1972) tested this assumption with 32 infants aged between 6 and 20 weeks using 6- and 18-cm white cubes located at 30 and 90 cm. The intention was to compare the degree of recovery from habituation of visual fixation of an 18-cm cube at 90 cm under four conditions. These were (1) 18-cm cube at 90 cm (the habituation condition), (2) 18-cm cube at 30 cm, (3) 6-cm cube at 90 cm, and (4) 6-cm cube at 30 cm. If size and distance were discriminated and size constancy operated as indicated in Bower's experiments it was to be expected that recovery from habituation would be least for 1 (same object at same distance), greater for 2 and 3 (same object at different distance, and different object at same distance), and greatest for 4 (different object at different distance).

These expectations were not realized. In the first place habituation over ten trials with the 18-cm cube at 90 cm did not occur and, in the second place, increased fixation in the test trials occurred only when either of the two cubes was presented at 30 cm. There was no change in duration of fixation when either of the two objects was presented at the greater distance.

In summary, whereas in Bower's experiments the subjects responded to object size and object distance, in McKenzie and Day's experiment they appeared to respond exclusively to object distance. This difference could have been due to the different procedure and indexing responses and, in particular, to the effect of the reinforcement procedure on the attention-capturing quality or "salience" of the object itself. This possibility is considered in more detail below.

SIZE CONSTANCY AND DISTANCE DISCRIMINATION

It is to be noted that in McKenzie and Day's (1972) experiment to check Bower's (1964, 1965) findings, the stimulus objects were stationary, white cubes with visual subtenses between about 3.3° and 33.3°, close to the range of 5.7°–48.5° for the objects in Bower's experiments. The absence of habituation of visual fixation over ten trials to one of these cubes at 90 cm and the markedly greater durations of fixation of both cubes when at 30 cm than when at 90 cm strongly implicates object distance as a factor in visual attention to stationary objects when no reinforcement methods are involved. The outcomes suggest that such objects are only of continuing interest to infants 6–12 weeks old when they are nearer than about 100 cm.

There is support for this view in the early observations of Stern and of Compayré briefly described by Koffka (1924/1959). Stern is quoted as stating that the "near space," the space within which very young infants attend to objects when they are straight ahead, extends for only about 33 cm with the distance for a particular object depending on various stimulus properties including luminance. With infants of about 3-weeks-of-age, Compayré is reported as demonstrating that a candle flame was attended to when it was at 3 m but not when it was at 4–5 m. Gesell, Ilg, and Bullis (1949) obtained similar results for the effects of viewing distance on attention.

To examine the effect of distance in more detail McKenzie and Day (1972) conducted a second experiment involving two groups of 16 infants aged between 6 and 20 weeks who viewed an object of either constant real of constant angular size located at four distances. For the former group there was an 18-cm cube at 30, 50, 70, and 90 cm and for the latter group 6-, 10-, 14-, and 18-cm cubes respectively at the same four distances. The objects that were white with a black cross proportional to their size on their near surfaces were presented twice to each subject for 20 sec. The score throughout was once again duration of fixation. At 30 cm the mean fixation time for both groups was about 10 sec. With increases in object distance there was a linear decline in fixation times. There was no difference between the two groups or between younger (6–12 weeks) and older (13–20 weeks) subjects.

McKenzie and Day's results have since been confirmed. Field (1975) found that with infants of about 22-weeks-of-age, looking time also decreased as a function of distance. Furthermore, in a later experiment McKenzie and Day (1976) compared visual fixation of the same object—a patterned cylinder—when it was rotating and stationary at distances of 30, 50, 70, and 90 cm. Decrements in fixation time with distance occurred with 9- and 16-week-old infants when the object was stationary but not when it was moving. Later, de Schonen, McKenzie, Maury, and Bresson (1978) showed that for infants between about 9 and 22 weeks both the occurrence and latency of saccadic shifts of fixation from a central to a peripheral object varied with distance. Near, peripheral objects were detected at greater eccentric angles than more distant ones. This tendency was modified by both the age of the subjects and the distance (30 or 90 cm) of central fixation.

It is unlikely that loss of attention to far objects is due to visual acuity. The outcomes of experiments by Fantz, Ordy, and Udelf (1962), Salapatek, Bechtold, and Bushnell (1976) and Atkinson, Braddick, and Moar (1977) are firmly in agreement in showing that even with infants as young as about 5 weeks visual acuity does not vary significantly with distance. This is probably due in part to the increased depth of focus in infant vision, which compensates for poorer accommodation (Green, Powers, & Banks, 1980). In any case the demonstration by Ihsen and Day (1981) that moving three-dimensional stimulus objects are both attended to and discriminated at distances up to 10 m strongly suggests that loss of acuity is not the basis of attentional failure with distance.

In summary, early and recent data on the effect of object distance on visual fixation of stationary, patterned objects is consistent in showing that for infants up to about 20 weeks there is a decline in fixation time as a function of distance. This decline is unlikely to be due to loss in visual acuity with distance.

It is possible that for infants movement increases the salience of objects, thus sustaining attention to them as distance increases. If so, a resolution of the inconsistency between the data reported by Bower (1964, 1965) and McKenzie and Day (1972) is suggested. The salience, i.e., "attention-capturing quality," of objects might also be enhanced and sustained by reinforcement of responses to them. However, until this issue is fully addressed and those factors that make for greater salience identified this suggestion for a resolution must remain speculative. It is also tautologous. What is clearly required is a series of experiments involving convergent operations, that isolate the stimulus and procedural variables associated with perceptual salience. For the time being the view that Bower's demonstration of responses to real size at a much greater (3 m) distance was due to the enhanced attention-capturing quality of the object consequent on reinforcement must be treated cautiously.

RECENT EXPERIMENTS

The data from the first of two recent studies (Day & McKenzie, 1981; McKenzie, Tootell, & Day, 1980), both employing recovery from habituation of visual fixation as an index of size constancy, showed that size constancy occurs at 26-weeks-of-age and possibly at 18 weeks. The second experiment involving a modified habituation-recovery procedure with an approaching and receding object confirmed that capacity to perceive the true size of an object with changes in distance is clearly evident at 18 weeks.

McKenzie et al. (1980) adopted the strategy of beginning their program with

26-week-old infants with the intention of testing 18-week-olds if constancy was evident at 26 weeks and 33-week-olds if it was not. The stimulus objects were chosen because of their potentially greater interest to the subjects. They were colored "realistic" models of human heads which were presented at 30 and 60 cm, well within the range of visual attention found earlier for white cubes with a black cross (McKenzie & Day, 1972). The large head was of about the normal size for an adult head and the other half that size in all dimensions and details. The design of the experiment involved habituation of visual fixation to a pre-determined criterion under one of four conditions of object size and distance. The test condition which followed was the same for all four habituation conditions. The conditions to which separate groups of 8 subjects of about 26 (Experiment 1), 33 (Experiment 2) and 18 weeks (Experiment 3) were assigned were (A) the large head at 60 cm, (B) the large head at 30 cm, (C) the small head at 60 cm, and (D) the small head at 30 cm. The test condition throughout was (A) the large head at 60 cm.

The habituation condition involving the large head at 60 cm was referred to as the control (Co) since the test condition was the same as it in all respects. The large head at 30 cm was referred to as the size constancy (SC) condition since in the test only size was the same, the small head at 60 cm as the distance (Di) condition since only distance was the same, and the small head at 30 cm as the visual angle (VA) condition since only visual angle was the same. The logic of this design was that if size constancy were operative, recovery from condition SC could be expected to be most similar to Co and that from Di and VA could be expected to be greater. If, on the other hand, apparent size were determined by the retinal projection, i.e., by visual angle, recovery from VA could be expected to be similar to Co, and Di and SC to be greater.

The outcomes of the first experiment with 26-week-old infants are shown in Fig. 4.1. It can be seen that the mean recovery for SC was similar to that of Co and that both were slight, whereas recoveries for Di and VA were greater. This pattern clearly favors an interpretation in terms of size constancy. The second and third experiments showed that while the pattern of recovery for 33-week-old infants was similar to that for 26-week-olds, that for 18-week-olds was not. The results for these two experiments are also shown in Fig. 4.1. Thus, it is reasonable to conclude that in terms of the habituation-recovery procedure, visual size constancy is operative at 26 weeks but not at 18 weeks. However, as is noted below, a more detailed analysis of the data for the third experiment modified this conclusion and led to a further experiment (Day & McKenzie, 1981).

In a fourth experiment—McKenzie et al. (1980) presented separate groups of 26-week-old infants with patterned cubes and model heads at the greater distances of 100 and 200 cm. The aim was to ascertain the effect of different stimulus objects, (patterned cubes), and greater viewing distances. In the event, the recovery scores were undifferentiated with both types of object and thus

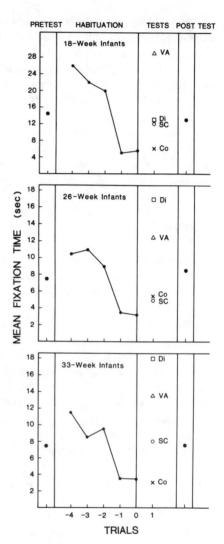

FIGURE 4.1. Mean visual fixation times for 18, 26-, and 33-week-old infants in four test conditions after habituation: (Co)- same object at same distance (Sc)- same object at different distance, (Di)- different object at same distance, (VA)- different object at different distance. The fixation times for the pretest and posttest controls for attention loss, and for the last five habituation trials are also shown. For 26- and 33-week-old infants the times for Di and VA were different from Co while that for SC was not, indicating the presence of size constancy. For 18-week-old infants the differences between these means were not significant (from McKenzie, Tootell, & Day, 1980).

failed to accord with expectations for either visual angle or size constancy. This outcome confirmed that infants in this age range are relatively insensitive to stationary objects at distances beyond about a meter.

As noted above, the recovery scores in the third experiment for conditions Co, SC, Di, and VA did not indicate that size constancy was evident at 18 weeks. However, more detailed analysis of the data showed that subjects with low variance relative to the median variance exhibited a pattern of recovery from habituation of fixation similar to that of older (26-week-old) subjects. Those with high variance did not; recovery scores were more or less the same across the four conditions. This outcome led to the tentative conclusion that although *some* infants at 18 weeks may perceive the invariant size of an object with change in its distance, others do not.

There are two further observations that lead to the view that size constancy might be better developed at 18 weeks. Both have already been pointed out (Day & McKenzie, 1981). The first is that in all the experiments on size constancy so far considered the stimulus objects were stationary, and stationary patterns appear to have markedly lower attractiveness for young infants than moving ones (McKenzie & Day, 1976; Volkman & Dobson, 1976; Wilcox & Clayton, 1968). Second, visual shape constancy has been shown to occur at about 12 weeks (Caron, Caron, & Carlson, 1979; Caron, Caron, Carlson, & Cobb, 1979). While there is no *a priori* reason why shape constancy should not precede size constancy in perceptual development, a difference of some 14 weeks between the emergence of these two depth-dependent constancies seems intuitively to be excessive. In this regard it can be noted that in the shape constancy experiment reported by Caron et al. (1979), subjects were "desensitized" to slant during the habituation stage by varying slants over a wide range. Thus responsiveness to shape during the recovery phase could be evaluated independently of both slant and retinal shape.

With these considerations in mind the experiment by Day and McKenzie (1981) with 18-week-old infants involved an habituation phase in which one stimulus object (a model head as before) moved towards and away from the infant along the median axis and a test phase in which an object of a different size moved through the same range of distances and visual angles as that of the habituation phase. Thus recovery from habituation in the test phase could be attributed to the size of the object independently of either distance or visual angle to which "desensitization" could be presumed to have occurred.

The experimental arrangement for this experiment is shown in Fig. 4.2. The data from 30 infants showed that recovery from habituation to a predetermined criterion was greater for a moving object of a different size than for the same object. This result indicated that the infants perceived and responded to the invariant physical size of the object as its visual angle varied. That is to say, visual size constancy obtained. A second finding was that after habituation to the smaller of the two heads there was a notably greater recovery to the larger head than to the smaller. However, when the larger head was used in the habituation phase and the smaller head in the test phase recovery was greater than for the opposite arrangement. This asymmetrical outcome can reasonably be attributed to the additive effects of object salience and dishabituation with a novel stimulus object. The larger head can be taken to have been more salient than the smaller. The greater recovery to the larger head after habituation to the smaller is in accord with the data on the salience of larger objects reported by Ruff and Turkewitz (1979) and Lawson and Ruff (1984).

In a review of these experiments by McKenzie et al. (1980) and Day and

FIGURE 4.2. Experimental arrangement used by Day and McKenzie (1981). The model head above the screen could be moved towards and away from the infant through a preset distance.

McKenzie (1981) on size constancy, Banks and Salapatek (1983) have commented that too often experiments designed to index a particular skill in infancy yield discordant results. In this case ''the same researchers testing the same age group with generally similar stimuli and procedures obtained different results'' (p. 524). This comment is quite unjustified. The stimuli were not generally similar. In the first experiment they were stationary and in the second they approached and receded over a common range of distances and within a common range of visual angles. Approach and recession were, as pointed out earlier, designed to enhance the salience of the stimulus objects while the common range of distances and visual angles rendered recovery a less ambiguous index of size recognition. Together these modifications were successful in revealing the operation of size constancy at 18 weeks.

DISCUSSION

In their detailed review of visual perception in infancy Cohen, DeLoache, and Strauss (1979) after considering the data then available on visual size constancy arrived at the conclusion that:

To date, there has been no unequivocal demonstration of size constancy in the first 6 months of life, perhaps because distance is a more potent variable for young infants than size. If a multiple-habituation paradigm were used and infants habituated to the same cube at a number of different distances, distance per se might become irrelevant and evidence for size constancy might emerge. Unfortunately, such an experiment has not yet been conducted. (p. 422)

This conclusion is no longer valid. The experiments by McKenzie et al. (1980) and Day and McKenzie (1981), both of which are reviewed in the last section, have shown by different methods that size constancy is clearly evident in the first 6 months of infancy. The first group of experiments identified it at 6 months and older and adduced some evidence for its occurrence at 4 months. The second study confirmed by means of the procedure recommended by Cohen et al. (1979), i.e., habituation to the same object at a number of different distances, the earlier tentative conclusion that size constancy is operative at 18 weeks.

Although size constancy in the first half year can be taken as established the question of how early in that period it begins to operate remains open. As noted above, the experiment by Day and McKenzie (1981) with the same "interesting" objects approaching and receding indicated that it is operative by about 18 weeks. It is conceivable that still more sensitive methods would identify it even earlier. In this regard it will be recalled that Bower (1964) using a conditioning procedure found evidence for size constancy with infants of 10–12 weeks, and later (Bower, 1965) with infants of 6–9 weeks. These observations have not been confirmed and clearly it is of interest to do so. As pointed out, it is possible that the reinforcement of naturally occurring responses such as head turns in the presence of an object constitute an even more sensitive means of identifying perceptual capacities such as size constancy early in infant development. It is relevant to note that McKenzie and Day (1971) demonstrated the efficacy of operant conditioning in studying pattern perception with infants aged 6–12 weeks.

Incidentally, Walk (1981) in a brief commentary on size constancy in infancy stated that in the light of the results reported by McKenzie et al. (1980), Bower's (1964, 1965) earlier results remain firm. Unfortunately, this conclusion is unjustified. As pointed out earlier, the subjects in Bower's (1964, 1965) experiments were aged 6–12 weeks and those in McKenzie, Tootell, and Day's (1980) experiment 18 weeks. This is not to split hairs; a minimum difference of 6 weeks and a maximum of 12 weeks so early in development could be of considerable significance.

A point that deserves some emphasis is that although reaching responses, conditioned head turning, and recovery from habituation can indicate the operation of size constancy in infancy they cannot reliably indicate the *degree* of constancy, as estimates of size by matching and other psychophysical means do with older observers. Thus, while it is now possible confidently to conclude that visual size constancy is operative in infancy, it is not yet possible to state how comlete it is.

In this connection it will be recalled from the earlier discussions of size constancy in childhood and adulthood (see above) that at 3–4 years marked underconstancy appears to obtain, at about 10–11 years constancy appears to be more or less complete, and that with adults overconstancy obtains. That is to say, there seems to be a progressive trend from marked underconstancy in early childhood to slight overconstancy in adulthood (see Wohlwill, 1963b). From this it might be concluded that constancy is incomplete and that underconstancy obtains in infancy. Such a view must be tempered by the unknown contribution of instructions and their capacity to invoke some degree of cognitive control over the perceptual processes associated with size constancy, as demonstrated by Gilinsky (1955). It is not inconceivable that size constancy in infancy is as great or greater than it is in childhood and adulthood. That is to say, that the basic perceptual processes associated with size constancy are fully operative whereas the cognitive processes that modulate it are not.

Another issue that warrants a concluding comment concerns the role of the perceptual saliency of stimulus objects. This point has been mentioned in connection with Bower's (1964, 1965) experiments in which response reinforcement in the presence of one object could conceivably have enhanced its salience and, therefore, the distance at which its physical size was perceived. The same point was made in the context of Day and McKenzie's (1981) experiment in which approaching and receding objects were used. It is quite possible that because of the much greater salience of moving objects as demonstrated in numerous experiments (McKenzie & Day, 1976; Volkman & Dobson, 1976; Wilcox & Clayton, 1968) and, in particular, more recently in the experiment reported by Ihsen and Day (1981), size constancy was demonstrated when it might not have been with less salient objects. Ihsen and Day (1981) showed that with infants aged 8 to 14 weeks patterned objects rotating at 7.5 rpm attracted as much attention at 10 m as at 3 m. By inducing habituation to a rotating object of one shape at 10 m and then testing for recovery with that of the same and another shape it was shown that infants can discriminate between the original and a novel object at this distance. These observations involving distances of up to 10 m suggest that rotating patterned objects have particularly high salience for infants of 8–14 weeks. They suggest too a means of testing for size constancy over much greater distances than hitherto.

Another issue worthy of comment concerns the role of various classes of stimulus information, i.e., "cues," for distance. Whereas there is now sufficient data to support the view that size constancy is operative in the first 6 months, the role of the various sources of information for distance, e.g., retinal disparity, motion parallax, ocular accommodation and convergence, and "pictorial" information is not known. It will be recalled that Bower (1965) found no difference between binocular and monocular vision in his size constancy experiment. This finding is not easily reconcilable with the recent finding by Granrud, Yonas, and Petterson (1984) that there are large differences between monocular and binocular viewing in infants' discrimination of the distance of objects. However, it is to be noted that both the distances involved and the indexing responses (conditioned head turns and reaching) differed in the two studies. More to the point, there is now a substantial body of data on the involvement of the various sources of information for distance and depth perception in infancy. Yonas and Granrud (1984) have commented in detail on the development in infancy of sensitivity to kinetic, binocular, and pictorial depth information. They argue that some sensitivity to kinetic (motion) information may be present at or soon after birth, to binocular information between about 13 and 22 weeks, and to static monocular (pictorial) information between about 22 and 31 weeks. It would be of interest for theories of size perception (as well of interest in its own right) to investigate the relationship between sensitivity to the three classes of distance information in these age groups and the degree of visual size constancy.

Such an inquiry would go to the heart of the long-standing debate about the basis of size constancy; whether it is essentially relationally determined as implied by the work of Gibson (1950) and Rock and Ebenholtz (1959) or whether it is dependent on "taking distance into account." Hochberg (1972) has pointed out that the first interpretation implies a direct response by the visual system to a relational feature (e.g., retinal image size and surrounding texture or frame) and the other a response to image size modified by distance cues. The first is essentially a basic "sensory" explanation and the second a cognitive view. This distinction leads immediately to a final point.

Perhaps the most fundamental and as yet unresolved issue to emerge from this commentary on visual size constancy in infancy is that of the processes involved in its initiation and control. While it is reasonable to conclude that there is a basic perceptual process which operates very early in development and which is associated with perception in simpler species than man (see Ewert & Burghagen, 1979; Ingle, 1968) there is also evidence from this analysis that implicates higher-order cognitive processes that are triggered by instructions (Carlson, 1977; Epstein, 1963; Gilinsky, 1955). This observation is not meant artificially to distinguish between perceptual and cognitive processes but to emphasize that visual size constancy does not derive exclusively from "lower-level" neural processes that are activated by particular stimulus patterns. If instruction-initiated cognitive processes exercise a degree of control over the perception of object size as distance varies, thus permitting the observer to switch between the visual-angle, apparent, and real-size "viewing attitudes," it follows that visual size constancy will depend in part on the development of cognitive abilities. If this is so then it is reasonable to take the view that the development of visual size constancy in infancy and early childhood as reported by numerous investigators (see above) reflects the emergence of cognitive processes including those associated with language and language comprehension.

In these terms it is not unreasonable to contemplate the hypothesis that the basic perceptual processes underlying visual size constancy in early infancy are close to being fully developed and that the changes with age are due to the emergence of cognitive skills. Now that visual size constancy has been shown to be operative in the first 6 months of infancy the challenge for future enquiry seems to be the nature of the processes that are associated with it and the manner of their development and of their interactions with increasing maturity.

REFERENCES

Akishige, Y. (1937). *Experimentelle Untersuchungen uber die Struktur des Wahrnehmungsraumes. Part II. Mitteilung.* Juristischliterarische Fakultat. Kyushu University, *4*, 23–118.

Allik, J., & Valsiner, J. (1980). Visual development in ontogenesis: Some reevaluations. In H. W. Reese & L. P. Lipsitt, *Advances in child development and behavior, Vol. 15.* (pp. 1–52). Orlando, FL: Academic Press.

Atkinson, J., Braddick, O., & Moar, K. (1977). Contrast sensitivity of the human infant for moving and static patterns. *Vision Research, 17*, 1045–1047.

Banks, M. S., & Salapatek, P. (1983). Infant visual perception. In P. H. Mussen (Ed.), *Handbook of child psychology: Vol. 2.* (pp. 435–571). New York: Wiley.

Berkeley, G. (1969). *A new theory of vision and other writings.* London: Everyman's Library. (Original work published 1734).

Beyrl, F. (1926). Uber die Grossenauffassung bei Kindern. *Zeitschrift fur Psychologie, 100*, 344–371.

Boring, E. G. (1942). *Sensation and perception in the history of experimental psychology.* New York: Appleton-Century.

Bower, T. G. R. (1964). Discrimination of depth in premotor infants. *Psychonomic Science, 1*, 368.

Bower, T. G. R. (1965). Stimulus variables determining space perception in infants. *Science, 149*, 88–89.

Bower, T. G. R. (1972). Object perception in infants. *Perception, 1*, 15–30.

Bruner, J. S., & Koslowski, B. (1972). Visually preadapted constituents of manipulatory action. *Perception, 1*, 3–14.

Brunswik, E. (1933). Die Zuganglichkeit von Gengenstanden fur die Wahrnehmung. *Archiv fur die Gesamte Psychologie, 88*, 377–418.

Carlson, V. R. (1960). Overestimation in size-constancy judgments. *American Journal of Psychology, 73*, 199–213.

Carlson, V. R. (1962). Size-constancy judgments and perceptual compromise. *Journal of Experimental Psychology, 63*, 68–73.

Carlson, V. R. (1977). Instructions and perceptual constancy judgments. In W. Epstein (Ed.) *Stability and constancy in visual perception: Mechanisms and processes* (pp. 217–254). New York: Wiley.

Caron, A. J., Caron, R. F., & Carlson, V. R. (1979). Infant perception of the invariant shape of objects varying in slant. *Child Development, 50*, 716–721.

Caron, R. F., Caron, A. J., Carlson, V. R., & Cobb, L. S. (1979). Perception of shape-at-a-slant in the young infant. *Bulletin of the Psychonomic Society, 13*, 105–107.

Chalmers, E. L. (1952). Monocular and binocular cues in the perception of size and distance. *American Journal of Psychology, 65*, 415–423.

Cohen, L. B., DeLoache, J. S., & Strauss, M. S. (1979). Infant visual perception. In J. D. Osofsky (Ed.), *The handbook of infant development* (pp. 393–438). New York: Wiley.

Cruikshank, R. M. (1938). The development of size-constancy in early infancy. *Onzième Congres Internationale de Psychologie*. Paris: Imprimeria Moderns.

Cruikshank, R. M. (1941). The development of visual size constancy in early infancy. *The Journal of Genetic Psychology, 58*, 327–351.

Dannemiller, J. L., & Banks, M. S. (1983). Can selective adaptation account for early infant habituation? *Merrill-Palmer Quarterly, 29*, 151–158.

Day, R. H. (1968). Perceptual constancy of auditory direction with head rotation. *Nature, 219*, 501–502.

Day, R. H., & McKenzie, B. E. (1977). Constancies in the perceptual world of the infant. In W. Epstein (Ed.), *Stability and constancy in visual perception: Mechanisms and processes* (pp. 285–320). New York: Wiley.

Day, R. H., & McKenzie, B. E. (1981). Infant perception of the invariant size of approaching and receding objects. *Developmental Psychology, 17*, 670–677.

Denis-Prinzhorn, M. (1961). Perception des distances et constance des grandeurs (etude genetique). *Archives Psychologie, Geneve, 37*, 181–309.

de Schonen, S., McKenzie, B., Maury, L., & Bresson, F. (1978). Central and peripheral object distances as determinants of the effective visual field in early infancy. *Perception, 7*, 499–506.

Drever, J. (1960). Perception and action. *Bulletin of the British Psychological Society, 45*, 1–8.

Edgren, R. D. (1953). *A developmental study of motion perception, size constancy, recognition speed and judgment of verticality*. Unpublished doctoral dissertation, Stanford University.

Epstein, W. (1963). Attitudes of judgment and the size-distance invariance hypothesis. *Journal of Experimental Psychology, 66*, 78–83.

Ewert, J.-P., & Burghagen, H. (1979). Ontogenic aspects of visual "size constancy" phenomena in the midwife toad. *Alytes obstetricans* (Laur.). *Brain, Behaviour & Evolution, 16*, 99–112.

Fantz, R. L., & Fagan, J. F. (1975). Visual attention to size and number of pattern details by term and preterm infants during the first six months. *Child Development, 46*, 3–18.

Fantz, R. L., Fagan, J. F., & Miranda, S. B. (1975). Early visual selectivity. In L. B. Cohen & P. Salapatek (Eds.), *Infant perception: From sensation to cognition: Vol. 1. Basic Visual Processes*. Orlando, FL: Academic Press.

Fantz, R. L., & Nevis, S. (1967a). Pattern preferences and perceptual-cognitive development in early infancy. *Merrill-Palmer Quarterly, 13*, 77–108.

Fantz, R. L., & Nevis, S. (1967b). The predictive value of changes in visual preferences in early infancy. In J. Hellmuth (Ed.), *The exceptional infant* (Vol. 1, pp. 351–413). Seattle: Special Child Publications.

Fantz, R. L., Ordy, J. M., & Udelf, M. S. (1962). Maturation of pattern vision in infants during the first six months. *Journal of Comparative & Physiological Psychology, 55*, 907–917.

Fechner, G. T. (1966). *Elements of psychophysics, Vol. 11*. (H. E. Adler, Trans.). New York: Holt, Rinehart and Winston. (Original work published 1860.)

Field, J. (1975, May). *The adjustment of reaching behavior to object distance in early infancy*. Paper presented at the Second Experimental Psychology Conference, Sydney.

Gesell, A., Ilg, F. I., & Bullis, G. E. (1949). *Vision: Its development in infant and child*. New York: Paul Hoeber.

Gibson, J. J. (1950). *Perception of the visual world*. Cambridge: The Riverside Press.

Gibson, J. J. (1968). *The senses considered as perceptual systems*. London: George Allen & Unwin.

Gilinsky, A. S. (1955). The effect of attitude upon the perception of size. *American Journal of Psychology, 68*, 173–192.

Granrud, C. E., Yonas, A., & Petterson, L. (1984). A comparison of monocular and binocular depth perception in 5- and 7-month-old infants. *Journal of Experimental Child Psychology, 38*, 19–32.

Green, D. G., Powers, M. K., & Banks, M. S. (1980). Depth of focus, eye size, and visual acuity. *Vision Research, 20*, 827–835.

Hastorf, A. H., & Way, K. S. (1952). Apparent size with and without distance cues. *Journal of General Psychology, 47,* 181–188.

Held, R. (1961). In "Symposium on Sensory Deprivation". *Journal of Nervous and Mental Disease, 132,* 1–38.

Hillebrand, F. (1902). Theorie der scheinbaren Grösse bei binocularen Sehen. *Derksschriften Akademie Wissenschaftlichen Wien, 72,* 255–307.

Hochberg, J. (1972). Perception: II. Space and movement. In J. W. Kling & L. A. Riggs (Eds.), *Woodworth & Schlosberg's Experimental Psychology* (pp. 475–550). London: Methuen.

Holway, A. H., & Boring, E. G. (1941). Determinants of apparent visual size with distance variant. *American Journal of Psychology, 54,* 21–37.

Ihsen, E., & Day, R. H. (1981). Infants' visual perception of moving objects at different distances. In A. R. Nesdale, C. Pratt, R. Grieve, J. Field, D. Illingworth, & J. Hogben (Eds.), *Advances in child development. Theory and research* (pp. 1–8). University of Western Australia.

Ingle, D. (1968). Visual releasers of prey-catching behaviour in frogs and toads. *Brain, Behaviour & Evolution, 1,* 500–518.

Izzet, T. (1934). Gewicht und Dichte als Gegenstande der wahrnehmung. *Archiv fur die Gesamte Psychologie, 91,* 305–318.

Koffka, K. (1959). *The growth of the mind: An introduction to child psychology.* (R. M. Ogden, Trans.). Paterson, New Jersey: Littlefield, Adams.

Lambercier, M. (1946). Recherches sur le développment des perception: VI. La constance des grandeurs en comparaisons sériales. *Archives de Psychologie, 31,* 1–204.

Lawson, K. R., & Ruff, H. A. (1984). Infants' visual following: Effects of size and sound. *Developmental Psychology, 20,* 427–434.

Lockmann, J. J., & Ashmead, D. H. (1983). Asynchronies in the development of manual behavior. In L. P. Lipsitt (Ed.), *Advances in infancy research: Vol. 2* (pp. 113–136). Norwood, NJ: Ablex.

Marr, D. (1982). *Vision: A computational investigation into the human representation and processing of Visual Information.* San Francisco: W. H. Freeman and Co.

McKenzie, B. E. (1972). *Visual discrimination in early infancy.* Unpublished doctoral thesis, Monash University.

McKenzie, B. E., & Day, R. H. (1972). Distance as a determinant of visual fixation in early infancy. *Science, 178,* 1108–1110.

McKenzie, B. E., & Day, R. H. (1976). Infants' attention to stationary and moving objects at different distances. *Australian Journal of Psychology, 28,* 45–51.

McKenzie, B. E., Tootell, H. E., & Day, R. H. (1980). Development of visual size constancy during the 1st year of human infancy. *Developmental Psychology, 16,* 163–174.

Martius, G. (1889). Ueber die scheinbare Grosse der Gegenstande und ihre Beziehung zur Grosse der Netzhautbilder. *Philosophische Studien, 5,* 601–617.

Miranda, J. B., & Fantz, R. L. (1971). Distribution of visual attention of newborn infants among patterns varying in size and number of details. *Proceedings of the American Psychological Association,* Washington, D.C.

Misumi, J. (1951). Experimental studies of the development of visual constancy in early infancy. *Bulletin of the Faculty of Literature.* Kyushu University, *1,* 91–116.

Mohrmann, K. (1939). Lautheitskonstanz im Entfernungswechsel. *Zeitschrift fur Psychologie, 145,* 146–199.

Piaget, J., & Lambercier, M. (1943). Recherches sur le developpement des perceptions: II. La comparaison visuelle des hauteurs a distances variables dans le plan fronto-parallel. *Archives Psychologie, Geneve, 29,* 173–253.

Piaget, J., & Lambercier, M. (1951). Recherches sur le developpement des perceptions: XII. La comparaison des grandeurs projectives chex l'enfant et chex l'adulte. *Archives Psychologie, Geneve, 33,* 81–130.

Piaget, J., & Lambercier, M. (1956). Recherches sur le developpement des perceptions: XXIX.

Grandeurs projectives et grandeurs relles avec etalou eloigne. *Archives Psychologie, Geneve, 35,* 257–280.

Rapoport, J. L. (1967). Attitude and size judgment in school age children. *Child Development, 38,* 1187–1192.

Rock, I., & Ebenholtz, S. (1959). The relational determination of perceived size. *Psychological Review, 66,* 387–401.

Ruff, H. A., & Turkewitz, G. (1979). Changing role of stimulus intensity as a determinant of infants' visual attention. *Perceptual and Motor Skills, 48,* 815–826.

Salapatek, P., Bechtold, A. G., & Bushnell, E. W. (1976). Infant visual acuity as a function of viewing distance. *Child Development, 47,* 860–863.

Tada, H. (1956). Overestimation of farther distance in depth perception. *Japanese Journal of Psychology, 27,* 204–208.

Thouless, R. H. (1931). Phenomenal regression to the real object. *British Journal of Psychology, 21,* 338–359.

Volkmann, F. C., & Dobson, M. V. (1976). Infant responses of ocular fixation of moving visual stimuli. *Journal of Experimental Child Psychology, 22,* 86–99.

Vurpillot, E. (1976). *The Visual World of the Child* (W. E. C. Gillham, Trans.). New York: International Universities Press. (Original work published 1972.)

Walk, R. D. (1981). *Perceptual Development.* Monterey, California: Brooks/Cole.

Walk, R. D., & Gibson, E. J. (1961). A comparative and analytical study of visual depth perception. *Psychological Monographs, 75(15),* no.519.

Wilcox, B. M., & Clayton, F. L. (1968). Infant visual fixation of the human face. *Journal of Experimental Child Psychology, 6,* 22–32.

Wohlwill, J. F. (1963a). Overconstancy in distance perception as a function of the texture of the stimulus field and other variables. *Perceptual and Motor Skills, 17,* 831–846.

Wohlwill, J. F. (1963b). The development of "overconstancy" in space perception. In L. P. Lipsitt & C. C. Spiker (Eds.), *Advances in child development and behavior: Vol. 1.* (pp. 265–312). Orlando, FL: Academic Press.

Yonas, A., & Granrud, C. E. (1984). The development of sensitivity to kinetic, binocular and pictorial depth information in human infants. In D. Ingle, D. Lee, & M. Jeannerod (Eds.), *Brain mechanisms and spatial vision.* Amsterdam: Martinus Nijhoff Press.

Zeigler, H. P., & Leibowitz, H. (1957). Apparent visual size as a function of distance for children and adults. *American Journal of Psychology, 70,* 106–109.

5 The Origins of Form Perception

Michael Cook
Australian National University

THE PROBLEM OF FORM PERCEPTION

This chapter discusses only a small fragment of the available material relating to infant form perception. It considers only the infant's ability to see the forms of rigid objects which are three-dimensional, either in the sense that they are solid, or in the sense that they are planar and oriented out of the fronto-parallel. That is to say, the following discussion is concerned with what is often described as the problem of infant "shape constancy." While consideration is given to certain questions relating to the infant's visual organization of form, no attempt is made to review or discuss the relatively large body of infant shape-perception literature which concerns the perception of flat patterns, and no attempt is made attempt to provide a developmental account of infant shape-constancy. The following discussion, and the research presented here, is concerned simply with providing a descriptive account of the young infant's ability to see the spatial structure of a rigid object.

Such an object has a variety of spatial properties. Its *structure* is specified by those attributes which are independent of its position in space. Its *form* is specified by those structural attributes that specify relationships between points on its surface, which would be invariant if it were expanded uniformly. Attributes specifying form may be distinguished from attributes which specify the absolute *size* of its parts (lengths, areas, and curvatures). As seen in Chapter 4, there is an experimental literature which is unambiguously directed to the problem of infant size perception. It is unambiguous because it has investigated discriminations between objects of constant form which vary in size. However, the research which has nominally been directed to the problem of infant form perception, is somewhat less clearly directed to its putative target. Typically, these experiments have measured the infant's capacity to distinguish between objects which differ in form. However, two objects which differ in form inevitably differ with respect to their linear dimensions, their surface areas and the volumes of their parts. That is they differ in *size* in numerous ways.

Experiments on infant form perception have not usually attempted to incorporate the controls which would be necessary to establish that the reported discriminations were based on relational rather than absolute attributes of the stimuli. Strictly speaking, then, this research simply concerns the infant's ability to distinguish between objects with different forms. The findings are neutral as to the nature of the attributes employed by the infants in making these discriminations. It will be seen that most of the experiments described here fall into this category, investigating discriminations between objects with different forms, rather than the perception of form per se. However, the question of form, as opposed to size, perception is addressed directly by Experiment 3. It will be concluded that the object discriminations reported in this chapter were probably based upon differences between the forms of the stimuli, rather than differences in the sizes of their parts.

That adults are able to see the structure of objects is usually taken for granted. Research on adult space perception has consequently concerned itself primarily with the questions of how, and how well, they are able to do this. On the other hand, it has not been taken as self-evident that infants perceive object structure, and, in the infant research, both the nature of the mechanism of infant form perception and the question of how well it works, have been subordinated to the question of whether the infant perceives the spatial structure of the stimulus object at all.

DO INFANTS SEE SPATIAL FORM?

The Problem of Demonstrating Form Perception in Young Infants

In a typical study of adult form perception, the subject is asked to judge which of a range of objects presented in a particular orientation has the same form as a standard object presented in another orientation. Our conviction that such judgments are indeed manifestations of the perception of the spatial attributes of these objects (as opposed to the proximal stimuli which they generate) does not derive from the experimental method. It is based on a variety of external sources, which include our knowledge that the subjects could, if asked, employ the spatial vocabulary of their language correctly to describe the objects, and that they could carry out precisely tuned actions upon these objects. The belief also reflects in no small measure our intuitions about the nature of our own spatial experience.

With young infants we cannot rely upon any of these supplementary sources of evidence. Clearly, our spatial intuitions are irrelevant here, since one of the major points at issue concerns the similarity of the infant to the adult. Similarly, we can neither instruct prelinguistic infants to make comparisons on the basis of spatial structure, nor ask them to describe it. An essential first step, therefore, in the study of infant form perception, is to establish that infants do indeed perceive spatial structure.

It has been claimed that infants are capable of visually directed prehensile behavior in the earliest weeks of life, and, furthermore, that this behavior is appropriately adjusted to spatial properties, such as the sizes and distances of stimulus objects (Bower, 1972, von Hofsten, 1982). Such a finding would provide strong evidence that young infants are perceiving the spatial structure of the stimuli. However, the phenomenon of spatially adjusted reaching has proved difficult to confirm, and conclusions based on this avenue of investigation are controversial. To date, the major evidence concerning the existence of infant perception of spatial structure has been provided by discrimination experiments.

This evidence is reviewed below. It is seen that the experimental approaches that have been employed have several elements in common. In each case, a demonstration of discrimination between objects with different forms has been accompanied by evidence which is intended to establish that this discrimination is not simply based on uninterpreted characteristics of the retinal images of the stimuli. The need to exclude this last possibility requires some comment.

The ability to see the spatial structure of an object is based on information which is available in the light which enters the eyes. The information is provided, in particular, by the spatial distributions of the light falling upon the retinas. The retinal image in each eye is a polar spherical projection of the stimulus object, and there is a systematic correspondence between the structure of the object and the structure of its images. The classical analysis of space perception supposes that perception of object structure is possible because use is made of (primarily) three sources of information in the retinal images. These are, first, static perspective cues which are provided by the structure of either one of the retinal images at a given moment in time, second, binocular parallax cues provided by differences between the images in the two eyes and, third, motion perspective cues provided by the continuous changes in the image structures which are generated by motion of the perceiver and/or the object. According to this analysis, the adult perception of the object's spatial structure is mediated by a mechanism which encodes this information and a mechanism which interprets it.

Under normal conditions, two objects differing in structure will produce different retinal stimulation patterns. As a consequence, a demonstration that an infant can discriminate between the two will be ambiguous. It might imply that the infant is, like the adult, perceiving the spatial structure of each object and responding to the difference between these perceptions. But it is also possible that she or he is responding directly to the differences between the retinal stimulation that each generates, without interpreting this information in terms of spatial structure. Research on infant form perception has generally taken this possibility as a kind of Null Hypothesis, and researchers have seen themselves as obliged to offer positive evidence in refutation of it. There are no doubt many reasons why this position might be adopted. For example, a purely sensory explanation of discrimination is more parsimonious than a perceptual one. However, the primary reason seems to lie in the history of psychology. Since Empiricism has traditionally provided the dominant theoretical framework underlying perceptual research, it is to be expected that any evidence that challenges this position must be compelling.

It should be made clear that, in entertaining the hypothesis that discrimination might be based on differences in retinal stimulation rather than differences in spatial structure, the researcher is not necessarily implying that the infants might be "seeing" their retinal images—although Empiricist theories of perception are sometimes interpreted as implying that this is precisely what infants do see. Similarly, if it is demonstrated that discrimination is based on the spatial structures of the stimuli this does not necessarily imply that the infants "see" these structures in the same sense as the adult does. The issue is simply whether the mechanism underlying the infant's discriminating behavior is driven directly by an internal coding of the proximal stimuli, or whether it is mediated by some sort of representation of the spatial structure of the stimulus objects.[1] This question can be asked without taking any particular position concerning the nature of the infant's experience (the terms "see" and "perceive" will nevertheless be employed in the present discussion for reasons of stylistic convenience).

---

[1]Most accounts of perception have postulated in one way or another that perception involves the derivation of an internal representation of the viewed object from an internal representation of the proximal stimulus. For such accounts, the question of whether a discrimination is based on the spatial structure of the object, or upon characteristics of the proximal stimulus, presents no problems. However, the meaningfulness of this question is vigorously challenged by proponents of the neo-Gibsonian view of perception which is currently influential in many quarters. This view postulates, firstly, that there is a one-to-one relationship between perceptible attributes of the stimulus object and properties of the ambient optic array (invariants). Secondly, the Gibsonian position asserts that the perceptual system, in "perceiving" an attribute, is merely registering the presence of the corresponding invariant in the optic array. If this is the case, it would be argued, a discrimination is *always* based upon characteristics of the optic array, and the distinction between responding to the object and responding to the proximal stimulus is meaningless. In place of this distinction, the Gibsonian position would ask whether the discrimination made by the infant is based upon the stimulus invariants which convey information about object structure, or upon other characteristics, which do not. In the view of the present writer, the choice between the language used in the text and the Gibsonian alternative, is a matter of taste. If it were really true that every object attribute is represented by a stimulus invariant (and it is by no means obvious that is the case), and if we were capable of probing the infant's nervous system directly, it is not clear how a neural representation of a particular structural attribute of the seen object could be distinguished from a representation of the invariant which corresponds to that attribute.

Each of the studies considered here has attempted to demonstrate that discriminations between particular stimulus objects are directed by their spatial attributes, rather than by the proximal stimuli that the objects generate. The approaches adopted by these studies have the following four characteristics in common:

1. the infant's responses to changes in stimulus form have been compared with the responses to changes in stimulus orientation,

2. the form changes have been selected so that they mimic the proximal consequences of an orientation change,

3. the infants have been shown to be sensitive to the changes in form but insensitive to the changes in orientation (either spontaneously or as a consequence of desensitisation), and

4. the lack of a response to the orientation change is used as evidence that the form discrimination was directed by the spatial structure of the stimulus object.

Of course, the aim of selecting a shape change which mimics the proximal consequences of an orientation change cannot be realized exactly. If this were possible, the perceiver would have no basis for discriminating between the two. In particular, the changes in the binocular disparity and motion parallax information generated by the two cannot be matched. On the other hand, it is possible to match approximately the changes in the static organization of the retinal images experienced in the two cases (I refer to the static organization of an object's image as its "retinal shape"). It is this last control which is usually seen as most important in these studies, reflecting the Empiricist tradition which offers the hypothesis that the infant's form perception is determined by the retinal shape of the object as the alternative to the hypothesis that it is determined by its spatial structure.

A complication that arises in this methodology is the fact that the retinal image cannot be controlled precisely under the conditions of these experiments. Because viewing is usually binocular and the infant's head movements are necessarily unrestrained, the stimulus objects do not have single, unique retinal images. Statements made about retinal shape in both the published literature and the following discussion are therefore only an approximation to the facts. Strictly speaking, the statements refer to projective shape, which is computed by taking the polar projection of the stimulus object at a single, more or less representative viewing location (the midpoint of the interocular axis when the head is in the normal position).

Three different versions of the approach described here have been reported. These comprise the study by Bower (1966) using an operant conditioning/generalization paradigm, a study by Day and McKenzie (1973) based on rates of habituation of fixation, and a study by Caron, Caron, and Carlson (1979), which used a recovery-from-habituation technique.

Bower (1966) used operant techniques on 6-week infants. He established a discriminant behavior—head-turning in the presence of a slanted square (which projected a trapezoidal retinal image). In subsequent generalization tests he found that the operant was evoked by the presence of a fronto-parallel square, but not by the presence of a frontoparallel trapezoid. Thus, the behavior generalized to the familiar square form presented in a novel orientation, in spite of the novelty of its (square) retinal image. It did not generalize to the novel trapezoidal form in spite of the familiarity of its (trapezoidal) retinal image. These results imply that the infants saw a commonality between the presentations of the square in its different orientations, while at the same time they distinguished the tilted square from the frontoparallel trapezium. While Bower's data seem to provide a clear demonstration that the subjects' behavior was directed by the spatial structure of the stimulus objects, there have been no published repetitions of this study and the subsequent studies have employed different methods. These are described below.

Some Further Evidence Concerning the Existence of Form Perception in Young Infants

The number of studies purporting to demonstrate the existence of spatial form perception in young infants is small, and these studies can be criticized (e.g., Cohen, DeLoache, & Strauss, 1979). In view of this, further research is necessary before a definitive conclusion concerning this question can be drawn. This section describes two further experiments which indicate the existence of infant form perception. These are based on the studies by Day and McKenzie (1973) and Caron et al. (1979). A third experiment which attempted to determine whether the infants in the earlier experiments were responding on the basis of object form, as opposed to object size is described in the next section.

Experiment 1: The Infant's Perception of a Cube in Varying Orientation[2]

The method employed by Day and McKenzie (1973) was based on habituation of fixation. When a cube was presented repeatedly to groups of 2- and 3-month-old infants, there was a progressive reduction in fixation time. Day and McKenzie obtained the same habituation curve when the cube orientation was

---

[2]Seven experiments will be described in this paper. Experiment 1 is described in detail in Cook, Hine and Williamson (1982). Experiments 2, 3 and 4 are described in Cook and Birch (1984). Experiment 7 (with larger sample size) and most of Experiment 6 are described in Cook, Birch, and Griffiths (1986). Experiment 5 is unpublished at the time of writing.

fixed and when its orientation changed between presentations. The fact that the orientation changes did not reduce habituation rate was interpreted as indicating that the infants were perceiving the constant cubical form of the object in spite of its changing retinal projection. In an additional experimental condition, the infants were habituated to a sequence of photographs of the cube in varying orientation. Fixation was found to be longer during the initial presentation of the photograph than the solid cube and the infants did not habituate to the sequence of photographs. This finding was interpreted as indicating that "stimulus features associated with the object's depth or solidity were closely involved in the preservation of shape constancy" (Day & McKenzie, 1973, p. 319).

This study does not provide unequivocal evidence that their subjects were perceiving the spatial structure of the stimuli. The fact that the infants responded equivalently to fixed- and varied-orientation sequences of presentations could simply have been due to poor resolution of the stimuli. Evidence in support of this interpretation is provided by the results of Cook, Field, and Griffiths (1978), who found that the habituation curve obtained when the cube was alternated with another convex polyhedron (either a wedge or a truncated pyramid) did not differ from that obtained when the cube was merely varied in orientation.

In principle, much stronger evidence that the infants were responding to the stimuli on the basis of their spatial structure is provided by Day and McKenzie's second finding—that while there was habituation to repeated presentations of the solid cube, there was no habituation to a sequence of photographs of the cube in different orientations. This means that the infants' behavior towards a sequence of retinal images generated by physically different objects (the photographs) differed from their behavior towards a similar retinal sequence generated by changes in orientation of a single object. Unfortunately, this evidence is weakened by the fact that longer fixation to the photographs than the solids was obtained even on the first presentation. If the subjects initially found the photographs more interesting than solids, it is not surprising that they habituated more slowly to the photographs than to the solids (Cohen et al., 1979). Of course, the mere fact that the photographs aroused greater interest provides some evidence that the infants were responding on the basis of spatial structure rather than retinal shape. However, this evidence is capable of other explanations. Moreover, other studies have either found greater fixation to solids than photographs (Fantz & Nevis, 1967; Field, 1976) or no difference between the two (Cook et al., 1978). This raises the possibility that the fixation difference obtained in the Day and McKenzie (1973) study might have been due to some extraneous stimulus variable. However, the following experiment, using a slight modification of the Day and McKenzie (1973) procedure, provides confirmation of their key findings, and clear evidence of the perception of object structure in young infants.

The stimuli were seen by the infants from a distance of 30 cm. They subtended approximately 12° and were seen in front of a blue rear screen (these viewing conditions were employed for all the experiments reported in this chapter). There were four groups of twelve 3-month-old infants. For each subject, total fixation time was recorded on each of a sequence of eight 20-sec stimulus presentations. The Fixed-solid group saw a cube in the same orientation on every trial. This object was painted white with a coarse granular surface. For the Varying-solid group, the cube orientation changed between presentations (a mixture of two- and three-face views). The Varying-photo group saw a sequence of photographs of the cube (cut out and mounted) in its various orientations, while the Fixed-photo group received repeated presentations of a single photograph of the cube in one of its orientations. The photographs were taken from the subject's viewing position and were adjusted to match the solids as closely as possible in size, contrast, and luminance.

Figure 5.1 shows mean total fixation times for each group on each trial. The significant points are, first, that similar habituation curves were obtained for the two groups who saw the solid cube. Therefore, as in Day and McKenzie's experiment, the infants' behavior was indifferent to changes in the orientation of the cube. Second, the Fixed-photo group showed substantially more habituation than the Varying-photo group. The infants' behavior was not, therefore, indifferent to the differences between the photographs. This difference in behavior towards the solids and photographs cannot be attributed to differences in the subjects' intrinsic level of interest in photographs and solids since (in contrast to Day and McKenzie's results) the initial fixation times did not differ for solids and photographs, while the habituation curve for the Fixed-photo condition was similar to that for the two Solid conditions throughout the eight trials.

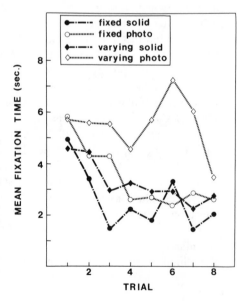

FIGURE 5.1. Results of Experiment 1: Mean fixation for real cubes in fixed and varying orientation, and for photographs of cubes in fixed and varying orientation. *Note.* From "The perception of solidity in early infancy" by M. Cook, T. Hine, & A. Williamson, 1982, *Perception, 11,* p. 680. Copyright 1982 by Pion Ltd. Reprinted by permission.

The infants' behavior provides evidence that they could distinguish between the different photographs, but no evidence of discrimination between the different orientations of the cube. Given the proximal similarity of the two stimulus sequences, this finding strongly suggests that the infants were perceiving the spatial forms of the stimulus objects—that they found a succession of plane polygons which changed in shape and surface pattern between presentations (i.e., the photographs) more discriminable (or more interesting) than a sequence of changes in orientation of a single unpatterned object. This demonstration that the infants were responding on the basis of spatial, as opposed to retinal form (see above), is not incontrovertible. The proximal sequences presented under Varying-solid and Varying-photo conditions were similar, but not identical, and the motion and binocular parallax cues generated by the solids would have been different from, and somewhat more complex than, those generated by the photographs. It is conceivable that the added complexity of the proximal stimuli in the Varying-solid condition simply masked the changes in retinal shape between presentations. Nevertheless, the results yielded by this method do offer a prima facie case for the perception of spatial form by young infants.

The results of this experiment carry an interesting additional implication. This is that variations in form are more discriminable (or salient) for the infant than variations in orientation. If this were not the case, the Varying-solid group would also have shown a reduction in habituation rate. This finding confirms Bower's (1966) conclusions. It is perhaps not surprising. As pointed out by Bower, the world is largely constructed of objects which move in space, but do not change in shape. Even objects which change shape do so in highly constrained ways (which do not resemble the changes encountered by the subjects in this experiment). But that the 3-month-old infant apparently perceives continuity of form and ignores change in orientation is interesting, because it suggests that the infant possesses at least the rudiments of the concept of an "object."

Experiment 2: The Perception of a Plane Tilted Form

An experiment reported by Caron et al. (1979) provides the third of the approaches that have been taken to the problem of demonstrating form perception in infants. As in the Bower (1966) experiment, an attempt was made to show that an acquired behavior would generalize to a familiar form in a new orientation, but not to a novel form. In this case, the "behavior" was habituation of fixation.

In the study by Caron et al. (1979), groups of 3-month-old infants received repeated presentations of a rectangle which was tilted out of the fronto-parallel plane. These continued until fixation time dropped to a criterion level. The tilt of the stimulus was varied between presentations so that the subjects would become used to change in orientation. They were then presented with either the familiar rectangle in a novel, frontoparallel orientation, or with a novel, trapezoidal form in the novel, frontoparallel orientation. In the test trials, a significant recovery of fixation was obtained for the frontoparallel trapezoid, but not for the frontoparallel rectangle. A corresponding result was obtained with groups who were habituated to a trapezoid in varying orientation and tested for recovery to either a frontoparallel rectangle or a frontoparallel trapezoid. This pattern of recoveries demonstrates that the subjects recognized the novelty of the new forms in the test trials even though they were presented in novel orientations. This was not a response to novelty of orientation, since the subjects did not respond to the familiar forms when they were presented in novel orientations. These results are consistent with the conclusion that the infants were perceiving the spatial structure of the stimulus objects.

As has been pointed out, if the method used by Caron et al. (1979) is to provide a convincing demonstration that the infants perceive spatial structure, it is necessary to establish that their subjects' ability to detect novelty of form was not based on the uninterpreted retinal projections of the stimuli. The interpretation of Caron et al.'s result is therefore complicated by the fact that the retinal projections of the novel forms used were themselves novel. Those subjects who were habituated to a tilted rectangle received a sequence of trapezoidal retinal shapes during habituation. While the novel frontoparallel trapezoid seen on the recovery trial also projected a trapezoidal retinal image, this lay outside the range of shapes encountered in the habituation sequence. For those subjects who were habituated to the tilted trapezoid, the problem is more substantial. In this case, a sequence of trapezoidal images was encountered during habituation, while the novel form presented in the recovery trial projected a rectangular retinal image.

Caron et al. acknowledge this problem. They reject the suggestion that the recoveries to the novel forms could have been responses to novelty of retinal shape, on the grounds that the groups who saw the familiar object in frontoparallel in the recovery tests had also encountered novel retinal images. It is argued that, since these groups did not recover, the responses to novelty of form were not based on retinal novelty. This argument is not unconvincing, but it depends on accepting that the novelty of retinal shape encountered in the novel-stimulus test trials was equivalent to that encountered in the familiar-stimulus test trials. To that extent, the strength of the Caron et al. (1979) study is weakened. The following experiment was based on the Caron et al. (1979) study, but the problem of retinal novelty was avoided by a slight modification of their procedure.

Subjects were habituated in a sequence of 20-sec trials to presentations of a planar form seen at various tilts out of the frontoparallel plane (the objects were tilted $+-20, +-40, +60$ degrees about the horizontal axis and were painted orange). Habituation proceded until total fixation dropped to a criterion level equivalent to that used by Caron et al. The subjects then received three further test trials in counterbalanced orders. These comprised a Control test in which they saw the familiar, habituation stimulus in a familiar (60°) orientation, a Novel-orientation test in which the habituation stimulus was presented in a novel (frontoparallel) form presented in the novel, frontoparallel projection. The novel stimulus seen in this trial was generated by tilting the habituation stimulus at 60° and computing its polar projection onto the frontoparallel (this form will be referred to as the "60° projection" of the habituation stimulus). There were two groups of 24 infants. For the Rectangle group, the object presented in the habituation sequence was a rectangle. For the Irregular-form group, the habituation stimulus was an irregular quadrilateral. The familiar and novel forms for each group are shown in Fig. 5.2.

Figure 5.2 shows mean total fixation times for each group on the first and last six habituation trials and for each test trial. Recovery from habituation is indicated when fixation time for a test trial exceeds that for the Control trial. The Rectangle group showed a recovery of fixation in the Novel-form test, but not the Novel-orientation test. These subjects therefore responded to the novel spatial form, even though its retinal shape (the 60° projection of the rectangle) was

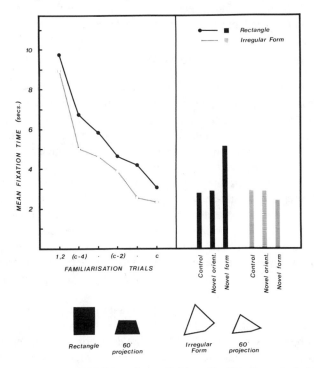

FIGURE 5.2.   Results of Experiment 2: Mean fixation times on habituation and test trials for Rectangle and Irregular-form groups. The forms seen by the two groups in the habituation and test trials are shown below the graph. *Note.* From "Infant perception of the shapes of tilted plane forms" by M. Cook & R. Birch, 1984, *Infant Behavior and Development, 7,* p. 392. Copyright 1984 by Ablex Publishing Corporation. Reprinted by permission.

familiar. They did not recover in the Novel-orientation test, even though the retinal shape here was novel. The recovery in the Novel-form test was not due to the novelty of the frontoparallel stimulus orientation, since they did not recover to this orientation in the Novel-orientation test. Taken as a whole, these results provide strong support for the conclusion that the behavior of the Rectangle group was directed by the spatial structure of the stimulus objects. They imply that the subjects were able to see the constant, rectangular form of the habituation stimulus in spite of its changes in orientation. They strongly confirm the findings of Caron et al. (1979).

In contrast, the data for the Irregular-form group do not confirm Caron et al.'s findings. They provide no evidence of spatial form perception, since the infants in that group did not recover to either novel test object. This negative result could be taken to imply that the infants were not perceiving the spatial structure of the irregular stimuli at all. But this seems unlikely. It is more plausible to suppose that it reflects limitations in the quality of the infants' resolution of these forms. This question is considered further in the next section.

Experiment 3: Form or Size Perception?

Each of these experiments has demonstrated that a 3-month-old infant can recognize when one object is substituted for another of different form. In each case we can conclude that the discrimination was based on attributes of the objects which were independent of their orientations, i.e., "structural" attributes. However, it was pointed out earlier that this demonstration does not establish that the infants were responding to changes in *form* as opposed to other structural attributes. Thus, the two objects seen by the Rectangle group in Experiment 2 were a rectangle and a trapezoid. The "forms" of these objects are specified by relational properties such as the angles of their corners and their height-to-width ratios. It is possible that the discrimination made by that group of infants was based on attributes of this type. However, it would also have been possible to distinguish the stimuli on the basis of their relative areas, or the lengths of their sides. The same consideration applies for Experiment 1 and the other studies reviewed above.

Studies of "size-constancy" in young infants might be expected to throw some light on this question. If the infant cannot detect a uniform change in the size of the object, it would seem unlikely that detections of changes in form are based on local size discriminations. There is some evidence of size-constancy in young infants (Bower, 1965; Day & McKenzie, 1981). However, the existing studies of size-constancy cannot be applied directly to this situation. They have all tested the infant's ability to compare sizes of objects with the same orientation but lying at different distances. If the "form-discriminations" described in this chapter were really based on perceptions of size, they would require an ability to compare sizes in different *orientations*. The ability to make such comparisons was examined in the following experiment, designed to determine the basis of the rectangle-trapezoid discrimination observed in Experiment 2.

The experiment was based on the procedure used for the Rectangle group in Experiment 2. A group of twenty-four 3-month-old infants was habituated to a rectangle seen at various tilts out of the frontoparallel. The habituation procedure and the stimuli were identical to those used in the earlier experiment. Three test trials were then given in counterbalanced order. As in the earlier experiment, the test trials included a Control test, in which the subjects saw the familiar rectangle in the familiar 60° orientation, and a Novel-form test, in which a trapezoid (the 60° projection of the rectangle) was presented in frontoparallel. In the earlier experiment, the third test trial was a Novel-orientation test, in which the rectangle used in the habituation sequence was presented in frontoparallel orientation. In place of this, subjects in this experiment received a Novel-size test. This was the same as the earlier Novel-orientation test, but the rectangle was reduced in size so that its area was the same as that of the trapezoid seen in the Novel-form test. The stimuli employed in the three posttests are shown in Fig. 5.3.

Figure 5.3 shows mean total fixation times for the first and last six habituation trials and for each test trial. As in Experiment 2, recovery from habituation is indicated when fixation time for a test trial exceeds that for the Control trial. The

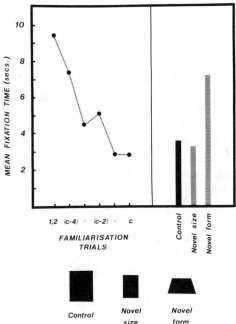

FIGURE 5.3. Results of Experiment 3: Mean fixation times on habituation and test trials. The forms seen in the habituation and test trials are shown below the graph. *Note.* From "Infant perception of the shapes of tilted plane forms" by M. Cook & R. Birch, 1984, *Infant Behavior and Development, 7,* p. 396. Copyright 1984 by Ablex Publishing Corporation. Reprinted by permission.

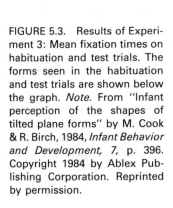

figure shows a recovery of fixation in the Novel-form test, but no recovery in the Novel-size test.

The positive results for the Novel-form test show that the subjects could distinguish the rectangle from the trapezoid. This merely confirms the findings of Experiment 2 and Caron et al. (1979). The negative results for the Novel-size test are more significant. The fact that no recovery was produced by a simple change in size suggests that the recoveries which occurred in the Novel-form tests, both here and in Experiment 2, were not due to the size differences between the trapezoid and the habituated rectangle. However, while the objects seen in the two novel-stimulus test trials were matched in area, they inevitably differed with respect to a variety of linear measurements (base lengths, heights etc.). It is possible, therefore, that the subjects were basing their discrimination between the rectangle and the trapezoid on one of these uncontrolled dimensions. Nevertheless, the result of this experiment does seem to establish an insensitivity to changes in size of the order encountered in the rectangle-trapezoid discrimination, and hence does imply that this discrimination was based on relational attributes of the stimuli—that is, on a perception of object *form*.

Conclusions: The Existence of Infant Form Perception

In summary, each of the three approaches distinguished earlier, including the modified repetitions of the Day and McKenzie (1973) and Caron et al. (1979) studies described above, has yielded evidence that young infants see the structures of objects in three-dimensional space—that their behavior towards objects is not simply directed by characteristics of the retinal image. Furthermore, the results of Experiment 3 indicate that the discriminations manifested in Experiment 2 and in the Caron et al. (1979) study were based on a perception of object form rather than size. Taken as a whole, this evidence constitutes a very strong case that the perception of object structure is established by the age of 3 months (Day & McKenzie, 1973; Caron et al., 1979; Experiment 1; Experiment 2), 2 months (Day & McKenzie, 1973) or even 6 weeks (Bower, 1966). It remains to be established whether it is present in infants of even younger age. Furthermore, little is known concerning the nature of the stimulus information employed by the infants in these studies. Their perception could have been based on a variety of binocular or monocular cues. It has been shown that infants can encode retinal disparities by the age of 14 weeks (Fox, Aslin, Shea, & Dumais, 1980). But all of the studies described here have used binocular viewing conditions, and the monocular controls necessary to establish that stereopsis was the basis of infants' spatial form perception have yet to be used. Meanwhile, we may note that the fact that, to the infants, a sequence of solids and a corresponding sequence of photographs are not equivalent (Day & McKenzie, 1973; Experiment 1 above) implies that static perspective cues do not provide the sole basis of their spatial form perception.

HOW GOOD IS INFANT PERCEPTION
OF SPATIAL FORM?

The research reviewed to this point was directed primarily to the question of whether young infants do indeed perceive the spatial forms of objects. It appears that the answer to that question is positive. Given this answer, it is appropriate to ask how good the infant's perception of form is. This section describes three experiments concerned with this problem. The first of these (Experiment 4) provides some information concerning the infants ability to discriminate between various plane forms. It constitutes an extension of Experiment 2, designed to examine some possible explanations for the results of the earlier experiment. The second experiment in this section (Experiment 5) assessed the infants' capacity to distinguish between various solid forms. The last two experiments (Experiments 6 and 7) were designed to examine some possible reasons for an inconsistency in performance with plane and solid forms observed in the earlier experiments.

Experiment 4: The Infant's Ability to Discriminate
Between Different Plane Forms

The experiments described above provide some information on this question. In particular, the results of Bower (1966), Caron et al. (1978, 1979) and Experiments 2 and 3 all imply that young infants can see sufficient of nonfrontoparallel plane forms to distinguish between a rectangle or square and a trapezoid when the two are presented in different orientations. That the infant subjects were able to make these discriminations implies a resolution of these forms which is broadly comparable to that of the adult. A more precise comparison between adult and infant performance is not possible on the basis of existing data. However, it could in principle be provided by using, say, the recovery-from-habituation procedure of Experiments 2 and 3 to test infants for discrimination between a rectangle and a range of trapezoids. The data yielded by such a study would provide the infant equivalent of the results of the standard adult shape constancy study.

In Experiment 2 the infants who had been habituated to a rectangle manifested a recovery of fixation to a trapezoid (a perspective transformation of the rectangle). The infants who were habituated to the irregular quadrilateral did not recover when presented with the equivalent perspective transformation of that object. These results suggest that the subjects perceived sufficient of the structures of the rectangle and trapezoid to distinguish between them, but did not resolve the two irregular forms at a level sufficient to make a discrimination. Why should a change made to an irregular quadrilateral be less discriminable than a metrically equivalent change made to a rectangle?

To the adult, the infant's behavior is comprehensible. The rectangle belongs to a well-established class of regular figures. The trapezoid belongs to a different class. We have effective schemes for coding and remembering the differences between these two forms. On the other hand, we do not have equivalent schemes for dealing with the differences between the irregular forms illustrated in Fig. 5.2, which both belong to the class of "irregular quadrilaterals." It does not, of course, follow that the 3-month-old infant's view of these stimuli fully conforms to that of the adult. However, the results of Experiment 2 do suggest that the roots of the adult view are present at an early age. An additional experiment was performed in an attempt to clarify the behavior of the infants in Experiment 2. The method used in that experiment was applied to two additional stimulus objects which were selected to isolate the key stimulus variables operating in the earlier experiment.

Several variables could have provided the basis for the pattern of discriminations observed in Experiment 2. In the first place, both the objects seen by the Rectangle group were bilaterally symmetrical, while the objects seen by the Irregular-form group were asymmetrical. It is conceivable that symmetrical forms are better encoded by the infant. Second, the discrimination made by the Rectangle group could have been based on the distinction between the converging edges of the trapezoid and the parallel edges of the rectangle. Third, it could have been based on the distinction between the orthogonality of the rectangle edges and the nonorthogonality of the trapezoid edges.

In order to distinguish between these possibilities, the procedure used in Experiment 2 was repeated with two additional groups of twenty-four 3-month-old infants. For one of these groups, a parallelogram was presented (in varying tilt) during the habituation sequence. For the second group, the habituation stimulus was a trapezoid. As before, there were three test trials, comprising a Control trial, in which the habituation stimulus was presented at $+60°$ tilt, a Novel-orientation trial in which the habituation stimulus was presented in frontoparallel, and a Novel-form trial, in which the $+60°$ polar projection of the habituation stimulus was presented in frontoparallel. The habituation and novel stimuli for each group are shown in Fig. 5.4.

Figure 5.4 shows mean total fixation times during the habituation sequence and on each test trial, for the Trapezoid and Parallelogram groups. Neither of these groups showed a recovery of fixation to the novel form (or the novel orientation). We may draw the following conclusions from this finding. First, the infants' failure with the irregular forms in Experiment 2 was not simply due to their irregularity, since both the parallelogram and trapezoid were "regular" forms. Second, the failure with the irregular forms was not due to their asymmetry, since the figures seen by the Trapezoid group were symmetrical. Third, the recovery by the Rectangle group in Experiment 2 was not based on a discrimination between the parallel sides of the rectangle and the converging sides of the trapezoid. This follows because the Parallelogram group in Experiment 4 did not recover even though this cue was also available to them.

If we consider only the three alternatives offered above, the results leave us

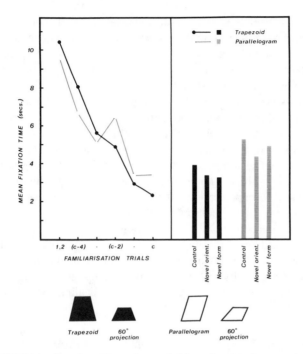

FIGURE 5.4.   Results of Experiment 4: Mean fixation times on habituation and test trials for Trapezoid and Parallelogram groups. The forms
seen by the two groups in the habituation and test trials are shown
below the graph. *Note.* From "Infant perception of the shapes of tilted
plane forms" by M. Cook & R. Birch, 1984, *Infant Behavior and Development, 7,* p. 398. Copyright 1984 by Ablex Publishing Corporation.
Reprinted by permission.

with the conclusion that the recovery manifested by the Rectangle group was
based on a discrimination between the orthogonality of the edges of the rectangle
and the nonorthogonality of the edges of the trapezoid. (Interestingly, the infants
in the Parallelogram group did not respond to the contrast between the regular
parallelogram and its irregular perspective projection, although this distinction is
quite manifest to the adult eye.) However, we cannot eliminate the possibility
that some other stimulus variable was operating. One possibility is that the
infants in the Rectangle group were recognising the *rectangularity* of the habituation stimulus (rather than the orthogonality of its corners). If this were the case,
they might be unable to discriminate between a nonrectangular right-angled
polygon (such as an L-shape) and its 60° projection.

It should be noted that the infants' apparent ability to distinguish orthogonality from nonorthogonality was operating in these experiments for non-front-
oparallel objects, so that the discriminated objects always projected trapezoidal
retinal images. This implies that the infants possessed a sophisticated capacity to

respond to angular relations in three-dimensional space. It should also be noted that the conclusions drawn from this experiment broadly confirm the conclusion (Experiment 3) that the rectangle-trapezoid discrimination in Experiment 2 was based on relational (i.e. form) attributes rather than perceptions of the absolute dimensions (i.e., size) of the stimuli.

These results could also be taken to imply that rectangularity has a special status in the infants' perceptual world. In Experiments 2 and 3, a rectangle was distinguished from a non-rectangle, but in Experiments 2 and 4, the subjects were unable to make a number of quantitatively equivalent discriminations involving nonrectangular forms. That rectangularity should have a special status at an age as young as three months clearly bears on the question of the role of learning in visual form perception. However, while these results are suggestive, they do not necessarily demonstrate that the special status of the rectangle is unlearned. The infants in this study were not neonates, and their participation in the experiments had been preceded by three months experience in highly carpentered environments. Their performance could be attributed to this experience. If so, this implies a capacity to learn from observation alone, since at 3 months infants would have had little opportunity for active dealings with the carpentered structures of their distant surroundings.

Experiment 5: The Effect of Orientation on the Infant's Perceptions of a Plane Form—Square vs. Diamond

One question that can be raised concerning the result of Experiment 2 and 3 (and the studies of Bower, 1966, and Caron et al., 1979) is whether the discriminations between rectangle and trapezoid were really based on perceptions of relationships between the objects' edges, or whether they were dependent on the relationships between the edges and the infants' primary spatial axes. In all these studies, the rectangle was oriented so that its edges were parallel to the primary visual planes of the subject, and it is possible that this provided the basis for the discriminations made in these studies. The following experiment confirms that the placement of a stimulus relative to these planes can indeed play a role in the infant's capacity to perceive orthogonality, although, in this case, investigation was limited to rotations within the frontoparallel plane.

The experiment used the same recovery-from-habituation procedure as was used in Experiments 2–4, with the exception that the orientations of the habituation stimuli were unchanged during the habituation trials. Two groups of twelve 3-month-old infants were used. Members of the Square group were habituated to repeated 20-sec presentations of a frontoparallel, orange square, oriented so that its base was horizontal. When the criterion fixation level was reached, the subjects received (in counterbalanced order) two test trials. In one of these they again saw the habituation stimulus. In the other test trial, they were presented with a new stimulus, namely a parallelogram. For the Diamond group, the procedure was identical with the exception that the stimuli were rotated in the frontoparallel plane through 90°, so that the old and new forms were both oriented as "diamond" shapes. The stimuli are shown in Fig. 5.5.

Figure 5.5 also shows mean total fixation times for each group during the habituation sequence and the test trials. There was a recovery of fixation (i.e., a difference in fixation time between the old and new test stimuli) for the Square group, but not for the Diamond group. The performance of the Square group shows that the infants could distinguish the square from the parallelogram. On the other hand, the Diamond group showed no evidence of making the same discrimination when the two stimuli had been rotated out of the horizontal. The implications of these results are twofold. First, they suggest that the infant view of these stimuli conforms to that of the adult (the rotated square and parallelogram are seen as both belonging to a single class of "diamonds"). In turn, this carries interesting implications concerning the role of the vertical and horizontal axes in the infant's perception of symmetry. Second, the results show that the ability to discriminate orthogonality from non-orthogonality can depend on the alignment of the stimuli with the infant's visual axes.

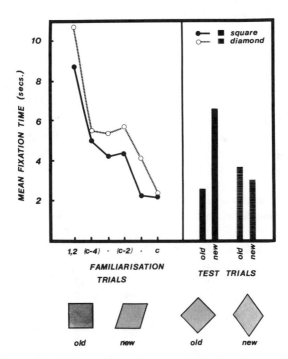

FIGURE 5.5.   Results of Experiment 5: Mean fixation times on habituation and test trials for the Square and Diamond groups. The forms seen by the two groups in the habituation and test trials are shown below the graph.

The finding that the square was only distinguished from the parallelogram when the bases of these forms were horizontal, suggests that the rectangle/trapezoid discriminations made in Experiments 2 and 3 might have been dependent on the stimulus orientations used there. In turn, this implies that the results of Experiments 2 and 4 should be interpreted with caution. The ability to distinguish the rectangle from the trapezoid may have been based on the relations of the objects' edges to the primary visual axes, rather than upon angular relationships within the objects. A direct test of this possibility would be provided by examining the ability to discriminate between the two forms when presented in more complex orientations, oblique to the primary visual axes. Data pertaining to this question are described in Experiment 7 (Single-face group). Although the stimuli used in the later experiment differed slightly from those employed in Experiments 2–4, the results confirm that the infants are capable of discriminating between a "rectangle" (a square) and a trapezoid, even when the stimuli are presented in complex orientations.

Experiment 6: The Infant's Ability to Discriminate Between Different Solid Forms

Experiments 2–4 were concerned with the infants' capacity to perceive the shapes of planar objects. They yielded evidence that the infant might have problems in resolving the forms of certain classes of plane quadrilateral forms (at least, when they are presented out of the frontoparallel plane). The results of Cook et al. (1978) could be taken to imply that 3-month-old infants also have problems in resolving the forms of solid objects. They found that the rate of habituation of fixation to a cube was not reduced when the cube was alternated with either a wedge or a truncated pyramid. On the other hand there was significant reduction in habituation rate when the cube was alternated either with a photograph of a cube, or a concave parallelipiped (an "L-form"). They interpreted these findings as indicating that their subjects' resolution of the spatial structure of the cube was insufficient to enable it to be distinguished from either the wedge or the truncated pyramid. However, their result for the truncated pyramid seems paradoxical in the light of the finding that the infants can distinguish between a rectangle and trapezoid (Bower, 1966; Caron et al., 1979; Experiment 2). Given this capacity, why did Cook et al.'s (1978) subjects not discriminate the square face of the cube from the trapezoidal faces of the truncated pyramid?

The apparent contradiction between the two findings might be taken to imply that young infants experience special problems in resolving the forms of solid objects. However, it is possible that Cook et al.'s results might merely reflect insensitivity in their index of discrimination. They relied on the expectation that habituation rate to a homogenous stimulus series would be greater than to a mixed sequence of discriminably different stimuli. Cook, Hine, and Williamson (1982) showed this method to be insensitive. In the second experiment reported by them, the subjects were habituated to presentations of a cube in a fixed orientation. Subsequent presentation of the cube in a novel orientation generated a recovery of fixation, demonstrating that the infants could distinguish between the two orientations. Yet their first experiment (reported here as Experiment 1, above) had obtained the same habituation rates for cubes presented in fixed and varying orientation. The following experiment was therefore carried out to reexamine discriminations between a cube and other solid forms, using the more sensitive recovery-from-habituation technique.

The method employed was identical to that used in Experiments 2–5. The infants were habituated to criterion with a series of presentations of an orange-painted cube. They then received three test trials, in which they were presented with a cube and two novel solid forms (in counterbalanced order). Their were four groups of twelve 3-month-old infants. For Groups 1–3, the orientation of the cube was varied during habituation. For Group 4, the cube orientation was fixed. Discrimination was examined between the cube and six novel forms, which were selected to provide a range of structural similarity to the cube. They were distributed across the three varied-orientation groups as follows: Group 1— a rhomboidal prism and a cylinder; Group 2—a triangular prism (wedge) and a truncated pyramid; Group 3—a sphere and the L-form employed by Cook et al. (1978). Figure 5.6 shows the various stimulus objects in the orientations seen in the test trials.

The variations in cube orientation during habituation for Groups 1–3 were made by rotating the stimulus about the subject's line of sight. While this rotation did not alter the geometry of the object's retinal projection, it substantially altered its position in space—tilting it forward and back, laying it on its side, etc. The rotation would have had a substantial effect on the binocular and motion parallax cues to the object's structure. This varying-orientation procedure corresponded to that employed in Experiments 2–4. The fixed-orientation orientation procedure employed for Group 4 provided a partial control designed to assess the contribution of the orientation changes seen by Groups 1–3 to any discrimination failures by them. The novel objects seen in the test trials by this Fixed-orientation group were the cylinder and the truncated pyramid.

The purpose of the varying-orientation procedure here differed from that in Experiments 2–4. In the earlier experiments, the varying-orientation procedure was intended to desensitize the infants to changes in orientation. In this experiment, its function was to desensitize the infants to *change* per se. The intention was to present the infants with a changing sequence of visual stimuli. In the initial part of the experiment (the habituation sequence), the changes would be due to changes in orientation, subsequently (the test trials), they would be due to changes in form. In order to respond to the novel test forms, the infant would

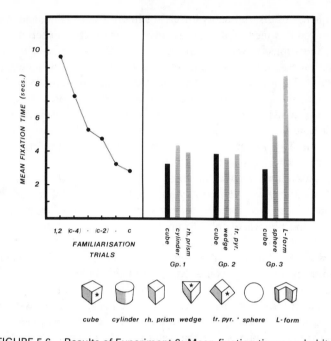

FIGURE 5.6.   Results of Experiment 6: Mean fixation times on habituation and test trials for the varying-orientation groups (Groups 1–4). The forms seen by the two groups in the habituation and test trials are shown below the graph. *Note.* Adapted from "Discrimination between solid forms in early infancy" by M. Cook, R. Birch & K. Griffiths, 1986, *Infant Behavior and Development, 9,* p. 193. Copyright 1986 by Ablex Publishing Corporation. Adapted by permission.

need to distinguish the proximal changes due to changes in form from those due to changes in orientation. Discriminations manifested under these conditions could plausibly be attributed to perception of object form.

Figure 5.6 shows the results for the three Varying-orientation groups. It shows mean fixation times during the habituation sequence for all infants combined, and mean times for each group on each test trial. The only stimulus to yield a clear recovery of fixation was the L-form seen by Group 3. The difference for this group between their fixation to the sphere and the test cube approached significance and the result for this stimulus should consequently be regarded as indeterminate. The results for the Fixed-orientation group (Group 4) are shown in Fig. 5.7. This group showed a significant recovery to both the cylinder and the truncated pyramid, even though neither of these objects yielded recoveries under the varying-orientation procedure.

The results of this experiment present problems of interpretation. In the first place, they confirm, with a more sensitive technique and a broader range of forms, the findings of Cook et al. (1978) that, in a varying-orientation environment, discrimination performance involving a cube and other solid forms is poor. But, in the second place, they suggest that this poor performance (for the cylinder and truncated pyramid at least) is a consequence of the orientation variations encountered during habituation.

Two contrasting interpretations of the discriminations manifested by the Fixed-orientation group suggest themselves. Firstly, they could be taken to imply that the performances by the varying-orientation groups underestimated the infants' perceptual capacity. Perhaps the infants were capable of perceiving the differences in form between the cube and the other objects, but this was masked in some way by the varying orientation procedure (for example, perhaps habituation generalised from orientation changes to form changes).

Alternatively, the performance by the varying-orientation groups could be taken as the true measure of the infants' resolution of form. The fixed-orientation performance required only a capacity to resolve the stimulus at a level which enabled a perception that some change had occurred in the test trials (for example, it could have been based on perceptions of the absolute locations in space of points on the stimulus surfaces). However, in order to recognize the novelty of the test stimuli under varying-orientation conditions, the subjects needed to perceive the spatial properties of the cube, which remained invariant as it changed orientation from one presentation to the next. That is, to perceive the objects' *structure*. According to this interpretation, the results for Groups 1–3

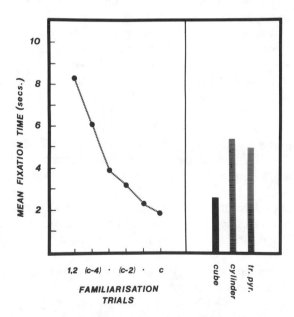

FIGURE 5.7.   Results of Experiment 6: Mean fixation times on habituation and test trials for the fixed-orientation group (Group 4).

imply that they were able to abstract sufficient of these properties to distinguish the cube from an L-form and, possibly, a sphere. However, their grasp of its structure was apparently insufficient to enable it to be distinguished from either a rhomboidal prism, a wedge, a truncated pyramid or a cylinder.

The results of Experiments 2 and 3 imply that the second of these interpretations is the correct one. The infants in those experiments manifested discrimination between a rectangle and a trapezoid in spite of the use of a varying-orientatation procedure (this is confirmed in Experiment 7 under conditions which corresponded precisely to those employed in this experiment). We may conclude therefore, that the poor performance by the varying-orientation groups here was due to the nature of the stimuli employed rather than insensitivity of the method. That is, this experiment appears to confirm the conclusions of Cook et al. (1978), that the 3-month-old infant's resolution of the form of a cube is poor.

Experiment 7: Do Infants Have Difficulty in Resolving Solid Forms?

Experiment 6 confirms that the 3-month-old infant does not distinguish (in a varying-orientation environment) between a cube and a truncated pyramid. This finding raises again the question of why the subjects were not distinguishing the square face of the cube from the trapezoidal face of the truncated pyramid. The infants in Experiment 2 were able to make this discrimination perfectly well when the shapes were presented in isolation.

One possible explanation for the apparent contradiction between the results of the two experiments lies in the differences between the orientations of their respective stimuli. In Experiment 2, the rectangle and trapezoid were always seen with their bases horizontal and frontoparallel. In Experiment 6, the solids were always oriented so that their edges and surfaces bore a complex relationship to the infants' primary visual axes. But Experiment 5 showed that the infants' ability to make form discriminations (in that case, between a rectangle and a parallelogram) can depend on the alignment of the stimuli relative to the primary visual axes. This could be the reason why the square surfaces of the cube were not discriminated from the trapezoidal surfaces of the truncated pyramid in Experiment 6.

It can be argued that the results of Experiment 5 do not necessarily demonstrate a general difficulty in resolving the forms of objects seen in complex orientations. The difficulties experienced by the Diamond group in Experiment 5 may have occurred because the stimuli were oriented so that they were symmetrical about the vertical axis. The discrimination difficulties may have been peculiar to that particular circumstance. It was therefore considered necessary to determine directly whether the infants would be capable of discriminating between one (square) face of the cube, seen in isolation but in the particular orientations used in Experiment 6, and isolated faces of some of the other objects used in that experiment. A trapezoidal face of the truncated pyramid and a triangular face of the wedge were selected for the purpose.

In order to examine this question, a group of twelve 3-month-old infants (the Single-face group) was habituated to repeated presentations of a square in varying orientation. The habituation sequence was followed by three test trials, in which the subjects saw the familiar square, a trapezoid and a triangle. In the test trials, the positions of the stimuli relative to the subject, their sizes, orientations, color and illumination all corresponded precisely to those of the object faces marked with (*)s in Fig. 5.5, and the procedure corresponded to that employed in Experiment 6. In effect, the subjects saw the cube, truncated pyramid, and wedge of Experiment 6 with all but a single distinctive face removed.

Positive evidence of discrimination by the Single-face group in this experiment would demonstrate that the failures with the corresponding solids in Experiment 6 were due to the presence of the additional faces of these objects. If, on the other hand, it turned out that this Single-face group was unable to distinguish the trapezoid from the square, this would imply that the failure with the truncated pyramid in Experiment 6 was a consequence of the particular orientations (or values of some other stimulus parameter) of the stimuli involved in that discrimination.

If the presence of the additional object faces were the cause of the poor discriminations in Experiment 6, this might suggest that the encoding of non-planar forms presents special problems for the 3-month-old infant. However, there could be a more prosaic explanation for such a result. It is conceivable that the poor performance in Experiment 6 was due to the relatively poor color contrast between the critical stimulus surfaces and the neighboring regions of the visual field, rather than to the solidity of the objects per se. Each face of the relevant stimulus objects seen in Experiment 6 was adjoined by two neighboring faces of like color. In segmenting the stimulus surface, the subject would need to rely upon the available depth cues, assisted by the luminance contrast between the adjoining faces. On the other hand, the boundaries of the plane forms seen by members of the Single-face group in Experiment 5 would be delineated (as were those seen by the subjects in Experiment 2) by the additional cue of the chromatic contrast between the orange of the object surface and the blue of the background. It is possible that the absence of this additional cue was responsible for the infants' inability to segregate the individual faces of the solids in Experiment 6.

In order to control for this possibility, a second group of twelve infants (the Painted-face group) was tested. The procedure was the same as for the Single-face group, but the stimuli were the cube, wedge and truncated pyramid used in Experiment 5. These were modified so that the faces marked with (*)'s in Fig. 5.6 were painted orange while the remaining faces of the objects were painted white. In effect, the stimuli for this group were identical to those for the Single-face group, with the addition of two adjoining white surfaces. Recovery to the novel stimuli by this group would suggest that the poor discriminations in Experiment 6 were indeed due to an inability to segment the homogeneously colored stimulus surfaces.

Figure 5.8 shows mean fixation times during habituation and on each test trial, for both the Single-face and Painted-face groups. In all trials, longer fixation times were recorded for the Painted-face group than for the Single-face group. Perhaps the infants found the more complex stimuli more interesting. The key result is that, for the Single-face group, fixation times in the test trials were longer for both novel stimuli than for the familiar habituation stimulus, while there was no corresponding evidence of recovery of fixation by the Painted-face group.

The performance of the Single-face group shows that the infants in Experiment 6 would have been capable of distinguishing the trapezoidal faces of the truncated pyramid and the triangular face of the wedge from the square face of the cube, if these had been seen in isolation. We may therefore conclude that the

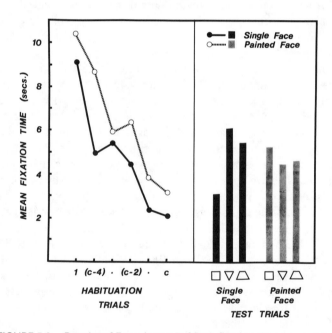

FIGURE 5.8.   Results of Experiment 7: Mean fixation times on habituation and test trials for the Single-face and Painted-face groups. *Note.* Adapted from "Discrimination between solid forms in early infancy" by M. Cook, R. Birch & K. Griffiths, 1986, *Infant Behavior and Development, 9,* p. 196 & p. 199. Copyright 1986 by Ablex Publishing Corporation. Adapted by permission.

difficulties experienced with these objects in Experiment 6 were not due to the orientations of their individual faces. It seems that the presence of the multiple faces of the solids (for the truncated pyramid and wedge at least) somehow interfered with the infants' capacity to discriminate between the forms of their individual faces. The performance of the Painted-face group in the present experiment implies, moreover, that this interference was not due to reduced color contrast. The interference occurred here even though the additional faces had been made chromatically distinct.

An additional implication of the performance by the Single-face group in this experiment, is that the rectangle/trapezoid discriminations made in Experiment 2 and 3 were not dependent upon alignment of the object edges with the primary visual axes. It seems then that the difficulties experienced by the infants in Experiment 5 when the square was rotated into the "diamond" position may have been due specifically to the infants' propensity to make use of the left-right symmetries of the stimuli used in that experiment. It seems that they do not have a general difficulty in resolving plane forms presented in complex orientations in which they are not aligned with primary visual axes.

Why should the presence of the additional faces of the solids seen in Experiments 6 and 7 have interfered with discrimination? This seems surprising since the solids provided more discriminative cues (for example, *two* squares and *two* trapezoids) than the faces seen in isolation. An obvious answer to this question is that the infants were simply not seeing the individual faces of these objects. This could have happened for many reasons, and it is not possible to decide between these on the basis of existing data. It is conceivable, for example, that 3-month-old infants do not follow our practice of segmenting the surfaces of solids into "faces," that they see these surfaces as continuous. Or perhaps they perceive objects in terms of the space enclosed by their surfaces, rather than attributes of the surfaces themselves. In either case, the cube and square, triangle and wedge, etc. seen in these experiments, would, from the infants' point-of-view, have been entirely unrelated structures. Another possibility is that the problems arose from the relative complexity of the solids. It may be that the strains placed on the infants' processing capacity by the task of resolving the global forms of these structures left insufficient capacity for the resolution of the forms of individual faces. Or the problem may have arisen from the distribution of the infants' attention. It may be that the subjects were not seeing the shapes of individual faces because they were more concerned with the forms of the solids as wholes. If this last possibility were the case, it might be possible to achieve a discrimination between, say, the cube and truncated pyramid, by directing the subject's attention to the distinguishing faces of these objects. The fact that the infants in the Painted-face group of Experiment 7 did not make this discrimination when the distinctive faces were chromatically isolated provides some prima facie, though not conclusive, evidence against this explanation.

CONCLUDING REMARKS

The research described in this chapter considered a range of specific issues which related to two broad questions. The first was whether young infants are capable of perceiving the forms in space of three-dimensional objects. A positive answer to this question, for infants aged between 6 and 12 weeks, has been suggested by three other studies (Bower, 1966; Day & McKenzie, 1973; Caron et al., 1979). This conclusion was supported by two of the experiments described here (Experiments 1 and 2), which constituted repetitions of the studies by Day and McKenzie and Caron et al., modified to overcome certain deficiencies in the earlier studies. In each of these experiments, the infants' behavior was directed by the structures of the stimulus objects in space, rather than their retinal projections. Considered as a whole, this research strongly supports the conclusion that some capacity to perceive the spatial structure of an object is either present at birth, or develops within the first few months of life.

Although work in this area is generally described as being concerned with the perception of object form, these studies have not demonstrated that it is form, as opposed to size, which provided the basis of the observed discriminations. Nevertheless, the results of Experiment 3 seem to establish that the rectangle/trapezoid discrimination in Experiment 2 (and, by implication, the similar discriminations studied by Caron et al. (1979) and Bower (1966) were in fact based on a perception of relational attributes of the stimulus objects. They suggest that the same might be true of studies which have used solid forms (Cook et al., 1982, reported here as Experiment 1; Day & McKenzie, 1973).

The second question considered in this chapter was how well young infants perceive the spatial forms of three-dimensional objects. In considering this question, the infants' performance under the varying-orientation conditions of Experiments 2–4, 6 and 7 has been considered most relevant, since these conditions require the subjects to abstract attributes of the stimulus structure which were invariant under changes in orientation—they preclude a response to mere *change*. Under varying-orientation conditions, the infants did manifest discriminations between forms. They were able to distinguish between a rectangle and a trapezoid (Experiment 2), between a square and trapezoid (Experiment 7) and between a square and triangle (Experiment 7). In Experiment 6, they were able to distinguish a cube from an L-form, and, possibly, a sphere. However, taken as a whole, the results obtained in those experiments do not suggest a high level of resolution of form by 3-month-old infants—the subjects gave no evidence of discrimination between a variety of nonrectangular plane quadrilaterals (Experiments 2 and 4), and no evidence of distinguishing the cube from a wide range of other convex solid forms (Experiment 6).

The conclusions drawn from the experiments reported here have been based in large measure on negative experimental results. Of course, negative evidence is weak. It is always subject to the argument that a technique which has failed to demonstrate a discrimination is statistically insensitive, or that the paradigm somehow prevents the manifestation of a discrimination which the infants are in fact making. It was seen in Experiment 6, for example that infants could distinguish the truncated pyramid and wedge from the cube in fixed-orientation habituation procedure, but did not manifest the same discriminations when the cube orientation had varied during habituation. It is conceivable that the subjects really did see the differences between these objects under both conditions. Perhaps the heterogeneity of orientation experienced during habituation merely reduced the novelty-value of a shape change so that it was not able to generate a recovery of fixation in the test trials.

The strongest argument against such objections is a demonstration that the procedure employed can produce positive results. This argument applies in the present case. The method which failed to demonstrate discriminations for the nonrectangular forms in Experiments 2 and 4, did yield positive results for the rectangle/trapezoid comparison in Experiment 2. Similarly, while the technique employed in Experiment 6 failed to demonstrate a cube/truncated pyramid discrimination, an identical procedure was able to demonstrate a discrimination between a square and trapezoid in Experiment 7. These demonstrations testify to the sensitivity of the present techniques, and hence lend strength to the conclusion that the negative results reported here were genuine failures of discrimination.

Nevertheless, the present negative conclusions should be regarded with circumspection. It is always possible that some more sensitive technique might demonstrate that the subjects were, after all, distinguishing between the forms used in these experiments. Or perhaps the results reflect failures of attention rather than perceptual deficiencies. The subjects might have been *capable* of perceiving the differences between the objects, but may not have noticed them under the conditions of these experiments. In this case, they could perhaps be led to do so by an appropriate procedure. In any case, we should bear in mind the relatively good discrimination displayed when a fixed-orientation procedure was employed (Experiment 6). Although it was argued that this result did not negate the conclusions based on the varying-orientation results, this finding must inject a note of caution.

Given that the discrimination failures were genuine, there is a more intractable problem concerning their interpretation. Any perceptual study based on discrimination methods inevitably taps the mechanisms of both perception and memory. In order to compare two stimuli, the subject must perceive them in sequence and retain the information about the first which is necessary to make the comparison with the second. Where a successful discrimination has been made, this is clear evidence that the distinctive attributes of the two have been both perceived and retained. But a discrimination failure is ambiguous, since it can always be attributed to inadequacies of either perception or retention. For example, it is entirely possible that in Experiment 6 the infants perceived all the stimulus objects at a level that would have enabled discriminations to be made between them, and that the failures were due to an inability to retain this information during the (approximately 5 sec) interval that separated the stimulus presentations. This possibility cannot be excluded. However, the performance by the Fixed-orientation group in Experiment 6 does suggest that the discrimination failures by the other groups in that experiment were not due to deficiencies in memory. The Fixed-orientation group made discriminations which were not evident in the Varying-orientation groups. If these failures were due to retention problems, why should these only have manifested themselves when the cube orientation was varied during habituation?

Taken at face value, the present results seem to imply only a limited grasp of object structure by 3-month-old infants. However, it may well be that the infants' performance with static geometrical forms underestimates their general perceptual capacity. Perhaps their performance with environmentally significant objects, or with moving objects would be better. Nevertheless, in spite of their likely irrelevance to the infants, the subjects did manifest some discriminative capacity with the forms presented to them in these experiments.

The discrimination failures observed in these experiments should not necessarily be interpreted simply as failures. Rather, they might be interpreted as evidence concerning the infants' taxonomy of object forms. For example, the subjects did not differentiate between a range of nonrectangular quadrilateral forms. This might imply that these objects were assigned to a common class ("blobs"?). Similarly, the results obtained here with solid forms could be explained by supposing that the cube, truncated pyramid etc. in Experiment 6 were simply classed as "convex lumps," in contrast to the L-form (a "concave lump"). In principle, a sufficiently large and systematic study could provide a definitive account of the classificatory system employed by the infants. However, the data provided in the studies reported here are too fragmentary to permit anything but speculation.

One final comment may be made concerning the broader implications of this study. In Experiments 2–4 (and 7), rectangles were distinguished from nonrectangular plane forms, while the subjects were unable to make a variety of discriminations involving nonrectangular forms. It was suggested that this might be taken to imply a special status for rectangularity in the perception of the 3-month-old infant. It was also suggested that this could be a consequence of the infant's experience with the orthogonal surfaces of its carpentered surroundings. The results obtained in Experiments 6 and 7 for the solid forms have some bearing on this question, because they imply that performance with solids is worse than that with plane forms. In particular, while discriminations were made between square, trapezoid, and triangle, in Experiment 7, no discriminations were manifest in Experiments 7 and 8 between the solid analogues of these forms, namely, the cube, truncated pyramid, and wedge. Since the solid cube is far more representative of the parallelipedal objects of the infants' surroundings than is the rectangle, these results detract somewhat from an environmental explanation of their performance with the rectangle.

ACKNOWLEDGMENT

The author wishes to thank Rosemary Birch for help in the preparation of this Chapter. Thanks are also due to the Infant Welfare Sisters of the Australian Capital Territory Health Commission for the help provided in obtaining subjects. This work was supported by A.R.G.C. Grant A79/15565.

REFERENCES

Bower, T. G. R. (1965). Stimulus variable determining space perception in infants. *Science, 149*, 88–89.

Bower, T. G. R. (1966). Slant perception and shape constancy in infants. *Science, 151*, 832–834.

Bower, T. G. R. (1972). Object perception in infants. *Perception, 1*, 15–30.

Caron, A. J., Caron, R. F., and Carlson, V.R. (1978). Do infants see objects or retinal images? Shape constancy revisited. *Infant Behavior and Development, 1*, 229–242.

Caron, A. J., Caron, R. F., & Carlson, V. R. (1979). Infant perception of the invariant shape of objects varying in slant. *Child Development, 50*, 716–721.

Cohen, L. B., DeLoache, J. S., & Strauss, M. S. (1979). Infant visual perception. In J. D. Osofsky (Ed.), Handbook of infant development (pp. 393–438). New York: Wiley.

Cook, M., & Birch, R. (1984). Infant perception of the shapes of tilted plane forms. *Infant Behavior and Development, 7*, 389–402.

Cook, M., Birch, R., & Griffiths, K. (1986). Discrimination between solid forms in early infancy. *Infant Behaviour and Development, 9*, 189–202.

Cook, M., Field, J., & Griffiths, K. (1978). The perception of solid form in early infancy. *Child Development, 49*, 866–869.

Cook, M., Hine, T., & Williamson, A. (1982). The perception of solidity in early infancy. *Perception, 11*, 677–684.

Day, R. H., & McKenzie, B. E. (1973). Perceptual shape constancy in early infancy. *Perception, 2*, 315–320.

Day, R. H., & McKenzie, B. E. (1981). Infant perception of the invariant size of approaching and receding objects. *Developmental Psychology, 17*, 670–677.

Fantz, R. L., & Nevis, S. (1967). Pattern preferences and perceptual-cognitive development in early infancy. *Merrill-Palmer Quarterly, 13*, 77–108.

Field, J. (1976). Relation of young infants' reaching behaviour to stimulus distance and solidity. *Developmental Psychology, 12*, 444–448.

Fox, R., Aslin, R. N., Shea, S. L., & Dumais, S. T. (1980) Stereopsis in human infants. *Science, 207*, 323–324.

von Hofsten, C. (1982). Eye-hand coordination in the new-born. *Developmental Psychology, 18*, 450–461.

6

The Development of Spatial Orientation in Human Infancy: What Changes?

B. E. McKenzie
La Trobe University

In order to orient themselves in space while moving from one place to another, mobile organisms take account of the direction and extent of their own movement and the spatial relationships between objects in their environment. In this chapter discussion is limited to the spatial orientation of infants in a stationary environment when the relative position of objects is unchanged but the infants' views of these objects vary as a consequence of their own self-induced (active) or imposed (passive) movement. The ability to perceive the identity of the spatial location of objects over variations in observer orientation and position has been called position constancy (McKenzie, Day, & Ihsen, 1984). The early development of position constancy—the conditions under which it is manifest and the measurement of its exactness—is reviewed. The question of central interest is when and how infants encode information that allows them to find a fixed target from different viewing points.

Human infants are slow in achieving self-mobility compared with most other animals. Once they begin to crawl or walk problems of spatial orientation arise frequently. This has led some investigators to suggest that active movement plays a special role in the abstraction of spatial information, triggering the subject to pay attention to stable features of the environmental layout. The notion of a developmental sequence in the manner of encoding this information as described by Piaget (1954) and others has become well accepted. Young infants are believed to lack an abstract system of axial coordinates in terms of which distance and relative position of objects within it are encoded. Rather than considering the self as one of a number of objects within this system, they are thought to encode object location solely in relation to their own body, i.e., egocentrically. For this reason they cannot apprehend the stability of a static array since their point of reference shifts with their own movement. It has been claimed that this early reliance on egocentric cues is later supplanted by a reliance on allocentric or environmental cues (see Acredolo, 1978; Cornell & Heth, 1979; Pick & Lockman, 1981). The transition from mainly egocentric to mainly allocentric frames of reference approximately coincides with the attainment of self-mobility.

It is argued here that locomotion is not a prerequisite for allocentric spatial reference and that the evidence for early egocentric spatial reference is not clear cut. Nevertheless, there are particular constraints on the kinds of features that can serve as environmental cues or landmarks for young infants. These constraints include the spatial relationships between landmarks and the target, the perceptual prominence of landmarks, and the type of information they convey. Cues for position may be provided by specific patterned features, by features associated with carpentered rooms (such as corners and surfaces) or by more general frames of reference (such as a rectangular wall).

Ability to orient spatially in an environment that is relatively featureless is also examined. In such conditions adults maintain spatial bearings by noting target location relative to themselves prior to moving, keeping track of the direction and extent of their own movements, and updating target location in accordance with these movements. In an unpatterned environment, one that is devoid of landmarks, localization is dependent on updating of target position on the basis of visual and proprioceptive information at the time of reorientation. A comparison of infants' ability to localize targets from novel viewing points in environments that are rich or poor in spatial features will serve to explicate the development of different strategies.

O'Keefe and Nadel (1978) distinguish two major systems of spatial reference, an orientation system and a guidance system. Whereas the former involves spatial coding relative to the self, the latter involves coding relative to the environment. An orientation system may operate in the absence of specific environmental cues. For example, a bushwalker wishes to reach a destination known to be one mile north in crow-flight distance from the starting point. There is no direct path; the sky is overcast and the destination is not visible as the bushwalker progresses through undulating wooded terrain. To remain oriented relative to the goal, the bushwalker must note deviations from the starting point and revise or update the position of the destination taking account of these deviations. This method of finding one's way involves the coding of target position relative to the self and requires the initiation and maintenance of an internal representation or sequence of movements. Knowledge of where the target is initially in relation to the self, of the direction and extent of movements and the integration of these two sources of information are required. The capacity of infants to use such a self-referent updating system has been studied in laboratory situations in featureless rooms.

The guidance system requires landmarks or environmental cues. Our bushwalker may note that the destination lies between a fire watching tower and a flowering gum tree. By choosing a route constantly directed towards this point the bushwalker is guided to the goal. Target location is coded in terms of its invariant relationship to objects in the environment and indirectly to the self. Continuous monitoring of deviations of the path from the starting point are not essential. The capacity of infants to use such an allocentric mode of reference has been studied by varying the characteristics of visible landmarks and environmental features such as the shape of the room in which testing occurs.

In the following review, studies concerning visual search for a target that is not directly visible are discussed. Reference to findings deriving from manual search and "detour" tasks are considered insofar as they clarify the interpretation of visual behavior.

LOCALIZATION OF A TARGET WITHOUT THE AID OF ENVIRONMENTAL CUES

The updating of target location relative to a new subject position and in the absence of specific environmental cues is exceptionally difficult for young infants. Accurate locational decisions under these conditions have not so far been demonstrated in the first year; they begin to appear early in the second.

In a longitudinal study, Acredolo (1978) tested infants aged 6, 11, and 16 months. They were seated at a round table in a square room with unpatterned walls and ceiling. There were two identical windows, one in each of two opposite walls. After being trained to anticipate an event at one of these windows, infants were moved through 180° around the table. Their direction of looking from this new position was observed. Looking first towards the true place where the event had occurred was more frequent in older subjects. At earlier ages the infants seemed not to take account of their own movement and continued to look mainly in the same egocentric direction after rotation as before. That is to say, they continued to look in the direction of the target relative to themselves during training—to the left or to the right.

It is interesting to consider how the older subjects were able to respond correctly. First, they must have assumed that the event would occur always at the one point in space. This is not a trivial consideration as it is conceivable that younger subjects did not make this assumption. They may have learned a motor response, for example, looking to the right, that was then continued when they were moved to the new position 180° removed from the old. The response therefore may not have indicated a locational decision but rather a learned direction of head and eye movement. Response perseveration, repetition of the trained response from the new position and orientation, is equivocal as an index of spatial reference. Whether or not it indicates an egocentric mode of responding is not clear. What is clear, however, is that perseveration is more frequent in younger than older subjects. Second, those older infants who looked toward the event site after rotation must have taken account of the direction and extent of their own movement. That is to say 16-month-old infants were more likely than younger infants to update target location on the basis of visual and proprioceptive information derived during their reorientation.

When testing 6-month-old infants in a spherical chamber without landmarks, Rieser (1979) also noted failure to adjust the direction of looking after rotation about the body axis through an angle of 90°. Results such as these have led some investigators to conclude that infants during their first year are unable to use information concerning their own movements to locate a target from a new position.

Before accepting this conclusion several procedural matters require careful consideration. The first concerns the training procedure. In each of these studies *one* direction of looking to the right or to the left was reinforced prior to rotation of the subject. Reproduction of this response after rotation may be interpreted as an instance of response generalization as well as one of spatial localization. A procedure that reduces this ambiguity is described below. A second issue concerns the type of change in subject position. In the studies by Rieser (1979) and Cornell and Heth (1979), subjects were simply rotated around the body axis whereas in that of Acredolo (1979) and Acredolo and Evans (1980) both rotation and relocation to a new point in space were involved. While rotation involves remaining in the same position but facing in a new direction, relocation involves a change in position in space. These several transformations may have separate effects (see Landau, 1984). A third issue is the magnitude of rotation from the training into the test position, 180° as compared with 90°. The former involves complete reversals of right-left and ahead-behind axes but the latter does not. Fourth, the number of elements contained in the stimulus array can vary widely; for example, there were only two potential target locations in Acredolo's study but four in Reiser's. To avoid confusion of egocentric responding (responses in the same relation to the body) with locational indecision and to provide a measure of the precision of localizational ability, more than two potential target locations are necessary. Finally, the shape of the room in which testing occurs may vary; Rieser (1979) tested in a circular room but Acredolo (1978), Acredolo and Evans (1980), and Cornell and Heth (1979) used a rectangular room. The latter provides cues such as contrasting surfaces and corners that are absent in the former.

In a recent study (Keating, McKenzie, & Day, 1986) an attempt was made to overcome these procedural problems. In one condition infants were trained and tested in a circular room without distinguishing features. They were seated in the center of this room and surrounded by a low circular enclosure from the top of which eight identical balls were suspended at 45° intervals. While facing and fixating one of these balls, they were trained to anticipate the appearance of the experimenter at another, either 45° or 90° to the left or right of the first. They were then faced towards another ball either 90° or 45° on the opposite side of the site of the experimenter's appearance. They had now to look in the opposite direction to witness this event. Having learned to look towards the one fixed location that was sometimes on their left and sometimes on their right, they were rotated into a new facing direction and the experimenter no longer appeared. Where they looked *first* on these test trials, when facing in a direction not used in training, was observed. This procedure was adopted in order to clarify the interpretation of behavior after reorientation. Because responses to both the left and the right had been reinforced during training neither one was more likely to be generalized to the test trials. The possibility of repetition of a simple operant response was thus avoided. Several potential target locations were each marked by identical balls; excluding the ball that served as the starting position for test trials and the one immediately behind the subject, six other locations remained. (A pilot study had shown that infants looked at balls rather than elsewhere.) It was thus possible to note whether subjects turned in the correct or incorrect direction to locate the target. As well, the accuracy of their first visual fixation could be determined. Subjects were rotated around their body axis to a maximum of 90° on either side of the target site and no relocation to a new position in space was involved. They were always rotated past the target site so that it remained potentially visible at the time of reorientation. The method of attracting attention to the ball to which the subject was faced on test trials prevented uninterrupted fixation on the target site and required eye movements of 90° to the left or right to locate it.

Under these conditions, without landmarks or room cues to guide them, 8-month-old infants were unable accurately to anticipate from a novel facing direction where the experimenter would have appeared. Of 16 subjects only 2 looked immediately towards the target on the first test trial. Furthermore, 14 additional subjects were tested in order to obtain a sample achieving the training criteria within the maximum trial limit. This number was notably greater than in the other experimental conditions where either a landmark or other environmental features were present (see later). It seems clear that localizing an exact position in space from a novel direction and without the aid of external spatial cues is not easily accomplished at this age. This contrasts markedly with the results described in the next section.

Analysis of errors in the direction of first looks suggested that subjects were not completely disoriented. Of the 14 subjects not looking immediately towards the target on the first test trial, 12 looked in the correct direction, but not far enough. The remaining two looked in the opposite direction. There are at least two possible interpretations of these results. It is conceivable that an updating strategy was used with respect to direction but that the information associated with reorientation was insufficient for precise localization. In these terms, the relative positions of subject and target were encoded, but imprecisely. The second and more likely interpretation is that infants had learned rather complex conditional rules in the training phase and that these were applied during testing. On control trials following the test trials, infants were faced in the directions that had been used in training. On the first of these, 11 subjects looked directly at the target and on the second, 8 subjects did so. Thus, in this circular room without a landmark more infants located the target on control than on test trials.

It is possible that, rather than having learned the location of the target, subjects had learned two specific movements each reversing the direction of turn into test position. For example, after rotation to the right, subjects may have learned to turn 90° to the left and after rotation to the left, 45° to the right. Such a strategy would lead to incorrect responses on test trials but correct responses on control trials. This pattern of results obtained for the condition involving a circular room without a landmark but was not as pronounced in the other conditions (Keating et al., 1986). In either case, whether subjects knew the direction of the target but not its precise location or whether they were using a conditional-rule strategy, it is clear that position constancy was not evident under these conditions.

Accurate search without the aid of external cues involves a self-referent updating strategy. This strategy has three requirements. First, the initial location of the target relative to the self needs to be encoded; since subjects had achieved the training criteria from two facing directions, this requirement appears to have been satisfied in our experiment. Second, the direction and extent of self-movement must be registered and represented. Subjects rarely looked in the wrong direction on test trials so it seems clear that direction of turn into test position was registered and remembered. Errors involved the magnitude of head and eye turns; most subjects undershot the true location on test trials. Little is known about the role and relative importance of proprioceptive and visual information as a basis for encoding the extent of self-movement, although visual information may outweigh proprioceptive information for stationariness and uprightness (Butterworth, 1981; Jouen, 1984). Certainly, visual cues concerning the extent of movement were impoverished in our study; the plain curtain walls were untextured and the balls marking possible locations were identical. That subjects were successful on control trials, however, suggests the likelihood that they had learned a response rather than a locational strategy under these conditions (see Keating et al., 1986). In addition there may be particular difficulties associated with the proprioceptive coding of rotatory as distinct from tranlocatory movement. The third requirement for accurate search in these circumstances is that movement information and initial target position must be integrated. Because subjects rarely mistook the direction of the target relative to themselves it would seem that direction of movement was integrated with the initial registration of target location. It is possible that either knowledge of the degree of self-movement is insufficiently precise or that integration of both aspects of movement— direction and extent—with target location is too complex for infants at this age. Updating of exact location in the absence of external cues has not been observed at 6 months (Acredolo, 1978; Rieser, 1979), 8 months (Keating et al., 1986) or 11 months, but may begin to appear around 16 months (Acredolo, 1978). Whether this reflects maturation in the accuracy of encoding of self-movements, in the integration of information regarding initial target location with that of self-movement, or both of these, is not known.

The results of several recent studies of locomotor problems confirm the suggestion that infants begin to use this self-referent updating strategy early in their second year. Rieser and Heiman (1982) examined the ability of 14- and 18-month-old infants to locate a target from a novel starting position. After having been trained to walk to one of eight identical windows in a circular, landmark-free room, infants were rotated through angles of more or less than 180° so that they were facing in a direction 90° from the target window. At both ages, infants learned to choose the shorter route to the target window, reversing the direction of movement into the test position in the case of a turn of 135° and continuing in the same direction after the 315° turn. These findings imply that infants from about 14-months-of-age have an understanding of the consequences of a 360° turn. In addition, information for self-movement must have been related to initial target location to infer a new and efficient path to the goal. Subjects were permitted alternative choices until they found the correct window and were given immediate reinforcement once they had pressed it. As the number of correct first choices was not given in the report, it is not possible to compare the performance of these subjects with that of the younger ones in our study (Keating et al., 1986). Nevertheless, it is clear that they exhibited spatially efficient navigation based on a process of updating target location in accordance with their own prior movements.

Rieser and his colleagues (Rieser, Doxsey, McCarrell, & Brooks, 1982) have also investigated toddlers' ability to perform inference-based navigation in situations involving detour problems in a round featureless chamber. Subjects were shown a side aerial view of the layout of barriers and a goal. Their selection of the open or blocked path to the goal from a frontal ground position was then observed. At 25-months-of-age subjects reliably selected the open route. This finding implies that they perceived the view from the air and the ground as different views of the same space and adapted their mental representation of the spatial layout from a side aerial view in terms of the frontal ground view. In this study subjects acquired knowledge in a "small-scale" space, i.e., when all aspects of the spatial layout were visible from a single viewing position, and had to demonstrate this knowledge in a "large-scale" space, i.e., when the spatial layout could not be apprehended from a single viewing position. It is conceivable that younger subjects may be able to register and remember spatial layouts and mentally transform information from one perspective view (e.g., the side) to another (e.g., the front) if within-scale comparisons are involved.

The findings of a study recently completed in our laboratory (Garino & McKenzie, in preparation) suggest that transfer of spatial information between

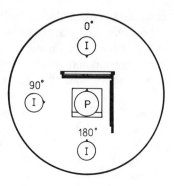

FIGURE 6.1. The experimental arrangement showing the three positions of the infant (I) at the front (0°), side (90°) and back (180°) of the maze. The parent (P) was the goal.

small- and large-scale views is difficult for infants, just as it is for older children (see Liben, Moore, & Golbeck, 1982). Operating in a large-scale space on the basis of information acquired from exposure to the same space in small-scale views may be particularly difficult. Garino and McKenzie found that when 18-month-old infants were given ground views of a maze from the front, side, or back and then tested from the front of the maze, they selected the shorter of two paths to the goal more often than when they were given similar aerial views from the front, side, or back of the maze (see Fig. 6.1). Subjects aged 18 months as well as those aged 24 months were able to represent and coordinate different *ground* views to select the shorter route. They were, however, less efficient after prior exposure to aerial views from different perspectives. That is to say, the coordination of varying perspectives between aerial and ground views was more difficult than the coordination of varying perspectives between ground views.

In summary, the ability visually to anticipate the appearance of a target at a particular point in space without the aid of environmental features appears to develop early in the second year. The process of updating target location on the basis of visual and proprioceptive information at the time of reorientation is clearly more difficult for young infants than the process of defining target location in terms of its invariant relationship to a visible landmark, as is noted in the next section. Findings from studies involving locomotor responses suggest that the updating strategy can be used by some infants at 14 months and by most at 18 months. Although it might reasonably be expected that localization by visual anticipation precedes locomotor responses, the relevant longitudinal data are not yet available.

LOCALIZATION OF A TARGET WITH THE AID OF ENVIRONMENTAL CUES

Several studies have been concerned with the ability of young infants to guide their visual search for a target by reference to visual environmental features or landmarks. The kind of landmarks made available in these studies has varied widely. First, a distinctive feature or features may be added to an environment that is otherwise featureless or, second, the information may be unspecified as is the case when testing occurs in a familiar room or a laboratory rich in spatial cues such as doors, windows, or wall pictures. Third, the landmark may be adjacent to or surround the target site or be indirectly associated with it, say on the opposite side of the room. Fourth, the features may be more or less prominent, e.g., flashing lights and moving stripes, or they may be of a more subtle nature, e.g., the corners and surfaces of a room.

In the following sections, studies that have been concerned with the role of landmarks in the localization of fixed objects and events are reviewed. For the sake of convenience these studies are grouped into those using landmarks that are directly associated with the target site, i.e., when a specific cue is situated at the site or surrounding it, and those using indirect landmarks or external cues that bear an invariant relationship to the target site but are physically separated from it. Of course, this classification is arbitrary; there are varying degrees of directness and indirectness in the relationship between landmark and target.

Direct Landmarks

In several studies Acredolo and her coworkers have found that the ability to make use of landmark information at the target site increases with age, with the prominence of the landmark, and with the infant's familiarity with the environment in which testing occurs (Acredolo, 1978, 1979, 1982; Acredolo & Evans, 1980). It is interesting to note that in these experiments, 6-month-old infants' performance was not significantly affected by visual cues that are known to be powerful elicitors of infant attention. When flashing lights and moving stripes surrounded the target window, infants at this age were unable reliably to look first towards it after they were reoriented in a new spatial location and facing in the opposite direction. It was not until after 6 months that objective responding was reliably demonstrated under these conditions. Repetition of the trained response was less pronounced in some conditions of Rieser's (1979) study with 6-month-old infants, possibly because the choice array was more numerous and simultaneously visible, infants were rotated but not relocated, and the degree of rotation was reduced. Nevertheless, Rieser concluded that the invariant relationship between the target and landmarks was not a reliable indicator of its true location for infants at this age. The tendency after rotation to look towards a location that stood in a constant relation to the body was reduced when the *true,* but not the egocentric, location was distinctively marked. However, when all locations other than the true location were patterned (the true location was distinctively unpatterned), repetition of the response acquired during training predominated.

These findings suggest that it is rare for 6-month-old infants to respond in terms of objective environmental cues. As has been noted earlier however, response repetition after rotation may be an instance of response generalization rather than of egocentric spatial reference. It is not without interest that this ambiguity in interpretation of responding applies mainly to infants around the age of 6 months or less. Since our purpose is to trace the development of position constancy and to specify the conditions under which it may first be demonstrated, it is important that the nonspatial interpretation of response repetition be excluded. In order to overcome this problem, McKenzie et al. (1984) trained infants to anticipate a target event from two facing directions, one on either side of the target. As in the study of Keating et al. (1986), accurate locational anticipations from a novel direction of facing required infants to select not only the right-left direction but also the magnitude of their eye and head turns towards the target. In this study the spatial cues associated with the test room were not excluded—windows, walls, and doors were fully visible. In the first experiment a specific landmark was also provided at the target location: the color and pattern of the ball at the event site was different from those at four other locations. Both 6- and 8-month-old infants anticipated the whereabouts of the target from the novel direction of facing and their visual fixation on this location was longer than at any other. Position constancy was evident for both age groups. In two further experiments with infants aged 8 months, direction of first looks after rotation was similarly accurate when the stimulus markers in the display were identical and when the angle of change in facing direction was increased from a maximum of 60° to 90° on either side of the target. Clearly, even 6-month-old infants do not define target location exclusively in terms of its original relationship to the self. However, it is not possible from this study to infer exactly what spatial information was used to determine target position. Cues associated with the room were present but whether and how they were involved was not examined.

In order to specify the kind of information that can serve as a basis for position constancy, the same procedure was used in a further study with subjects aged 8 months (Keating et al., 1986). Environmental features were varied in a factorial design. Infants were tested in a circular or square room with or without a patterned landmark surrounding the target location. The results for the circular room without the landmark have already been discussed. A comparison of accuracy of localization in the square and circular rooms without specific landmarks allowed a determination of whether corners or surfaces provided spatial referents. These room cues are not located at the target site and hence are not strictly relevant to this section. For the sake of clarity and contrast the results are included here. The design also made possible a comparison of visual search for the target in the presence and absence of the patterned landmark in the two rooms. There were 16 subjects in each of the four experimental conditions. The numbers of infants whose first look after rotation was towards the target site in the circular room, the circular room with the landmark, the square room and the square room with the landmark exceeded chance expectation in all but the first condition. Inability to update target location in the absence of external cues was discussed earlier. Of greater interest here is the observation that subjects could anticipate target location in the square room when the distinctive marker was not provided. These results suggest that the corners or surfaces of the square room function as cues for spatial orientation as does the specific marker.

The combination of square room and landmark produced the highest frequency of subjects whose first look was towards the target. These findings were supported by analysis of the duration of fixation on the target site. Subjects spent a greater proportion of time looking towards the target when the landmark was present than when it was not. They also looked longer towards the target in the square than in the circular room. Thus, several measures indicated that spatial orientation was poor in the absence of external cues and was improved by the presence of landmark information. Specific patterned features or more subtle cues deriving from the square room were necessary for position constancy.

Landmark information that directly distinguishes one spatial location from another can guide infants' search strategies. This effect is more than just a tendency to look to a patterned rather than an unpatterned area as is shown in Rieser's study (1979) where attention was directed differentially between patterned locations and, in some instances, at the true unpatterned location rather than at a patterned irrelevant location. In our studies the presence of a specific landmark resulted in infants directing their search towards a particular place. It is immaterial whether they looked first towards that place in order to see the landmark itself or towards that for which it was a marker. In either case, and in the square room without the landmark, the conclusion that 8-month-old infants have a mental place-keeping system—a representation of place—is supported.

Indirect Landmarks

Rieser (1979) noted that at 6-months-of-age infants did not use an allocentric strategy when the target location was distinctively unpatterned and the three other locations were patterned. Similarly, Acredolo and Evans (1980) found that only the performance of their oldest subjects (11 months) was influenced by the indirect landmark when the window opposite to the target window was surrounded by a distinctive pattern. Indirect spatial reference is clearly more difficult than direct spatial reference even for older children. De Loache and Brown (1983), for example, noted that memory for location in children aged 21 months was more fragile when the landmark was not intrinsic to the hiding place and associated with it in an arbitrary and indirect way.

The results of several unpublished studies with infants aged 8 months also indicate that landmarks distant from the target site do not promote position constancy. In the same experimental procedure as described earlier (McKenzie et al., 1984; Keating et al., 1986) we used single, paired, or several patterned figures as potential landmarks attached to the wall of the circular room. No pattern was less than 20° from the target. In another study the circular wall was curtained so that one half was blue and the other white. The vertical intersection of the two colored sections was offset 20° to the left or right of the target. When no marker was contiguous with the target site the numbers of infants looking first towards it after rotation did not exceed chance expectation in any experiment.

The outcomes of these experiments suggest that infants less than about 11-months-of-age seem to maintain their bearings precisely only in the presence of external cues that directly indicate the target site. The one significant exception to this conclusion is the performance of 8-month-old infants in the square room without a patterned landmark. It is possible that corners and surfaces provide reference cues of a different kind. Vertical surfaces and their junctions indicate the straight ahead, the right and left, and provide parallactic information as to the relative depth of objects in the visual field as the subject moves. Singly or in combination this information was sufficient for a significant number of subjects to locate the target site (Keating et al., 1986). The question then arises as to why the older subjects in Acredolo's study (1978) did not also respond objectively when they were tested in a square room without a landmark at the window where the experimenter had appeared. Considering only the first trial after reorientation, Acredolo noted that 4 out of 12 16-month-old infants looked to the true location whereas in our study 7 out of 16 8-month-old infants did so. Since the test rooms were similar in shape and size and the same target event was involved, it seems likely that differences in experimental procedure were implicated. As discussed earlier, these differences included training from two rather than one facing direction, rotation alone rather than rotation and relocation to a new position in space, and the presence of several potential event sites. Our findings show that under some circumstances room features by themselves are sufficient to sustain a place-keeping system. This information is not provided by the vertical junction of two colored surfaces in a circular room.

With the exception of the more natural cues provided by the carpentered environment, the ability to make referential use of specific features that are distant from the target site appears later than the ability to use coincident landmark information. Pick, Yonas, and Rieser (1979) also concluded that the ability to use landmarks at increasing distances from the target improved with age. Longitudinal data are, of course, required to confirm these suggestions.

THE ROLE OF SELF-PRODUCED MOVEMENT

Most human infants become independently mobile in the second half of their first year. It has been postulated that this active experience plays a special role in the development of spatial orientation by forcing infants to progress beyond a body-centered organization of space. Whether or not this egocentric reference has been unduly emphasized as a result of limitations in experimental procedures, infants become increasingly able to behave in accordance with an objective system of spatial coordinates that incorporates the relative position of objects and the metric relationships between them. This maturation is evident in visual, manual, and locomotor behavior.

Campos, Svejda, Berthenthal, Benson, and Schmid (1981) suggest that active movement is the basis on which infants develop those perceptual skills that are required to avoid the deep side of a visual cliff. It has also been suggested that crawlers more readily abstract the invariant shape of an object presented in varying orientations than do noncrawlers (Campos, Berthenthal, & Benson, 1980). McComas and Field (1984), on the other hand, found no difference in the behavior of infants of similar age but with high and low levels of crawling experience in a spatial orientation task like that of Acredolo (1978). If active movement is to be established as anything other than a correlate of spatial proficiency it is necessary to establish the processes through which it is operative.

Acredolo, Adams, and Goodwyn (1984) have investigated this problem. Rather than comparing infants with differing amounts of locomotor experience, they examined the accuracy of manual search for hidden objects in subjects who were passively moved or who had moved themselves into the test position. They concluded that self-produced movement enhanced visual fixation on the hidden object. This visual monitoring of target position while moving from one place to another improved the accuracy of searching in 12- but not 18-month-old infants. Acredolo and her coworkers suggest that mental representation of the spatial layout supplanted an earlier reliance on direct perception. Further research in this area could usefully be directed towards examining the possible interactive effects of type of movement and presence or absence of visual monitoring of the target. As noted earlier in this chapter although our method of training in visual search studies (McKenzie et al., 1984; Keating et al., 1986) did *not* allow continuous monitoring of target position, evidence for spatial representation of position in infants as young as 6-months-of-age was adduced. Because none of these infants were independently mobile and they had been passively reoriented throughout training and testing, it is clear that active movement is not a prerequisite for this ability.

THE DEVELOPMENT OF DETOUR BEHAVIOR

Despite the importance that Piaget (1954) attached to the invention of detours as marking the beginning of spatial representation, it is only recently that systematic investigation of the factors influencing the early development of this behavior has begun. Some of these studies have been described earlier (Rieser et al., 1982; Garino & McKenzie, in preparation). The ability of infants to select alternative routes to a goal making allowance for obstacles between themselves and the goal was examined also by Lockman (1984). In a longitudinal study he found that manual detours, i.e., reaching around barriers, preceded locomotor detours, i.e., crawling or walking around barriers, and that detours around opaque barriers preceded transparent ones. McKenzie and Bigelow (1986) did not confirm this finding concerning the effect of transparency of the barrier on locomotor detours. The cross-sectional design of this study was, however, less sensitive to sequential effects. Infants aged 14 months selected a more efficient route to the goal than did those aged 10 or 12 months. A more interesting outcome concerned the flexibility of detour behavior following relocation of the barrier. Subjects were given four trials with the unobstructed path to the goal on their right or left and then a further four trials with this path on the opposite side. On the first trial involving the new spatial arrangement, the reduction in the route efficiency score for the 10- and 12-month-old subjects was greater than the reduction for the 14-month-old subjects. A similar disruption in route efficiency was noted in 10-month-old subjects after only one successful trial prior to spatial rearrangement. Since spatial cues associated with the test room were available it was not possible to determine whether route selection was guided by environmental cues. In contrast to the study of Rieser et al. (1982) the open and the obstructed route to the goal were clearly visible from the starting point. Nevertheless, infants aged just under 1 year did not readily adapt their path towards the goal in accord with the rearrangement in spatial layout. These results suggest that the revision of the representation of spatial relationships between objects together with the displacement of the self relative to these objects is a complex skill that begins to be achieved early in the second year. The factors associated with the development of this skill are yet to be determined. In this respect the studies of Lockman (1984), Heth and Cornell (1980), Green and Rieser (1983), Rieser (1983), and Haake, Smith, and Pick (1984) are a promising beginning.

CONCLUSION

In this chapter a distinction has been drawn between two types of processing of spatial information: an orientation strategy involving the revision of target location on the basis of visual and proprioceptive cues arising during subject movement, and a guidance strategy based on the invariant relationship between the target and visual landmarks. Of course these strategies need not be mutually exclusive. It seems clear, however, that infants' ability to maintain spatial orientation without reference to visible cues is not well developed in the first year. In contrast, from at least 8-months-of-age they can anticipate the whereabouts of a target in terms of its stable relationship to another visible object at the target site and to the corners and surfaces of a room but not in terms of noncontiguous objects that are displaced from the target.

In the study of Keating et al. (1986) infants were unable to anticipate the place of the experimenter's appearance on test trials when there were no landmarks in a circular room. Yet, they had completed training and had remembered this information on control trials. Examination of the errors for this group suggested that, rather than abstracting a representation of the target location, they had acquired conditional responses of the form: "after rotation to the right, look 45° to the left; after rotation to the left, look 90° to the right." This permitted subjects to satisfy the various training criteria and respond correctly on control trials but lead them to make specific errors on test trials. A large proportion of subjects made errors of this kind. This interpretation cannot, however, account for the correct responses evident in the three other experimental groups where subjects could rely on environmental spatial features—landmarks or room cues—that provided a spatial referent or referents in relation to which the position of the target could be specified. A central issue for future research is to establish how place-keeping strategies in a featureless environment become transformed into the more mature spatial representation of toddlers 6 months later as shown in the study of Rieser and Heiman (1982). From 14 months toddlers search for a target using an orientation strategy that minimizes the length of the path to the goal. Although initially imprecise, the responses of sometimes reversing the direction of turn into test position and sometimes continuing in the same direction (depending on the extent of the turn) indicate development in coding of the degree of rotation and in the conception of spatial properties.

It is of interest to note that it is at about this age that infants exhibit greater flexibility in locomotor detours (McKenzie & Bigelow, 1986) and a little later they are able to coordinate their mental representation of a spatial layout between different ground views, and between aerial and ground views (Garino & McKenzie, in preparation; Green & Rieser, 1983).

With regard to the second strategy of spatial representation in which visual search is guided by reference to environmental features and their invariant relationship to the target position, some competence is evident in the first half year of life. Position constancy is operative in infants who have been passively moved from one facing direction to another provided that there is a visible marker at the target position or that room corners and surfaces are visible (Keating et al., 1986; McKenzie et al., 1984). The achievement of position constancy in the absence of visible environmental features or in the presence of noncontiguous landmarks appears to be a later development. This suggestion is yet to be confirmed using longitudinal methods. The localization displayed by 6- and 8-month infants in the study of McKenzie et al. (1984) may have been partially determined by the processing of cues associated with the rectangular room in which testing occurred. In the normal environment there is redundancy in the spatial cues specifying position. Although some infants may have been aided by the incidental coincidence of target and a particular room feature, the rectangularity cues could by themselves have been sufficient.

In a recent unpublished study we have noted even more reliable localization after translocation rather than rotation of subjects. Of 16 8-month-old infants who were translocated from one point in space to another, 15 successfully looked directly towards the site of the experimenter's appearance. Subjects were equally proficient when tested in a rectangular room with no reduction in spatial cues and when a patterned landmark surrounded the target site in a rectangular room with unpatterned surfaces. It is conceivable that translocatory movements are more readily encoded than rotatory movements. If this is the case, localization after translocation of the subject may occur at this age in a circular featureless room. This possibility has yet to be tested.

The ability to use a stable and objective set of spatial coordinates is dependent on a complex interaction of stimulus display features, response demands and procedural variables. In this, as in other areas of infant development, there is a need to distinguish those aspects of behavior that are task specific. The apparent egocentricity obtained by one experimental technique may not be evident in another. Outside the laboratory, place is not usually defined by a single cue but by a set of spatial relations obtaining in a stimulus constellation. How infants come to form mental representations of these relationships with the self as one item within the system will best be understood by examining their behavior over a range of spatial tasks.

ACKNOWLEDGMENT

This research was supported by grants from the Australian Research Grants Scheme to B. E. McKenzie and R. H. Day. The author wishes to thank E. Ihsen, B. Keating, H. Chandler, E. Bigelow and J. Monaco for research assistance.

REFERENCES

Acredolo, L. P. (1978). Development of spatial orientation in infancy. *Developmental Psychology*, *14*, 224–234.

Acredolo, L. P. (1979). Laboratory versus home: The effect of environment on the 9-month-old infant's choice of spatial reference system. *Developmental Psychology, 15,* 666–667.

Acredolo, L. P. (1982). The familiarity factor in spatial research. In R. Cohen (Ed.), *New directions for child development: Children's conceptions of spatial relationships*. San Francisco: Jossey-Bass.

Acredolo, L. P., Adams, A., & Goodwyn, S. W. (1984). The role of self-produced movement and visual tracking in infant spatial orientation. *Journal of Experimental Child Psychology, 38,* 312–327.

Acredolo, L. P., & Evans, D. (1980). Developmental changes in the effects of landmarks on infant spatial behavior. *Developmental Psychology, 16,* 312–318.

Butterworth, G. (1981). Object permanence and identity in Piaget's theory of infant cognition. In G. Butterworth (Ed.), *Infancy and epistemology: An evaluation of Piaget's theory*. Brighton: Harvester Press.

Campos, J., Bertenthal B., & Benson, N. (1980, April). *Self-produced locomotion and the extraction of form invariance*. Paper presented at the International Conference on Infant Studies, New Haven.

Campos, J., Svejda, M., Berthenthal, B., Benson, N., & Schmid, D. (1981, April). *Self-produced locomotion and wariness of heights: New evidence from training studies.* Paper presented at the Society for Research in Child Development, Boston.

Cornell, E. H., & Heth, C. D. (1979). Response versus place learning by human infants. *Journal of Experimental Psychology: Human Learning and Memory, 5,* 188–196.

De Loache, J. E., & Brown, A. L. (1983). Very young children's memory for the location of objects in a large-scale environment. *Child Development 54,* 888–897.

Garino, E., & McKenzie, B.E. (in preparation). The development of inference-based navigation in infancy.

Green, J. A., & Rieser, J. J. (1983, April). *The cognitive mapping of toddlers and young children.* Paper presented at the Society for Research in Child Development, Detroit.

Haake, R. J., Smith, R., & Pick, H. L. (1984, April). *Spatial orientation and wayfinding in an unfamiliar environment.* Paper presented at the International Conference on Infant Studies, New York.

Heth, C. D., & Cornell, E. H. (1980). Three experiences affecting spatial discrimination learning by ambulatory children. *Journal of Experimental Child Psychology, 30,* 246–264.

Jouen, F. (1984). Visual-vestibular interactions in infancy. *Infant Behavior and Development, 7,* 135–145.

Keating, M. B., McKenzie, B. E., & Day, R. H. (1986). Spatial localization in infancy: Position constancy in a square and circular room with and without a landmark. *Child Development, 57,* 115–124.

Landau, B. (1984, April). *Rotations and translations in infancy.* Paper presented at the International Conference on Infant Studies, New York.

Liben, L. S., Moore, M. L., & Golbeck, S. L. (1982). Preschoolers' knowledge of their classroom environment: Evidence from small-scale and life-size spatial tasks. *Child Development, 53,* 1275–1284.

Lockman, J. J. (1984). The development of detour ability during infancy. *Child Development, 55,* 482–491.

McComas, J., & Field, J. (1984). *Does crawling experience affect infants' emerging spatial orientation abilities?* Unpublished manuscript.

McKenzie, B. E., & Bigelow, E. (1986). Detour behaviour in young human infants. *British Journal of Developmental Psychology, 4,* 139–148.

McKenzie, B. E., Day, R. H., & Ihsen, E. (1984). Localization of events in space: Young infants are not always egocentric. *British Journal of Developmental Psychology, 2,* 1–9.

O'Keefe, J., & Nadel, L. (1978). *The hippocampus as a cognitive map.* Oxford: Oxford University Press.

Piaget, J. (1954). *The construction of reality in the child.* New York: Basic Books.

Pick, H. L., & Lockman, J. J. (1981). From frames of reference to spatial representations. In L. S. Liben, A. H. Patterson & W. Newcombe (Eds.), *Spatial representation and behavior across the life span: Theory and application.* Orlando, FL: Academic Press.

Pick, H. L., Yonas, A., & Rieser, J. J. (1979). Spatial reference systems in perceptual development. In M. C. Bornstein & W. Kessen (Eds.), *Psychological development from infancy: Image to intention.* Hillsdale, NJ: Lawrence Erlbaum Associates.

Rieser, J. J. (1979). Spatial orientation of six-month-old infants. *Child Development, 50,* 1078–1087.

Rieser, J. J. (1983). The generation and early development of spatial inferences. In H. L. Pick & L. P. Acredolo (Eds.), *Spatial orientation: Theory, research and application.* New York: Plenum Press.

Rieser, J. J., Doxsey, P. A., McCarrell, W. S., & Brooks, P. H. (1982). Wayfinding and toddlers' use of information from an aerial view of a maze. *Developmental Psychology, 18,* 714–720.

Rieser, J. J., & Heiman, M. L. (1982). Spatial self-reference systems and shortest-route behavior in toddlers. *Child Development, 53,* 524–533.

7 The Role of Movement in Object Perception by Infants

Denis K. Burnham
University of New South Wales

INTRODUCTION

Charles Darwin (1877) noted that shortly after birth visual fixation by his son, Doddy, could only be attracted by the flickering of a candle. We now know that newborn infants can also fixate upon static stimuli. However, we also know that movement is a highly captivating stimulus and that infants much prefer to fixate moving over stationary objects (Burnham, 1980, Burnham & Day, 1979; McKenzie & Day, 1976; Volkmann & Dobson, 1976; Wilcox & Clayton, 1968). Except in special experimental situations, movement is only evident when something moves. Relying as it does on objects for its perceptual manifestation, how does movement influence object perception? This question is especially important with regard to infants for whom it seems that movement is such a prepotent stimulus and for whom the distinction between an object and the manner in which it moves may not be as clear-cut as for adults. It is also of interest because its investigation throws light on some general issues relevant to the development of object perception.

Four possible roles of movement in the perception of objects by infants are examined in this chapter. These are movement as a suppressor of object perception, movement as a facilitator of object perception, movement as an incidental or secondary characteristic of objects, and movement as an object feature. Investigation of these will lead us to consider various theoretical and empirical aspects of object perception in infancy and some theoretical implications for adult perception. The view that movement acts as a suppressor of object perception is first discussed. This view arises out of T. G. R. Bower's views on limited processing ability and supramodal perception in early infancy. Consideration of Bower's original research in the light of methodological criticisms and more recent research by others results in rejection of the claim that movement acts *solely* to suppress object perception in early infancy. However, instances where movement does suppress object perception are described, as is a new effect concerning the suppression of the processing of stimulus compounds.

Two roles of movement as a facilitator of object perception are next investigated. First the facilitative role of movement on the detection and perception of objects over distance is considered. Then, in relation to Ruff's views, the facilitating role of movement in the perception of object structure is considered. It is concluded that some types of movement can facilitate object perception.

The third role relates to the development of the object concept in infancy, in particular the development of identity constancy over movement transformations. After discussing the Piagetian and Gibsonian positions on object concept development, the component abilities making up identity constancy are considered. A review of relevant research shows that infants can perceive object features over movement transformations. Although this is a necessary precursor of identity constancy, it is a rather low-level ability compared with the fully mature object concept. Consideration of two issues suggest that young infants' degree of identity constancy is limited to this low level. The first relates to the difficulty of operationally defining identity given the limited response repertoire of infants. A study is outlined which suggests that over different presentations of an object, infants respond to the similarity of features rather than to their identity. The new method used in this study is suggested as a fruitful means for the future differentiation of the perception of similarity and identity by infants. The second issue is that studies purporting to examine identity constancy have lacked an essential control. When this control is incorporated, the propensity to identify objects only by their features is called into question. A subsequent study suggests that while infants can form concepts, there seems to be no predisposition for them to form concepts based on constant object features.

This evidence leads to consideration of the final possible role of movement, namely movement as an object feature. It is argued that infants simply perceive movement as a feature of objects similar to, though more interesting than other object features such as shape and color. This raises issues about how adults perceive objects, especially moving objects, and how the development of perception may differ for biological and nonbiological objects. A summary and conclusions are presented in the third section.

FOUR POSSIBLE ROLES OF MOVEMENT

Movement as a Suppressor

Limited Capacity and Suppression of Object Features.   As young infants have limited capacity to process information, Bower believes that it is natural, and ecologically plausible, that they should attend selectively to the most informative aspects of ambient stimulation (Bower, 1974, 1975, 1978). In a

Gibsonian vein, Bower suggests that the important environmental events are those which convey information which is supramodal, relational, and dynamic rather than those events which convey only modality-specific, absolute, and static information. Thus, there are innate structures for the registration of environmental events such as occurrence, existence, location, and movement (Bower, 1978). A consequence of this is that for young infants the featural identity of objects is secondary to their position or movement in space. Thus, Bower claims that infants younger than about 20-weeks-of-age have an erroneous concept of object identity: An object is defined as a bounded volume of space in a particular place or on a path of movement (Bower, 1974, 1975). With regard to moving objects the implications are that until about 20-weeks-of-age infants (a) do not process the features of moving objects, (b) track trajectories rather than objects, and (c) do not perceive any relationship between an object when it is moving and when it is stationary (Bower, Broughton, & Moore, 1971; Bower & Paterson, 1973). The second and third claims are relevant in the third section but it is the first that is of particular interest here.

Perception of Features of Moving Objects.   Evidence that infants can perceive features of moving objects is now available. However, if any weight is to be attached to this evidence two preconditions must be met. First, infants must be able to perceive features when objects are stationary, i.e., the features must be perceived in the absence of movement otherwise feature perception could be the *result* of movement. Second, infants must be able to perceive movement and to discriminate between movement and stationariness otherwise there would be no phenomenal difference between the perception of features of objects which are stationary and features of objects which are moving. Regarding the first, it is now well established that from an early age infants perceive various features of stationary objects and patterns. From birth they can perceive pattern elements (Fantz, 1963; Salapatek & Kessen, 1966) and by around 2 months perceive color (Bornstein, 1976; Peeples & Teller, 1975), shape (Caron, Caron, & Carlson, 1979; Cook, Hine, & Williamson, 1982; McGurk, 1972; Salapatek, 1975; Schwartz & Day, 1979; see also Cook in this volume), and color-shape compounds (Mundy, 1985). With regard to the second precondition, it is evident that even at birth infants have the ability to perceive various classes of movement: nontranslatory, lateral, and approaching and receding movement (Burnham, 1980; Salapatek & Banks, 1978). Moreover, infants as young as 2 weeks prefer moving to stationary objects over a wide range of movement types which demonstrates their ability to discriminate movement and stationariness (Burnham & Day, 1979; Carpenter, 1974; Carpenter & Stechler, 1969; McKenzie & Day, 1976; Silfen & Ames, 1964; Volkmann & Dobson, 1976; Wilcox & Clayton, 1968). In addition, they can discriminate between aspects of movement. By at least 8 weeks infants discriminate different movement velocities both of rotating objects (Burnham & Day, 1979) and internal components of schematic faces (Girton, 1979). By this age they also track faster-moving objects better than slower-moving objects (Burnham & Dickinson, 1981; Kremenitzer, Vaughan, Kurtzberg, & Dowling, 1979). By at least 5 months infants discriminate rigid and nonrigid movement transformations (Gibson et al., 1978, 1979), by around 4 to 6 months they discriminate biological motion from nonbiological motion (Bertenthal, Proffitt, & Cutting, 1984; Fox & McDaniels, 1982) and by around 8 to 9 months they appear to discriminate between more and less human-like biological motions (Bertenthal, Proffitt, Spetner, & Thomas, 1985).

Infants perceive features of stationary objects, perceive different aspects of movement, and discriminate movement from stationariness. Can infants perceive features of moving objects? Positive evidence before the age of 20 weeks would conflict with Bower's notion that movement suppresses the processing of object features in early infancy.

Burnham and Day (1979) investigated whether young infants could perceive and remember the colored patterns of rotating cylinders. Infants of 8 to 19 weeks were shown cylinders which rotated about their central axes in the frontoparallel plane at angular velocities of either 42° per sec or 84° per sec. Following habituation of visual fixation to a rotating cylinder of a specific color, in test trials infants were shown rotating cylinders of the same or a novel color. In conditions where the cylinders rotated at 42° per sec infants of all ages were found to fixate novel-colored rotating cylinders significantly longer than familiar-colored rotating cylinders. Similar results were obtained with cylinders rotating at 84° per sec showing that infants as young as 2 months can discriminate between rotating objects on the basis of color. It could be argued that the color of objects may be particularly resilient to suppression by movement especially when such movement merely involves rotation in the frontoparallel plane. However, further work by Burnham and Kyriacos (1982) has produced similar results with a different feature, namely shape, and a different type of movement, namely rotation in depth. Infants of 17 and 26 weeks were habituated to a patterned object of a specific shape, which rotated in depth about its central axis at about 2 cycles per sec in a specific direction, e.g., up and down. In test trials infants of both ages fixated a rotating novel shape significantly longer than the familiar rotating shape. Together these two studies show that infants younger than 20 weeks can perceive the color and shape of objects rotating in various ways.

This conclusion has been supported by other investigations. In an habituation study similar to those already mentioned, Ihsen and Day (1981) found that 8- to 14-week-old infants discriminated between a patterned cylinder and a patterned cube each of which rotated about its central axis in the frontoparallel plane. This discrimination was evident even at distances of 4m and 10m. These findings extend those of Burnham and Day (1979) who found similar results at shorter viewing distances of 55cm and 1m. In another habituation study Gibson, Owsley, Walker, and Megaw-Nyce (1979) found that 15-week-old infants perceived the shape of objects undergoing rigid movement transformations (rotations in depth). Similar results have been obtained in investigations of infants' visual preferences. Hartlep (1979) and Ball (1980) presented infants with two patterned stimuli simultaneously rotating in circular orbits. Hartlep (1979) found that 11-week-old infants fixated a rotating cube longer than a rotating sphere and Ball (1980) found that 16- to 19-week-old infants fixated a rotating schematic face arranged normally longer than a scrambled face. Finally, in a recent series of visual preference and habituation studies Slater, Morison, Town, and Rose (1985) found that even newborn babies perceive the shape of objects rotating in the frontoparallel plane either around their central axes or when the objects described the circumference of a small circle without change of orientation.

These studies support the conclusion that young infants and even newborns can perceive various features of rotating objects. However, a limitation of most of these studies (Burnham & Day, 1979; Burnham & Kyriacos, 1982; Gibson et al., 1979; Ihsen & Day, 1981) is that they only involved nontranslatory movement. A further limitation is that the studies involved types of movement which are not of particular ecological significance to young infants. In the natural environment it is not often that infants would encounter objects rotating in the frontoparallel plane (Burnham & Day, 1979; Ihsen & Day, 1981; Slater et al., 1985), in depth (Burnham & Kyriacos, 1982; Gibson et al., 1979) or in a circular orbit in a regular rhythmic manner (Ball, 1980; Hartlep, 1979; Slater et al., 1985). In Bower's original studies objects translated across the infant's field of view (Bower et al., 1971; Bower & Paterson, 1973). Perhaps Bower's claim that movement suppresses feature perception is applicable only in those cases where object movement is translatory.

To investigate this possibility Burnham examined 11- and 17-week-old infants' perception of features of objects which translate laterally across their field of view (Burnham & Dickinson, 1981; Day & Burnham, 1981). By means of a camera moving with the object, precise frame-by-frame measures of visual pursuit were obtained. In one experiment shapes moved laterally at 4° per sec throughout habituation and test trials. Following a number of habituation trials with a particular shape, infants of both ages continued pursuit in test trials more readily for a novel than for the familiar shape (Day & Burnham, 1981). Evidence of a similar nature comes from a study by Hartlep (1983) involving simultaneous presentation of two objects moving laterally at approximately 7.5° per sec, about the same speed as that used in the studies by Bower et al. (1971). Hartlep found that 10- to 15-week-old infants preferred to track a checkerboard cube over a bulls-eye sphere. There is also evidence to suggest that newborn babies may be able to perceive the features of laterally moving objects. Goren, Sarty, and Wu (1975) found that newborn infants tracked a laterally moving schematic face better than a laterally moving scrambled face. This has recently received some support from a similar study by Maurer and Young (1983). Their results indicate at least some degree of pattern differentiation by newborns for laterally moving objects. Together these results show that newborns and young infants have the capacity to process features of moving objects even when movement is translatory.

Burnham, however, was unable to find similar results with a relatively fast translation velocity. While infants' tracking was better at 10° per sec than at 4° per sec (Burnham & Dickinson, 1981), evidence for shape discrimination was obtained only for those objects moving at the slower speed (Day & Burnham, 1981). It is conceivable that at the faster speed visual pursuit is more automatic or taxic and that this type of pursuit may interfere with the processing of object features (Burnham & Dickinson, 1981; Day & Burnham, 1981). The suggestion that some kinds of motion may inhibit infants' detection of object structure has also been made by Ruff (1982). She found that while 6-month-old infants could detect the structure of complex objects translating across the infants' visual field at a velocity of about 4.3° per sec, they could not do so when the movement was very complex, i.e., when the objects both translated *and* rotated.

Another limitation due to movement has been discovered recently in our laboratory. Burnham and Vignes (1983) investigated infants' ability to remember various compounds of movement, shape and color components. A trials-to-criterion variation on the habituation method used by Cohen (1973) was employed. In the first study five groups of 7-month-old infants, 16 per group, were tested. In the control group there was no change between habituation and test trials. The procedure for the four experimental groups is shown in Fig. 7.1. As can be seen the changes between habituation and test trials in the experimental groups always involved a novel recombination of familiar components. For recovery of visual fixation to occur, infants in each group would have had to store the compound specified—a color-movement compound in the first group (CM), a shape-movement compound in the second (SM) and a color-shape compound in each of the final two groups (CS and CS-stat). There was no

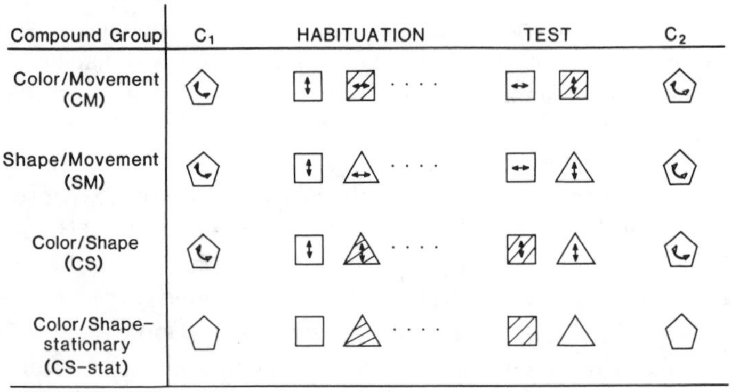

Compound Group	C₁	HABITUATION	TEST	C₂

FIGURE 7.1. Schematic representation of the procedure in the studies of compound processing by Burnham and Vignes (1983). C1 and C2 are the control stimuli presented before and after testing. The arrows represent the direction of movement—in the frontoparallel plane for the control stimuli and in depth about the fixed central axis for habituation and test stimuli. Absence of arrows indicates stationariness.

recovery in the no-change control group. In the experimental groups recovery was found in the CM and the CS-stat groups but not in the SM or CS groups. The CM and SM group results are discussed in greater detail in a later section. Here the CS versus CS-stat comparison is important.

A subsequent study was conducted with 4-, 7-, and 10-month-old infants using only the CS and CS-stat procedures. A within-subject design obviated the need for a separate control group. At all ages infants were found to recover to novel compounds in the CS-stat but not in the CS condition. Thus, movement appears to interfere with the storage of color-shape compounds over a wide age range. In a final study the locus of this interference was sought. Two groups, with equal representation by 4-, 7-, and 10-month-old infants, were tested. The procedure was similar to that in the CS-stat and CS groups except that the movement and stationariness of objects in habituation and test trials varied. In the stationary to moving group (S-M), stationary color-shape compounds were presented in habituation trials (as in CS-stat) while in test trials familiar and novel color-shape compounds were moving (as in CS). In the moving to stationary group (M-S) the opposite was the case: objects were moving in habituation and stationary in test. It was reasoned that if movement interferes with retrieval there should be no significant recovery in the S-M group despite the fact that a color-shape compound would have been encoded in habituation trials. If movement interferes with encoding there should be no significant recovery in the M-S group because, despite infants' ability to perceive color-shape compounds in the stationary test trials, no color-shape compound would have been stored in habituation trials. There was no significant recovery in either group, suggesting the possibility that movement interferes both with the ability to encode color-shape compounds and with the ability to retrieve such compounds once they are stored. This conclusion must as yet be drawn with caution because it is based on null results. Nevertheless, irrespective of the locus of the interference, movement does interfere with compound formation in some way. This interference is not simply at a perceptual level because, as evidence presented earlier shows, infants do perceive the features of objects moving in this manner (Burnham & Kyriacos, 1982; Gibson et al., 1979). Rather, it appears that the interference has to do with the type of processing which occurs once the features of moving objects are perceived.

In summary, infants detect the shape and structure of objects moving laterally at about 4° per sec (Burnham & Day, 1981; Ruff, 1982) and 7.5° per sec (Hartlep, 1983) but cannot do so when translation is combined with rotation (Ruff, 1982) or when translation velocity is increased to 10° per sec (Day & Burnham, 1981). In addition, for at least some types of movement only feature components and not feature compounds are processed (Burnham & Vignes, 1983). Nevertheless, in general, there is now substantial evidence from a number of different laboratories to suggest that infants perceive various features of objects moving in a variety of manners (Ball, 1980; Burnham & Day, 1979;

Burnham & Kyriacos, 1982; Gibson et al., 1979; Hartlep, 1979, 1983; Ihsen & Day, 1981). No differences across age have been observed. Indeed in some studies even newborns have been found to perceive features of moving objects (Goren et al., 1975; Maurer & Young, 1983; Slater et al., 1985). As a general rule movement does *not* suppress processing of object features, even for newborn infants. This suggests that any suppression of the perception or processing of features by movement is determined by stimulus characteristics rather than a general inability to process features of moving objects.

How can these results be reconciled with Bower's claim that movement suppresses feature perception for infants younger than 20 weeks? Bower based his conclusions on studies in which infants viewed objects moving behind a screen (Bower et al., 1971). Visual pursuit was analyzed when either the same object moving at the same velocity reappeared on the other side of the screen or when an anomolous event occurred such that a new object reappeared, the same object reappeared prematurely given its entry velocity, or a new object appeared prematurely. Visual tracking by infants younger than 20 weeks was found to be disrupted by an anomolous trajectory but not by an anomolous object, results which were taken as evidence that movement but not features were perceived. Detailed critical analysis of these studies has been made elsewhere (Burnham, 1980, 1981). However, it is worth taking note of a few points regarding the validity of Bower's response measures.

First, it is possible that the disruption of tracking with an "impossible" trajectory does not indicate cognitive surprise based on a dominance of movement over feature information. Rather, it could indicate infants' response to a difficult motor task. Nelson (1974) found that, in response to a change in trajectory which involved a change in the extent and speed of movement (long-fast to short-slow and vice versa), 6- to 8-month-old infants successfully generalized their learned tracking skill. The mid-trajectory disruption of tracking reported by Bower does not occur for all movement changes. The tracking disruption may have been due to difficulty with visual tracking without necessarily involving awareness of incongruity in trajectory information.

Second, with regard to the *lack* of tracking disruption when object features "changed" behind the screen, it may be argued that continuation of tracking does not necessarily imply that infants fail to notice the change of object features nor that they remain unsurprised by this change. The results from two experiments support this contention. In a lateral tracking task Goldberg (1976) presented 5-month-old infants with events in which an object either did or did not change features behind a screen. She found differential heart rate deceleration to these two events, indicating that infants registered the change in object features which occurred behind the occluding screen. Nevertheless, there was no difference in infants' visual fixation of the two events. Similarly, Meicler and Gratch (1980) demonstrated that when 5- and 9-month-old infants observed a transformed object emerge from behind a screen, they showed increased affective scores but still continued undisrupted tracking of the new moving object. These experiments show that 5- and 9-month-old infants notice feature changes of moving objects, which their tracking of the objects continues undisrupted. It seems that disruption of tracking is not a valid index of infants' concept of object identity.[1]

This point is emphasized by Muller and Aslin's (1978) systematic investigation of the causes of tracking disruption in 2-, 4-, and 6-month-old infants. They found no disruption of tracking when object features were changed during occlusion. Tracking was affected only by the speed of target movement (more disruption with slower speed), the size of the occluding screen (more disruption with larger screens), and by the interaction of these two features, occlusion duration. They conclude that "if disruptions in tracking are to be used as an indicator of a violation of an expectancy concerning an object's properties, then our data suggest that the level of false positive responding is too high to draw meaningful conclusions about object-related expectancies" (p. 315).

Presence or absence of tracking disruption in Bower's studies appears to be unrelated to infants' perception of object features. Measures based on fixation duration in conjunction with the habituation method would appear to be more valid in establishing whether object features are perceived. As reviewed earlier there is now much evidence that conflicts with Bower's conclusions. Nevertheless, the view that young infants can not perceive features of moving objects persists (Lugar, Bower, & Wishart, 1983; Lugar, Wishart, & Bower, 1984; Wishart & Bower, 1984). This view should be modified. While under some conditions infants' perception of features may be dominated by their perception of movement (Day & Burnham, 1981; Ruff, 1982), infants, even newborns, do perceive features of moving objects.

Movement as a Facilitator

There are two ways in which movement facilitates object perception in infancy. The first is that moving objects are detected and their features perceived at observer-object distances beyond limits established with stationary objects. The second is that certain movements facilitate the perception of object structure.

Facilitation over Distance.   In 1924 Koffka reviewed early research suggesting that in infancy objects beyond about a third of a meter blend into the general background of visual experience. Koffka added that this seems to depend on the

---

[1]This is a valid criticism of Bower's experiments even though his subjects were younger than those tested by Goldberg (1976) and Meicler & Gratch (1980). The specific point being made is not whether infants younger than 20 weeks can process the features of moving objects but whether disruption of tracking actually measures feature processing, given independent evidence that features are being processed.

kind of object seen. More recently McKenzie and Day (1972) found that visual fixation of a stationary cube by 6- to 20-week-old infants decreased markedly over viewing distances from 30 to 90cm irrespective of the cube's real or retinal size. McKenzie and Day (1976) confirmed this effect when groups of 9- and 16-week-old infants viewed a stationary cylinder. However, they found that infants fixated the cylinder significantly longer when it rotated in the frontal plane about its central axis and, most importantly, that fixation duration did *not* decrease over distance (30 to 90cm) when the cylinder was rotating. Ihsen and Day (1981) further investigated this effect at even greater viewing distances. They presented 8- to 14-week-old infants with large objects rotating about their central axes and found that fixation duration was unaffected by changes in viewing distance from 30cm right up to 10m.

These results suggest that young infants perceive moving objects over distances at which detection is either difficult or impossible with stationary objects. It would be interesting to determine whether movement simply enhances the *detection* of objects or whether it enhances the *perception* of objects. In other words, do infants simply perceive *movement* at such distances or do they perceive *moving objects?* As reported earlier Burnham and Day (1979) demonstrated that infants of 11 and 17 weeks perceive features of rotating objects. Their first two experiments showed this at a viewing distance of 55cm. It was also shown that infants perceived the features of stationary objects at this distance. In a third experiment infants were tested for feature perception with rotating objects at 100cm. This is beyond the maximum distance used by McKenzie and Day (1972, 1976) with stationary objects. Burnham and Day found that infants did discriminate between novel and familiar rotating objects at this distance. Ihsen and Day (1981) also obtained similar results at 4m and 10m though their studies should be repeated with procedural improvements as habituation to criterion was used without a control for regression to the mean. Nevertheless, it seems clear that at a moderate viewing distance of 1m, movement not only facilitates object detection but also the perception of object features (Burnham & Day, 1979). This may be the case up to at least 10m (Ihsen & Day, 1981). It is not certain whether this effect of movement is due to direct facilitation of detectability or increased attention due to increased salience, though evidence from Finlay and Ivinskis (in this volume) suggests the latter.

Facilitation of Object Structure.   Ruff (1980) suggests that rigid motion transformations of objects should enhance perception of their structure, i.e., the object's surfaces and edges and their relationship to one another. This is because rigid motion transformations allow the infant to perceive the structural invariance of objects despite variations in stimulation. There is evidence to support this notion. Ruff (1982) found that translation of complex three-dimensional objects actually facilitated later recognition of the objects by 6-month-old infants. A control condition involving the same orientation changes but restricted movement led to no such facilitation. There was also some indication that extended periods of experience with rotating objects facilitated recognition, however, translation was superior to rotation in its facilitative effect.

Similar evidence has also been reported recently for younger infants. Owsley (1984) discovered that under monocular conditions, 4-month-old infants perceived the shape of a solid wedge veridically when they were given experience of the wedge rotating about its vertical axis but not when their experience with the wedge involved either seeing it in different orientations from trial to trial, or stationary on each trial. Thus it appears that certain kinds of movement across various orientations facilitate object perception over and above simple changes from one static orientation to another. However, as mentioned previously, even in Ruff's experiment a complex motion (translation plus simultaneous rotation) hindered infants' perception of object structure. Thus movement does not always facilitate object perception; facilitation depends at least upon the type of movement and it is likely that the type of object, the viewing context, and the age of the child are also relevant.

In conclusion, movement facilitates object perception in two ways. First, it allows infants to detect objects and perceive object features at greater distances than when they are stationary (Burnham & Day, 1979; Ihsen & Day, 1981; McKenzie & Day, 1972, 1976). Second, movement facilitates the perception of the structure of certain types of objects (Owsley, 1984; Ruff, 1982), provided that the movement is neither too fast (Burnham & Day, 1981) nor too complicated (Ruff, 1982). Ruff (1982) claimed that movement may have a facilitatory effect on the perception of object structure but not that *all* movement should facilitate the perception of the structure of *all* objects. The data reviewed in this section support her claim. These results are contrary to Bower's claim that movement invariably suppresses the perception of object features for young infants. Under certain conditions facilitation occurs for infants of 2 months (Burnham & Day, 1979; Ihsen & Day, 1981; McKenzie & Day, 1976) 4 months (Owsley, 1984) and 6 months (Ruff, 1982).

Movement as an Incidental Characteristic of Objects

Along with John Locke it could be argued that there are some properties of an object which are primary and essential if its identity is to be sustained, and others which are secondary and incidental to its identity. Properties which fall into the first category are those such as color, shape, size, texture, and substance, while into the second fall such aspects as position in space, orientation, time of presentation, trajectory, and velocity. This distinction is implicit in the way the adult characterizes the world as being populated by objects which are permanent and relatively unchanging with an existence and identity independent of the observer. (We take the view that adults have a concept of permanent and unique objects, the "object concept," as a working hypothesis, but will comment on this assumption in a later section.) If infants also perceive the world in terms of permanent and unique objects, i.e., if infants have a mature object concept, then we should expect them to treat object features such as shape and color as integral to object identity, while other characteristics, in particular, movement information about trajectory and velocity, should be treated as incidental.

The Object Concept.   Piaget (1954) drew attention to the development of the object concept. He claimed that object concept development is the main achievement of the sensorimotor period (from birth to about 2 years).[2] In line with his interactive view of development and his assumption that the infant can only interact with the world by sensorimotor means, he claimed that no significant development of the object concept is apparent until stage III of the sensorimotor period—around 20 weeks of age. This, Piaget claimed, is the age when infants begin to interact manually with objects and to experience the intermodal concomitance of their features. Thereby they abstract the invariant object from the motor schemes in which it is embedded.

Bower follows the more realist-based Gibsonian view of developmental epistemology (E. J. Gibson, 1969; J. J. Gisbon, 1966). He claimed that all the information for the invariance of objects is "out there" for the infant to perceive directly (Bower, 1971, 1974). The task of the developing organism is to learn or to develop the ability to perceive objects veridically. Bower conducted and inspired various studies which investigated the object concept and its development more analytically than Piaget's studies had done. Along with this more analytic approach came the distinction between two aspects of the object concept, existence constancy and identity constancy, concerned with permanent existence and unique identity of objects respectively. Identity constancy can be defined as the ability to perceive an object to be the same object, despite extraneous or incidental changes to it, for example, in its time of presentation, position, orientation, trajectory, or velocity. Existence constancy can be defined as the ability to perceive or conceive the continued existence of an object despite its diminished or discontinued sensory representation. Based on his neo-Gibsonian views regarding limited processing and the prepotence of movement, and on the results of empirical studies (Bower et al., 1971; Bower & Paterson, 1973), Bower claimed that infants as young as 3 weeks can pick up the information for existence constancy contained in kinetic occlusion sequences, but that until 20-weeks-of-age they identify an object only by its movement characteristics and position in space and not by its features such as size, shape, and color. Therefore, young infants have a basic idea of object reality and existence and their main developmental task is to refine their notion of object identity. During

---

[2]Piaget used the term "object permanence." In the wake of more analytic studies concerning both the unique identity and the permanent existence of objects, the term "object permanence" with its specific connotations, has given way to the more general term "object concept."

Piaget's stages I and II, infants define an object as a bounded volume of space in a particular place or on a path of movement. Due to the supposed prepotence of movement, object features only enter into the infant's notion of identity in stage III, around 20-weeks-of-age (Wishart & Bower, 1984).

Moore, who participated in Bower's original studies (Bower et al., 1971), basically agrees with Bower's views on identity constancy but claims that existence constancy must follow identity constancy both logically and ontogenically. He claims that the only way in which the infant can build up an understanding of stability is by determining what has remained the same in spite of apparent flux. Therefore, the understanding of existence constancy must depend on the infant perceiving an object to be the same object before and after its disappearance. Moore claimed that while identity constancy is evident around 20 weeks, existence constancy only emerges at about 9 months after the repeated application of identity rules (Moore, Borton, & Darby, 1978; Moore & Meltzoff, 1978).

Feature Perception over Motion Transformations.   Identity constancy is the ability to recognize an object as the *same* object despite incidental changes. Here, the changes we are interested in are those due to movement. In order to demonstrate unequivocably an ability for identity constancy over movement transformations, it is necessary to show that the infant perceives an object in two different situations, e.g., when it is moving and when it is stationary, to be exactly the same object. This is a difficult task to set experimenters. It is also difficult to envisage how such a conclusion could ever be reached from the behavior of preverbal infants.

Given these difficulties, a useful heuristic for the experimental examination of identity constancy over movement transformations is to consider the component abilities it would be necessary for an infant to exhibit in order that identity constancy could be inferred. There are three such components. It would be necessary to show that:

1. infants perceive features of stationary objects, perceive movement per se, and perceive features of moving objects,
2. infants recognize features of objects despite movement transformations,
3. infants recognize *objects,* not just features, over movement transformations, and recognize an object to be exactly the same object despite such transformations.

Evidence for the first collection of abilities has been documented earlier. The second ability is the one of major concern in this section. It is shown here that infants do recognize at least the similarity of object features over movement transformations. The third ability is rather more difficult to demonstrate. Nevertheless, in the next two sections methods are outlined which have some potential for investigating this ability. The results of experiments using these methods are also relevant when considering whether infants treat movement as an incidental characteristic of objects.

Burnham and Day (1979) investigated whether infants' memory for the color of rotating objects generalizes over changes in angular velocity. They found that 8- to 19-week-old infants recognize familiar-colored patterns and discriminate them from novel-colored patterns over movement transformations from stationariness to 42° per sec and vice versa and from 42° per sec to 84° per sec and vice versa. This constitutes evidence that infants recognize the familiarity of object color over movement transformations, both when the transformation involves a change in the angular velocity of rotation *and* when the transformation involves a change from rotation to stationariness or stationariness to rotation. Gibson et al. (1979) conducted similar experiments in which they investigated the object feature of shape. With 15-week-old infants they found evidence for the perception of the shape of objects which were rotating in depth in one experiment and in another for generalization of this shape perception from rotating to stationary objects. The perception of shape was maintained over a movement to stationariness transformation.

Similar results have been obtained when objects do not simply rotate but rather translate from one position to another. Day and Burnham (1981), on the basis of their finding that 8- to 19-week-old infants perceive shapes of objects translating laterally at 4° per sec, conducted a further experiment in which, following habituation at 4° per sec, familiar and novel objects were stationary when presented in posthabituation test trials. Under these conditions infants maintained a low probability of fixating familiar shapes but had a significantly greater probability of fixating novel shapes. These data provide evidence for the recognition of the shape of objects over a slow movement to stationariness transformation, even when the movement involves translation across the infant's field of view. Results of a study by Hartlep and Forsyth (1977) confirm this conclusion. They used an operant conditioning method to train 10-week-old infants to fixate either a stationary cube or a stationary sphere when both were presented simultaneously. When both the objects subsequently moved in circular paths, generalization tests revealed that infants still fixated the object on which they were trained, indicating shape recognition over a transformation from stationary to moving objects.

Recently similar evidence for the generalization of shape perception over motion transformations has been obtained with newborn infants. Slater, Morison, Town, and Rose (1985) found that following habituation with either a stationary or moving stimulus newborn infants showed preference for a novel-shaped object in test trials despite either a stationary to moving or moving to stationary transformation from habituation to test. The movement involved objects describing a restricted circular path while remaining in a constant orientation. In a subsequent experiment when objects also changed orientation by rotating about their central axes, similar evidence was not obtained. Nevertheless, Slater et al. have shown that newborn infants can recognize the shape of objects over some movement transformations.

It is apparent from the above evidence that young infants have the ability to recognize the familiarity of features of objects (color, shape) over movement transformations. This ability is the second in the hierarchy of three abilities which were previously suggested to make up identity constancy. Without evidence regarding the third ability (the ability to recognize *objects* to be the *same* objects over movement transformations) no definite conclusions can be drawn about young infants' ability for identity constancy. Nevertheless, two less forceful conclusions are possible. The first is that infants *can* treat movement as an incidental characteristic of objects. Whether this role of movement in object perception is peculiar to movement is taken up shortly. The second conclusion is that young infants can organize their perception of objects in terms of featural similarities despite movement transformations.

This latter conclusion is at odds with both Bower's and Moore's claims that it is only by 20-weeks-of-age that infants begin to identify objects on the basis of object features (Bower, 1974; Bower et al., 1971; Lugar et al., 1983, 1984; Moore & Meltzoff, 1978; Wishart & Bower, 1984). It seems that there is at least some rudimentary ability in this regard even in newborn infants. This suggests that Bower's and Moore's views should be modified; infants have at least the potential for applying featural rules for identifying objects well before 20-weeks-of-age.

As the detection of the invariance of features over movement transformations occurs so early in life it is tempting to compare this ability with object constancies, e.g., size and shape constancy, which also appear early in life—by at least 12 and 16 weeks respectively (Caron et al., 1979; Day & McKenzie, 1981; see also chapters by Day and by Cook in this volume). In fact, the ability to perceive the invariance of features over motion transformations (or other transformations) could be considered to be one of the object constancies. It could be labeled feature constancy. At least one of these object constancies, size constancy, has been observed in lower animals (Ewert & Burghagen, 1979; Ewert & Gebauer, 1973). Size constancy is an ability which lower animals would certainly find advantageous for survival and it could be argued that object constancies in general, including feature constancy, would be advantageous. Seen in this light object constancies could be classed as rather low-level abilities which are evident in lower animals and in very young human infants. For lower animals it is unlikely that these object constancies precede or engender any higher-level concepts such as the object concept. However, it is possible that increasingly high-level concepts are formed from these in more phylogenetically advanced animals. This is consistent with evidence for stage IV development of the object concept development in cats (Gruber, Girgus, & Banuazizi, 1971) and stage VI object concept development in rhesus and squirrel monkeys (Vaughter, Smotherman, & Ordy, 1972; Wise, Wise, & Zimmerman, 1974).

According to this view identity constancy and existence constancy develop out of these lower level constancies. This does not sit easily with Bower's claim that existence constancy is evident as early as 3-weeks-of-age (Bower, 1966, 1967, 1971; Bower et al., 1971). However, evidence was reviewed earlier which suggests that it is necessary to reevaluate Bower's interpretations of infants' behavior when objects disappear (Burnham, 1980, 1981; Goldberg, 1976; Meicler & Gratch, 1980; Muller & Aslin, 1978; Nelson, 1974). In addition, adults have been found to make similar tracking errors to the infants in Bower's original studies (Chromiak & Weisberg, 1981). Moreover, there is evidence to support the view that existence constancy is a relatively late development. For instance, Moore et al. (1978) showed infants a laterally moving object which either did or did not appear in a gap between two occluding screens. They discovered that 9-month-old infants tracked the object as if they had an expectation that it would continue to exist in the gap between the screens, while 5-month-old infants did not. Similar evidence was found by Meicler and Gratch (1980). When an object went behind a screen for five times as long as it did on previous trials, it was found that while both 5- and 9-month-old infants showed increased affect, their visual behavior was different: 9-month-old infants stared at the screen or the ends of the screen, whereas 5-month-old infants looked away from the screen. This suggests that infants of both ages noticed something strange or unexpected about the situation, but that only the 9-month-old infants seemed to know that the object still existed behind the screen. Finally, Bull (1979) found that 4-month-old infants showed better anticipatory tracking when a moving object made a sound than when it did not, i.e., when information for the object's continued existence behind a screen was provided for the infant. As these experiments involved visual tracking as the dependent measure they are open to the criticisms of Bower's tracking studies which were outlined earlier. Nevertheless, their conflicting evidence allows us to question whether existence constancy is such an early development, and raises the possibility that low-level object constancies, including feature constancy over movement transformations, may be perceptual precursors of both identity and existence constancy.

In conclusion, the findings reported in this section conflict with Bower's and Moore's views regarding when infants can begin to identify objects by their features. They also contest Bower's view that existence constancy precedes this ability and open the possibility that the object concept arises out of the early ability to recognize the familiarity of features over transformations. While questioning specific claims of Bower and Moore, the suggestion that perceptual precursors of identity constancy are apparent in newborns supports a Gibsonian realist-based view of object concept development. In accord with this view the object concept originates in infants' perceptual activity, well before Piaget claims that object-related sensorimotor schemes begin to develop.[3]

---

[3]Piaget could object that in studies in which the objects move but do not change position (e.g., Burnham & Day, 1979; Gibson et al., 1979), the results indicate that infants could only recognize a motor schema previously associated with the object, not the object or its features as such (Piaget, 1954, p. 4–6). This objection does not apply to the lateral movement studies by Day and Burnham (1981) in which infants recognized the shape of an object originally seen moving laterally at 4° per sec, in the context of a *new* motor schema, i.e., when the object was stationary.

It must be stressed that the studies reviewed in this section do not constitute evidence for the early development of identity constancy. All that has been shown is that infants can treat movements as an incidental characteristic of objects which does not alter object features. In the next two sections we consider two further issues. The first is whether infants actually perceive an object to be the *same* object despite movement transformations. The second is whether the ability to recognize features over transformations is peculiar to those transformations, such as movement, which are incidental to object identity. The latter enquiry will lead us to question whether it is correct to characterize the role of movement in object perception as incidental.

Identity or Similarity?   There is a logical consideration which affects the interpretation of the studies reviewed above. In those studies it could be implicitly assumed that in test trials nonrecovery to a familiar stimulus and recovery to a novel stimulus implies that the infant recognizes the familiar feature to be exactly the same feature even if some transformation has taken place between habituation and test. Of course, this can never be concluded from these methods, a point which has also been made by Ruff (1980). It can only be concluded that the infant perceives some similarity between two presentations of an object, either the similarity of particular features or of the complete object.

However, it is possible to devise methods which may lead to more precise conclusions about the specific aspects of objects which infants recognize. In this regard consideration of a study by Burnham, Norman, Day, Ihsen, and Schoknecht (1982) is apt. The study concerned the perception of three-dimensional objects and their two-dimensional representations. Its method allows more precise conclusions to be drawn about the perception of similarity and identity.

Four groups of 5-month-old infants were tested in a familiarization-to-criterion adaptation of the recognition memory familiarization-test technique. The stimulus objects were small hollow objects of various shapes, all the same color and approximately the same size. These objects (3D) or their two-dimensional representations (2D) were presented in their frontoparallel plane (0°) in the four possible combinations of familiarization and test, 3D-3D, 3D-2D, 2D-3D, and 2D-2D. As an example, the procedure for the 3D-2D group is shown in Fig. 7.2. There were two phases of testing—a training phase and, when the training criterion was reached, an orientation change phase. Each trial involved familiarization with two identical stimuli and then tests for novelty preference. In the training phase two identical stimuli were presented side by side for 10 sec. Then in two 5-sec test periods one of the familiarization stimuli was presented side by side with a novel test stimulus. The position of familiar and novel stimuli were changed over the two test periods. This familiarization-test sequence continued until infants showed a visual preference for the novel stimulus on three consecutive trials. Then the orientation change phase was presented. This was similar to previous familiarization-test sequences except that in test periods the stimuli were tilted 45° in depth.

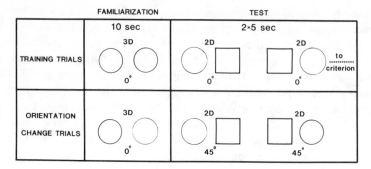

FIGURE 7.2.   Procedure in the 3D-2D group in the 3D-2D experiment by Burnham et al. (1982).

The purpose of the training phase was to determine whether infants could perceive some similarity between a three-dimensional object and its two-dimensional representation. In this regard the 3D-2D and 2D-3D groups were of greatest interest as they functioned to test generalization from 3D to 2D and vice versa. The 3D-3D and 2D-2D groups were controls to determine whether recognition occurred when no dimension change was involved. Almost all infants in all four groups reached criterion. For all four groups there was discrimination between the familiar and novel test stimuli which must have been based on some perception of similarity between the familiarization stimulus and the familiar test stimulus. In the 3D-2D and 2D-3D groups this discrimination must have been based on the perception of some similarity between a 3D object and its 2D representation.

Given that infants saw some similarity between familiarization stimuli and familiar test stimuli, the purpose of the orientation change phase was to ascertain whether infants gained enough knowledge of objects during familiarization to recognize the similarity between familiarization and test presentations when, in addition to the dimension change, an orientation change was introduced. Results for the orientation change phase showed that only infants in the 3D-3D group obtained novelty preference scores significantly greater than chance. This indicates that only in this group did infants perceive the object at 45° to be similar to the object at 0°.

Therefore infants in the 3D-2D and 2D-3D groups perceived some similarity between stimuli over a dimension transformation (as shown by their familiarization to criterion). However, when objects also changed orientation from familiarization to test, infants in these groups failed to discriminate a novel from a familiar object. Infants in the 3D-3D condition did not have any trouble with this task. Thus, the perceived similarity between 3D objects and 2D representations seems to have been based on topological information rather than on a very sophisticated notion of what constitutes the ''deep structure'' of an object.

These results demonstrate two points of importance. The first is that by the use of this double transformation design it has been shown that at 5 months infants do not have a very mature notion of constant object identity over transformations. Infants recognize similarities over dimension changes (as shown by the 3D-2D and 2D-3D groups reaching the novelty preference criterion in the training phase) and shape constancy for objects tilted in depth (as shown by the novelty preference in the orientation change phase by the 3D-3D group). However, they do not integrate these two elementary pieces of knowledge about the object. Thus, 5-month-old infants recognize some similarities between successive presentations of an object, but their knowledge of objects and object identity is rather limited.

The second important point demonstrated by this study is that it is possible to design experiments to investigate more precisely whether infants perceive an object presented on two different occasions to be the same or similar. If a novelty preference had been obtained by the 3D-2D and 2D-3D groups in the orientation change phase it would not indicate unequivocally that infants perceive the objects as the same objects over the two transformations. However, it would reduce the possibility that they only perceive some simple phenomenological similarity. This argument can be extended ad infinitum: if infants, perhaps older than those tested here, demonstrated novelty preferences in a number of phases with various orientation changes, and even with changes involving other transformations, e.g., position, distance, velocity, trajectory etc., then the experimenter could, by ruling out more and more alternative hypotheses, be progressively more certain that infants were demonstrating a knowledge of the common identity of the familiarization stimulus and the familiar test stimulus.

Feature Perception over Motion Transformations and Motion Perception over Feature Transformations.   The argument was considered earlier that, for infants, movement is a secondary characteristic of objects which is incidental to object perception. There are two forms of this argument. The strong form is that infants actually filter out movement information and attend only to object features. This lacks empirical support because it has been found that infants attend to and remember both featural *and* movement information about objects (Burnham & Day, 1979; Burnham & Kyriacos, 1982). A weaker form of the argument is that infants attend to both movement and featural information but attach only secondary importance to movement because it is not integral to object identity. This form of the argument can also be questioned.

Consider the design of the experiments concerned with feature perception over motion transformations. An infant is habituated to an object moving in a certain manner. Then in test trials the same object and one differing on a certain feature, e.g., shape, are presented moving in a novel manner. Longer fixation of the novel-shaped object is considered to demonstrate that infants perceive the similarity of the feature over the motion transformation. Consider, however, a reciprocal control condition in which, following the same habituation trials, the familiar movement and a novel movement are exhibited by a new object which differs in shape from the habituation stimulus. According to the same reasoning as above, longer fixation of the novel movement could be taken to indicate that infants perceive the invariant movement of objects despite shape transformations. Such evidence would suggest that infants believe objects to be defined by the particular motion they exhibit irrespective of feature changes (Burnham, 1980, 1981).

An experiment based on this reasoning has been conducted by Burnham and Kyriacos (1982). Infants of 4 and 6 months were habituated to an object of a certain shape which rotated in depth about its central axis either vertically (up and down), horizontally (side to side), or in one of two oblique directions. For any one infant object shape and direction of rotation were constant over habituation trials. Then infants were given test trials in which the same-shaped or a novel-shaped object either moved in the same or a novel direction. Infants of both ages looked longer at a novel shape than the familiar shape even when the shapes moved in a novel direction, thus confirming the results of previous experiments (Burnham & Day, 1979; Day & Burnham, 1981; Gibson et al., 1979; Hartlep & Forsyth, 1977; Slater et al., 1985). However, infants of both ages also looked longer at an object moving in a novel direction than one moving in the familiar direction, even when the movements were being exhibited by novel-shaped objects. This implies that infants recognize familiar movements despite feature transformations.

Following the reasoning outlined above these results could be taken to show that infants identify objects both by their features *and* by the movements they undergo. In contrast, it would appear that adults define objects primarily by their features, not by their movements. For instance, a red car traveling forward in a straight line at 60 km per hr is the same object as when it is traveling in reverse in a circular path at 10 km per hr. For infants to develop a mature notion of object identity, they should define objects primarily by their features rather than by the movements they happen to display. The problem is to test this empirically.

Burnham and Kyriacos (1982) conducted a second experiment in order to test whether 6-month-old infants identify objects primarily on the basis of features or movements. They used the same shapes and movements as those in the first experiment. (Another aim of the first experiment was to settle upon shape and movement changes which result in equivalent response recovery for infants. The shape and movement changes in the first experiment were equivalent in this regard for 6-month-old infants. Thus it serves as a control for differential recovery effects in this second experiment.) The concept learning or detection of invariance procedure pioneered by McGurk (1972) was employed. Of interest was whether infants would form a concept of a constant-shaped object undergoing various motion transformations more strongly than a concept of a number of objects all undergoing the same motion transformation.

Examples of the procedure in the constant shape concept group and the constant movement concept group are set out in Fig. 7.3. It was reasoned that if infants in the constant shape concept group formed the concept of a single object moving in various ways over habituation trials, then recovery to the first test stimulus—a novel exemplar of this familiar concept—should be minimal. On the other hand, recovery should occur for the second test stimulus, which is *not* an exemplar of this concept. Similarly, if infants in the constant movement concept group formed the concept of a number of objects moving in the same way, then there should be more recovery to the second test stimulus—a nonexemplar—than to the first test stimulus—a novel exemplar. It was also reasoned that if features are more integral to object identity than are movements then the constant shape concept should be formed more strongly than the constant movement concept. If this were so then recovery to the nonexemplar relative to recovery to the novel exemplar should be greater in the constant shape than in the constant movement group. (Such comparisons are only valid if the shape and movement changes are equivalent in terms of the dependent variable. This was found to be the case for the 6-month-old infants in the first experiment, which, in part, served as a control for this subsequent experiment.)

Both groups of infants habituated to criterion in an equal number of trials and both groups fixated the nonexemplar significantly longer than the novel exemplar. However, there was no difference in the relative degree of recovery in the two groups. Thus both groups of infants formed their assigned concepts and

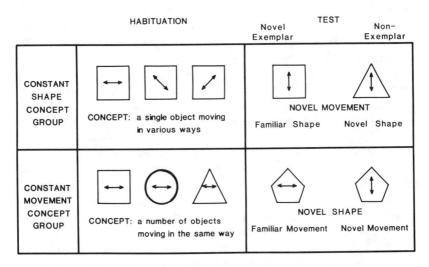

FIGURE 7.3. Procedure in experiments by Burnham and Kyriacos (1982) to test concept formation for a constant shape with varying movement, and for a constant movement with varying shape. Arrows represent direction of movement in depth about the fixed central axis.

formed them equally well. Interestingly, both groups also fixated the novel exemplar of the familiar concept significantly longer than they did the familiar exemplars at the end of habituation. It is therefore possible that infants in both groups had a good understanding of objects which were not exemplars of their assigned concepts, i.e., of what is *excluded* from the concept, but did not have a good understanding of which exemplars fell within their assigned concept, i.e., of what is *included* in the concept.

Burnham and Kyriacos conducted a third experiment with older infants to investigate (a) whether with development one concept came to be formed more strongly than the other, and (b) whether older infants would form concepts with tighter boundaries. Two groups of 8-month-old infants were tested and similar results were obtained. Both groups formed their respective concepts to an equal degree. Of note, however, was that in test trials infants did not fixate novel exemplars of the familiar concept significantly longer than the familiar exemplars at the end of habituation. Therefore 8-month-old infants still formed the two concepts equally well, but each concept had more clearly defined boundaries than did those of the 6-month-old infants.

Together these outcomes indicate that infants as young as 6 months are able to form simple concepts involving moving objects. To do so they must have the ability to pick up the invariance of certain dimensions despite flux in certain other dimensions. However, there is no evidence to indicate that certain types of invariance, e.g., constant shape, are picked up more readily than certain other types of invariance, e.g., constant movement direction. Thus, while these experiments show that infants are able to detect invariance and that this general ability improves between 6 and 8 months, the type of invariance appears to be unimportant to the infant. Young infants appear to identify objects both by their features *and* by their movement characteristics.

A Re-appraisal of Identity Constancy in Infancy.   The review of experiments in the preceding sections demonstrates that infants recognize the familiarity of object features despite movement transformations. This evidence supports the Gibsonian, as opposed to the Piagetian, notion that premotor infants can pick up invariance from the stimulus array. The experiments reviewed also demonstrate that both Bower and Moore were too conservative in their determination of when infants can begin to use featural invariance as a basis for identifying moving and stationary objects. However, it was argued that the ability demonstrated in these experiments is a perceptual ability that is a necessary but not sufficient condition for identity constancy and the object concept.

It was indicated that infants' notion of identity cannot be tested adequately using presently available methods. The results of an experiment with a new method, which allows a closer approximation to an operational distinction between similarity and identity judgments by infants, revealed that 5-month-old infants appear to recognize only the gross similarity of an object presented successively over different transformations. It was also shown that constancy is not specific to recognition of features over motion transformations. The opposite also applies: Infants respond differentially to familiar and novel movements even over feature transformations. Subsequent studies showed that 6- and 8-month-old infants readily form concepts but are not predisposed to form a concept based on constant featural identity over one based on constant movement direction. Together these results demonstrate that young infants are not tuned to process or interpret the world selectively on the basis of the featural identity of objects, i.e., they do not have a well-developed object concept.

Regarding the three component abilities necessary for identity constancy set out earlier, young infants (i) have the ability to perceive features of stationary objects, to perceive movement per se, and to perceive features of moving objects; (ii) have the ability to recognize the familiarity of features over movement transformations; but (iii) do *not* have the ability to perceive an object to be exactly the *same* object over movement transformations.

With regard to movement as an incidental characteristic of objects, it can be concluded that infants can treat movements to be incidental to the perception of object features such as shape. However, they can also treat a feature such as shape to be incidental to the way in which an object moves. Infants seem able to abstract the invariant characteristics of a situation irrespective of whether the invariant is a feature or the object's manner of movement.

Movement as a Feature

Movement has been shown to suppress object perception under some conditions, facilitate object perception under others, and under other conditions to be incidental to object feature perception. However, none of these is the *sole* role of movement in object perception, nor is it likely that movement is the sole necessary and sufficient condition for any one of these effects on object perception. Thus we arrive at the position that movement has no special or unique role in object perception. Rather, for infants movement is an object feature which has equivalent ontological status as other object features such as color and shape. Some of the consequences of such a position follow.

First, movement and other features should be equivalent in certain ways, for example, infants should be able to store compounds comprised of movement components and other featural components. Second, under certain conditions some feature components should be more salient than others. Finally, memory for objects should not necessarily be based on stimulus characteristics which are more central to object "identity." Some support for these three hypotheses was found in a study of 7-month-old infants' ability to perceive and remember compounds of visual stimulus components (Burnham & Vignes, 1983). Some of the results of this study were discussed earlier. Discussion of other results are relevant here. Refer to Fig. 7.1. It was found that there was significant recovery in the CM and CS-stat groups but not in the SM and CS groups. The following conclusions can be drawn from these results. First, they demonstrate that movement is treated as being equivalent to at least one other object feature, namely color, because infants formed color-movement compounds in memory. Second, they demonstrate that under one set of stimulus conditions, namely when objects are stationary, both color and shape are salient for the memorial representation of objects (indicated by recovery in the CS-stat group), while under another set of stimulus conditions, namely with moving objects, movement and color but not shape are salient (CM group recovery). Third, they demonstrate that memory for objects is not invariably based on those features which adults might consider to be integral to object identity, e.g., color and shape. This final point is also supported by Burnham and Kyriacos (1982). In this study infants' memory for objects was seen to be based on that feature, shape, or movement, which is kept invariant, rather than the feature (shape) more integral to object identity.

This view of the role of movement raises important questions about object perception, the notion of object identity, and memory for objects. In particular, how do adults perceive, identify, and remember objects, i.e., what is the mature ideal towards which infant behavior progresses? Certain findings suggest that even in adulthood perception of objects is not entirely independent of surrounding objects or frameworks. For example, there are context effects in memory (Thomson, 1972) and field effects in perception, e.g., the rod and frame effect (Witkin, 1959) and induced movement (Day, Millar, & Dickinson, 1979). Thus, to define object identity and object memory even for adults is not as easy as it seems. When object movement is considered the problem becomes even murkier. If movement can act as an object feature for infants, is this also the case for adults? Intuitively it would appear that when relatively meaningless objects undergo rigid transformations as in the experiments described here, adults should not define objects by their movements. However, this is yet to be tested. On the other hand intuition would suggest that when *nonrigid* movements of more *ecologically significant* objects are involved, movement could possibly enter into the adult definition of identity. In this regard it would be interesting to discover whether adults consider the potential motion transformations of an object, such as its ability to bend, bounce, sway in the wind, or walk, to be integral to object identity.

The results of recent experiments on biological motion (Johansson, 1978) are relevant to the last of these types of motions, namely walking. In these studies point sources of light are placed on various joints of a human body and viewing conditions are arranged such that observers can only see the lights and not the body. Of particular importance is the finding that under these conditions an observer can not perceive the identity of a familiar stationary human but can perceive the identity of a familiar walking human (Cutting & Koslowski, 1977). Thus it seems that the way in which humans move in some sense constitutes their identity. Recently it has been found that by about 3 to 6 months human infants discriminate between biological and equally complex nonbiological motion (Bertenthal, Proffitt, & Cutting, 1984), and prefer the former (Fox & McDaniels,

1982). Additionally by around 8 to 9 months infants appear to be sensitive to the structure of human form in such displays (Bertenthal, Proffitt, Spetner, & Thomas, 1985). This raises the possibility that infants may incorporate movement into the identity of biological objects.

It is clear that the way in which the notion of object identity develops requires further investigation both with biological and nonbiological objects and with infants, children, and adults. Nonetheless what is certain from studies reported here is that young infants are tuned to picking up invariance of various kinds from the perceptual array (Burnham & Kyriacos, 1982). Perhaps this ability to pick up invariance from whatever source, may be selectively tuned over development such that biological motion remains an integral part of the identity of biological objects, while rigid motion becomes less integral to the identity of nonbiological objects.

SUMMARY AND CONCLUSIONS

Four roles of movement in infants' perception of objects have been investigated—movement as a suppressor, as a facilitator, as incidental to object perception, and as an object feature itself. In the first section evidence was presented which contradicts Bower's claim (Bower, 1971, 1974; Bower et al., 1971) that movement serves invariably to suppress featural information in young infants' perception to moving objects. It was found that young infants have the requisite attentional and cognitive capacities to process both movement and shape information (Ball, 1980; Burnham & Day, 1979; Burnham & Kyriacos, 1982; Day & Burnham, 1981; Gibson et al., 1979; Hartlep, 1979, 1983; Ihsen & Day, 1981; Maurer & Young, 1983; Slater et al., 1985), although under some conditions movement can suppress featural information. In some cases this suppression appears to be a perceptual effect (Day & Burnham, 1981; Ruff, 1982) while in others the effect may be more central (Burnham & Vignes, 1983). Just as suppression of object perception by movement occurs under some conditions, in the second section it was found that under certain circumstances facilitation also occurs. Movement improves young infants' detection of, or attention to, distant objects (Ihsen & Day, 1981; McKenzie & Day, 1976) and even enables the features of such distant objects to be perceived (Burnham & Day, 1979; Ihsen & Day, 1981). Furthermore, under certain circumstances movement facilitates the perception of the invariance of object structure (Owsley, 1984; Ruff, 1982). In the third section it was found that infants perceive object features over movement transformations and can treat movement as an incidental property of objects (Burnham & Day, 1979; Day & Burnham, 1981; Gibson et al., 1979; Hartlep & Forsyth, 1977; Slater et al., 1985). However, it was argued that this ability is probably quite a low-level perceptual ability rather than an ability necessarily indicative of a mature object concept. Moreover, the results of an experiment using a procedure to differentiate more clearly between similarity and identity in infants' visual responses to objects suggest that 5-month-old infants operate on the basis of similarity rather than identity judgments (Burnham et al., 1982). Finally, the results of experiments by Burnham and Kyriacos (1982) show that the ability to treat a stimulus characteristic as incidental is not confined to movement, nor does this ability define the role of movement in object perception: Infants are able to form concepts equally well on the basis of invariant shape (with redundant direction of movement) and invariant movement direction (with redundant shape). In the fourth section it was concluded that for infants movement acts as an object feature with much the same properties as any other feature, albeit that movement is often a very salient feature.

This position raises two main issues. The first is that the way in which adults perceive, identify, and remember objects, especially moving objects, has not yet been clearly specified. The second is that biological movement and non-biological movement may play different roles in object perception over development. One possibility is that all movement, both biological and nonbiological, acts as an object feature for young infants, but that over development the organism comes to attend selectively to those types of movement which are important for the identification of objects, e.g., biological movement, and to filter out those types of movement which are unimportant for object identification, e.g., rigid, nonbiological movement.

It has been shown that while movement is a highly salient stimulus for infants, it does not have a single role in object perception. It can suppress, facilitate or be incidental to perception of object features. In general, the best description of the role of movement in object perception by infants is that movement itself serves as an object feature. Therefore, it seems that young infants have yet to learn what constitutes an object and, despite the recent advances in our knowledge of object perception in infancy, much the same could be said about those who study these infants.

ACKNOWLEDGMENT

Comments on an earlier draft of this chapter by B. E. McKenzie and R. H. Day were very useful and are greatly appreciated.

REFERENCES

Ball, W. A. (1980). Infants' perception of structure and form across orientations. *International Journal of Behavioral Development, 3,* 147–157.
Bertenthal, B. I., Proffitt, D. R., & Cutting, J. E. (1984). Infant sensitivity to figural coherence in biomechanical motions. *Journal of Experimental Child Psychology, 37,* 213–230.

Bertenthal, B. I., Proffitt, D. R., Spetner, N. B., & Thomas, M. A. (1985). The development of infant sensitivity to biomechanical motions. *Child Development, 56,* 531–543.

Bornstein, M. H. (1976). Infants are trichromats. *Journal of Experimental Child Psychology, 21,* 425–445.

Bower, T. G. R. (1966). *Object permanence and short-term memory in the human infant.* Unpublished manuscript.

Bower, T. G. R. (1967). The development of object permanence: Some studies of existence constancy. *Perception and Psychophysics, 2,* 411–418.

Bower, T. G. R. (1971). The object in the world of the infant. *Scientific American, 225,* 30–38.

Bower, T. G. R. (1974). *Development in infancy.* San Francisco: Freeman.

Bower, T. G. R. (1975). Infant perception in the third dimension and object concept development. In L. B. Cohen & P. Salapatek (Eds.), *Infant perception: From sensation to cognition. Vol. II: Perception of space, speech and sound.* Orlando, FL: Academic Press.

Bower, T. G. R. (1978). Perceptual development: Object and space. In E. C. Carterette & M. P. Friedman (Eds.), *Handbook of perception, Vol. VIII: Perceptual coding.* Orlando, FL: Academic Press.

Bower, T. G. R., Broughton, J. M., & Moore, M. K. (1971). Development of the object concept as manifested by changes in the tracking behavior of infants between 7 and 20 weeks of age. *Journal of Experimental Child Psychology, 11,* 182–193.

Bower, T. G. R., & Paterson, J. G. (1973). The separation of place, movement and object in the world of the infant. *Journal of Experimental Child Psychology, 15,* 161–168.

Bull, D. (1979, March). *Infants' tracking of auditory-visual events.* Paper presented at the meeting of the Society for Research in Child Development. San Francisco, California.

Burnham, D. K. (1980). *The perception of moving objects by infants and the development of the object concept.* Doctoral dissertation, Monash University.

Burnham, D. K. (1981). *Objects: How do Piagetians, Gibsonians and infants see them?* In A. R. Nesdale, C. Pratt, R. Grieve, J. Field, D. Illingworth, & J. Hogben (Eds.), *Advances in child development: Theory and research.* Perth, Western Australia: N.C.C.D.

Burnham, D. K., & Day, R. H. (1979). Detection of color in rotating objects by infants and its generalization over changes in velocity. *Journal of Experimental Child Psychology, 28,* 191–204.

Burnham, D. K., & Dickinson, R. G. (1981). The determinants of visual capture and visual pursuit in infancy. *Infant Behavior and Development, 4,* 359–372.

Burnham, D. K., & Kyriacos, E. (1982, August). *Development of the object concept in infancy.* Paper presented in a symposium on 'Growth of the mind: Psychological processing in infancy' at the 2nd National Child Development Conference, Melbourne.

Burnham, D. K., Norman, A., Day, R. H., Ihsen, E., & Schoknecht, C. (1982, May). *The perception by infants of two- and three-dimensional stimulus objects.* Paper presented at the 9th Annual Experimental Psychology Conference, University of Queensland.

Burnham, D. K., & Vignes, G. (1983, May). *Perception of stationary and moving colour-shape compounds by infants.* Paper presented at the 10th Annual Experimental Psychology Conference, University of Tasmania.

Caron, A. J., Caron, R. F., & Carlson, V. R. (1979). Infant perception of the invariant shape of objects varying in slant. *Child Development, 50,* 716–721.

Carpenter, G. C. (1974). Visual regard of moving and stationary faces in early infancy. *Merrill-Palmer Quarterly, 20,* 181–194.

Carpenter, G. C., & Stechler, G. (1969, March). *Effects of stimulus movement on attention in early infancy.* Paper presented at the meeting of the Society for Research in Child Development. Santa Monica, California.

Chromiak, W., & Weisberg, R. W. (1981). The role of the object concept in visual tracking: Child-like errors in adults. *Journal of Experimental Child Psychology, 32,* 531–543.

Cohen, L. B. (1973). A two-process model of infant visual attention. *Merrill-Palmer Quarterly, 19*, 157–180.

Cook, M., Hine, T., & Williamson, A. (1982). The ability to see solid form in early infancy. *Perception, 11*, 677–684.

Cutting, J. E., & Koslowski, L. T. (1977). Recognizing friends by their walk: Gait perception without familiarity cues. *Bulletin of the Psychonomic Society, 9*, 353–356.

Darwin, C. (1877). A biographical sketch of an infant. *Mind, 7*, 285–294.

Day, R. H., & Burnham, D. K. (1981). Infants' perception of shape and color in laterally moving objects. *Infant Behavior and Development, 4*, 341–357.

Day, R. H., & McKenzie, B. E. (1981). Infant perception of the invariant size of approaching and receding objects. *Developmental Psychology, 17*, 670–677.

Day, R. H., Millar, J., & Dickinson, R. G. (1979). Induced movement as nonveridical resolution of displacement ambiguity: Effect of enclosure and number of field elements. *Perception and Psychophysics, 25*, 23–28.

Ewert, J-P., & Burghagen, H. (1979). Ontogenetic aspects of visual 'size-constancy' phenomena in the midwife toad *Alytes obstetricians* (Laur.). *Brain, Behavior and Evolution, 16*, 99–112.

Ewert, J-P., & Gebauer, L. (1973). Grössenkonstanzphänomene im Beutefangverhalten der Erdkröte (Bufo bufo L.). *Journal of Comparative Physiology, 85*, 303–315.

Fantz, R. L. (1963). Pattern vision in newborn infants. *Science, 140*, 296–297.

Fox, R., & McDaniels, C. (1982). Perception of biological motion by human infants. *Science, 218*, 486–487.

Gibson, E. J. (1969). *Principles of perceptual learning and development.* New York: Appleton-Century-Crofts.

Gibson, E. J., Owsley, C. J., & Johnston, J. (1978). Perception of invariants by five-month-old infants: Differentiation of two types of motion. *Developmental Psychology, 14*, 407–415.

Gibson, E. J., Owsley, C. J., Walker, A., & Megaw-Nyce, J. (1979). Development of the perception of invariants: Substance and shape. *Perception, 8*, 609–619.

Gibson, J. J. (1966). *The senses considered as perceptual systems.* London: Allen & Unwin.

Girton, M. R. (1979). Infants' attention to intrastimulus motion. *Journal of Experimental Child Psychology, 28*, 416–423.

Goldberg, S. (1976). Visual tracking and existence constancy in 5-month-old infants. *Journal of Experimental Child Psychology, 22*, 478–491.

Goren, C. C. Sarty, M., & Wu, P. Y. K. (1975). Visual following and pattern discrimination of face like stimuli by newborn infants. *Pediatrics, 56*, 544–549.

Gruber, H. E., Girgus, J. S., & Banuazizi, A. (1971). The development of object permanence in the cat. *Developmental Psychology, 4*, 9–15.

Hartlep, K. L. (1979). Object perception and motion in infants. *The Journal of General Psychology, 100*, 167–174.

Hartlep, K. L. (1983). Simultaneous presentation of moving objects in an infant tracking task. *Infant Behavior and Development, 6*, 79–84.

Hartlep, K. L., & Forsyth, G. A. (1977). Infants' discrimination of moving and stationary objects. *Perceptual and Motor Skills, 45*, 27–33.

Ihsen, E., & Day, R. H. (1981). Infants' visual perception of moving objects at different distances. In A. R. Nesdale, C. Pratt, R. Grieve, J. Field, D. Illingworth, & J. Hogben (Eds.), *Advances in child development: Theory and research.* Perth, Western Australia: N.C.C.D.

Johansson, G. (1978). Visual event perception. In R. Held, H. W. Leibowitz, & H.-L. Teuber (Eds.), *Handbook of sensory physiology, Vol. VIII: Perception.* Berlin: Springer-Verlag.

Koffka, K. (1924). *The growth of the mind: An introduction to child psychology.* London: Routledge & Kegan Paul.

Kremenitzer, J. P., Vaughan, H. C., Kurtzberg, D., & Dowling, K. (1979). Smooth pursuit eye-movements in the newborn infant. *Child Development, 50*, 442–448.

Lugar, G. F., Bower, T. G. R., & Wishart, J. G. (1983). A model of the development of the early infant object concept. *Perception, 12*, 21–34.

Lugar, G. F., Wishart, J. G., & Bower, T. G. R. (1984). Modelling the stages of the identity theory of object-concept development in infancy. *Perception, 13,* 97–115.

Maurer, D., & Young, R. E. (1983). Newborns' following of natural and distorted arrangements of facial features. *Infant Behavior and Development, 6,* 127–131.

McGurk, H. (1972) Infant discrimination of orientation. *Journal of Experimental Child Psychology, 14,* 151–164.

McKenzie, B. E., & Day, R. H. (1972). Object distance as a determinant of visual fixation in early infancy. *Science, 178,* 1108–1110.

McKenzie, B. E., & Day, R. H. (1976). Infants' attention to stationary and moving objects at different distances. *Australian Journal of Psychology, 28,* 45–51.

Meicler, M., & Gratch, G. (1980). Do 5-month-olds show object conception in Piaget's sense? *Infant Behavior and Development, 3,* 265–282.

Moore, M. K., Borton, R., & Darby, B. (1978). Visual tracking in young infants: Evidence for object identity or object permanence? *Journal of Experimental Child Psychology, 25,* 183–197.

Moore, M. K., & Meltzoff, A. N. (1978). Object permanence, imitation, and language development in infancy: Toward a neo-Piagetian perspective on communicative and cognitive development. In F. D. Minifie & L. L. Lloyd (Eds.), *Communicative and cognitive abilities—Early behavioral assessment.* Baltimore: University Park Press.

Muller, A. A., & Aslin, R. N. (1978). Visual tracking as an index of the object concept. *Infant Behavior and Development, 1,* 309–319.

Mundy, P. C. (1985, April). Compound and component processing in three-month-old infants. *Journal of Genetic Psychology, 146,* 357–365.

Nelson, K. E. (1974). Infants' short-term progress toward one component of object permanence. *Merrill-Palmer Quarterly, 20,* 3–8.

Owsley, C. (1984). The role of motion in infants' perception of solid shape. *Perception, 12,* 707–717.

Peeples, D. R., & Teller, D. Y. (1975). Color vision and brightness discrimination in two-month-old infants. *Science, 189,* 1102–1103.

Piaget, J. (1954). *The construction of reality in the child.* (M. Cook, trans.). London: Routledge & Kegan Paul.

Ruff, H. A. (1980). The development of perception and recognition of objects. *Child Development, 51,* 981–992.

Ruff, H. A. (1982). The effect of object movement on infants' detection of object structure. *Developmental Psychology, 18,* 462–472.

Salapatek, P. (1975). Pattern perception in early infancy. In L. B. Cohen & P. Salapatek (Eds.), *Infant perception: From sensation to cognition. Vol. 1: Basic visual processes.* Orlando, FL: Academic Press.

Salapatek, P., & Banks, M. S. (1978). Infant sensory assessment: Vision. In F. D. Minifie & L. L. Lloyd (Eds.), *Communicative and cognitive abilities—Early behavioral assessment.* Baltimore: University Park Press.

Salapatek, P., & Kessen, W. (1966). Visual scanning of triangles by the human newborn. *Journal of Experimental Psychology, 3,* 155–167.

Schwartz, M., & Day, R. H. (1979). Visual shape perception in early infancy. *Monographs of the Society for Research in Child Development, 44,* (Whole No. 7).

Silfen, C. K., & Ames, E. W. (1964). *Visual movement preference in the human infant.* Revised version of a paper presented at the Eastern Psychological Association Meeting, Philadelphia.

Slater, A., Morison, V., Town, C., & Rose, D. (1985). Movement perception and identity constancy in the new-born baby. *British Journal of Developmental Psychology, 3,* 211–220.

Thomson, D. M. (1972). Context effects in recognition memory. *Journal of Verbal Learning and Verbal Behaviour, 11,* 497–511.

Vaughter, R. M., Smotherman, W., & Ordy, J. M. (1972). Development of object permanence in the infant squirrel monkey. *Developmental Psychology, 7,* 34–38.

Volkmann, F. C., & Dobson, M. V. (1976). Infant responses of ocular fixation to moving visual stimuli. *Journal of Experimental Child Psychology, 22,* 86–99.

Wilcox, B. M., & Clayton, F. L. (1968). Infant visual fixation on motion pictures of the human face. *Journal of Experimental Child Psychology, 6,* 22–32.

Wise, K. L., Wise, L. A., & Zimmerman, R. R. (1974). Piagetian object permanence in the infant rhesus monkey. *Developmental Psychology, 10,* 429–437.

Wishart, J. G., & Bower, T. G. R. (1984). Spatial relations and the object concept: A normative study. In L. P. Lipsitt & C. Rovee-Collier (Eds.), *Advances in infancy research: Volume 3.* Norwood, NJ: Ablex.

Witkin, H. A. (1959). The perception of the upright. *Scientific American, 200,* 50–56.

III BIMODAL PERCEPTION

8 The Development of Auditory-Visual Localization in Infancy

Jeff Field
University of Auckland

INTRODUCTION

Normal adults perceive a unity in the auditory and visual characteristics of many events in their world. When they look at and listen to a friend talking to them, they perceive the friend's voice to be spatially and temporally related to his or her mouth and its movements. As a consequence of their experience with such spatio-temporal relationships, adults can often predict where and how an object will sound from its appearance, or where and how an object will appear on the basis of its sounds. Adults' ability to perceive the invariant spatio-temporal characteristics of many multimodal objects and events reveals the impressive economy and stability of human perception.

This chapter is concerned with the development, in infancy, of one subcategory of intermodal perception: the emergence of the coordinated localization of sights and sounds. The meanings of the terms "localization" and "coordinated," as I use them, can cover quite a range of behaviors, depending upon the maturity of the particular human perceptual-motor systems under discussion. After outlining the nature of these behaviors in adult humans, the rest of the chapter is devoted to discussions of their qualities in developing infants. For adults, I use the term "localization" to refer to the perception of where objects and events are located, both in relation to one's own body, and in relation to other objects and events in the environment. Coordinated localization in adults also carries the meaning of being able to act upon a specific location by turning to look at it, or reaching for it, or locomoting to it. Of course, this broad definition of the term localization is equivalent to most writers' use of the words "space perception."

Under natural conditions, the intersensory localization of adult humans is strongly biased by their visual perception of events. Before discussing viewpoints and evidence on infant perceptual localization, the relative dominance of visual perception in adult localization deserves to be outlined, since it gives a clearer perspective on the ultimate direction of the development of infants' auditory-visual localization.

Visual Biasing in Adult Localization or Seeing is Believing

Although the issue is very complex, most perception researchers would agree that vision is particularly suited to the detection of detailed distal changes in spatial arrays, whereas audition is suited to the detection of sequences of events over time (see Welch & Warren, 1980). The adult visual perception system affords a great deal of rich and redundant information on the spatial layout of objects and events. In a general sense, this spatial information is continuously available to the observer, while acoustical spatial information is usually changing much more rapidly and can lack the continuity of visual spatial inputs. Evidence illustrating the great importance of visual information and experience for adult localization in normal environments can be drawn from three areas: studies of perceptually handicapped individuals, research on the accuracy of object distance perception afforded by audition and vision, and experiments examining the outcome of spatial conflicts between listening and looking.

The localization and mobility problems of blind people are a sad testimony to the typical importance of visual control over manipulation and locomotion development in humans. In a review of research on perception by the blind, Warren (1978) noted the frequent finding of superior capacities for spatial perception in blind persons who had experienced a period of early vision, relative to those with congenital blindness. Furthermore, although auditory localization becomes a critical ability for the blind person, laboratory studies have found that blindfolded, sighted subjects are equal to, or better than, blind people in their accuracy of auditory localization (Warren, 1978).

In normal adults the accuracy of auditory distance perception, particularly for unfamiliar sounds in far space, is very poor when compared with visual distance judgments made under average viewing conditions. In a recent summary of auditory distance perception, Moore (1982) concluded that: "In general, localization of sounds in depth is relatively inaccurate, and errors of the order of 20% are not uncommon for unfamiliar sources" (p. 181). However, the importance of accurate distance perception is very apparent from many adult activities. The basic hunting and food gathering capacities of adult humans, as well as many of our present-day transportation control skills, are dependent upon accurate, absolute judgments of distance in large-scale space. While visual distance information enables these kinds of activities, auditory distance perception can usually provide only a very crude guide for such actions.

Many everyday events, together with the magical experience of ventriloquism, illustrate the enormously powerful influence that visual perception can have over our auditory localization. Actors' voices are perceived to come from their faces on a large cinema screen, despite the locating of the speakers to the side of, or well behind, the screen. We mistakenly locate the sound of the ventriloquist's voice at the moving mouth of the dumb puppet and do not perceive any auditory-visual "detachment." This visual biasing of auditory location is at least partly due to our familiarity with many sight and sound contiguities in our world. Thus, when Jackson (1953) artificially distorted the relative locations of the sight of a kettle puffing steam and the sound of its whistling, he found that his naive adult subjects frequently attributed the whistle locations to puffs of steam which were laterally separated by 30° and even 60° from the actual whistle positions. Likewise, after Witkin, Wapner, and Leventhal (1952) had artificially dislocated the sound of a man's voice from his visibly talking face, their naive subjects only reported an apparent sensory detachment if the man's voice was located more than about 33° from his moving mouth. It has also been shown that, just as a visual target may affect the perceived apparent direction of a sound, so in many situations the existence of a visual object may greatly influence judgements of a sound's apparent distance (Mershon, Desaulniers, Kiefer, Amerson, & Mills, 1981). Of course, both this and the previous examples of conflict research are not meant to imply that visual and auditory localization do not normally work in concert. Indeed, one of the main functions of auditory localization seems to be that of bringing events to the "attention" of foveal vision. Rather, it is my intention to emphasize appropriately the functional significance of visual space perception in normal ecological conditions permitting multimodal localization.

In summary then, both the presence of a visual framework and even the past experience of a visual framework leads to greater accuracy in adults' auditory localization (Warren, 1970, 1978). Absolute judgments of the distance of sounds are very inaccurate in comparison to parallel visual localization capacities. These inaccuracies in auditory distance localization are no doubt due partly to the extreme subtlety of auditory information for distance (Coleman, 1963) and partly to the heavy reliance on stimulus familiarity in such perception. Nevertheless, the normally enhanced accuracy of visual spatial information relative to auditory spatial information results in a tendency for visual localization to dominate or bias auditory localization in situations of intermodal conflict. In such situations adults usually will attend more to what they see than what they hear. Whether this biasing by visual space perception is evident from birth and/or is gradually enhanced by some combination of experiential and maturational factors will be discussed in subsequent sections devoted to empirical findings on infant localization. The main theoretical viewpoints on the development of intermodal localization do not address the question of intermodal biasing directly. They concentrate instead on the more general issue of the origins of intermodal unity in space perception.

Theoretical Viewpoints on the Development
of Intermodal Localization

Do infants possess a coordinated, multimodal representation of the world from birth, or is this integration of the senses only gradually achieved with experience? Although there are widely varying answers to this question, it is also possible to detect much common ground between theoretical positions. Most modern theorists would agree that there is ever-increasing differentiation within and between perceptual modalities in the early years of life. All theorists also probably agree that an adult's intermodal perception is partly dependent upon learning. We come to expect to hear ringing sounds colocated with telephones, due to our experience with such man-made objects. Spelke (in press) has also pointed out that most theorists would probably acknowledge that there has to be some innate potential to detect relationships between two modalities, otherwise we could never learn to relate information gained from each of them. Of course, there may be disagreements about the developmental timing of the emergence of such an innate detection ability, and about its specific nature.

Two general theoretical perspectives have currently quite a marked influence over research design and interpretation of intermodal development. I call them differentiation and constructionist theories. There are potential subcategories of both general viewpoints and, in fact, two versions of differentiation theory are discussed here. Modern differentiation theory has been best articulated by Eleanor J. Gibson. She describes perceptual development as a process of more and more efficient, or better differentiated, extraction of relevant information enabling effective action on the part of the child. Gibson (1977) has said that: "we should speak of learning and development in perception as differentiation rather than construction; that the relevant processes are more akin to discovery and abstraction than to association and integration . . ." (p. 171). Although Eleanor Gibson has rarely discussed newborn perception directly, one can infer that she would argue that newborns are equipped with a coordinated listening and looking system ready for the detection of amodal information available for object and event perception. Another differentiation theorist, T. G. R. Bower, takes a very strong initial unity viewpoint. He does not seem to assume that modality discrimination is even available to the newborn infant. Bower (1979) has argued that the neonate responds only to the abstract, amodal properties of stimuli, such as their general location or intensity. He has described newborn intermodal perception as showing a "primitive unity" (Bower, 1974) and he suggests that the ability to respond differentially to input from the different senses emerges gradually in early infancy.

The perceptual differentiation viewpoints of E. G. Gibson and T. G. R. Bower are in marked contrast to the constructionist perspective on intermodal perceptual development taken by Piaget (1954). Very briefly, Piaget argued that although the newborn perceptual systems are functional at birth their operations are simply reflexive, and initially no coordination or appropriate sequencing exists between the systems. Piaget claimed that integrated multimodal perception only emerged through infants' active use of their perceptual-motor systems over the first 3 months, followed by the integration of active touch with vision and hearing after 3-months-of-age.

The bearing of empirical findings on these differentiation and constructionist views of the development of auditory-visual localization is discussed during the course of the following review of the infant localization literature. The review has been organized into three sequential age periods: the first 6 weeks; from 6 weeks to 6 months; and from 6 months to 18 months. It should not be inferred however, that these age periods represent any clearly distinct psychological stages in intermodal perceptual development. Rather, my intention is simply to try and emphasize the considerable changes in auditory-visual localization during infancy.

THE FIRST 6 WEEKS: COORDINATION OF REFLEXES?

Many researchers argue that newborns' auditory and visual orientation is simply reflexive, but others suggest there are elements of voluntary behavior in some of the more complex orientation responses of neonates to sights and sounds. Although this issue cannot be resolved as yet, the relevant findings and interpretations are outlined in this section. Since auditory and visual space perception are not known to undergo marked functional changes within the first 6 weeks after birth, the term *newborn* is abnormally stretched here to provide a shorthand name for this 6-week period. The findings of studies on newborns' visual and auditory localization is first summarized separately, and then research on newborns' responsiveness to auditory-visual dislocation is reviewed.

The immature motor-neuronal systems of newborn babies may permit only very crude auditory and visual localization of objects and events. Newborns show horizontal saccadic localization of visual targets up to about 30° from the midline when a central target is removed from view (Aslin & Salapatek, 1975; Harris & MacFarlane, 1974). If the central target remains visible, then the field of peripheral visual attention is reduced to 15° (Harris & MacFarlane, 1974). The vertical extent of peripheral attention is limited to only about 10° (Aslin & Salapatek, 1975). Newborns' visual localization is slow, requiring several seconds for the gaze to be directed to the target (Tronick, 1972) and their saccades are adjusted grossly to the peripheral extent of objects by 1-month-of-age (Aslin & Salapatek, 1975). Both the probability and the radial extent of very young infants' visual attention are also reduced markedly by increases in the distance of objects, even from 30 to 90cm, with retinal image size held constant (de-Schonen, McKenzie, Maury, & Bresson, 1978; McKenzie & Day, 1972, 1976). Despite these attentional limitations on newborns' looking behavior, when they do look toward stimuli they can do so accurately. The same cannot be said for their auditory localization responses.

Auditory localization in newborns has been assessed by recording their eye movements toward brief lateral sounds (Castillo & Butterworth, 1981; Crassini & Broerse, 1980; Hammer & Turkewitz, 1975; Mendelson & Haith, 1976; Turner & MacFarlane, 1978; Wertheimer, 1961) and by observing both head and eye movements to lateral sounds with longer durations (Alegria & Noirot, 1978; Clifton, Morrongiello, Kulig, & Dowd, 1981; Field, Muir, Pilon, Sinclair, & Dodwell, 1980; Muir & Field, 1979; Muir, Abraham, Forbes, & Harris, 1979). The latter procedure has more ecological validity, as humans normally localize sounds with active directional head and eye movements, which are not possible under the head restraint conditions that are necessary for accurate eye-movement recording.

Over recent years Muir and his colleagues have advanced our knowledge of young infants' auditory localization considerably. Muir and Field (1979) found that about 80% of optimally alert, 2- to 3-day-old infants would turn their heads reliably toward continuous, 80dB, rattle sounds located 90° from the midline in the horizontal plane. The turns were often slow, taking on average 2.5 sec to begin and 5.5 sec to end. Preterm infants have been found to be even slower, taking an average of 12 sec to complete lateral turns (Muir et al., 1979) and this points to the probable importance of neuromotor maturation in very early orientation to sound stimuli. In work carried out with his graduate student Brian Forbes, Muir (1982) has found that newborns' average extent of spontaneous head turning to a frontal 0° speaker was 26°, and they averaged 53° and 68° turns to speakers placed laterally at 45° and 90°. In orienting to the 45° speakers the newborns showed longer latencies in making their maximum turn and more vacillation movements. Muir (1982) suggests that: "Perhaps this was due to the baby's continual efforts to balance the two inputs to the two ears competing with the tendency for the head to be pulled down to one side through the joint actions of gravity and fatigue" (p. 229).

Similar neuromuscular immaturity problems could contribute to Muir's (1985) recent report on newborn localization of sounds in the vertical plane. With the subject held in the usual test position, which is nearly supine, it was found that newborns would crudely turn toward rattle sounds placed at 70° in the medial vertical plane. They did not show corresponding "downward" looks to stimuli below eye level, presumably because of the motoric difficulty of such responses. In the supine position "downward" head turns would require anti-gravitational effort.

Although motoric immaturity seems to be one obviously important constraint on newborns' localization, there is also some evidence that they have more subtle neurophysiological immaturities which may mean that their auditory localization behavior is subcortically mediated. In a series of studies Clifton and her colleagues (Clifton, Morrongiello, Kulig, & Dowd, 1981) have reported that newborns fail to orient appropriately to precedence effect stimuli, where one of two bilaterally presented sounds leads the other in arrival time at the head by 7 msec. On the other hand, 5-month-old infants do turn in the direction of the leading sound, just like adults. Since neurophysiological experiments on cats and monkeys have implicated auditory cortex function in the localization of such precedence effect stimuli, Clifton et al. (1981) have suggested that newborns' auditory localization behavior may be subcortically controlled and that cortical control may emerge sometime between 2- and 5-months-of-age.

Although our knowledge of the accuracy of newborns' perceptions of the *direction* of sounds has advanced considerably, our ignorance about their perception of the externality and distance of sounds remains almost complete. Very little consideration has been given to the issue of whether young infants perceive sounds initially to come from inside or outside their heads. Even if they are born with the ability to make this subjective/objective discrimination, then the further matter of infants' perception of the distance of sounds needs research attention. The same comment has even been made about adult auditory localization research (Wightman & Kistler, 1980). Certainly the information for the externality of sounds is directly available from the joint operation of a binaural detection system on a moving head, as Gibson (1966) has pointed out. Hence, under natural conditions a continuing balance of binaural input during head movements through orthogonal planes should specify that a sound is coming from within the head. Whether this information is used by very young infants remains an open question, however.

Apart from research into the accuracy of auditory-visual localization, there have also been investigations of newborns' responsiveness to disruptions in the natural spatial contiguity between sights and sounds. The main intent of the newborn studies on this topic, which are summarized in Table 8.1, has been to question whether the spatial correspondence of sights and sounds can be detected soon after birth. The experiments also speak directly to the more general issue of the nature of the interaction between auditory and visual stimulation in newborn perceptual exploration. At this point, I shall consider only the results of studies which have included infants less than 6-weeks-of-age. Discussion of the general problems of interpretation of the spatial dislocation experiments are reserved for the next section dealing with the 6 weeks to 6 months period.

Three conclusions can be derived from the experiments outlined in Table 8.1 that have involved very young infants. First, there is only one study (Aronson & Rosenbloom, 1971) that has claimed to show any emotional disturbance in very young infants to unnatural auditory-visual dislocation of the normal spatial correspondence between a person's voice and face. The design faults of this work and the failures to replicate the findings with more adequate methods (Condry, Haltom, & Neisser, 1977; McGurk & Lewis, 1974) greatly decrease its significance. Second, it seems that when young infants are attending to a central visual stimulus and are presented subsequently with a spatially separated sound, there is

TABLE 8.1

Summary of Studies on the Responsiveness of Infants to Spatially Dislocated Auditory and Visual Events

Authors	Subjects	Dislocated Stimulus Situation	Results and Interpretations
Aronson & Rosenbloom (1971)	eight infants aged 30 to 55 days	Mothers talking from 60cm away in front of their infants for 2 to 5 min, with the mothers' voices coming from speakers 90° to the left or right of each infant.	There were "often" increases in distress over a previous congruent test period and a significant increase in tongue protrusions were reported. However, the dislocation phase was always the last half of the test session.
Castillo & Butterworth (1981)	twenty-four newborns	While subjects were looking straight ahead stationary circle patterns were presented 30° to one side and a 1-sec, 62dB, tone burst was presented 30° to the other side for 10 trials.	Initial eye movements were significantly more frequent toward the visual stimulus. However, even in a group tested with only the lateral sound, ipsilateral turning was at chance level and therefore the sound stimulus may not have been salient.
Condry, Haltom, & Neisser (1977)	eight infants aged 39 to 58 days	Mothers talking at 60cm distance in front of their infants for two, 1-min periods, with the mothers' voices coming from right or left speakers.	No increases in tongue protrusions or emotional negativity were found during the dislocation periods. There was a nonsignificant trend for ipsilateral head turning toward the sound sources.
Field, DiFranco, Dodwell, & Muir (1979)	twelve infants aged 62 to 88 days	While each infant was looking straight ahead a female experimenter's face (40cm distant) appeared 50° to one side and her recorded voice was triggered simultaneously at 50° away to the opposite side.	There was no significant difference in the direction and latencies of the initial looking responses on the dislocated and other coincident trials. The infants looked initially toward the face without exception.

Study	Sample	Procedure	Results
Fisher-Fay (cited by Muir, 1985)	twenty newborns	In a darkened room, a circular diode pattern was presented 30° to one side of the newborn's midline and an 80dB rattle sound was simultaneously presented 90° to the other side.	Only 36% of initial head turns were directed toward the sound source. On trials without any competing visual stimulus 78% of initial head turns were ipsilateral to the rattle sound.
Lyons-Ruth (1975)	six infants at 3 months, eight at 4 months, and eight at 5-months-of-age	Eight, 5-sec periods of a moving toy directly in front of the subject (50cm distant) with a simultaneous chime located 90° to the right side.	"Limb and body movements" were more pronounced during the dislocation trials than during other coincident trials. These increased movements seemed to be an outcome of orientation responses to the sound locus.
McGurk & Lewis (1974)	eleven infants at 1 month and twelve at 4 and 7 months-of-age	Two, 30-sec periods of the mothers' talking from 125cm distance in front of the infants were used. The maternal voice was relayed over speakers 90° to either side.	All infant groups showed some ipsilateral looking toward the voice location but this was only reliable at 4 and 7 months-of-age. The face-voice dislocation did not result in changes in smiling, frowning, fretting, tongue protrusion or vocalization at any age.
Mendelson & Haith (1976)	sixteen infants aged 1 to 3 days	Newborns were presented monocularly with a white, vertical bar to one side of their line of sight while a continuous 40-sec voice sound emanated from 90° on the other side.	Infants initially fixated in the direction of the sound and then away from it in the latter half of the 40-sec trials.

only a small probability of a change in their looking patterns (Condry et al., 1977; McGurk & Lewis, 1974). Third, when newborns are presented simultaneously with a peripheral visual stimulus of moderate complexity on one side of their midline and an auditory stimulus on the other side, the visual stimulus initially attracts their attention on most occasions (Castillo & Butterworth, 1981; Fisher-Fay, 1981, cited in Muir, 1985). Both of the latter findings indicate the dominance, even from birth, of visually controlled over acoustically controlled perceptual exploration. This more powerful attention-getting quality of visual stimulation has led to the necessity of carrying out experiments on newborns' auditory localization in almost complete darkness (Muir, 1985).

Summary and Discussion of the First 6 Weeks

Listening and looking around is very primitive at birth. There is much evidence of immature motor-neuronal systems placing constraints on young infants' perceptual capacities (see also Atkinson & Braddick, 1982). Hence, newborns are very slow to respond to peripheral sights and sounds. Their poor control of neck/head movements seems to contribute heavily to their difficulties both in tracking visual and auditory stimuli and in steadily fixating the location of such stimuli.

Are these newborn orientation responses uncoordinated and purely reflexive? Newborn listening and looking are coordinated in the sense of being properly sequenced and this sequencing occurs reliably under optimal stimulus conditions. This is not to say that newborns' orientation responses have the same intentionality and planning as adult localization behavior, however. In view of evidence concerning maturational changes in auditory localization that is discussed next it does seem necessary to conclude that, for about the first 6 weeks, auditory-visual orientation reflects the operation of a subcortically controlled system of coordinated reflexes. There is some recent evidence (Clarkson, Clifton, & Morrongiello, 1983) that newborns' orientation to sound may not be dependent upon the availability of a continuous or long-duration stimulus. Given more research on the nature of newborn auditory localization, it may be necessary to revise our conceptions of newborn head movements to sound as being tropistic and requiring only lateralization abilities rather than some kind of representation of space (e.g., Muir & Field, 1979).

The findings on newborn auditory-visual localization provide some support for the differentiation viewpoint on the development of intermodal perception. It does seem as though we are born with naturally coordinated perceptual systems that are ready to detect spatial correspondence between sights and sounds. However, the questions of whether the detection of intermodal invariances is actually operating during the newborn period and of what the exact nature of such invariances may be, remain difficult to answer. The claim by Bower (1979) that newborns do not discriminate between sights and sounds is somewhat contradictory to the evidence on the dominance of visual attention over auditory orientation. However, a clear refutation or confirmation of such theoretical positions is not yet possible in the area of newborn perception research.

FROM 6 WEEKS TO 6 MONTHS: THE DISAPPEARANCE AND REEMERGENCE OF ACTIVE EXPLORATION OF SOUND LOCATIONS

Between about 6 weeks and 12-weeks-of-age, infants' overt responsiveness to the location of sounds undergoes a marked decline from the level exhibited in the newborn period. Field et al. (1980) carried out monthly tests for auditory orientation responses on a group of infants from birth to 3-months-of-age. On each test occasion the same procedures were used as those that Muir and Field (1979) found effective for eliciting head turns from newborns. At 2-months-of-age the infants showed a significant increase in *failure to turn at all*. This unresponsiveness to novel sounds began to abate by 3-months-of-age. Similar findings of a decline in auditory localization responses between about 2- and 3-months-of-age have been reported by Muir et al. (1979).

In contrast with the diminution of auditory localization responses, the reliability and efficiency of visual localization seems to continue to improve throughout the 2- and 3-month period (deSchonen et al., 1978; Tronick, 1972). One electro-oculargraphic study of 2-month-old infants has shown that their eye movements towards lateral sounds are slower, less consistent, and less accurate than eye movements toward visual stimuli in the same locations (Bechtold, Bushnell, & Salapatek, 1979). In comparing the localizing eye movements toward peripheral sights and sounds, Bechtold et al. (1979) concluded that 2-month-olds "turn their eyes toward peripheral auditory stimuli with considerably less consistency and with no precision at all; the features of this response are more characteristic of voluntary behavior in the process of being acquired" (p. 8). In fact, this speculation about the emergence of voluntary orientation is very similar to the explanation offered for the 2-month decline by Muir (1982, 1985), after his consideration of many alternative possibilities.

Muir (1985) has argued that the downturn in responsiveness to auditory spatial information is not due to the dominance of visual attention consequent upon the marked improvements in visual perception around this time (see, for example, Atkinson & Braddick, 1982). Infants tested in complete darkness, and hence without visual distraction, appear to exhibit the same 2-month decline (Muir et al., 1979). Muir (1985) also reports preliminary results from a follow-up study of auditory localization in infants born at least 6 weeks before term. The 2-month decline was temporally related to the infants' conceptual age and not their postnatal age, indicating the likely important role of maturation in the phenomenon. Muir suggests that these data further support an hypothesis of an initially reflexive orientation response to sound being gradually inhibited by the emergence of cortically controlled auditory localization around 3-months-of-age.

Although infants' overt sound localization emerges as a more reliable and motorically efficient response after 3 months, there are several important immature and involuntary features about the behavior, at least prior to 5-months-of-age. Localization of sounds in the vertical plane is still almost three times as slow, and a great deal less accurate, than horizontal plane performance (Muir, 1985). One involuntary characteristic is the insensitivity of 4- and 5-month-old infants to the visual consequences of their orientation responses. Thus, Field (1981) reported that 5-month-olds did not show habituation of head turning over 16 trials when no spatially contiguous, visual rewards were presented at the sound loci. In a similar vein, Moore, Wilson, and Thompson (1977) found that visual rewards did not maintain unilateral head turns toward a sound until after 5-months-of-age.

Another related characteristic of young infants' listening and looking is that they make very little use of the auditory spatial information provided by objects and events in order to guide their visual and manipulative exploration of such stimuli. McGurk and MacDonald (1978) presented 3-, 6-, 9- and 12-month-old infants with two widely separated, visually identical patterns and a sound was played from the position of one of the patterns, with the right-left location of the sound varying randomly across trials. The 3-month-olds spent only slightly more time looking at the patterns colocated with the sound, while the older infants spent approximately twice as much time looking at the sounding stimuli. Similarly, Bull (1978) found that 4-month-olds' visual search for the reappearance of a moving visual target which disappears temporarily behind a screen is only slightly facilitated by adding a continuous sound to the target. Spatially discordant sounds did not affect the infants' tracking behavior. In apparent contrast to these examples of visual dominance there has been one claim that 4- and 5-month-old infants will reach for sounding objects in total darkness (Wishart, Bower, & Dunkeld, 1978). However, it is difficult to accept the conclusions derived from these data, since the reaching measurements did not discriminate between intentional and unintentional arm movements and no appropriate control condition of a silent object in the dark was used. Aitken and Bower (1982) have also claimed that congenitally blind infants of 5- and 6-months-of-age can use the auditory guidance of an electronic echolocation device in order to reach toward objects. Once again, however, the published descriptions of this work to date have not given clear details on the precise measurements of reaching and on the exclusion of tactual-kinesthetic guidance from the infants' performance.

A further indication of the low salience of auditory-visual spatial contiguity for young infants has been provided by studies of their reaction to artificially dislocated sights and sounds. By referring again to Table 8.1 it can be seen that studies on this topic have used some quite dramatic distortions of the normal spatial relationships between sights and sounds and have examined the reactions of subjects from birth to at least 7-months-of-age. As noted earlier, these studies have shown that young infants have an apparently high tolerance for auditory-visual spatial dislocation. In fact, research on infants' perception of auditory-visual events has often relied on this tolerance of *spatial* dislocation in its exploration of other characteristics of their intermodal perception (e.g., Kuhl & Meltzoff, 1982; Spelke, 1979). In an unpublished study by the author, ten infants aged 9 to 10 months were familiarized with the talking face of a female experimenter for approximately 2 min. All the subjects then experienced repeated 15-sec exposures of the experimenter's face silently mouthing the words of a nursery rhyme, while her voice recording of the rhyme was played simultaneously through a small, invisible speaker. The speaker was during some periods kept stationary just below her mouth and at other times moved vertically through 30° elevations at positions 70° (65cm distant) from her mouth. There was no general evidence of differences in surprise or distress between these conditions of colocated and dislocated recordings, or between such situations and further natural or unrecorded rhyme-recital periods.

There are, however, problems in attempting to use young infants' emotional responses as indices of their perception and understanding, and these have become more widely recognized in the last few years. Even the presence of a surprise or distress reaction does not necessarily imply the perception or understanding of normal auditory-visual contiguity. Distress could even arise from competing tendencies to orient to both the separated sight and sound at the same time (Lawson, 1980), without any perception of an abnormal spatial dislocation.

Although the interpretation of these auditory-visual dislocation results by themselves remains unclear, when they are combined with the evidence indicating that young infants' visual search is not greatly influenced by auditory spatial information and that they are insensitive to the visual spatial consequences of sounds, then one is forced to conclude that their perception and understanding of the normal *spatial* correspondence between sights and sounds is poorly developed. In more concrete terms, this means that by 6-months-of-age infants have no strong expectancies that familiar voices will be located invariably and quite precisely at the location of their familiar faces. It does not mean that they cannot perceive and even recognize a familiar voice as corresponding generally to a familiar face (e.g., Spelke & Owsley, 1979), nor does it mean necessarily that such young infants cannot *detect* auditory-visual spatial contiguity. However, it does mean that their perception of auditory-visual spatial contiguity is still too inaccurate to enable them to *predict,* and hence also remember, the location of specific visual stimuli on the basis of their specific auditory spatial stimulation.

Such intermodal perception and knowledge continues to develop slowly throughout infancy as we shall see.

Summary and Conclusions on the 6 Weeks to 6 Months Period

From approximately 6 weeks to 12 weeks after birth there is an actual decline in the consistency of infants' overt auditory localization behavior. The reasons for this decline are still unclear, but there do seem to be important maturational factors involved, as the timing of the decline correlates highly with conceptual age. Between 3- and 6-months-of-age there is a reemergence of more consistent visual searching toward sounds, but the auditory localization responses to sounds in the vertical plane remain slower and much less accurate. During this time infants' orientations to sounds retain certain passive qualities. Prior to 5-months-of-age their auditory localization responses are not enhanced by the specific colocation of interesting visual consequences at sound locations. Furthermore, while young infants may be able to *detect* artificial spatial dislocations of faces from voices in experimental situations, they have not developed very precise *expectancies* about the normal limits of such face-voice dislocations. Of course, these findings may reflect the lack of specificity of the spatial information afforded by sounds to infants. Given the poorly developed accuracy of infant auditory localization and given the general inferiority of human auditory to visual space perception, it seems little wonder that young infants would attach a low attentional priority to sound localization in their perception of objects and events.

FROM 6 TO 18 MONTHS: PERCEPTION AND UNDERSTANDING OF THE SPATIAL CONTIGUITY OF SIGHTS AND SOUNDS IS STILL IMMATURE

After 6-months-of-age infants show a marked increase in their responsiveness to sounds accompanied by interesting sights. It is after this time that conditional head-turning studies of auditory localization become a viable proposition (Schneider, Trehub, & Bull, 1979). Infants' orientation to sounds not only becomes more purposeful, but also increases in reliability above and below the horizontal plane (Chun, Pawsat, & Forster, 1960; Northern & Downs, 1978). However, these improvements in accuracy of auditory localization appear to be very gradual over the next 12 months and they have yet to be clarified by systematic experimentation. In fact, experimental investigations of the general accuracy of auditory localization between 1 and 3 years are just beginning (Ashmead & Perris, 1986; Morrongiello & Rocca, 1986). Siegenthaler and Aungst (1968) have carried out such work with children from the age of 3 years.

Using male speech sounds and speaker separations of 3° around the frontal azimuth, they reported mean localization errors of 18° and 12° in the 3- and 4-year-old subjects, respectively. The mean error dropped to 5° by 7 years. Siegenthaler and Aungst only reported average localization errors for all the frontal azimuthal region, but one might generalize cautiously from this work to suggest that 1-year-old infants may have average error rates of between 10° and 20° in their most accurate, frontal-horizontal region of sound localization.

Two of the most important psychological advances of the 6- to 18-month period of infancy are the emergence of active, distal exploration of the environment by means of manipulation and locomotion, and the development of the perception and conception of the permanence of objects (Piaget, 1954). Of course, both of these areas of achievement seem to be interrelated and both reflect improvements in the visual control of infants' behavior. How does auditory perception contribute to such developments? I now consider the possible role of auditory space perception in infants' active manipulative and locomotive exploration of objects and events.

When Wishart et al. (1978) presented continuously sounding toys within the reaching distance of 6- to 9-month-olds, the infants did not reach out for the toys if they were presented in total darkness. Even at 11-months-of-age the accuracy of any reaching for the sounding toys in darkness was very poor, unless the infants accidentally touched them with some part of their body. So at 11 months the invisible, sounding toys did not elicit reliable reaching without prior tactual-kinesthetic localization. The auditory spatial information from the toys was insufficient to support or elicit accurate reaching.

Studies of the development of blind infants' auditorially guided reaching have also revealed that such reaching lags well behind the emergence of visually guided reaching in normal infants (Fraiberg, 1977; Harris & Muir, 1980, cited in Muir, 1985). The initial reaching attempts of blind infants also seem to be guided initially by tactual-kinesthetic cues (Fraiberg, 1977), and auditory control emerges soon after such tactual-kinesthetic localization of objects. Fraiberg (1977) and others have related the findings on blind infants' coordination of listening and looking to the use of sound by sighted infants in their search for hidden objects. Fraiberg and her colleagues have suggested that the use of sound in active search for objects emerges at the same time in blind and sighted infants and therefore reflects the maturation of perception and understanding of object permanence around 9- to 10-months-of-age (Fraiberg, 1977; Freedman, Fox-Kolenda, Margileth, & Miller, 1969). This conclusion seems an oversimplification when we look in detail at the studies of infants' use of sound in search tasks, which are summarized in point form in Table 8.2.

Two related generalizations can summarize effectively the results outlined in Table 8.2. First, sound cues afford very little help to infants in their attempts to find objects completely hidden from view. Second, this inability to make good use of auditory spatial information in their searching persists well into the second

TABLE 8.2

Summary of Experiments on Infants' Use of Sound in Searching for Objects

Authors	Subject's Age Range	Hiding Tasks with Sound	Results
Bigelow (1983)	7 to 19 months	- partial hiding - complete hiding - successive visible displacement - single invisible displacement - successive invisible displacements - complete hiding during distraction	Some stage IV infants performed at higher level tasks with sound, but the complexity of hiding continued to influence search performance.
Freedman, Fox-Kolenda, Margileth, and Miller (1969)	5 to 12 months	complete hiding during distraction	Use of sound was said to emerge at about the same time that search for completely hidden silent toys was achieved.
Ginsburg & Wong (1973)	all 6 months	complete hiding	Significantly more frequent searching occurred with sounding than with silent toys.
Field (1984)	12 to 13 months	- single invisible displacement - complete hiding during distraction	Sound did not lead to better performance than silent presentations.
Uzgiris & Benson (1980)	9 to 12 months	- complete hiding during distraction at 'A' - complete hiding during distraction at 'B' - invisible displacement from 'A' to 'B'	71%, 54% and 46% of infants searched successfully on the first, second and third of these tasks, respectively.
Wishart, Bower, & Dunkeld (1978)	4 to 12 months	complete hiding by darkness of objects in midline, 30° to left and right of the subjects.	Reaching to sounding objects was said to decline after 5 months and re-emerge after 10 months, but occurred mainly after tactual contact in the latter case.
Zucker & Corter (1981)	all 9 months	Trial 1: complete hiding of mother at place 'A' during distraction. Trial 2: complete hiding of mother at place 'B' during distraction.	On trial 1, 89% of locomoting infants made a correct choice of place from which mother's voice emanated, but on trial 2 only 50% of responders made a correct choice.

year, especially on tasks involving very complex visual disappearance. It is the latter conclusion which reveals the oversimplification of the suggestions of Fraiberg (1977) and Freedman et al. (1969). Sighted infants do not simply acquire the ability to use sound in their search for objects at the stage IV level of Piagetian object concept development (Piaget, 1954). It appears that their successful search for objects continues to be adversely affected by the relative visual-spatial complexity of the hiding events presented to them. Let me now outline some of the empirical findings leading to such a conclusion.

Data from the most influential investigator of infants' searching behavior are missing from Table 8.2. Piaget's (1954) observations on object concept development in his own children did not include much systematic exploration of their use of sound cues in searching for hidden objects. For those observations at the stage III, IV and V levels where he did make use of at least temporarily sounding objects in hiding tasks, he reported no enhancement of search for sounded objects over the equivalent, purely visual, hiding conditions. Ginsburg and Wong (1973) did report that 6-month-old infants "searched" significantly more often for a music box when it was continuously sounding during and after occlusion, than when it was not. However, it seems as though "searching" was also occurring during silent trials and this makes the task situation incomparable with the conventional finding that 6-month-old infants do not normally search for completely hidden objects. In addition, there have been two failures to replicate this result of Ginsburg and Wong on 6- and 7-month-olds (Bigelow, 1983; Bull, 1978).

Some tendency to use sound as an aid in object search has been reported for 9- and 10-month-old infants in three different studies (Bigelow, 1983; Freedman et al., 1969; Uzgiris & Benson, 1980). However, clear interpretation of these findings is not possible because of the failure of all of the investigators to include appropriate visual control tasks for the particular sounding object conditions that were employed. All three studies made use of a visual distraction procedure during the complete hiding of sounding objects. While the subject was visually distracted, the object was surreptitiously hidden under a cloth. No parallel silent control tasks, involving visual distraction followed by the presentation of a silent hidden object, were ever used in order to check upon spontaneous search levels. It seems likely that infants who can search for a silent toy that is seen to be hidden, may also search in the same social situation for one that is not seen to be hidden. This suggestion is supported by the only study that has included appropriate silent control conditions in its design. Field (1984) examined the search performance of 12-month-old infants on Piagetian invisible displacement tasks where half the subjects experienced silent objects and half experienced continuously sounding objects. Both the "visual" and "auditory-visual" groups also experienced a distraction condition, where they were visually distracted before seeing (and/or hearing) the object hidden in a box. Field found no significant difference in the search performance of infants on the silent and sounding trials, irrespective of whether the standard or distraction conditions were used.

The results of Field's (1984) work and of a longitudinal study by Bigelow (1983) indicate that infants aged from 9- to 18-months do not necessarily utilize auditory information for the location and continuing existence of an object, when that object undergoes complex visual disappearance movements. On the other hand, it might be argued that these studies have not used sufficiently salient auditory stimuli to be fair tests of the potential utility of sound for infants' searching behavior. Certainly the sounds of music boxes and buzzers may have a reduced salience, but what about the calling voice of a mother who has surreptitiously disappeared from sight? Do infants use such biologically relevant sounds to search accurately, even in visually complex hiding situations? A preliminary study by Zucker and Corter (1981) suggests that they do not. Zucker and Corter tested the ability of crawling, 9-month-old infants to search out their mothers, who had disappeared through one of two doorways in a laboratory room, while each infant was distracted with toy playing. When the mothers simply called to their infants repeatedly through one of the doorways, the great majority of the babies crawled toward the correct door. However, when the same procedure was used on a second trial, only with the mother now calling from the other doorway, only 50% of the infants crawled toward the correct, novel location. These results paralleled their previous findings on a similar visual search task. So this procedure involving highly salient sound stimuli confirms the outcome of the manipulative search tasks; the availability of object sound cues does not enhance searching behavior beyond the level of competence shown under purely visual disappearance conditions. In other words, salient auditory spatial information did not eliminate the stage IV error characteristic of 9-month-old infants.

Summary and Conclusions on the 6- to 18-Months Period

From 6 months onwards, infants' orientation to lateral sounds is much more purposeful and more responsive to the spatial contingencies of sights and sounds. The significance of the visual-spatial control of exploratory behavior also increases markedly in the second half of the first year. Initially, reaching and prehension, and subsequently locomotion, come under strong visual control in the early phases of their development, while the potential contribution of auditory-spatial control lags well behind. Hence 6- to 9-month-old infants do not reach out for sounding objects when there is no possible guidance from visual-spatial information for their reaching (Wishart et al., 1978). After some months of skill development in reaching and locomotion, the heavy dependence on direct visual guidance seems to decline (Bushnell, 1981) and infants may be able to attend more to tactual- and auditory-spatial information as visual control becomes increasingly automatic. However, when older infants are presented with the problem of finding an object which has undergone a visually complex disappearance, but which continues to provide them with constant, directional, auditory information about its existence, they seem to attend to the detailed, but confusing, visual information and not the simple, but perhaps unspecific, auditory information. In other words, at least into the first half of the second year, infants do not seem to be able to use the spatial information afforded by the sounds of objects, to help them overcome being confused by complex visual-spatial changes that occur when objects are hidden temporarily from view.

GENERAL CONCLUSIONS

The account of developments in auditory-visual localization that I have presented accords more closely with the perception-centered theoretical perspective of James and Eleanor Gibson, than the action-centered perspective of Jean Piaget. Infants seem to be born with auditory and visual systems that are organized to listen to and look around their environment in a coordinated manner. This listening and looking may be initially of a reflexive nature and it is certainly quite inaccurate, at least in part, because of the immaturity of the neuromotor control systems for neck, head, and eye movements. However, the newborn infants' capacity to detect spatial correspondences between sights and sounds does not seem to depend on developments in the coordination of active touch with vision and hearing, as Piaget has suggested. Spatial information does seem to be picked up by any perceptual system alone, or with any combination of perceptual systems, at least from the time of birth. Piaget's invoking of the role of prehension in intermodal coordination is a reversion to the old empiricist notion that touch teaches vision and hearing. Thus, one legacy of this empiricist notion has been the tendency, even in recent times, to think of intermodal space perception as derived from separate channels of sensory experience, which have to be cross-validated by touch (Gibson, 1966). Another legacy has been the failure to recognize adequately the dominant role played by vision in space perception from early infancy onwards.

To argue that vision most frequently plays a dominant role in human space perception throughout life is not necessarily inconsistent with J. J. Gibson's rejection of the channels of sensation approach in theories of perception (see Pick, 1974). Nor should the use of the word "dominance" be taken to imply that the visual and auditory perception systems do not play mutually supportive roles under normal ecological conditions. The idea of the visual coding of nonvisual spatial information in human perception is also not new (Pick, 1974; Rock, 1966). However, in more general discussions of infant intermodal perception there is often a tendency to ignore the *relative* importance of the visual space perception system from the time of birth. While humans are born with the potential for highly effective *temporal* discrimination between sounds, their auditory *space* perception capacities in early infancy are extremely crude in comparison with their visual space perception. Of course, this difference in auditory and visual localization capacities is narrowed a little during the early years, but it always remains a characteristic of human space perception. A direct contrast with the special significance of visual space perception for humans is provided by the example of bats, who are heavily reliant on sound localization for their survival. As a consequence, bats have not only developed an echolocation system for more accurate perception of the distance of sounds, but also use a special external ear structure to localize sounds very accurately in the vertical plane (Lawrence & Simmons, 1982).

We have only just begun to explore the actual nature of infants' auditory localization capacities. Throughout this chapter I have emphasized the need for more research on the specificity of the auditory-spatial information detected by infants. There is also a continuing need to relate the findings on infants' auditory-visual localization to similar work in the animal behavior (Kelly, 1982) and neurophysiological areas (Heffner, 1978; Middlebrooks & Pettigrew, 1981). Clifton and her colleagues (Clifton et al., 1981) have made laudable moves in this regard and they have stressed that we are still very ignorant about the nature of the spatial representations underlying infants' head and eye orientations to sounds. There needs to be much more work on infants' ability to localize sounds distally, by reaching and locomoting to their precise positions in space. Research on normal infants' multimodal perception should also clarify the specific potential for auditory- and tactual-spatial information to support the reaching and locomotion development of visually handicapped infants.

ACKNOWLEDGMENT

I wish to thank the Auckland University Research Committee for a grant which has aided the preparation of this chapter. Darwin Muir, Dan Ashmead and John Irwin provided many helpful comments on an earlier draft of this work.

REFERENCES

Aitken, S., & Bower, T. G. R. (1982). Intersensory substitution in the blind. *Journal of Experimental Child Psychology, 33*, 309–323.

Alegria, J., & Noirot, E. (1978). Neonate orientation behaviour towards human voice. *International Journal of Behavioural Development, 1*, 291–312.

Aronson, E., & Rosenbloom, S. (1971). Space perception in early infancy: Perception within a common auditory-visual space. *Science, 172*, 1161–1163.

Ashmead, D. H., & Perris, E. (1986, April). *Accuracy of auditory localization in 7-month-old human infants.* Paper presented at the Fifth International Conference on Infant Studies, Los Angeles.

Aslin, R. N., & Salapatek, P. (1975). Saccadic localization of peripheral targets by the very young human infant. *Perception and Psychophysics, 17*, 293–302.

Atkinson, J., & Braddick, O. (1982). Sensory and perceptual capacities of the neonate. In P. M. Stratton (Ed.), *Psychobiology of the human newborn,* Chichester: Wiley.

Bechtold, A. G., Bushnell, E. W., & Salapatek, P. (1979, March). *Infants' visual localization of visual and auditory targets.* Paper presented at the Society for Research in Child Development, San Francisco.

Bigelow, A. A. (1983). The development of the use of sound in the search behaviour of infants. *Developmental Psychology, 19,* 317–321.

Bower, T. G. R. (1974). *Development in infancy.* San Francisco: Freeman.

Bower, T. G. R. (1979). The origins of meaning in perceptual development. In A. D. Pick (Ed.), *Perception and its development: A tribute to Eleanor J. Gibson.* Hillsdale, NJ: Lawrence Erlbaum Associates.

Bull, D. (1978) *Auditory-visual coordination in infancy: The perception of moving sights and sounds.* Paper presented at the 1st International Conference on Infant Studies, Providence, Rhode Island.

Bushnell, E. W. (1981, April). *The decline of visually-guided reaching in infancy.* Presented at the biennial meeting of the Society for Research in Child Development, Boston.

Castillo, M., & Butterworth, G. (1981). Neonatal localization of a sound in visual space. *Perception, 10,* 331–338.

Chun, R. W. M., Pawsat, R., & Forster, F. M. (1960). Sound localization in infancy. *Journal of Nervous and Mental Disorders, 130,* 472–476.

Clarkson, M. G., Clifton, R. K., & Morrongiello, B. A. (1983, April). *Newborns show head orienting toward brief stimuli.* Paper presented at meetings of the Society for Research in Child Development meeting, Detroit.

Clifton, R., Morrongiello, B. A., Kulig, J. W., & Dowd, J. M. (1981). Developmental changes in auditory localization in infancy. In R. N. Aslin, J. R. Alberts, & M. R. Petersen (Eds.), *Development of perception: Psychobiological perspectives* (Vol. 1). Orlando, FL: Academic Press.

Coleman, P. D. (1963). An analysis of cues to auditory depth perception in free space. *Psychological Bulletin, 60,* 302–315.

Condry, S. M., Haltom, M., & Neisser, U. (1977). Infant sensitivity to audio-visual discrepancy: A failure to replicate. *Bulletin of the Psychonomic Society, 9,* 431–432.

Crassini, B., & Broerse, J. (1980). Auditory-visual integration in neonates: A signal detection analysis. *Journal of Experimental Child Psychology, 29,* 144–155.

deSchonen, S., McKenzie, B., Maury, L., & Bresson, F. (1978). Central and peripheral object distances as determinants of the effective visual field in early infancy. *Perception, 7,* 499–506.

Field, C. J. (1984). *One-year-old infants' use of sound in searching for hidden objects.* Unpublished master's thesis, University of Auckland.

Field, J. (1981). Looking and listening in the first year of infancy. In A. R. Nesdale, C. Pratt, R. Grieve, J. Field, D. Illingworth, & J. Hogben (Eds.), *Advances in child development: Theory and research.* Nedlands: National Conference on Child Development.

Field, J., DiFranco, D., Dodwell, P., & Muir, D. (1979). Auditory-visual coordination of 2½-month-old infants. *Infant Behaviour and Development, 2,* 113–122.

Field, J., Muir, D., Pilon, R., Sinclair, M., & Dodwell, P. (1980). Infants' orientation to lateral sounds from birth to three months. *Child Development, 51,* 295–298.

Fraiberg, S. (1977). *Insights from the blind.* New York: Basic Books.

Freedman, D. A., Fox-Kolenda, B. J., Margileth, D. A., & Miller, D. H. (1969). The development of the use of sound as a guide to affective and cognitive behaviour—A two phase process. *Child Development, 40,* 1099–1105.

Gibson, E. J. (1977). How perception really develops: A view from outside the network. In D. LaBerge & S. J. Samuels (Eds.), *Basic processes in reading: Perception and comprehension.* Hillsdale, NJ: Lawrence Erlbaum Associates.

Gibson, J. J. (1966). *The senses considered as perceptual systems*. Boston: Houghton-Mifflin.

Ginsburg, H. L., & Wong, D. L. (1973). Enhancement of hidden object search in six-month-old infants presented with a continuously sounding hidden object. *Developmental Psychology, 9,* 142.

Hammer, M., & Turkewitz, G. (1975). Relationship between effective intensity of auditory stimulation and directional eye-turns in the human newborn. *Animal Behaviour, 23,* 287–290.

Harris, P. L., & Macfarlane, A. (1974). The growth of the effective visual field from birth to seven weeks. *Journal of Experimental Child Psychology, 18,* 340–348.

Heffner, H. (1978). Effect of auditory cortex ablation on localization and discrimination of brief sounds. *Journal of Neurophysiology, 41,* 963–976.

Jackson, C. V. (1953). Visual factors in auditory localization. *Quarterly Journal of Experimental Psychology, 5,* 52–65.

Kelly, J. B. (1982). Developmental aspects of sound localization. In R. W. Gatehouse (Ed.), *Localization of sound: Theory and application*. Groton, CT: Amphora.

Kuhl, P. K., & Meltzoff, A. N. (1982). The bimodal perception of speech in infancy. *Science, 218,* 1138–1141.

Lawson, K. R. (1980) Spatial and temporal congruity and auditory-visual integration in infants. *Developmental Psychology, 16,* 185–192.

Lawrence, B. D., & Simmons, J. A. (1982). Echolocation in bats: The external ear and perception of the vertical positions of targets. *Science, 218,* 481–483.

Lyons-Ruth, K. (1975, April). *ntegration of auditory and visual spatial information during early infancy*. Paper presented at the biennial meeting of the Society for Research in Child Development, Denver.

McKenzie, B., Day, R. H. (1972). Object distance as a determinant of visual fixation in early infancy. *Science, 178,* 1108–1110.

McKenzie, B., & Day, R. H. (1976). Infants' attention to stationary and moving objects at different distances. *Australian Journal of Psychology, 28,* 45–51.

McGurk, H., & Lewis, M. (1974). Space perception in early infancy: Perception within a common auditory-visual space? *Science, 186,* 649–650.

McGurk, H., & MacDonald, J. (1978). Auditory-visual coordination in the first year of life. *International Journal of Behavioural Development, 1,* 229–240.

Mendelson, M. J., & Haith, M. H. (1976). The relation between audition and vision in the human newborn. *Monographs of the Society for Research in Child Development, 41,* No. 4.

Mershon, D. H., Desaulniers, D. H., Kiefer, S. A., Amerson, T. L., & Mills, J. T. (1981). Perceived loudness and visually-determined auditory distance. *Perception, 10,* 531–543.

Middlebrooks, J. C., & Pettigrew, J. D. (1981). Functional classes of neurons in primary cortex of the cat distinguished by sensitivity to sound localization. *The Journal of Neuroscience, 1,* 107–120.

Moore, B. C. J. (1982). *An introduction to the psychology of hearing*, 2nd Edition. London: Academic Press.

Moore, J. M., Wilson, W. R., & Thompson, G. (1977). Visual reinforcement of head-turn responses in infants under 12 months of age. *Journal of Speech and Hearing Disorders, 42,* 328–334.

Morrongiello, B. A., & Rocca, P. T. (1986, April). *Infants' localization of sounds in the horizontal plane*. Paper presented at the Fifth International Conference on Infant Studies, Los Angeles.

Muir, D. W. (1982). The development of human auditory localization in infancy. In W. Gatehouse (Ed.), *Sound Localization: Theory and Application*. Groton, CT: Amphora.

Muir, D. W. (1985). The development of infants' auditory spatial sensitivity. In S. E. Trehub & B. A. Schneider (Eds.), *Auditory development in infancy*. New York: Plenum.

Muir, D. W., Abraham, W., Forbes, B., & Harris, L. (1979). The ontogenesis of an auditory localization response from birth to four months of age. *Canadian Journal of Psychology, 33,* 320–333.

Muir, D. W., & Field, J. (1979). Newborn infants orient to sounds. *Child Development, 50,* 431–436.

Northern, J. L., & Downs, M. P. (1978). *Hearing in children.* Baltimore: Waverly Press.

Piaget, J. (1954). *The construction of reality in the child.* London: Routledge & Kegan.

Pick, H. L., Jr. (1974). Visual coding of nonvisual spatial information. In R. B. MacLeod & H. L. Pick, Jr. (Eds.), *Perception: Essays in honor of James J. Gibson.* Ithaca, NY: Cornell University Press.

Rock, I. (1966). *The nature of perceptual adaptation.* New York: Basic Books.

Schneider, B. A., Trehub, S. E., & Bull, D. (1979). The development of basic auditory processes in infants. *Canadian Journal of Psychology, 33,* 306–319.

Siegenthaler, B. M., & Aungst, R. B. (1968). Auditory localization for speech in children. *The Journal of Auditory Research, 8,* 433–438.

Spelke, E. S. (1979). Exploring audible and visible events in infancy. In A. D. Pick (Ed.), *Perception and Its Development: A Tribute to Eleanor J. Gibson.* Hillsdale, NJ: Lawrence Erlbaum Associates.

Spelke, E. S. (in press). The development of intermodal perception. In L. B. Cohen & P. Salapatek (Eds.), *Handbook of infant perception.* Orlando: FL: Academic Press.

Spelke, E. S., & Owsley, C. J. (1979). Intermodel exploration and knowledge in infancy. *Infant Behaviour and Development, 2,* 13–28.

Tronick, E. (1972). Stimulus control and growth of the infant's effective visual field. *Perception and Psychophysics, 11,* 373–376.

Turner, S., & MacFarlane, A. (1978) Localization of human speech by the newborn baby and the effects of pethidine ('meperidine'). *Developmental Medicine and Child Neurology, 20,* 727–734.

Uzgiris, I. C., & Benson, J. (1980, April). *Infants' use of sound in search for objects.* Paper presented at the International Conference on Infant Studies.

Warren, D.H. (1970). Intermodal interactions in spatial localization. *Cognitive Psychology, 1,* 114–133.

Warren, D. H. (1978). Perception by the blind. In E. C. Carterette & M. P. Friedman (Eds.), *Handbook of perception* (Vol. 10). Orlando, FL: Academic Press.

Welch, R. B., & Warren, D. H. (1980). Immediate perceptual response to intersensory discrepancy. *Psychological Bulletin, 88,* 638–667.

Wertheimer, M. (1961). Psychomotor coordination of auditory and visual space at birth. *Science, 134,* 1962.

Wightman, F. L., & Kistler, D. J. (1980). A new "look" at auditory space perception. In G. Van den Brink & F. A. Bilsen (Eds.), *Psychophysical, physiological and behavioural studies in hearing.* The Netherlands: Delft University Press.

Wishart, J. G., Bower, T. G. R., & Dunkeld, J. (1978). Reaching in the dark. *Perception, 7,* 507–512.

Witkin, H., Wapner, S., & Leventhal, T. (1952). Sound localization with conflicting visual and auditory cues. *Journal of Experimental Psychology, 43,* 58–67.

Zucker, K. J., & Corter, C. M. (1981, April). *Infant's use of sound in search for mother during brief separation.* Paper presented at the biennial meeting of the Society for Research in Child Development, Boston. (Abstract).

9 Visual and Haptic Bimodal Perception in Infancy

Sharne Rolfe-Zikman
Monash University

INTRODUCTION

We live in a world full of objects and events that provide multimodal stimulation, i.e., stimulation to two or more sensory modalities. For example, we not only see the glow of an open log fire, but we feel its warmth on our skin, hear the logs crackling, and smell the odor of the burning wood. The world of the human infant is also multimodal. It is now clear that at birth or soon after, the human neonate perceives visual, auditory, tactile, olfactory, and gustatory stimulation (Fantz, 1963; Haith, 1966; Mendelson & Haith, 1976; Nemanova, as cited by Pick, 1961; Rovee, Cohen, & Shlapack, 1975; Sherman & Sherman, 1925). In the usual course of events, the mother or other caregiver provides the infant with integrated multimodal stimulation from birth since people in general, and caregivers in particular, can be seen, heard, felt, and so on. However, once visually directed reaching develops at around 5-months-of-age (White, Castle, & Held, 1964) infants become adept at gaining one particular kind of multimodal stimulation for themselves. At this stage in development, infants begin to look at objects that they hold and during the second half year, simultaneous visual and haptic exploration of objects occurs frequently during an infant's interaction with the environment.

This chapter is concerned with multimodal perception of this kind, i.e., visual and haptic bimodal perception. Three main issues are discussed. First, what is the role of manipulation in learning about objects and events? Do infants learn better under bimodal (i.e., visual and haptic) or unimodal (i.e., visual) conditions? Second, what do infants learn about or attend to during periods of visual and haptic exploration? A number of investigations have been concerned with this question when stimuli are presented visually (e.g., Fagan, 1977) but few for visual and haptic bimodal conditions. Third, is there concordance between visual and haptic responsiveness to novelty and, related to this, what are the optimal conditions for demonstration of differential haptic responsivity? These three issues are considered in detail in the following sections.

THE ROLE OF MANIPULATION IN LEARNING
ABOUT OBJECTS AND EVENTS

From the standpoint of theory, the role of "action," including haptic manipulation, in the perception of objects and space has been a long standing issue in perceptual and cognitive development. At least three theoretical positions which accord "action," "activity," and "manipulation" a key role in the origin and development of knowledge about the world can be identified in current research (Bruner, 1964; Bruner, Olver, & Greenfield, 1966; Piaget, 1952, 1954; Piaget & Inhelder, 1956; Zaporozhets, 1965, 1973). The implication of these theories is that learning should be better were subjects permitted to undertake practical manipulative activity with an object, as compared with the more passive process of looking alone.

The suggestion that motor activity provides the basis of perception led to a number of studies in the 1960s and 1970s concerned with how the addition of haptic experience to visual experience affects memory for objects in preschool, school-age, and adult subjects (e.g., Butter & Zung, 1970; Cashdan & Zung, 1970; De Leon, Raskin, & Gruen, 1970; Denner & Cashdan, 1967; Millar, 1971; Zung, Butter, & Cashdan, 1974). In the main, these studies did not provide empirical support for the enhancement of visual perception and memory as a result of concurrent haptic exploration. Certainly *consistent* facilitative effects have not been reported. The possibility remains, however, that for younger children and infants, manipulation may have a specific facilitative effect not found with older subjects. In the theoretical positions of Piaget and Bruner, what is defined as an "action" is very much dependent upon the developmental level of the individual. It is possible that in infancy, when visually directed reaching first develops, "motor acts" of the type executed during haptic manipulation may be more important than at later stages, when knowledge of the world through internalised "cognitive actions" has emerged. Others have suggested that haptic manipulation may have an enhancing effect on learning in infancy simply because it occurs so frequently in an infant's behavior (Rose, Gottfried, & Bridger, 1979) or because infants are visually inexperienced (Ruff, (n.d.)). Consequently, a facilitative effect of haptic manipulation could conceivably be found with young infants but not with older subjects.

To the writer's knowledge, the first published attempts to investigate the relative effects of unimodal (i.e., visual) and bimodal (i.e., visual and haptic) experience with objects in infancy were reported by Gottfried, Rose, and Bridger (1978) and Rose et al. (1979). In these experiments, 6- and 12-month-old infants received either visual, or visual and haptic experience with an object or a transparent box in which the object was enclosed. Following a brief familiarization period during which infants accrued 20 sec of direct looking at the frontal perspective of the object, the infants were presented visually with the familiar and a novel object—a new form—and their visual interest in these objects observed. In both experiments, it was found that 12-month-old infants could visually recognize the familiar object, as indexed by greater attention to the novel object, following both uni- and bimodal famliarization. However, in contrast to the expected outcome, there was no evidence for enhanced recognition in the bimodal groups, and furthermore, visual recognition in the younger infants was *impaired* following bimodal familiarization. In both experiments, the younger infants looked significantly more at the novel test object following visual familiarization, but there was no evidence for recognition following visual and haptic experience with either the object itself or the encased object.

These results were provocative and unexpected, both on theoretical grounds and because a number of earlier studies with 6-month-old infants had reported discrimination between novel and familiar objects following bimodal familiarization (Rubenstein, 1974, 1976; Ruff, 1976; Schaffer & Parry, 1969, 1970; Schaffer, Greenwood, & Parry, 1972). In all these experiments—which are discussed in detail in the section to do with visual-haptic concordance—infants who visually and haptically explored an object during familiarization looked significantly longer at the novel object in the test phase. In some cases, infants also manipulated the novel object more.

In considering these data, Gottfried et al. proposed that the discrepancy in outcomes resulted from the use of a much shorter familiarization period of 20 sec in their experiment, compared with periods of 2–10 min in the other studies. They suggested that 6-month-old infants may be unable to process multimodal stimulation when the familiarization period is brief. However, there is another possibility; it is conceivable that it is the form of test, or more specifically, the similarity between the familiarization and test phases, that is critical. In the experiments of Gottfried et al. (1978) and Rose et al. (1979) a unimodal (visual) test phase followed both uni- and bimodal familiarization, whereas in the other experiments bimodal familiarization was followed by a bimodal test phase. Recognition memory in 6-month-old infants was only evident when the conditions of familiarization and testing were identical in terms of their uni- or bimodality.

It is not unreasonable to suggest that similarity and dissimilarity between familiarization and test may affect memory for the object with which an infant is familiarized. Recently, a number of studies have been directed to this issue, variously described as the effect of context (Ruff, 1981) or in the parlance of the adult memory literature, as the influence of encoding and retrieval conditions (Mackay-Soroka, Trehub, Bull, & Corter, 1982; Rovee-Collier & Fagen, 1981; Sullivan, 1982; Sullivan, Rovee-Collier, & Tynes, 1979). The important implication of this contextual viewpoint is that nondifferential attention to novel and familiar stimuli may not indicate memory loss, but simply that memories are inaccessible. Such an approach of course owes a great deal to the position of Tulving and his associates (Thomson & Tulving, 1970; Tulving & Osler, 1968; Tulving & Pearlstone, 1966). Tulving, working on verbal learning in adult subjects found that many items available in the memory store that could not be recalled under noncued recall conditions were recalled—became accessible—in the presence of appropriate retrieval cues. Tulving further found (Tulving & Pearlstone, 1966) that a retrieval cue is effective if and only if the information about its relation to the to-be-recalled (TBR) item is stored at the same time as the TBR item itself. Tulving and his associates called this the encoding specificity principle.

If the contextual viewpoint is valid, similarity between the familiarization and test phases may facilitate retrieval during a retention test. Dissimilarity between familiarization and test may inhibit retrieval. It is possible, therefore, that the absence of recognition memory in the experiments of Gottfried et al. (1978) and Rose et al. (1979) was quite unrelated to the manner in which the familiarization objects were explored, i.e., bimodally, and instead reflected the sensitivity of memory to contextual change. This possibility was investigated in two experiments (Rolfe & Day, 1981).

In the first experiment, 6-month-old infants received either unimodal (visual) or bimodal (visual and haptic) familiarization with two identical objects until the infants had looked at the objects for a total of 20 sec. This was followed by a test phase in which the familiar object and an object of a novel form were presented visually, i.e., out of reach. This was similar to the procedure used by Gottfried et al. and Rose et al. (1979). In the second experiment, the same procedure was used except that familiarization was followed by a bimodal test phase. If the interpretation proposed by Gottfried et al. and Rose et al. is valid (i.e., that 20 sec is insufficient time for infants to process bimodal stimulation) confirmation of their findings would be expected regardless of the test conditions. However, if the similarity between the conditions of the familiarization and test phases is critical, confirmation of their results would be expected only in the first experiment. In the second experiment, recognition memory would be expected only in those subjects familiarized bimodally.

The results of the experiments were consistent with a contextual viewpoint. Recognition memory was only evident in the unimodal group in Experiment 1 and the bimodal group in Experiment 2. In other words, it was the similarity between the way in which familiarization and test objects were presented that determined whether visual recognition memory for form was evident.

This effect has now been confirmed several times (Mackay-Soroka et al., 1982; Ruff, 1981). As with all null results, however, two possible interpretations must be considered. The first is that infants did not remember the familiar stimulus and the second is that infants recognized the "changed" familiar object but nevertheless attended to it and the completely novel object equally. These possibilities are considered in turn.

In relation to the first, Goodnow (1971) has discussed why changes in the manner in which objects are inspected may influence recognition memory. Her position owes much to the contextual model of memory described earlier. Goodnow considered that the critical determinant of recognition is the extent to which there is overlap in the stimulus properties perceived on two inspections of an object or event. While her discussion was directed to the role of modalities in perceptual and cognitive development, changing the modality of inspection between the familiarization and test phases—as in cross-modal matching tasks—is only one way in which there may be mismatch between the stimulus properties sampled. Another way is for the experimenter to allow bimodal exploration in one phase and unimodal exploration in the other. Such dissimilarity may reduce the possibility of the infant detecting the critical amount of overlap required for recognition. For example, if an infant perceives an object on one occasion as having properties 1, 2, and 3 (e.g., yellow, Y-shaped and touchable) and on another occasion as having properties 1, 2, and 4 (i.e., yellow, Y-shaped, but now out of reach) the occurrence of one changed feature may interfere with recognition despite overlap in the other features. However, it is probably not whether there is or is not similarity that is important, but the nature of the dissimilarity. For some objects, dissimilarity in one feature may not be enough to disrupt recognition given the presence of similarity in other features. The question thus reduces to that of how much a stimulus or event can be changed before it is perceived as a new stimulus or event, or responded to as if it was novel. This has to do with the object concept—identity constancy—and since this is discussed elsewhere in this book (Burnham, Chapter 7) it is not considered further here.

The foregoing discussion rests, of course, on the assumption that nondifferential attention to the novel and familiar test objects reflects lack of recognition. The second possibility is that infants recognized the familiar object but continued to look at it nonetheless. Support for the possibility that infants maintain attention to "changed" familiar objects comes from cross-modal matching studies, both of form (e.g., Ruff & Kohler, 1978), and substance, i.e., whether an object is soft or hard (Gibson & Walker, 1984). The outcomes of these studies indicated that when a familiar object is available to be explored in a novel way, i.e., to look at an object previously only explored haptically—infants may attend more to the familiar object. It is intuitively reasonable that in some circumstances, a familiar object which is in some way(s) novel may be just as interesting, or indeed more interesting, than a completely novel object. This will probably depend on the feature(s) of the object changed, the time course of change, and the object or event undergoing change. This is so for adults as well as infants.

The issue of context effects in infant memory therefore remains unresolved and will possibly remain so while evidence for discrimination and memory relies upon differential attention to novel and familiar stimuli. However, in terms of the role of manipulation, the results reported by Rolfe and Day (1981) simply added to the already considerable body of evidence that the addition of manipulation to visual inspection is not consistently facilitative. Provided the appropriate testing conditions were employed, recognition was equivalent whether exploration had been visual, or visual and haptic. It now seems, with the benefit of hindsight, that it may be naive to expect some absolute effect of adding manipulation to vision.

This is so because the role of manipulation can only be understood with due regard to the "ecological significance" of the haptic modality, i.e., the function of the hands in real-world encounters with objects. Among others, Ruff (1982) has discussed the two functions of manipulation. The most obvious is that it provides haptic (i.e., tactual and kinesthetic) information about an object. But manipulation has another role—it can act as a "pedestal" for vision. For example, manipulation serves vision when the hands move an object so that its various perspectives can be seen. However, these two types of information, i.e., haptic and visual, additional to that available when a stationary object is only looked at, are relevant or useful for only certain tasks or certain object features.

For example, haptic manipulation cannot provide any relevant information additional to that available visually in the case of visually specific features such as color or brightness. For other features, such as shape or texture, information arising from haptic manipulation is to some extent redundant since these so called "amodal" features can be perceived visually or haptically. For still other features, haptic manipulation has a more critical role. For example, haptic manipulation may be critical in the perception of substance or solidity, in that it is when an object is haptically manipulated (by oneself or by another) that the visual correlates of haptic differences in substance are produced.

This point can be amplified by reference to some of the studies in which perception of stimuli has been compared under visual and visual-haptic conditions. In many of these experiments, the task of the subjects was to recognize two-dimensional shapes. Although three-dimensional forms may have been used during familiarization, the subjects' task was to identify the object on the basis of one frontal perspective of that form (e.g., Millar, 1971; Zung et al., 1974). For adults, at least, vision usually dominates touch in shape perception if the two modalities provide discrepant information (e.g., Rock & Victor, 1964). Why then should perception of shape be any better when manipulation is added to vision? A more appropriate task may involve recognition of the structural invariants of a three-dimensional form, or a stimulus feature of particular relevance to the haptic modality such as substance.

That detection of the invariants specifying form may be enhanced when manipulation *and* vision are used is suggested by work reported by Ruff (1982). In two experiments, 12-month-old infants detected the invariant shape or texture of objects but not their color or surface pattern when the objects were visually and haptically explored. However, when the objects were encased in clear plastic thereby preventing haptic involvement with the objects themselves, infants of the same age detected color but not shape invariants. It must be noted, however, that infants were still manipulating *something,* although not "the object" as specified by the experimenter. Presumably then, the encased object was still seen in its various perspectives, i.e., the hand was able to fulfil its "pedestal" role. That structural invariants were not detected in this situation is puzzling, and as Ruff concludes, suggests a primary role for the haptic, not visual consequences of manipulation.

Within the wider context of the role of manipulation, the most likely conclusion would seem to be that the addition of manipulation to visual fixation may be helpful, harmful, or have no effect depending upon the information that is being picked up during exploration. In other work comment has been made about the possible significance of the object features used in experiments in which the stimulus objects are explored visually and haptically (Gottfried et al., 1978; Rose et al., 1979). For example, Gottfried et al. concluded that "it may be more accurate to consider object manipulation not as a general basis for cognitive or perceptual functioning and development, but rather as a specific type of experience that provides unique information about objects in the world" (p. 311). Rose et al. (1979) made much the same point and suggested that in their experiments infants may have learned about object features other than shape—such as texture and flexibility—during bimodal familiarization. Given longer familiarization times, they concluded that infants "may obtain a more complete understanding of the object's qualities" (p. 65) under bimodal learning conditions. Certainly, it would seem that more attention should now be given to just what features infants attend to and learn about when manipulation accompanies visual inspection. This issue is considered in the next section.

WHAT DO INFANTS ATTEND TO WHEN EXPLORING AN OBJECT VISUALLY AND HAPTICALLY?

While it is clear from the experiments of Rolfe and Day (1981) that infants can remember at least the form or shape of objects explored briefly and bimodally, this research leaves unresolved the more general issue of what parts of the multimodal stimulus package infants attend to while exploring an object in this way. It is not clear whether infants attend to the visual stimulation, the haptic stimulation, or both. This is so because the feature of the object that was remembered in these experiments was shape, which can be perceived both visually and haptically. Memory for shape would occur even if only visual or haptic information had been attended during the familiarization phase.

When infants explore objects visually and haptically it is not necessarily the case that both the visual and haptic consequences of the exploration are registered. It is possible that one type of stimulation, say the visual, may preclude attention to the haptic, at least in the short term, or indeed, that the haptic information may be ignored. Certainly, information *can* be acquired by the hand (and mouth). This has been indicated by studies of cross-modal matching of form when the familiarization period is haptic only, and the test phase visual only (Rose, Gottfried, & Bridger, 1981; Ruff & Kohler, 1978; Meltzoff & Borton, 1979) and in haptic intramodal tasks (Soroka, Corter, & Abramovitch, 1979). This does not indicate, however, that haptic information is attended to during bimodal exploration, just as experiments using visual-only presentation conditions cannot establish whether attention to visual stimulation occurs when there is concurrent haptic stimulation. A bimodal learning context may not be the simple sum of the two unimodal contexts of which it is comprised.

To test directly whether haptic and/or visual information is attended during bimodal exploration requires memory for an haptically specific, or visually specific object feature to be demonstrated following visual and haptic familiarization. For example, if infants demonstrated recognition memory for the weight of an object following bimodal experience then attention to haptic information during the familiarization phase could be inferred. Similarly, if recognition memory for color obtained then attention to visual information would be established.

Research directed to this issue has only just begun. In one experiment (Bushnell, Shaw, & Strauss, 1985), 6-month-old infants were familiarized bimodally with an object of a particular temperature—warm or cool—and color—red or blue. In the test phase, infants were presented with an object novel only visually, i.e., of a novel color, or novel in temperature only, and in the usual way, their visual and haptic responses to the object observed. Bushnell et al. reported significant visual and haptic novelty percentages when the test object was of a novel temperature, thereby indicating that infants had attended to the tactual consequences of their manipulation. Surprisingly, differential responsiveness to color novelty was not observed, in either the visual or the haptic modality. They interpreted these outcomes as possibly indicating "tactual capture"—i.e., that infants "may be so engrossed with the tactual characteristics of an object that attention to its visual properties is diluted" (p. 591). Certainly, given current knowledge of infant color vision, an explanation in terms of attentional considerations rather than a discrimination failure would seem plausible. Nevertheless, since recognition memory for the colors used in this experiment was not established using visual-only familiarization, it remains possible that a discrimination failure explains the data.

That infants' attention to visually specific information may be facilitated in the absence of haptic manipulation was given some support by the experiments of Ruff (1982). In these experiments, infants did not detect the unchanging color of objects which they manipulated but did so when the objects were encased in plastic. Of relevance also are the outcomes of three unpublished experiments by the writer. The stimulus features used in these experiments were color and substance but for the present discussion it is the outcomes in relation to color, a visually specific feature, which are of major interest.

In the first two experiments, 6-month-old infants were familiarized bimodally (i.e., visually and haptically) with small spherical objects of a particular color— red or blue—and substance—hard or soft. Familiarization continued until 55 sec of looking at the objects had been accrued. In both experiments the familiarization phase was followed by two, 15-sec test trials in which bimodal exploration was also allowed. While infants spent some of the time looking at an object, but not manipulating it, or manipulating it without visual inspection, most infants spent most of the time simultaneously looking at and manipulating the same object.

The design of the first experiment is shown in Fig. 9.1. Thirty-two 6-month-old infants were familiarized bimodally with two identical spheres, either soft red (SR), soft blue (SB), hard red (HR) or hard blue (HB). After familiarization, infants were randomly assigned by sex to either an Experimental or Control group. In both groups, the novel test object differed from the familiar object in substance. However, the Experimental and Control groups differed in the color novelty of the test objects. For the Control group both test objects were presented in the familiar color. For example, if infants had been familiarized with SR spheres, the novel object was HR, and the familiar SR. For the Experimental group, however, both test objects were presented in a novel color. For example, following familiarization with SR spheres the test objects were HB and SB. This manipulation was used because the outcomes of some pilot work suggested that perception of substance may be potentiated in the presence of color novelty.

The data were first analyzed using the standard t-test analysis of novelty percentages. The outcomes of these analyses are only referred to in passing as they bear on recognition memory for substance. Briefly, there was no evidence of recognition memory for substance in either the visual or haptic modality, although infants showed a spontaneous preference for the soft object.

A second analysis of the data compared the absolute durations of fixation and manipulation of the test objects across groups, using analyses of variance. The most interesting outcome was a nonsignificant main effect of condition. Infants in the Experimental group neither looked at nor manipulated the test objects more than Control group subjects. More visual fixation of the test objects would have been expected in the Experimental group if these infants perceived the color of

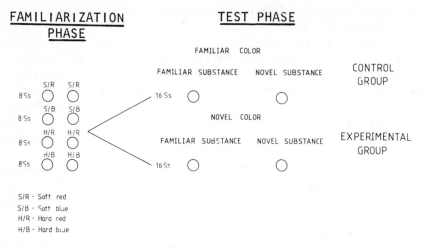

FIGURE 9.1.   Design of Experiment 1

the test objects to be novel. Since previous work has shown that color vision is essentially adult-like by 6-months-of-age (Bornstein, 1981) and since infants look longer at novel colors in a visual intramodal task after 30-sec familiarization (Fagan, 1977), this nonsignificant result was surprising.

The findings of the second experiment, however, confirmed those of the first in terms of memory for color. The design was similar but the test objects differed in color novelty. The design is shown in Fig. 9.2.

In this experiment, infants had to discriminate between the test objects on the basis of color novelty. The Experimental and Control groups differed in the

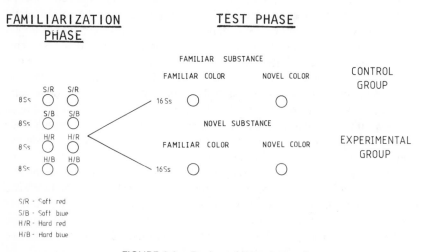

FIGURE 9.2.   Design of Experiment 2

substance novelty of the test objects. For the Control group, both test objects were of the familiar substance; for the Experimental group both test objects were of a novel substance. This manipulation was used to assess in another way whether substance was remembered and is not discussed further here.

The results in terms of t-test analyses of novelty percentages are presented in Table 9.1.

Although the fixation novelty percentages just reached significance for subjects in the Experimental group, visual recognition memory for color was not evident when the test objects were of a familiar substance, i.e., in the Control group, and furthermore, when the data for the 32 subjects were combined, the novelty percentages were not significant. Manipulation novelty percentages were also nonsignificant.

To determine whether these results indicated some interference from the concurrent haptic manipulation or whether the colors used were simply difficult to discriminate, a third experiment was conducted using visual-only presentation conditions throughout. One group of eight infants was tested. All subjects were familiarized visually with two identical spheres—Red or Blue—until they had accrued 55-sec visual familiarization, as in Experiments 1 and 2. The familiarization phase was followed by a visual-only test phase in which the familiar-colored object was paired with a novel-colored object. Analysis of the novelty percentages using t-tests was again used. The mean novelty percentage was 68.35% and this was significant at the .01 level. Unequivocal recognition memory for color was therefore demonstrated in the absence of concurrent haptic manipulation.

Since recognition memory for color following bimodal familiarization was not shown in the absence of substance novelty in Experiment 2, or when the data

TABLE 9.1
Mean Novelty Percentages and t-Test Outcomes for Experiment 2

	Group	
	Experimental	Control
Mean percentage of fixation of novel stimulus object	55.69	51.24
SD	11.79	13.46
t-value	1.92[a]	.37
Mean percentage of manipulation of novel stimulus object	49.24	44.12
SD	18.06	16.35
t-value	.17	1.43

[a] $p < .05$

from the Experimental and Control groups in Experiment 2 were combined, it seems that infants' attention to visually specific information may be facilitated in the absence of haptic manipulation. Unfortunately, however, these three experiments do not resolve the issue. This is so principally because familiarization and test phase conditions were confounded. The experiments in which infants explored the objects bimodally differed from the experiment in which exploration was only visual not only in the conditions of familiarization but also in the conditions of the test phase. This could not be avoided since the experiments of Rolfe and Day (1981) had established that recognition memory is only evident in 6-month-old infants when there is similarity between the familiarization and test phase contexts. With 6-month-old infants, therefore, it was necessary to follow unimodal familiarization with a unimodal test phase and bimodal familiarization with a bimodal test phase.

This confounding in test phase conditions is a problem because the observed effect may have been due to interference in retrieval rather than encoding. Being able to manipulate the test objects may interfere with the expression of preferential looking behavior, for example, if the object of manipulation appropriates visual regard. Lewis and Bryant (1982) have established that visual exploration of shapes is different in the presence and absence of haptic manipulation. Both normal and Down's syndrome infants looked less frequently but for longer durations at objects which they also manipulated. Therefore it may take longer for infants to show memory for *any* feature if the test objects are manipulated as well as visually inspected. The problem may thus reduce to a methodological one, in that certain procedures, allowing longer, or infant-controlled test trial lengths, may be more optimal for the *expression* of memory than others when manipulation is allowed in the test phase. This is taken up in the next section.

Another resolution to the dilemma of familiarization-test phase confounding is suggested by the research of Gottfried et al. (1978) and Rose et al. (1979). As outlined in an earlier section, they did not find recognition memory for form in 6-month-old infants when bimodal familiarization was followed by a unimodal test phase. However, this sort of interference was not found for 12-month-old infants. Infants of this age showed recognition memory for form, even when there was dissimilarity between the conditions of the familiarization and test phases. Therefore, it may be possible to compare directly recognition of color following brief uni- and bimodal familiarization simply by using older subjects. Of course the possibility remains that recognition may be potentiated even in 12-month-old infants when the conditions of familiarization and testing are similar. This was suggested by the experiments of Gottfried et al. and Rose et al. in which higher novelty preferences were found when the conditions of familiarization and testing were the same. For this reason, the preferred approach would be to follow both uni- and bimodal familiarization with a unimodal test for half the subjects and a bimodal test for the others. Similar research could usefully be directed to the equally interesting question of whether recognition of haptically specific information is inhibited through concurrent visual inspection. This would involve comparing unimodal (haptic) experience with visual and haptic experience.

Clearly, the issue requires more research using a variety of stimulus features. What the few studies conducted thus far suggest, however, is that some tactile features are attended to in a bimodal learning situation but, at least in the initial stages of exploration, this may not be so for visually specific characteristics like color. Explanations of these observations are at best speculative. Bushnell et al. (1985) have suggested that "purely visual characteristics such as color and surface pattern may not determine an object's identity for infants" (p. 599) at least in the context of bimodal exploration, or that certain tactual features e.g., temperature may have greater salience than certain visual features such as color. The findings of other work (e.g., Schaffer & Parry, 1969, 1970; Schaffer et al., 1972) in which infants were given more extended familiarization indicate that such "tactual capture" if it can be confirmed, may be a short-term phenomenon. In these experiments, infants showed memory for the color of objects explored bimodally following six, 30-sec habituation trials. This prompts one to speculate that visual and haptic stimulation may be processed serially.

Finally, it should be noted that while research using visually or haptically specific features makes it possible to determine whether haptic and/or visual information is attended to in a bimodal learning situation, it is nonetheless the case that this approach still leaves unanswered the question of whether infants attend to haptic information when the feature of the object to be discriminated is amodal and available to the visual modality. Haptic information for such features is redundant and may therefore be ignored. However, some insight into this problem can be gained from procedures like that used by Ruff (1982). She compared memory for object features when either the object itself or the object encased in clear plastic was manipulated. Recognition of the invariant form of objects was enhanced when infants could manipulate the object itself. This seems to indicate that the haptic information must have been registered, although it is not clear whether the effect was due to facilitation in the "unencased" condition, or interference in the "encased" condition, since in this latter condition the visual and haptic information was in some sense discrepant. The procedure is an interesting one and warrants further attention.

VISUAL-HAPTIC CONCORDANCE

A final issue to be discussed concerns visual-haptic concordance. Visual-haptic concordance refers to "the agreement between fixation and manipulation in the direction and extent of preference for or attention to stimuli" (Ruff, 1976, p. 868). In one series of experiments, Schaffer and others (Schaffer, 1975; Schaffer & Parry, 1969, 1970; Schaffer et al., 1972) reported that it is not until around 8-

to 9-months-of-age that an infant displays differential haptic as well as visual exploration of objects as a function of their familiarity. In all these experiments, differential manipulative responsiveness—both in terms of the time to commence manipulation of a novel object and duration of manipulation—and differential visual responsiveness were observed in infants of 8 months and older, but 6-month-old infants showed differential visual responsiveness only. Schaffer and Parry (1970) concluded that it is only at the older ages that the visual system controls manipulative behavior with respect to the features of familiarity and novelty. However, in contrast to Schaffer's results, Rubenstein (1974, 1976) reported that 6-month-old infants looked at *and* manipulated a novel object longer than a familiar object.

It has been suggested that the equivocality of these results may be due to the stimulus features varied by the experimenters (Steele & Pederson, 1977). In all of Schaffer's studies, the novel object differed from the familiar object only in its visual properties, i.e., the novel object was of a new color. In Rubenstein's experiments, the novel object differed from the familiar object both visually and haptically since the stimulus objects used were common household objects such as purses and plastic spoons. According to Steele and Pederson, it is possible that for young infants, novel haptic cues are necessary to control haptic exploration of objects.

To examine this possibility, Steele and Pederson conducted two experiments with 6-month-old infants. The infants were repeatedly presented with an object and, when responding in both the visual and haptic modalities habituated, they were shown a second object that was different in color only, or in form and texture. Both visual fixation *and* manipulation recovered upon introduction of an object that was of a new form or texture but the novel-colored object elicited an increase in looking only. These results supported the suggestion that whether or not concordance between the visual and haptic modalities is observed depends on the specific features of the object that are novel. Concordance was found when the feature was amodal and therefore relevant to both the visual and haptic modalities but not when the feature was visually specific.

As discussed in the preceding section, however, Bushnell et al. (1985) have recently reported increased visual and tactual interest in a novel temperature. Increased tactual interest only should have been observed if Steele and Pederson's account is valid.[1] In the light of this finding, consideration must be given to another possibility, i.e., that duration of manipulation may simply be a less sensitive measure of attention than fixation, when the short term, paired comparison procedure is used (Ruff, 1976; Willatts, 1983; Zikman, 1983). In this procedure, brief familiarization is followed by simultaneous presentation of fa-

---

[1]Bushnell et al. (1985) note, however, that their experiment could not determine whether the increase in looking at the object of a novel temperature was a truly exploratory behaviour, or whether it was in some way "recruited" by the haptic modality's search for information.

miliar and novel stimuli. For unimodal (visual) presentation conditions, the cooccurrence of the stimuli is generally considered advantageous since infants can compare the stimuli directly (Cohen & Gelber, 1975). However, when the objects are to be explored haptically as well as visually it is conceivable that paired presentation of the novel and familiar stimuli may be detrimental. This is so because the hands can act independently—i.e., both test objects can be manipulated at the one time. Since manipulation was scored in most of these studies whenever *contact* with (rather than haptic manipulation of) an object occurred, "inattentive" responses such as "a hand resting on a stimulus" (Ruff, 1976, p. 870) would nonetheless add to the duration of manipulation for that stimulus, thereby introducing an inaccuracy in any comparison of manipulation durations between stimuli.

When different objects are manipulated simultaneously it is also possible, although untested empirically, that processing of stimulus information is more demanding than when only one object is manipulated, by either one or both hands. Ruff (n.d.) has recently suggested that the processes underlying visual behavior are likely to be more complex under bimodal—i.e., visual and haptic, than unimodal conditions. When two objects are explored simultaneously these processes are likely to be even more complex and this may make processing of stimulus features difficult, especially for younger infants. Until such processes are better understood it may be preferable to use single object presentation. Although one can only speculate on whether this procedure would enable a more sensitive evaluation of memory and discriminative capacity, it would certainly test the visual and haptic responses under more similar conditions (Ruff, 1976).

Of course, the use of simultaneous object presentation is only a problem to the extent that infants *do* manipulate two objects simultaneously. Fenson, Kagan, Kearsley, and Zelazo (1976) reported that at 6-months-of-age infants typically play with one object at a time. However, more recently, Willatts (1983) found that 6-month-old infants tested with paired presentation of a novel and familiar stimulus "spent almost half the manipulation time in contact with both objects simultaneously" (p. 148).

Another aspect of the paired comparison procedure which may reduce the likelihood of differential manipulative responsiveness to novelty has to do with the use of brief, fixed-length test trials. For fixation, the use of brief test trials has provided generally sensitive measures of differential responsiveness (e.g., Fagan, 1974). However, earlier work has indicated that in the presence of some types of novelty, infants may show long latencies to manipulation (e.g., Schaffer & Parry, 1969, 1970; Schaffer et al., 1972). While these findings were derived from experiments with older infants, my own casual observations of a number of 6-month-olds participating in experiments using short test trials suggested that manipulation of the test objects did not begin at the start of the trials, but commenced some seconds later and may have continued beyond the end of the trial had the objects not been removed.

It is therefore possible that allowing a longer test trial when the conditions are visual and haptic may yield more sensitive haptic data and possibly visual data as well. Certainly, attention should be directed to what Cohen (1976) has called the "attention-releasing process." For visual fixation, "attention-getting" and "attention-holding" processes have been distinguished (Cohen, 1973), and as Cohen (1976) stated:

> the attention-releasing process, like attention getting and holding involves more active control by the infant than had previously been assumed. Understanding the nature of this control and how it develops requires much more information than is currently available. (p. 235)

The same comments may hold for haptic manipulation.

Although speculative, the argument being put forward here is that differential manipulative responsiveness (and indeed, differential visual responsiveness in the presence of manipulation) may be observed more reliably if adequate time is given for infants to demonstrate it. In this regard it is relevant that both Steele and Pederson (1977) and Bushnell et al. (1985) used an infant control procedure and trials did not terminate until the infant simultaneously ceased looking *and* manipulating the object. This degree of infant control is absent when a fixed trial length is used. This may be particularly problematic when the test trials are brief. Identification of the optimal trial length requires further observation and experimentation on the course of habituation of manipulation in infants of this age (e.g., Hutt, 1967).

Of course, appropriate attention should also be given to the question of individual differences. Just as one infant will fixate a stimulus for the entire exposure duration while another may glance only briefly at it (Kagan, 1971), so the "tempo" of manipulative exploration no doubt differs from individual to individual. It would be interesting to compare manipulative responsiveness to novelty in infants who characteristically manipulate for long or short periods of time in a manner akin to the analysis of visual fixation data of so called rapid and slow habituators and short lookers (McCall & Kagan, 1970).

Finally, comment should be made on the tendency to rely exclusively on *duration* measures of haptic exploration. When an object is explored visually, duration measures such as total duration and duration of first fixation probably provide a satisfactory summary of the exploration. However, when an object is explored haptically, the time taken to commence manipulation may be as important as for how long it is subsequently explored. Further, it is possible that for haptic manipulation, evidence for discrimination—particularly for some object features—would be obtained if the *manner* in which the objects were manipulated had been quantified. This type of approach is exemplified in the area of human ethology in which attempts are made to quantify the occurrence of well defined "molecular" units of behavior. For example, Hutt (1967) provided detailed information about the manner in which a 7-month-old infant manipulated objects differing in novelty, as well as measuring duration of manipulation and the number of "drops."

More recently, attempts to describe manipulation of objects in terms of the actions performed have been reported. For example, Gibson and Walker (1984) investigated, *inter alia*, whether infants discriminate soft and hard substances. They defined several distinct behaviors, which were subsequently combined into five categories—"presses," "touches," "drops/throws," "mouths," and "strikes." Exploratory manipulation was found to differ according to the substance of the object. Frequency of striking was signifciantly higher with the hard object while pressing occurred more frequently with soft objects. Because these observations were made during familiarization—the test phase being visual—memory processes were not investigated. However, memory for substance could be evaluated using this approach. For example, it may have been instructive to observe how infants initially attempted to manipulate the test objects. If this manipulation was appropriate to the familiarization object, memory could be inferred.

To summarize, it is clear that whether or not differential manipulative responsiveness to novelty is observed and therefore whether visual and haptic responses are concordant or not—may depend as much on procedural aspects as on the ability of the infants to discriminate the novel and familiar stimulus objects and remember the familiar one. In future research, consideration must be given to the optimum conditions for the demonstration of response capabilities in the haptic modality. This must be based on due regard for the purpose of and manner in which haptic manipulation is used in the real-world encounters infants have with objects about them.

GENERAL CONCLUSIONS

In this chapter I have outlined some important issues in research on visual and haptic bimodal perception in infancy. In much of this research too little attention has been paid to the ecological significance of the haptic modality in terms of the questions to which experiments have been directed and the procedures used. It is also true that visual and haptic bimodal functioning is more complex than has hitherto been acknowledged. What is now needed is research in which both factors are given due regard.

ACKNOWLEDGMENT

This chapter is based in part on the author's doctoral dissertation which was submitted to the Department of Psychology, Monash University in August 1983.

REFERENCES

Bornstein, M. H. (1981). Psychological studies of color perception in human infants: Habituation, discrimination and categorization, recognition, and conceptualisation. In L. P. Lipsitt & C. J. Rovee-Collier. *Advances in Infancy Research* (Vol. 1). Norwood, NJ: Ablex.

Bruner, J. S. (1964). The course of cognitive growth. *American Psychologist, 19,* 1–15.

Bruner, J. S., Olver, R. R., & Greenfield, P. M. (Eds.). (1966). *Studies in cognitive growth.* New York: Wiley.

Bushnell, E. W., Shaw, L., & Strauss, D. (1985). Relationship between visual and tactual exploration by 6-month-olds. *Developmental Psychology, 21,* 591–600.

Butter, E. J., & Zung, B. J. (1970). A developmental investigation of the effects of sensory modality on form recognition in children. *Developmental Psychology, 3,* 276.

Cashdan, S., & Zung, B. J. (1970). Effect of sensory modality and delay on form recognition. *Journal of Experimental Psychology, 86,* 458–460.

Cohen, L. B. (1973). A two-process model of infant attention. *Merrill-Palmer Quarterly, 19,* 157–180.

Cohen, L. B. (1976). Habituation of infant visual attention. In T. J. Tighe & R. C. Leaton (Eds.), *Habituation: Perspectives from child development.* New York: Wiley.

Cohen, L. B., & Gelber, E. R. (1975). Infant visual memory. In L. B. Cohen & P. Salapatek (Eds.), *Infant perception: From sensation to cognition* (Vol. 1). Orlando, FL: Academic Press.

De Leon, J. L., Raskin, L. M., & Gruen, G. E. (1970). Sensory-modality effects on shape perception in preschool children. *Developmental Psychology, 3,* 258–362.

Denner, B., & Cashdan, S. (1967). Sensory processing and the recognition of forms in nursery-school children. *British Journal of Psychology, 58,* 101–104.

Fagan, J. F. (1974). Infant recognition memory: The effects of length of familiarisation and type of discrimination task. *Child Development, 45,* 351–356.

Fagan, J. F. (1977). An attention model of infant recognition. *Child Development, 48,* 345–359.

Fantz, R. L. (1963). Pattern vision in newborn infants. *Science, 140,* 296–297.

Fenson, L., Kagan, J., Kearsley, R. B., & Zelazo, P. R. (1976). The developmental progression of manipulative play in the first two years. *Child Development, 47,* 232–236.

Gibson, E. J., & Walker, A. S. (1984). Development of knowledge of visual-tactual affordances of substance. *Child Development, 55,* 453–460.

Goodnow, J. (1971). The role of modalities in perceptual and cognitive development. In J. Hill (Ed.), *Minnesota Symposium in Child Psychology* (Vol. 5). Minneapolis: University of Minnesota Press.

Gottfried, A. W., Rose, S. A., & Bridger, W. H. (1978). Effects of visual, haptic and manipulatory experiences on infants' visual recognition memory of objects. *Developmental Psychology, 14,* 305–312.

Haith, M. M. (1966). The response of the human newborn to visual movement. *Journal of Experimental Child Psychology, 3,* 235–243.

Hutt, C. (1967). Effects of stimulus novelty on manipulatory exploration in an infant. *Journal of Child Psychology and Psychiatry, 8,* 241–247.

Kagan, J. (1971). *Change and continuity in infancy.* New York: Wiley.

Lewis, V. A., & Bryant, P. E. (1982). Touch and vision in normal and Down's syndrome babies. *Perception, 11,* 691–701.

MacKay-Soroka, S., Trehub, S. E., Bull, D. H., & Corter, C. M. (1982). Effects of encoding and retrieval conditions on infants' recognition memory. *Child Development, 53,* 815–818.

McCall, R. B., & Kagan, J. (1970). Individual differences in the infant's distribution of attention to stimulus discrepancy. *Developmental Psychology, 2,* 90–98.

Meltzoff, A. N., & Borton, R. W. (1979). Intermodal matching by human neonates. *Nature, 282,* 403–404.

Mendelson, M. J., & Haith, M. (1976). The relation between audition and vision in the human newborn. *Monographs of the Society for Research in Child Development, 41,* (Serial No. 167).

Millar, S. (1971). Visual and haptic cue utilisation by preschool children: The recognition of visual and haptic stimuli presented separately or together. *Journal of Experimental Child Psychology, 12,* 88–94.

Piaget, J. (1952). *The origins of intelligence in children.* New York: Norton.

Piaget, J. (1954) *The construction of reality in the child.* New York: Basic Books.

Piaget, J., & Inhelder, B. (1956). *The child's conception of space.* London: Routledge and Kegan Paul.

Pick, H. L. (1961). Research on taste in the Soviet Union. In M. R. Kane & B. P. Halpern (Eds.), *Physiological and behavioural aspects of taste.* Chicago: University of Chicago Press.

Rock, I., & Victor, J. (1964). Vision and touch: An experimentally created conflict between the two senses. *Science, 143,* 594–596.

Rolfe, S. A., & Day, R. H. (1981). Effects of the similarity and dissimilarity between familiarization and test objects on recognition memory in infants following uni- and bi-modal familiarisation. *Child Development, 52,* 1308–1312.

Rose, S. A., Gottfried, A. W., & Bridger, W. H. (1979). Effects of haptic cues on visual recognition memory in fullterm and preterm infants. *Infant Behavior and Development, 2,* 55–67.

Rose, S.A., Gottfried, A. W., & Bridger, W. H. (1981). Cross-modal transfer in 6-month-old infants. *Developmental Psychology, 17,* 661–669.

Rovee, C. K., Cohen, R. Y., & Shlapack, W. (1975). Life-span stability in olfactory sensitivity. *Developmental Psychology, 11,* 311–318.

Rovee-Collier, C. K., & Fagan, J. W. (1981). The retrieval of memory in early infancy. In L. P. Lipsitt (Ed.), *Advances in infancy research* (Vol. 1). Norwood, NJ: Ablex.

Rubenstein, J. (1974). A concordance of visual and manipulative responsiveness to novel and familiar stimuli in six-month-old infants. *Child Development, 45,* 194–195.

Rubenstein, J. (1976). Concordance of visual and manipulative responsiveness to novel and familiar stimuli: A function of test procedure or of prior experience. *Child Development, 47,* 1197–1199.

Ruff, H. (1976). The coordination of manipulation and visual fixation: A response to Schaffer (1975). *Child Development, 47,* 868–871.

Ruff, H. A. (1981). The effect of context on infants' responses to novel objects. *Developmental Psychology, 17,* 87–89.

Ruff, H. A. (1982). Role of manipulation in infants' responses to invariant properties of objects. *Developmental Psychology, 18,* 682–691.

Ruff, H. A. (n.d.). *The role of manipulation in infants' detection of invariance.*

Ruff, H. A., & Kohler, C. J. (1978). Tactual-visual transfer in six-month-old infants. *Infant Behavior and Development, 1,* 259–264.

Schaffer, H. R. (1975). Concordance of visual and manipulative responses to novel and familiar stimuli: A reply to Rubenstein (1974). *Child Development, 46,* 209–211.

Schaffer, H. R., & Parry, M. R. (1969). Perceptual-motor behaviour in infancy as a function of age and stimulus familiarity. *British Journal of Psychology, 60,* 1–9.

Schaffer, H. R., & Parry, M. R. (1970). The effects of short-term familiarisation on infants' perceptual motor co-ordination in a simultaneous discrimination situation. *British Journal of Psychology, 61,* 559–569.

Schaffer, H. R., Greenwood, A., & Parry, M. H. (1972). The onset of wariness. *Child Development, 43,* 165–176.

Sherman, M., & Sherman, J. C. (1925). Sensorimotor responses in infants. *Journal of Comparative Psychology, 5,* 53–68.

Soroka, S. M., Corter, C. M., & Abramovitch, R. (1979). Infants' tactual discrimination of novel and familiar tactual stimuli. *Child Development, 50,* 1251–1253.

Steele, D., & Pederson, D. R. (1977). Stimulus variables which affect the concordance of visual and manipulative exploration in 6-month-old infants. *Child Development, 48,* 104–111.

Sullivan, M. W. (1982). Reactivation: Priming forgotten memories in human infants. *Child Development, 53,* 516–523.

Sullivan, M. W., Rovee-Collier, C. K., & Tynes, D. M. (1979). A conditioning analysis of infant long-term memory. *Child Development, 50,* 152–162.

Thomson, D. M., & Tulving, E. (1970). Associative encoding and retrieval: Weak and strong cues. *Journal of Experimental Psychology, 86,* 255–262.

Tulving, E., & Osler, S. (1968). Effectiveness of retrieval cues in memory for words. *Journal of Experimental Psychology, 77,* 593–601.

Tulving, E., & Pearlstone, Z. (1966). Availability vs accessibility of information in memory for words. *Journal of Verbal Learning and Verbal Behaviour, 5,* 381–391.

White, B. L., Castle, P., & Held, R. (1964). Observations on the development of visually directed reaching. *Child Development, 35,* 349–364.

Willatts, P. (1983). Effects of object novelty on the visual and manual exploration of infants. *Infant Behaviour and Development, 6,* 145–149.

Zaporozhets, A. V. (1965). The development of perception in the preschool child. *Monographs of the Society for Research in Child Development, 30,* (Serial No. 100).

Zaporozhets, A. V. (1973). The development of perception and activity. *Early Child Development and Care, 2,* 49–56.

Zikman, S. A. R. (1983). *Bimodal perception of form, color and substance in infancy.* Unpublished doctoral dissertation, Monash University.

Zung, B. J., Butter, E. J., & Cashdan, S. (1974). Visual-haptic form recognition with task delay and sequenced bimodal input. *Neuropsychologia, 12,* 73–81.

10 Can Human Neonates Imitate Facial Gestures?

Ray Over
La Trobe University

Recent demonstrations that infants within hours of birth are capable of copying facial gestures, such as mouth-opening and tongue-protrusion, have challenged claims by Piaget (1962) about the ontogeny of imitative behavior. Piaget argued that prior to about 8-months-of-age infants are able to imitate only those gestures that they can see or hear themselves perform. Opening and closing the hand is one such gesture. Imitation of behaviors within this category is considered to become possible after infants link their own visible actions with the associated motor movements. When observing a model presenting the visual component of such a visual-motor circular reaction, the infant produces the motor component.

Piaget has contended that infants are unable to imitate facial gestures before 8 to 12-months-of-age. They can perform the specific actions, the rate of the behaviors can be modified through learning (pseudo-imitation), but duplication in response to observation of a model does not occur. In order to imitate a gesture such as mouth-opening, infants need to match their own nonvisible actions with the visible movements of the model. This skill entails translating information via one modality to behavior within another such that the spatial and temporal characteristics of the action are maintained. Piaget has claimed that it is not until the child has developed the capacity for intermodal comparison and integration that facial expressions become imitated. Deferred imitation, where the gesture to be copied is no longer visible, is considered to have an even later onset.

Several large-scale studies (Abravanel, Leven-Goldschmidt, & Stevenson, 1976; Abravanel & Sigafoos, 1984; Kaye & Marcus, 1982; Uzgiris, 1972; Uzgiris & Hunt, 1975), in which either cross-sectional or longitudinal designs were employed in surveying children across the first year of life, have yielded data that generally are consistent with Piaget's position. At the same time, there have been suggestions in the literature that infants are capable of imitation at a much earlier age than Piaget had supposed. Gardner and Gardner (1970), for example, assessed a single infant at 6-weeks-of-age. In limited testing, they found that the infant copied facial as well as manual gestures.

The most direct challenge to Piaget's position has come from several recent studies undertaken within an experimental paradigm that was developed with the intention of eliminating the possibility of several forms of artifact. Meltzoff and Moore (1977) reported that infants aged 12 to 21 days can duplicate facial and manual gestures that the infants have seen performed by an adult model. Subsequent research indicated that infants within the first few hours of life can copy not only tongue-protrusion and mouth-opening (Meltzoff & Moore, 1983a), but facial expressions that are correlated with such emotions as happiness, sadness, and surprise (Field, Woodson, Greenberg, & Cohen, 1982). Evidence of neonatal imitation suggests that infants possess information processing and motor programming skills at a level well beyond that accepted by Piaget. On the basis of their data, Meltzoff and Moore (1983a) proposed that infants undertake intermodal mapping, since infants generate mouth movements (which they cannot observe visually) that match the mouth movements they have seen the model performing.

Claims that the human neonate is capable of imitating gestures should not be accepted uncritically. First, as mentioned above, several large-scale studies have instead provided evidence of developmental staging. Second, even when neonatal imitation has been claimed, infant behavior has not been highly selective to the gesture performed by the model. Third, several investigators who used much the same paradigm as Meltzoff and Moore (1977) found little or no evidence that young infants imitate gestures (Abravanel & Sigafoos, 1984; Hayes & Watson, 1981; Koepke, Hamm, Legerstee, & Russell, 1981; McKenzie & Over, 1983). Fourth, correspondence in adult-infant behavior, when it does occur, may be open to explanation in terms other than imitation. Fifth, imitation requires a range of sensory, categorization, memory, and output skills that seem beyond the level of competence of infants. For example, it is questionable whether an infant within a few hours of birth is able to perceive gestures in sufficient detail to permit their reproduction. The visual acuity of infants at 1 month is only 0.7 cycles per degree, whereas adult acuity is 30 to 40 cycles per degree (Atkinson, Braddick, & Moar, 1977). Finally, investigators who have used the paradigm which Meltzoff and Moore developed in order to study imitation have abruptly confronted an infant with a strange adult performing odd actions for a short period of time. Why should the infant be expected to duplicate the adult's behavior rather than to show curiosity, surprise, or distress? In addition to asking whether imitation occurs, it is reasonable to inquire why it should occur.

The objective in this chapter is to examine the question of whether human neonates are capable of imitation in the context of methodological issues. The commentary is divided into three sections. The different aspects of the paradigm that Meltzoff and Moore developed for the study of imitation in infancy are first discussed. Studies that have demonstrated imitation, as well as those that have not, are then evaluated in some detail. The question of whether neonates imitate is discussed in the final section in terms wider than the operational perspective adopted by Meltzoff and Moore. It is argued that convergent evidence, rather than replication of earlier studies, will be needed in order to accept the conclusion that neonatal infants imitate. The objective in further research should be to explore the contexts in which infant-adult correspondence is found, if at all. One strategy might involve establishing whether imitation occurs as part of a process of social exchange and communication. Attention could then, for example, be given to issues such as the degree to which infant behavior is flexible when a number of task requirements, including the role of the model, are varied.

RESEARCH METHODOLOGY

In everyday language, to imitate means to copy, duplicate, or match. However, Meltzoff and Moore (1977), when they were developing a paradigm within which neonatal imitation can be assessed, sought not only to determine whether there is correspondence between infant and adult behaviors, but to eliminate the possibility that any isomorphism which is found can be conceptualized in terms other than imitation. Duplication of gestures as a consequence of shaping or selective reinforcement of infant behavior by the model would not constitute imitation. It is also necessary to ensure that the infant's behavior is directly linked to the gesture that was modeled, and that it is not just a product of social stimulation. As a further test of specificity, the possibility that what may seem to be imitation is instead a fixed action pattern released by a sign stimulus that is incorporated within the modeled gesture needs to be considered. The issue of blind methodology in coding infant behavior is also important. Interpretative bias in scoring is less likely when each sample of infant behavior is coded by a person who lacks information about which gesture the model has performed. The method which Meltzoff and Moore developed in order to cope with these problems represents a considerable advance on earlier research.

Meltzoff and Moore favored study of neonatal imitation within the laboratory rather than through field investigation on the grounds that standardized conditions and exacting methods can be employed. An infant, when judged to be alert and attentive, is confronted by an adult model who performs a series of standardized gestures. Imitation obviously can be studied only with reference to actions that are within the infant's behavioral repertoire. The gestures employed by Meltzoff and Moore (1977) were tongue-protrusion, lip-protrusion, mouth-opening, and sequential finger movement. These different gestures were modeled so that they had the same temporal characteristics (for example, a specific gesture was repeated 4 times within a 20 sec segment, with an interval of 1 sec between each act). Standardization was intended not only to produce exact categorization of the modeled gestures, but to reduce the possibility that the model would selectively reinforce or shape infant behavior. It is fundamental not only that the infant observe the model while the gestures are being demonstrated, but that the gestures be discriminable by the infant. Instead of undertaking an independent test of discriminability, Meltzoff and Moore have argued that the gestures they employed were discriminable on the grounds that the gestures were imitated by infants. Field, Woodson, Greenberg, and Cohen (1982) have used an habituation paradigm in order to undertake a formal test of discriminability. A problem with this method is discussed later.

In order to demonstrate imitation, it is necessary to show that there is selectivity in the matching of infant to adult behaviors. It is not legitimate to conclude that imitation has occurred when infants engage in a particular gesture more often after they have seen the model perform this act than when the model was passive. The infant's behavior under such conditions may simply have been elicited by the social stimulation provided by an active model. To eliminate the possibility that what may seem to be duplication is simply a by-product of social stimulation or generalized arousal, imitation must be indexed in terms of selectivity in the relative frequency with which behaviors occur. Thus, infants should engage in a higher rate of tongue-protrusion after the model has demonstrated tongue-protrusion than mouth-opening, and at the same time a higher rate of mouth-opening after the model has demonstrated mouth-opening rather than tongue-protrusion.

The possibility that what may seem to be imitation is instead a fixed action pattern triggered by a sign stimulus incorporated within the modeled gesture needs also to be considered. In the most direct evaluation of this issue, Jacobson (1979) compared behavior after the infant had observed the model and an inanimate object that was moved in a manner that duplicated the gesture performed by the model. The indirect test undertaken by Meltzoff and Moore (1977) was based on the assumption that fixed action patterns are released immediately. Meltzoff and Moore studied delayed imitation by preventing an infant from engaging in the behavior that was to be copied over the period that the gesture was being modeled. A pacifier was kept in the infant's mouth while the model demonstrated mouth-opening or tongue-protrusion, and it was only when the gesture ceased that the pacifier was removed. Meltzoff (1981) has also argued that gestural duplication by infants lacks the rigid stereotypic properties that are characteristic of fixed action patterns.

The virtue of the paradigm developed by Meltzoff and Moore (1977) is that it offers an operational specification of imitation. The possibility that correspondence in adult-infant behavior is a product of reinforcement by the model, generalized arousal, or observer bias in behavioral classification can be eliminated. At the same time, there has not been complete uniformity in the methods used by investigators. In comments directed towards studies that have failed to provide evidence of neonatal imitation, Meltzoff and Moore (1983b, 1983c) placed considerable emphasis on procedural and measurement factors that they believe to be of critical importance. Their supposition is that investigators who fail to demonstrate imitation by young infants have used inappropriate or insensitive methods. Some of these claims are considered later. However, the issue of whether specific aspects of method are as critical for the demonstration of neonatal imitation as Meltzoff and Moore have supposed is one to be decided through research rather than by argument.

RESEARCH FINDINGS

In addition to studies confirming the report by Meltzoff and Moore (1977) that infants are capable of imitation, there are negative findings. The aim in the present section is to evaluate research that has been undertaken within the general paradigm described earlier. Attention is directed mainly to questions of design and procedure, as well as validity of interpretation.

In the first of the two experiments reported by Meltzoff and Moore (1977), six infants aged 12 to 17 days observed a model engaging in lip-protrusion, mouth-opening, tongue-protrusion, and sequential finger movement. Observers then tried to identify which gesture the model had performed by looking at infant behavior recorded in the 20 sec after completion of each gesture. Although these classifications proved to be accurate at a level above chance accuracy, infant behavior proved to be a noisy indicator of which action the model had demonstrated. McKenzie and Over (1983) used signal detection analysis to assess the strength of the relationships identified by Meltzoff and Moore. Discriminability measures (d') were established by calculating the observer's hit rate (probability of correctly reporting that gestures were of a specific kind) and false alarm rate (probability of incorrectly reporting that gestures were of a specific kind) for each of the gestures performed by the model. The discriminability values index the accuracy with which the observer, relying only on samples of infant behavior, could distinguish that the model had performed a specific gesture rather than one of the other three gestures. A d' value of zero signifies that the observer was not able to identify gestures at above chance accuracy, whereas a value of 3.00 or greater would signify a high level of discriminability. The observers used by Meltzoff and Moore performed only slightly better than chance in relying on samples of infant behavior to identify which gesture the model performed. The d' values were only 0.45 for mouth-opening (hit rate .18, false alarm rate .12), 0.25 for tongue-protrusion (hit rate .23, false alarm rate .17), and 0.40 for sequential finger movement (hit rate .20, false alarm rate .11).

In an attempted replication of Meltzoff and Moore, Koepke et al. (1983) found that the gesture performed by the model could not be identified from observation of infant behavior. McKenzie and Over (1983) reported that although tongue-protrusion could be differentiated from some other states of the model by reliance on information conveyed in infant behavior, active states of the model could not be distinguished from the passive state, nor facial gestures from manual gestures, nor one gesture from another belonging to the same class. The possibility that their results reflected insensitivity on the part of the observers was checked by McKenzie and Over. They compared the frequency and the duration of specific infant behaviors during and after execution of each gesture by the model. This further step yielded no evidence of similarities between infant behavior and the actions of the model.

Even if the discriminability indices in the above studies had been high, the observer may have been able to identify which gesture the model had performed from looking at the infant behavior without the infant having imitated the model. There could be a contingent relationship between the actions of the model and the infant without the two sets of behaviors being structurally similar or even related. For example, an observer may be able to differentiate states of the model by relying on eye-movements, pattern of fixation, or any characteristic that might vary in kind or frequency across gestures.

The objective of Meltzoff and Moore (1977) in their second experiment was to test for imitation by reference to structural similarity. Delayed imitation was assessed by comparing the relative frequencies of tongue-protrusion and mouth-opening following observation of each gesture and a passive face. The pacifier which had been placed in the infant's mouth to limit facial gestures during modeling was removed when the gesture had been demonstrated. Although Meltzoff and Moore claimed that both gestures were imitated, the 12 infants between them made only 12 mouth-openings in total over a period of 90 min. It is only for tongue-protrusion that data seemingly consistent with imitation were obtained.

In a cross-sectional analysis of 155 infants at 4–6, 10–12, 15–17, and 20–21 weeks-of-age, Abravanel and Sigafoos (1984) assessed imitation by scoring partial as well as complete duplication of gestures. In the first study none of the five gestures (tongue-protrusion, mouth-opening, eye-blinking, hand-opening, chest-tapping) performed by the model had selective influence on infant behavior. In the second study three gestures (tongue-protrusion, hand-opening, chin-tapping) were each modeled continuously over a 3-min period. Modeling of tongue-protrusion had no effect on complete tongue-protrusion by infants. Although infants at 4–6 weeks showed higher rates of partial tongue-protrusion, such selectivity was not evident at an older age. Because neither a linear nor a curvilinear developmental function was found, Abravanel and Sigafoos argued that the limited gestural correspondence observed at 4–6 weeks should be interpreted as a fixed action pattern rather than as imitative behavior.

In studies that were designed as replications of Meltzoff and Moore (1977), both Hayes and Watson (1981) and Koepke et al. (1983) found that the rate at which young infants engaged in mouth-opening or tongue-protrusion was independent of the gesture the model had demonstrated. McKenzie and Over (1983) found no evidence of structural correspondence in infant and adult behavior across manual as well as facial gestures. Hayes and Watson (1981) suggested that the delayed imitation claimed by Meltzoff and Moore was primarily artifactual. They showed that the type of behavior (mouth-opening vs. tongue-protrusion) in which infants engage after a pacifier has been removed from the mouth is related to the type of mouthing (passive release vs. tongue pressure) found just prior to removal of the pacifier. In noting that there was a subjective element in termination of the modeling period, Hayes and Watson (1981) argued that ". . . the fact that the modeler controlled the beginning of the response period could permit the experimenter to wait until the infant seemed more likely to emit the response that matched the model" (p. 657).

As noted above, whether or not neonates can imitate must be evaluated by reference to the relative frequency of behavior. Although Meltzoff and Moore (1977) reported statistical analyses showing that the extent of correspondence in adult-infant behavior over the testing session is only slightly higher than would be expected by chance, they, as did Field et al. (1982), included in their article "sample photographs" which might lead a reader to conclude that neonatal imitation is a robust phenomenon. In terms of the noisy relationships demonstrated through statistical analysis, it seems improbable that these photographs were drawn at random from the total set available. Both Hayes and Watson (1981) and McKenzie and Over (1983) noted correspondence within some of the segments they recorded, but in many other instances an infant engaged in one behavior when the model had performed a quite different gesture.

The recent study by Meltzoff and Moore (1983a) produced what seemingly is unequivocal evidence of neonatal imitation. Infants aged from 1 to 71 hours watched a model who alternated between an active and a passive state every 20 sec over a period of 4 min while demonstrating a gesture. Mouth-opening and tongue-protrusion were modeled, and for each gesture the behavior of infants was structurally similar to the action of the model at a level above chance expectancy. In contrast to the low rate of mouth-opening (0.15 times per min) found in the 1977 study, the infants in the 1983 experiment carried out this behavior an average of 1.56 times per min. The basis for such a difference is not clear, although Meltzoff and Moore (1983a) suggested that burst-pause stimulation over a 4-min period during modeling is much more salient than the stimulation provided when a single active state of 20 sec is followed by a passive state, during which the behavior of the infant is recorded. Unfortunately Meltzoff and Moore (1983a) did not report whether their data analysis was based on infant behavior coded throughout the 4-min period, only when the model was passive (as in the 1977 study), or only when the model was active. Comparison of infant behavior during active and passive states of the model bears on the question of whether gestural selectivity is best conceptualized in terms of fixed action patterns that are triggered by an immediate stimulus. Further, although they suggested that infants sometimes gradually approximated the response that was to be imitated, Meltzoff and Moore did not analyze temporal variation in infant behavior. The need for such fine-grain analysis is discussed later.

Field et al. (1982) reported that human neonates can imitate facial expressions. Unlike other investigators, Field et al. used an habituation paradigm to show that the gestures which were modeled could in fact be discriminated from each other by the infants. The infants (average age 36 hours) watched an adult demonstrate three facial expressions (happy, sad, surprised). Trials continued with a particular expression until habituation in visual fixation of the model's face occurred. Visual fixation was then monitored to establish whether dishabituation resulted when another facial expression was shown. Because dishabituation was found for each facial stimuli, the three expressions could be discriminated from each other. However, dishabituation simply means that change in information has been detected. It is not necessarily the case that the displays were distinguished by infants on the basis supposed by the experimenter.

In conjunction with the measurement of habituation, an infant's facial movements (brow, eyes, and mouth) were coded for each display by an observer. The facial movements of infants selectively matched the facial expressions that had been modeled. Thus, an infant exhibited widened eyes and wide mouth most often when surprise was being modeled, while lip widening was linked with the happy expression of the model. Tightened-mouth-protruding-lips accompanied by a furrowed brow occurred when the model adopted a sad expression. The possibility that response coding was open to observer bias must be kept in mind. The observer was able to identify which gesture had been modeled at a level of accuracy well above chance. Because the observer ". . . stood behind the model in order to see the infant's face" (p. 179), it cannot be certain that discrimination was based solely on information derived from infant behavior. The observer could, for example, have been influenced by the model's head or body movements in deciding whether the model was displaying a happy or a sad gesture.

It is clear from the statistical analyses reported by Field et al. (1982) that the facial movements of infants often did not match the expression displayed by the model. Similarly, not every infant demonstrated dishabituation for every expression. It is therefore important that the degree of selectivity in the facial movements exhibited by an infant be compared for expressions that had been discriminated relative to those that had not. No such analysis was attempted.

Neither Meltzoff and Moore (1983a) nor Field et al. (1982) provided a direct test of the possibility that the gestural selectivity they obtained can be conceptualized as a response released by a sign stimulus rather than as imitation. Results obtained by Jacobson (1979) point to the need for an explicit test of this possibility. Infants observed not only a model engaging in tongue-protrusion, but a white ball or a black felt-tip pen which was moved towards the infant over a distance and at a rate that approximated tongue-protrusion. Infants also watched an orange plastic ring being dangled as well as the model opening and closing one hand. Jacobson found that for infants aged 6 weeks the ball and the pen were as effective as exposure to modeling of tongue-protrusion in eliciting long-tongue protrusions by the infant. All three stimuli were more effective than observation of the moving hand or the ring. At 6 weeks hand opening occurred at a low rate, and it was not selective to modeling. The rate had increased by 14 weeks, when exposure to the ring was as effective as exposure to the model's hand. Both of these stimuli elicited higher rates of hand opening by the infant than did modeling of tongue-protrusion or display of either the pen or the ball.

In a second stage of testing, Jacobson requested mothers to model tongue-protrusion daily with their infants between 6- and 14-weeks-of-age. When they were subsequently tested, the infants demonstrated a higher rate of tongue-protrusion after this gesture had been modeled than when either the pen or the ball was displayed. However, because the training probably involved some degree of reinforcement and shaping of infant behavior by the mother, the selectivity to modeling that was found following training may well constitute what Piaget (1962) has termed pseudoimitation.

The implication from Jacobson's study is that exposure to a small object moving towards the mouth is sufficient to elicit tongue-protrusion by the neonate, just as observation of an object contracting or expanding within certain limits is presumably sufficient to elicit mouth-opening. However, it is questionable whether infant behavior which is selective simply to patterning within stimulation should be conceptualized as imitative. Even if infants sometimes duplicate the actions of a model, they may not have perceived, encoded, or reproduced the gestures as such. The suggestion by Meltzoff and Moore (1983c) that imitation entails crossmodal translation requires not that behaviors such as mouth-opening and tongue-protrusion can be passively elicited by visual expansion or contraction, but that the infant is actively attempting to reproduce what has been recognized and encoded as a motor sequence. To be performing in an imitative manner, the infant must be sensitive not just to transformations in stimulation, but to episodes that are categorized as events. Jacobson (1979) has shown that several different episodes, each entailing specific stimulation, can elicit mouth-opening and tongue-protrusion. It thus does not follow that infants who engage in mouth-opening or tongue-protrusion after observation of a model are responding to the event demonstrated by the model, rather than to specific stimulation. Although it is difficult to assess within the imitation paradigm whether infants are engaging in event perception, the issue is one of importance.

In commenting on several studies that failed to demonstrate neonatal imitation, Meltzoff and Moore (1983b, 1983c) have adopted the position that ". . . neonatal imitation can be elicited under certain conditions, but it may easily be obscured through procedural errors. Evidently neonates have the capacity to imitate; but one can arrange situations that are better or worse for eliciting and demonstrating the optimal behavioural performance of young infants'' (Meltzoff & Moore, 1983b, pp. 285–286). Some of the factors that they suggest are critical can be noted. Meltzoff and Moore contend that prior contact between the infant and the model reduces the saliency of the model. The lighting and background within the experimental situation should be arranged so that the infant's attention is centered on the model. The use of wide-range photography in recording infant behavior has been criticized on the grounds that fine motor movements will be missed. Meltzoff and Moore argue that only those behaviors that match exactly the gesture performed by the model should be taken as imitative. For example, they specify mouth-opening as ''. . . an abrupt jaw drop opening the mouth across the entire extent of the lips (followed by) the return of the lips to their closed resting position'' (Meltzoff & Moore, 1983a, p. 704). The implication is that use of a less stringent criterion (for example, an approximation to the model's gesture, or partial matching) in coding behavior will result in signals (imitative responses) being obscured by noise (ongoing activity that is not imitative). In contrast, it will be argued later that the focus in analysis should be on degree of similarity. Meltzoff and Moore may be defining as not worthy of investigation certain aspects of infant behavior that are in fact regulated by exposure to the model.

As noted earlier, it is an experimental issue as to whether the claims that Meltzoff and Moore have made about specific factors being critical for the demonstration of neonatal imitation are valid. The situation at present is that there are major discrepancies in research findings and conclusions. Claims made from some studies are contradicted by claims developed from other research. Since the different experiments have not entailed exact replication, it may be, as Meltzoff and Moore contend, that the diversity in findings reflects subtle differences in experimental conditions. If this conclusion is adopted, one objective in further research could be to attempt exact replication. An alternative is to diversify the paradigm and the conditions under which neonatal imitation is studied in order to gather convergent evidence on whether and why infants duplicate adult behaviors. In adopting this broader approach, it is useful to consider the literature on imitation by older infants.

IMITATION BY OLDER INFANTS

In studies yielding data generally consistent with Piaget's position on imitation, it has been found not only that different actions are most likely to be imitated at different ages, but infants often exhibit approximations to the modeled behavior well before the action is duplicated exactly. The degree of flexibility in timing and context that is demonstrated with older infants might suggest that imitative behavior has functional significance. Several writers have proposed that imitation occurs not simply because the infant has the capacity to duplicate an adult's behavior and does so, but because imitation is appropriate behavior on the part of an infant in the context of the infant's ongoing interaction with an adult. The proposition is that imitation is primarily a communicative activity which is not only elicited by social stimulation, but serves the function of regulating behavior within dyadic interaction.

In an experiment concerned with imitation, the model can be assigned one of two roles. In the intransitive case, the task of the model is simply to display gestures to the infant. The model is required to be insensitive to any of the infant's actions. Since it is questionable whether neutrality can be fully maintained in practice, the infant should perhaps see a filmed model rather than a live model. In the transitive case, the model is responsive to and able to interact with the infant, even though the model may be programmed to display specific gestures or to behave in a particular manner in the course of the interaction. Neonatal imitation has so far been studied only within the intransitive case.

Even when there has been intransitive modeling, imitation by older infants does not occur as though it were simply a by-product of information processing. Kaye and Marcus (1981), who tested infants each month from 6- to 12-months-of-age, found qualitative changes in imitation with age. Approximations became progressively closer to the structure of the gesture performed by the model. Further, ". . . the infants did not share our understanding about the divisions of the session into separate trials: They did not stop producing features of one task just because we had gone on to another task. What they did do, however, was nearly always perform a gesture for the first time during the appropriate task. After this occurrence, a feature was often performed later in the session, perhaps also with even greater frequency. It might then also occur in later sessions, even before the experimenter modeled the task of which it was supposed to be a feature" (p. 261).

Several investigators have noted that infants may fail to duplicate at an older age actions which they readily imitated at a younger age. For example, Abravanel et al. (1976) found that infants imitated facial gestures in complete form from about 9 months-of-age, but before long ". . . (infants) found the nonobject actions to be strange or atypical for an adult to model, and, accordingly, actively inhibited imitation. For example, we have the distinct impression that by 12 months and older some infants were perplexed by actions (of the model) involving tongue protrusion, shaking the head, and smacking the lips" (p. 1042). The implication is that actions are open to imitation only if they are appropriate to the norms of social exchange.

Pawlby (1977), who studied infants from 17 to 43 weeks during unstructured interaction with the mother, scored tapes to identify all instances where the behavior of an infant matched an action which the mother had just performed (MI sequence), or where the infant initiated the action and the mother followed (IM sequence). In all, imitative activity occurred over about one-sixth of the time that the mother and her infant spent in interaction. Sequences initiated by the mother predominated initially, and although they remained relatively stable in frequency over time, their nature changed. As infants grew older, IM sequences occurred more frequently. Further, there was a shift from duplication of facial and manual gestures to the display and imitation of activities involving the manipulation of toys. Speech sounds were also increasingly imitated. Sustained sequences occurred such that imitation seemed not just a response to a gesture, but itself a signal inviting a reply. Since there was mutual control (turn-taking) in mother-infant interaction involving imitation, Pawlby argued that the developmental course of imitative behavior by infants must be considered in the context of social communication.

FUNCTIONS OF IMITATION

In subjecting neonatal imitation to laboratory investigation, Meltzoff and Moore sought to avoid the problems that arise when imitation is studied at a descriptive level through observations of unstructured adult-infant interactions. The research paradigm used by Meltzoff and Moore was developed with emphasis on methodological rigor. Not only must procedures be standardized, but control conditions need to be used to eliminate the possibility of artifact. Imitation was defined in strictly operational terms. Infants can be said to imitate only if the frequency with which they engage in specific behaviors varies selectively with the gestures that the adult has modeled. The objective of research undertaken within this paradigm has been to ask not only whether neonatal imitation occurs, but how soon after birth it can be demonstrated. The youngest infant to be tested so far was 42 minutes-of-age!

The question of why neonates might imitate has had little impact on research methodology and strategy. In studies of neonatal imitation, it is as though a predetermined methodology has defined the phenomenon under investigation. Infants are brought into a strange situation where they come face-to-face with a strange adult for a brief period of time. Although the stereotyped actions performed by the adult may not necessarily be strange (in the sense of being unfamiliar to the infant), the adult behaves in a manner which is unique to the laboratory. The adult must act in accord with the experimenter's timetable, not the infant's. No matter what the infant does, the model is to remain noninteractive. In their quest for methodological rigor through operational definition, Meltzoff and Moore not only restricted the activities of the adult, but they disregarded what may be important aspects of infant behavior. Only actions of the infant that occur within a restricted period of time are scored, since attention is given solely to behaviors of the infant that match what the adult did. The possibility that infants engage in behavior, within or outside the defined period, in an attempt to initiate an adult-infant sequence has not been considered. Further, Meltzoff and Moore (1983b) continue to maintain that only behavior that constitutes an exact match to the modeled gestures should be scored. Nevertheless Meltzoff and Moore (1983a) noted that ''. . . infants corrected their responses over successive efforts, often beginning by producing partial approximations of the model—small tongue movements in the oral cavity (not scored as imitation according to the operational definitions used here)—and then converged toward more accurate matches of the adult's display over successive efforts'' (p. 707).

If gestural imitation serves social functions, the context in which neonatal imitation is most likely to be demonstrated is social interaction. In future studies the model should be allowed to do more than simply display gestures. At one limit, it can be asked whether there is adult-infant and infant-adult matching as well as turn-taking when the adult is allowed to engage in unstructured interaction with the infant. In contrast, the actions of the adult can be programmed so that the effects of different forms of adult responsiveness to infant behavior are open to assessment. Such conditions might include the case where the adult never duplicates a gesture performed by the infant, and the case where the actions of the adult mirror those of the infant. The importance of temporal aspects of contingency can also be assessed. The objective of such research should be not simply to establish whether infants copy what adults do, but to identify the influence that different aspects of adult-infant interaction, including feedback, have on duplication of adult behavior by infants. Because some conditions might elicit curiosity, surprise, or distress rather than imitation, a more diverse response classification than that used by Meltzoff and Moore is required. They in fact disqualified from their study any infant who exhibited distress or who seemed inattentive during modeling of the gestures. The response coding system must also be sensitive to gradations in behavior so that approximations to imitation can be assessed.

Neonatal imitation has to date been evaluated by observing the behavior of infants over a matter of minutes. In most studies a single trial has typically lasted less than 1 minute. Imitation needs instead to be studied in the context of extended interaction, and preferably within a developmental design. In addition, the adult serving as the model has characteristically been a stranger to the infant. The issue of whether an infant's history of interaction with the adult affects the likelihood of imitation is only one of many questions that are concerned with the situational and contextual specificity of imitation.

The proposal is not that laboratory investigation of neonatal imitation be discontinued, but that the paradigm within which imitation is examined be made more ecologically valid. The modifications that have been proposed do not necessarily entail loss of experimental rigor. Blind methodology can still be used in scoring infant and adult behaviors. Operational specification of behavior can be maintained, although a more detailed and complex response code will be needed. Imitation will still be assessed by determining whether a particular action is more likely to be performed by an infant in association with certain behavior of an adult rather than other behavior. Controls for artifact can be employed. When imitation during social interaction is studied, the issue of whether learning is involved can be evaluated by comparing the relationships found when different contingencies have been in operation. The question of whether infants are responding to events rather than simply to transformations in stimulation is open to study by presenting in place of the model an inanimate object which undergoes specific transformations. As an example, Frye, Rawling, Moore, Myers, and Myers (1983) studied social selectivity by comparing the behavior of infants to an episode (approach-withdrawal) involving an adult and the same sequence of stimulation involving an object. Infants behaved differently to the two circumstances at 10 months-of-age, but not at 3 months. As a further research strategy, transformations can be made contingent on infant behavior.

CONCLUSIONS

My objective in this chapter has been not only to review research on gestural imitation by neonates, but to ask why young infants might be expected to imitate gestures such as tongue-protrusion and mouth-opening. Although it would not be meaningful to ask why infants imitate without having demonstrated that they do imitate, consideration of the functional significance of imitation is necessary to identify the context in which the capacity for imitation should be studied. Noenatal imitation has only recently been subjected to systematic examination, and the research to date has employed the intransitive modeling paradigm developed by Meltzoff and Moore (1977). The different studies have yielded far from uniform results, and there is no strong empirical basis for the claim that human neonates imitate facial and manual gestures. Although some studies have demonstrated correspondence between the behaviors of an infant and the model, it is a matter of dispute as to whether the correspondence, which typically has been limited in extent, is best conceptualized in terms of imitation.

The concern in recent research has been with whether effects reported by Meltzoff and Moore (1977) can be replicated. It will be more profitable, however, to diversify the paradigm under which imitation is studied in order to gather convergent evidence on whether and why young infants duplicate adult gestures. The question of whether human neonates engage in imitation needs to be studied in the context of social interaction and communication.

REFERENCES

Abravanel, E., Levan-Goldschmidt, E., & Stevenson, M. B. (1976). Action imitation: The early phase of infancy. *Child Development, 47,* 1032–1044.

Abravanel, E., & Sigafoos, A. D. (1984). Exploring the presence of imitation during early infancy. *Child Development, 55,* 381–392.

Atkinson, J., Braddick, O., & Moar, K. (1977). Development of contrast sensitivity over the first three months of life in the human infant. *Vision Research, 17,* 1037–1044.

Field, T. M., Woodson, R., Greenberg, R., & Cohen, D. (1982). Discrimination and imitation of facial expressions by neonates. *Science, 218,* 179–181.

Gardner, J., & Gardner, H. (1970). A note on selective imitation by a six-week-old infant. *Child Development, 41,* 1209–1213.

Hayes, L. A., & Watson, J. S. (1981). Neonatal imitation: Fact or artifact? *Developmental Psychology, 17,* 655–660.

Jacobson, S. W. (1979). Matching behavior in the young infant. *Child Development, 50,* 425–430.

Kaye, K., & Marcus, J. (1981). Infant imitation: The sensori-motor agenda. *Developmental Psychology, 17,* 258–265.

Koepke, J. E., Hamm, M., Legerstee, M., & Russell, M. (1983). Neonatal imitation: Two failures to replicate. *Infant Behavior and Development, 6,* 97–102.

McKenzie, B., & Over, R. (1983). Young infants fail to imitate facial and manual gestures. *Infant Behavior and Development, 6,* 85–96.

Meltzoff, A. N. (1981). Imitation, intermodal coordination, and representation in early infancy. In G. Butterworth (Ed.), *Infancy and epistemology.* Brighton: Harvester.

Meltzoff, A. N., & Moore, M. K. (1977). Imitation of facial and manual gestures by human neonates. *Science, 198,* 75–78.

Meltzoff, A. N., & Moore, M. K. (1983a). Newborn infants imitate adult facial gestures. *Child Development, 54,* 702–709.

Meltzoff, A. N., & Moore, M. K. (1983b). The origins of imitation in infancy: Paradigm, phenomena, and theories. In L. P. Lipsitt & C. Rovee-Collier (Eds.), *Advances in infancy research* (Vol. 2). Norwood, NJ: Ablex.

Meltzoff, A. N., & Moore, M. K. (1983c). Methodological issues in studies of imitation: Comments on McKenzie and Over and Koepke et al. *Infant Behavior and Development, 6,* 103–108.

Pawlby, S. J. (1977). Imitative interaction. In H. R. Schaffer (Ed.), *Studies in mother-infant interaction.* London: Academic Press.

Piaget, J. (1962). *Play, dreams, and imitation in childhood.* New York: Norton.

Uzgiris, I. C. (1972). Patterns of vocal and gestural imitation in infants. In F. J. Monks, W. W. Hartup, & J. deWitt (Eds.), *Determinants of behavioral development.* Orlando, FL: Academic Press.

Uzgiris, I. C., & Hunt, J. McV. (1975). *Assessment in infancy.* Urbana: University of Illinois Press.

IV SPEECH PERCEPTION

11 The Development of the Categorical Identification of Speech

Denis K. Burnham
Lynda J. Earnshaw
Maria C. Quinn
University of New South Wales

INTRODUCTION

Two important developments have provided impetus for research on speech perception. The first, almost 3 decades ago, was the development at Haskins laboratories of rules for synthesizing speech at the phoneme level (Liberman, Ingemann, Lisker, Delattre, & Cooper, 1959). From this came the finding that speech sounds which vary continuously along certain dimensions are perceived categorically by adults. That is, adults' ability to discriminate between sounds on various continua was found to be limited by their ability to label or identify such sounds as belonging to different categories (Liberman, Harris, Hoffman, & Griffiths, 1957). This was taken as evidence for a special form of processing of speech by adults. In 1971 the second important development occurred when Eimas, Siqueland, Jusczyk, and Vigorito introduced a method to study speech discrimination in infancy. They found that infants as young as 1 month discriminate speech categorically, which strongly suggested that the special manner in which humans process speech is innate. This chapter is concerned with these two claims and their subsequent modification. We also report research that we believe has an important bearing on these claims.

The claim that speech perception is categorical rests on the limiting effect that phonetic identity is supposed to have upon listeners' ability to discriminate between sounds. However, due to procedural difficulties, identification of speech continua by infants has not been investigated effectively. The claim that humans innately perceive and process speech in a special manner is now questioned and it is believed that linguistic experience is involved to some extent. Nevertheless, mainly infant-adult and some child-adult studies have been conducted. No single study has investigated speech perception across development from infancy to prelinguistic childhood to postlinguistic childhood to adulthood. Furthermore, in the main, only contrasts which are phonemic[1] in the child's primary linguistic environment have been investigated. For a comprehensive view, the development of speech perception for both phonemic and nonphonemic contrasts should be studied across the various stages of linguistic development. These problems are overcome in the research reported later in this chapter in which infants, 2-year-olds, 6-years-olds, and adults are tested for their identification of phonemic and nonphonemic speech contrasts.

This chapter is concerned with two main themes—the *identification* of speech sounds, and the *development* of speech perception.[2] The chapter is organized into six sections. Following this introduction, we define categorical perception and present the results of early studies with infants and adults. A brief review of subsequent work shows that the categorical discrimination of speech by infants does not constitute evidence for a special innate mode of speech processing in humans. In the third section we consider the evolution of language and the ontogenetic development of speech perception in humans. Theories from each of these areas and empirical evidence regarding ontogenetic development suggest that speech perception is initially psychoacoustic in nature and only comes to have a phonological basis as a result of experience. Following this, methodological issues regarding infant discrimination procedures, the differences between infant and adult procedures, and the differences between discrimination and identification are described. Consideration of these issues demonstrates the need for an infant speech identification procedure. Finally, we present the results of the first study to use an infant speech identification procedure successfully. Evidence from this study suggests that perception of speech in infancy is *not* truly categorical but becomes increasingly so with experience, especially with

---

[1]A phonemic contrast is one which is meaningful or phonologically relevant in the particular language in question. For example, the difference between /b/ and /p/ in English is phonemic because substitution of one for the other, e.g., in 'bin' versus 'pin', involves a change of meaning. On the other hand the aspirated phone [pʰ] as in 'pin' and the unaspirated phone [p] as in spin are both examples of the phoneme /p/. Thus in English this phonetic difference is nonphonemic. In this chapter the distinction between phonemic and nonphonemic contrasts is vital but the distinction between phonetic and phonemic levels of processing is not. Therefore the term *phonological* is usually used to refer to both levels and its use is meant to contrast with the term *psychoacoustic* (see footnote 4).

[2]The interested reader may like to consult Aslin, Pisoni, and Jusczyk (1983) for a comprehensive review of auditory and speech perception development in infancy; Aslin and Pisoni (1980b) and Walley, Pisoni and Aslin (1981) regarding developmental processes and the role of experience; Morse (1978) and Kuhl (1978) on phylogenetic and evolutionary aspects of speech perception and also on context effects and perceptual constancy; Eilers (1980) and Aslin and Pisoni (1980b) for systematic reviews of research on the various types of speech contrasts; and Eilers (1980) and Morse (1978) regarding further questions of method.

the active experience involved in language acquisition between 2 and 6 years. Summary and conclusions are then provided.

CATEGORICAL PERCEPTION

Definition of Categorical Speech Perception and Studies of Adults

Categorical perception is the tendency to perceive a physical continuum discontinuously, i.e., for the relevant perceptual system to group stimuli on a continuum such that discrete categories are perceived. Within such categories, stimuli taken from various points along the continuum are perceived to be similar and are discriminated only with difficulty, while stimuli taken from different categories are discriminated with ease. For instance, both adults and infants categorically perceive the physical continuum of visible wavelengths as separate hues with quite sharp category boundaries (Bornstein, Kessen, & Weiskopf, 1976).

In a similar fashion, speech sounds synthesized so as to vary along physical continua are perceived categorically. Researchers have taken a somewhat stronger view of categorical perception where speech is concerned, claiming that discriminative ability is limited *completely* by the listener's ability to identify the sounds with different phonemic labels. Both *identification* (labeling) and *discrimination* functions are required in order to determine whether areas of discriminability coincide with boundaries between sounds that are identified differently (Studdert-Kennedy, Liberman, Harris, & Cooper, 1970). Results in accord with this view have been found for various continua along which speech sounds vary. For example, consonants can vary in their place of articulation, i.e., the locus of maximum airstream constriction, such that the locus is the lips, e.g., the bilabial /b/; the tongue tip and the alveolar ridge, e.g., the alveolar /d/; or the back of the tongue and the velum, e.g., the velar /g/. Consonants can also vary in voicing, or more quantitatively, voice onset time (VOT), which is the time between the release burst and the onset of larangeal pulsing. For example, a bilabial can be voiced /b/, voiceless /p/, or even prevoiced /-b/ in some languages. Early research in speech perception revealed that consonants are perceived categorically when they vary along the place of articulation continuum with voicing constant (Liberman, Harris, Hoffman, & Griffith, 1957), or when they vary along the VOT continuum with place of articulation constant (Liberman, Harris, Kinney, & Lane, 1961; Lisker & Abramson, 1964). Such results were taken to indicate that speech is processed in a special manner by humans (Liberman, Cooper, Shankweiler, & Studdert-Kennedy, 1967; Liberman, 1970; Mattingly, Liberman, Syrdal, & Halwes, 1971).

Categorical Speech Perception in Infancy

Eimas, Siqueland, Jusczyk, and Vigorito (1971) introduced the high-amplitude sucking (HAS) procedure for investigating speech perception by infants. In this procedure infants are conditioned to suck a nonnutritive nipple at consistently high rates for the presentation of a certain auditory stimulus. Familiarization with this sound typically results in habituation of the high-amplitude sucking. After habituation, any dishabituation of high-amplitude sucking when a second sound replaces the first is interpreted as showing that the infants recognize the second sound as novel and discriminate between the two sounds. Failure to dishabituate can be interpreted in a number of ways, one of which is that the infants fail to discriminate between the two sounds. Using this HAS procedure Eimas et al. (1971) discovered that 1- and 4-month-old human infants discriminate between bilabial stop consonants in a categorical manner. (Since these original findings, similar evidence for categorical discrimination has been found for many different speech contrasts—see, for example, Aslin & Pisoni, 1980b; Aslin et al., 1983; and Eilers, 1980.) On the basis of these findings Eimas et al., drew three conclusions:

1. that infants perceive speech in a manner approximating categorical perception,
2. that the mechanisms underlying such perception may well be innate in humans, and
3. that human infants perceive speech in a linguistic mode.

The implications of Eimas' findings and conclusions are far-reaching. Before 1971 the categorical perception of speech sounds, and thus any special processing that speech sounds might undergo, was assumed to be the result of extensive linguistic experience. Eimas' discovery raised the possibility that such experience is not necessary and that infants are biologically tuned to perceive speech in some selective and special manner. This interpretation sat well with the popular notion at the time that there is an innate species-specific language acquisition device which facilitates language acquisition in humans (Chomsky, 1965).

The original study by Eimas and similar studies that followed are still taken to indicate categorical discrimination of speech sounds by human infants. However, all three conclusions which Eimas drew have been criticized. Let us briefly consider each of these. His third conclusion, that human infants perceive speech in a linguistic mode, has three implications: (a) that the categorization of speech sounds is unique to humans, (b) that categorization of auditory stimuli is specific to speech sounds, and (c) that speech perception proceeds by way of feature detectors tuned to respond to peculiarly phonetic features. There are problems with each of these implications. Contrary to the species specificity implication, it has been discovered that chinchillas (Kuhl & Miller, 1975, 1978), and macaque (Kuhl & Padden, 1982, 1983) and rhesus monkeys (Morse & Snowdon, 1975) perceive speech sounds categorically. Contrary to the signal specificity implication, it has been found that music-like sounds which vary continuously in rise-time are categorized into "plucks" and "bows" both by adults (Cutting & Rosner, 1974) and infants (Jusczyk, Rosner, Cutting, Foard, & Smith, 1977).[3] In addition, two-tone complexes which vary continuously in tone onset time (TOT) are perceived categorically both by adults (Pisoni, 1977) and infants (Juszcyk, Pisoni, Walley, & Murray, 1980). Regarding the feature detector implication Eimas (1975, 1978) argues for phonetic feature detectors on the basis of selective adaptation effects with adults (Cooper, 1979; Eimas, Cooper & Corbit, 1973; Eimas & Corbit, 1973). Contrary to Eimas' argument Pisoni and Tash (1975) have suggested an auditory explanation of the results of selective adaptation studies. Remez (1975) and Simon and Studdert-Kennedy (1978) have also questioned Eimas' claims. In addition, as Eimas (1975) acknowledges, selective adaptation studies have not yet been possible with infants.

The second conclusion that Eimas et al. (1971) drew from their results was that categorical speech perception is innate in humans. In its extreme form this would imply that there is no role for linguistic experience in the development of speech perception. Research conducted since 1971 has shown such a strong claim to be untenable: linguistic experience does modify categorical speech perception. This is one of the two major themes of this chapter and evidence regarding the development of categorical speech perception is considered in detail in the next section.

The first conclusion that Eimas et al. (1971) drew from their results, and one that underlies the others, was that their results indicate categorical perception of speech in infancy. This claim can be questioned because until now no identification functions for the perception of speech continua in infancy have been obtained. Furthermore, there are now grave doubts that even adult speech perception is categorical in the sense defined by Studdert-Kennedy et al. (1970). It may be more like the categorical perception of hue where discriminably different hues, e.g., orangey-yellow and greeny-yellow, are still identified as the same color, i.e., yellow. The need for identification functions in infancy is the second major theme of this chapter and research and issues concerning this are considered in the section on methodological issues.

---

[3]However, note recent evidence that this continuum is not perceived categorically (Rosen & Howell, 1981) and even later evidence that it is only perceived categorically under certain conditions (Cutting, 1982). Such evidence does not affect results regarding the categorical perception of other nonspeech sounds such as noise-buzz sequences and two-tone complexes which vary in TOT.

DEVELOPMENT OF CATEGORICAL PERCEPTION
OF SPEECH

Evidence that categorical perception is not peculiar to speech or peculiar to humans suggests that there is some role for linguistic experience in the development of speech perception. This has implications for both the evolution of language and the ontogenetic development of speech.

Evolution of Language

Evolutionary influences on human speech capacities have been studied primarily with regard to production (Stevens, 1972) rather than perception and thus there has been little theoretical speculation about the phylogenetic development of categorical perception. However, Kuhl (1978) has offered some suggestions. She accepts the notion that categorical perception can be explained in terms of psychoacoustic processes (Cutting & Rosner, 1974; Hirsh, 1959; Jusczyk et al., 1977, 1980; Pisoni, 1977). Some acoustic continua may be automatically partitioned into "natural categories" by the human auditory system because changes along such continua are only perceived if they cross a kind of perceptual threshold. This process is seen to be psychoacoustic[4] in nature rather than phonetic because animals with similar auditory systems to our own similarly categorize speech sounds (Kuhl & Miller, 1975, 1978; Kuhl & Padden, 1982, 1983; Morse & Snowdon, 1975). Kuhl (1978) further suggests that continua with these properties were selected for in the evolution of language systems, i.e., that speech is not perceived categorically because it is speech, but that speech *is* speech because it is perceived categorically. Thus, the development of language systems by humans did not depend only on articulatory constraints but upon how possible articulations are perceived by the auditory system.

If Kuhl's ideas are correct then certain predictions about categorical perception over both phylogeny and ontogeny follow. In the case of phylogeny it seems reasonable to expect that mammals (including humans) should be more likely to perceive categorically those contrasts which are phonemic over a large number of languages (e.g., the voiced and voiceless categories of stop consonants—Lisker & Abramson, 1964) rather than those not so universal across languages. This is yet to be tested empirically.

With regard to ontogeny it would seem reasonable to expect that if language has been tailored to accommodate the human auditory system, and if speech continues to be psychoacoustically based up to adulthood, the categories perceived by infants and by adults should have the same boundaries. If this on-

---

[4]*Psychoacoustic* here means having to do with the interaction of acoustic (not necessarily phonetic) dimensions and the human (or a similar) auditory system. It is a particular application of the generic term *psychophysical*.

togenetic prediction were not upheld and it was still wished to maintain Kuhl's position, one of two assumptions would need to be adopted. First, it could be assumed that differences between infant and adult categories are due to maturation or general sharpening of the auditory system. Second, it could be assumed that the natural categories perceived by infants, which by Kuhl's definition should be based on psychoacoustic attributes of sounds, have undergone a boundary shift by adulthood due to linguistic experience. Thus, it is conceivable that natural psychoacoustically based categories gradually come to have a more phonological basis as a result of specific linguistic experience. Therefore, it can be seen that while there may be an evolutionary phylogenetic basis for categorical perception, a complex interplay of the initial state of the auditory system, its general maturation and improvement over time, and of specific linguistic experience may take place. It is this complex interplay to which we now turn our attention.

Ontogenetic Development

Trehub (1979) and Aslin and Pisoni (1980b) observed that there is a need for developmental studies to trace the ontogeny of speech perception. At present it is very difficult to piece together the various studies with infants of a variety of ages in various linguistic environments. Improvement in speech synthesis during the years spanned by these studies further hinders comparison. In addition, there are problems such as the lack of identification data in infant studies, and the questionable comparability of adult and infant data and of different infant discrimination procedures.

Until recently there has also been some conceptual confusion about the specific role which experience might play in speech perception development. This confusion has largely been allayed by an organizational framework set up by Aslin and his colleagues. Aslin (1981; Aslin & Pisoni, 1980b; Aslin, Pisoni, & Jusczyk, 1983; Walley, Pisoni, & Aslin, 1981) has differentiated between four different theories. These are maturation theory and three theories concerned with experiential processes—perceptual learning theory, universal theory, and attunement theory. Each of these differs in terms of the degree of perceptual expertise assumed to be available to the infant at birth, and on the influence which linguistic experience has on perceptual development. Evidence relevant to each of these approaches is considered in turn.

Maturation

In a maturational account of speech perception development the ability to discriminate a particular phonetic contrast is assumed to be independent of any specific early experience. Instead, it is proposed that development occurs in accordance with some predetermined sequence. In its extreme form, this view results in two predictions. First, there should be no differences in the perception of phonologically relevant and irrelevant contrasts. Second, there should be consistent developmental change in discrimination of contrasts irrespective of whether they are relevant in the particular linguistic environment.

Evidence consistent with the first prediction has come from studies investigating discrimination of bilabial stops by infants from non-English speaking communities. Lasky, Syrdal-Lasky, and Klein (1975) used the heartrate (HR) deceleration procedure to test 4- to 6½-month-old Guatemalan infants from a Spanish language environment. (The HR procedure is similar to the HAS procedure, the main difference being that another response is used.) Streeter (1976b) tested 2-month-old Kikuyu infants with the HAS paradigm. The voiced /b/ versus voiceless /p/ distinction in bilabial stops is not phonologically relevant in either Spanish or Kikuyu. The Spanish phonemic boundary for the bilabial stop VOT continuum occurs at approximately 0 msec VOT, i.e., between previoced prevoiced /-b/ and voiced /b/ regions of the continuum. In Kikuyu there exists only one bilabial stop, a prevoiced /-b/ with an average VOT of −64 msec. Despite this, infants from both of these language backgrounds exhibited heightened discriminability at two regions along the voicing dimension, corresponding to the prevoiced/voiced and voiced/voiceless boundaries. The Guatemalan infants discriminated contrasts of +20 versus +60 msec VOT, and −20 versus −60 msec VOT, but were unable to discriminate a contrast which crossed the adult Spanish phonemic boundary, i.e., −20 versus +20 msec VOT (Lasky et al., 1975). Kikuyu infants were able to discriminate contrasts of −30 versus 0 msec VOT, and +10 versus +40 msec VOT, but a contrast of +50 versus +80 (within an English phonemic category) was not reliably discriminated. Similar cross-language results have been obtained for adults. Adult speakers of Kikuyu (Streeter, 1976a) and Spanish (Williams, 1977a, 1977b) are also capable of discriminating a voiced/voiceless bilabial stop distinction which crosses the English boundary but which is not phonemic in either Kikuyu or Spanish.

These results show that there is sensitivity to the voiced/voiceless distinction even when it is not phonemic in the listener's language. Is the same true when the prevoiced/voiced distinction is nonphonemic in the listener's language? Studies by Eilers and her colleagues suggest not (Eilers, Wilson, & Moore, 1979; Eilers, Gavin, & Wilson, 1979). They used a visually reinforced infant speech discrimination (VRISD) procedure in which a head-turn to a change in a repeating background stimulus is reinforced visually. In their experiment 6- to 8-month-old infants from Spanish-speaking and English-speaking families were presented with a contrast which crossed the Spanish adult phoneme boundary (−20 versus +10 msec VOT), and one which crossed the English adult phoneme boundary (+10 versus +40 msec VOT). While the Spanish infants demonstrated reliable discrimination of both contrasts, the English infants were only capable of discriminating the contrast which crossed the English voiced/voiceless boundary.

This suggests that the ability to perceive the prevoiced/voiced contrast in infancy requires specific early experience.

However, Eilers' studies (Eilers, Wilson, & Moore, 1979; Eilers, Gavin, & Wilson, 1979) have been criticized on various grounds (Aslin & Pisoni, 1980a; see also the reply by Eilers, Gavin, & Wilson, 1980). In a later study Aslin, Pisoni, Hennessy, and Perey (1981) investigated cross-language discrimination on the bilabial VOT continuum using a more rigorous procedure. English infants between 6 and 12 months reliably discriminated the phonemic voiced/voiceless distinction. Infants also reliably discriminated the nonphonemic (in English) prevoiced/voiced distinction, though their discriminative sensitivity at this boundary was less than at the voiced/voiceless boundary. They also found similar results for English-speaking adults. However, it is important to note that comparison of infant and adult discrimination functions suggested that the adults' perception of the phonemic but not the nonphonemic distinction had been modified by experience. (This finding is discussed in more detail later with regard to attunement theory.) This result is inconsistent with the second prediction of maturation theory.

Together these results provide some evidence for the first prediction of the maturational view of speech perception development. That is to say, studies have shown perception of the distinction between both phonemic and nonphonemic contrasts by both infants and adults (Aslin et al., 1981; Lasky et al., 1975; Streeter, 1976a, 1976b; Williams, 1977a, 1977b). This suggests an independence of speech perception processes from specific early experience. However, the second prediction, that there should be consistent developmental change for both phonemic and nonphonemic contrasts, has not been upheld, as Aslin et al. (1981) have found selective improvement in discrimination of a phonemic contrast between infancy and adulthood. This finding suggests that specific linguistic experience is involved in speech perception development. For maturational processes to be the *sole* cause of any development of speech perception it is necessary that *both* predictions are upheld. As the second prediction is not upheld the data presented above are not inconsistent with the view that experience modifies speech perception.

Induction due to Experience: Perceptual Learning Theory

According to perceptual learning theory, speech perception abilities are undeveloped at birth and specific early experience with any given contrast is essential if that contrast is to be discriminated by infants or adults. One of the main implications of this view is that phonologically irrelevant contrasts will never be discriminated due to the paucity or absence of these contrasts in the listener's linguistic environment. Quite clearly this view is not upheld by research reviewed earlier which demonstrated infants' ability to discriminate phonologically irrelevant speech contrasts (Aslin et al., 1981; Eilers, Gavin, & Wilson, 1979; Lasky et al., 1975; Streeter, 1976b). Thus, it appears that the ability to perceive speech contrasts does not necessarily require induction by prior linguistic experience.

Maintenance by Experience: Universal Theory

In universal theory all contrasts are discriminable at birth and experience maintains this ability. The theory is most clearly defined by its corollary in which lack of specific linguistic experience with a certain contrast results in the selective loss of perceptual ability with that contrast. Thus, universal theory would predict that infants should perceive all possible speech contrasts while adults should only perceive those that are phonemic in their native language.

Evidence cited above showing the perception of nonphonemic contrasts by adults clearly argues against this theory (Aslin et al., 1981; Streeter, 1976a; Williams,1977a, 1977b). However, there is other evidence consistent with universal theory. Eimas (1975) has demonstrated that English language environment infants of 2- to 3-months can discriminate the liquids /r/ and /l/, and has suggested that this ability may be present at birth. Adult English speakers are also capable of making this discrimination. However, Miyawaki, Strange, Verbrugge, Liberman, Jenkins, and Fujimura (1975) have demonstrated that Japanese adults, for whom the /r/ versus /l/ contrast is not phonologically relevant, can not discriminate the two sounds. It has also been found that young infants from an English language environment reliably discriminate the strident distinction between the fricatives /z/ and /ř/ (phonemic in Czech) while their adult counterparts were confused about the distinction (Trehub, 1976). Universal theory would attribute these inabilities respectively to the lack of the /r/ versus /l/ distinction in the Japanese language and the /z/ versus /ř/ distinction in the English language.

A series of developmental studies with stop consonants by Werker and Tees and their colleagues also support universal theory. They obtained similar results for two contrasts, the dental stop /t/ versus the retroflex stop /ʈ/ (Werker et al., 1981; Werker & Tees, 1984), and the velar stop /k̇/ versus the uvular stop /q̇/ (Werker & Tees, 1983, 1984). The /t/ versus /ʈ/ contrast is phonemic in Hindi but not Englsih, while /k̇/ versus /q̇/ is phonemic in Thompson (spoken by North American Indians) but not English.[5] Seven-month-old English language environment infants could discriminate both contrast, as could members of the relevant adult populations (Hindi and Salish respectively) (Werker et al., 1981; Werker & Tees, 1984). However, for both contrasts there was a progressive loss of discriminative ability from 7- to 9- to 11-months (Werker & Tees, 1984). These losses

---

[5]The sound [ʈ] is produced by curling the tongue back and placing the tongue tip posterior to the alveolar ridge prior to the release burst; [q̇] is produced by stopping the airflow prior to release with the back of the tongue behind the velum, rather than against the velum as is the case in [k].

appear to be permanent as English-speaking adults could discriminate neither contrast. In addition, 4-, 8-, and 12-year-old English-speaking children could not discriminate the /t/ versus /ṭ/ contrast (Werker & Tees, 1983). Thus, both of these unusual contrasts are discriminated early in life but are lost permanently in the second half of the first year if specific linguistic experience is absent.

Werker and Tees have also investigated the ontogenetic modulation of discrimination of the voiceless aspirated dental stop /tʰ/ versus the voiced breathy dental stop /dʰ/ (VOT 130 and −120 msec respectively). This contrast is phonemic in Hindi and more common in natural languages than the other stops they tested but is nevertheless not phonemic in English. Werker et al. (1981) found that 100% of their adult Hindis and 83% of their 7-month-old English language environment infants perceived this contrast. Only 40% of English-speaking adults perceived the contrast but with additional training this improved to 70%. In a follow-up study with children Werker and Tees (1983) found that none of their sample of 12 4-year-olds could perceive the contrast, while 33% of 8- and 12-year-olds could do so—a percentage similar to the untrained adults. Thus, in support of universal theory, the ability to perceive /dʰ/ versus /tʰ/ is present for infants but is lost by 4 years if it is not phonologically relevant in the language environment. However, inconsistent with universal theory, there is a partial resurgence of this ability by at least 8 years and training with the contrast is effective with adults. This curvilinear developmental trend is unexpected. It is discussed further in relation to a similar trend in our own data.

There is support for universal theory with some contrasts. However, for many speech contrasts universal theory is either not applicable or only partially applicable as adults can discriminate some nonphonemic contrasts. The ability to discriminate nonphonemic contrasts is not inconsistent with the final theory to be considered.

Facilitation by Specific Linguistic Experience: Attunement Theory

According to attunement theory specific linguistic experience enhances, realigns, or sharpens the boundaries between categories for which discriminative abilities are incompletely developed at birth. This theory allows that infants and adults may perceive both phonemic and nonphonemic contrasts. It implies that infants' and adults' perception of nonphonemic contrasts will be equivalent, but that at least for some phonemic contrasts boundaries will become enhanced, realigned, or sharpened over development. There is evidence that all three of these attunement processes occur.

Enhancement. Eilers and Minifie (1975) studied 1- to 4-month-old infants' perception of naturally produced fricatives using an HAS procedure. They found that some contrasts could be discriminated, e.g., /s/ versus /v/, and /ʃ/ versus /s/ (as in ship and sip respectively). However the /s/ versus /z/ contrast could not be discriminated. It is likely that this lack of discrimination between a voiceless and a voiced fricative early in life can be accounted for by attunement theory, a possibility which is supported by further research. Eilers, Wilson, and Moore (1977) used their VRISD procedure to study the development of the perception of fricatives by infants in two age groups, 6 to 8 months and 12 to 14 months. Infants of both ages discriminated the /s/ versus /z/ contrast which suggests that this discriminative ability had developed between 4 (Eilers & Minifie, 1975) and 6 months (Eilers et al., 1977). However, different methods were used in the two studies. In addition, the study in which no discrimination was found (Eilers & Minifie, 1975) employed the HAS procedure. It is difficult to interpret negative results unequivocally when this procedure is used (see section on methodological issues).

Better evidence for the progressive development of enhanced discriminative abilities comes from further studies by Eilers et al. (1977). Using the VRISD procedure for each age group, it was found that while 6- to 8-month-old infants generally did not discriminate the fricatives /f/ and /θ/ (as in fought and thought respectively), 12- to 14-month-old infants did discriminate between these sounds. This evidence for enhanced discriminative ability over age is quite compelling because the same method was used with each age group. In addition, the negative results of the younger infants were not due to their inability to respond because the method revealed discrimination of other contrasts by both age groups, e.g., /s/ versus /z/. Is this developmental improvement due to maturation of an ability or to the enhancing effects of repeated linguistic experience with the specific contrast? Results of a study by Holmberg, Morgan, and Kuhl (1977) suggest the latter. They found that 6-month-old infants given extensive training on the /f/ versus /θ/ contrast ($\bar{X} = 68$ trials) did actually discriminate the difference. This extensive training presumably caused a short-term enhancement of infants' discriminative abilities. In the natural course of events this attunement process probably takes much longer.

Evidence presented here could be seen to support an inducing rather than an enhancing role of experience. The evidence has been taken to support enhancement here because some fricative contrasts are perceived while others are not, indicating some sensitivity to fricative differences. Final differentiation between enhancement and induction can only come with more sensitive test techniques.

Realignment.   There is also evidence for the realignment of category boundaries as a function of linguistic experience. On the VOT continuum Spanish adults do not naturally discriminate between bilabials with different positive VOT values as they have only one bilabial boundary at about 0 msec VOT. On the other hand, English adults discriminate between bilabials on either side of a +25 msec boundary and Thai adults do the same on either side of a +40 msec boundary (Lisker & Abramson, 1964). It appears that the boundary in infancy is around +20 to +40 msec VOT (Aslin et al., 1981; Eimas et al., 1971; Lasky et al., 1975; Streeter, 1976b) for English, Spanish, and Kikuyu infants. From this apparently universal threshold value in infancy (a "natural" threshold in Kuhl's terms), linguistic experience presumably affects the boundary value differently depending upon the linguistic environment. In fact there is evidence that Spanish infants discriminate between tokens on either side of the natural boundary (in a +20 versus +60 msec VOT test) but not between tokens on either side of the boundary used by their parents (in a −20 versus +20 msec VOT test) (Lasky et al., 1975).

Sharpening.   The sharpness of a category boundary can be operationally defined in two ways. With respect to identification functions the sharpness of the boundary is inversely related to boundary width, while with respect to discrimination functions the sharpness of the boundary is inversely related to the difference limen at that boundary. There is evidence for developmental sharpening of each of these.

Zlatin and Koenigsknecht (1975) conducted one of the few studies of categorical identification with children. Two-year-olds, 6-year-olds, and adults were tested for their identification of bilabial, alveolar, and velar stop consonants which ranged from the voiced to the voiceless areas of the VOT continuum. The stimuli were synthesized words, e.g., bear/pear, dime/time, goat/coat. Adults were instructed to identify the perceived initial phoneme by writing the initial letter of these words. Children were asked to point to one of two pictures for a candy reward. Significant age-related differences were found. Two-year-olds had significantly wider phoneme boundaries than 6-year-olds and adults on all three continua, and 6-year-olds had significantly wider phoneme boundaries than adults for the velars. Thus, category boundaries became sharper over development, i.e., perception became more clearly categorical as a function of age.

It could be argued that this increased sharpness of category boundaries over age is not necessarily a function of specific linguistic experience. It could, for example, be due to general auditory maturation or to general linguistic or psychoacoustic experience. The possibility that the increased sharpness may be due to psychoacoustic rather than linguistic development gains force when the results of tone onset time (TOT) studies with infants and adults are considered. Jusczyk, Pisoni, Walley, and Murray (1980) found that infants perceived three categories of two-tone complexes and that the two category boundaries were between −70 and −40 msec TOT and +40 and +70 msec TOT.[6] However, Pisoni (1977) found that for adults the category boundaries between perceiving simultaneity of the two tones and perceiving either the low tone preceding, or the low tone

---

[6]TOT stimuli are usually constructed from a 500 Hz and a 1500 Hz tone. TOT is measured relative to the lower tone, thus a negative TOT value indicates that the onset of the lower tone precedes that of the higher tone, while a positive TOT value indicates that the onset of the lower tone lags behind onset of the higher tone.

following the higher tone had reduced to −20 and +20 msec TOT respectively. This suggests that the perception of asynchrony becomes more acute with age, a possibility which is quite reasonable given other increases in perceptual acuity over age. If, as Pisoni (1977; Pisoni & Tash, 1975) suggests, speech perception is basically a psychoacoustic phenomenon in which the perception of linguistic dimensions such as voicing are determined by underlying acoustic correlates such as TOT, it could be argued that any developmental changes in the sharpness of VOT category boundaries are the result of the same general process which causes developmental changes in the sharpness of TOT boundaries.

While this view may be partly correct, evidence from the study by Aslin, Pisoni, Hennessy, and Perey (1981) shows that specific linguistic experience plays a role in attunement over and above any general psychoacoustic tuning of category boundaries. Aslin et al. investigated the categorical perception of the VOT continuum for bilabial stops and found that infants and adults from an English language environment discriminated synthesized tokens which straddled both the phonemic and the nonphonemic boundary. Nevertheless, the difference limens were generally less for the phonemic voiced/voiceless boundary. Experience did not affect category boundary values which were approximately the same for adults and infants (i.e., there was no realignment due to English language exposure). However, difference limens generally decreased from infancy to adulthood, indicating, perhaps, a general improvement in perceptual acuity over age. Most importantly, over and above this general improvement, adults showed a marked reduction in difference limens around the phonemic voiced/voiceless boundary which was not evident in the infants' data.

Together the results reviewed here show that linguistic experience can facilitate the categorical perception of speech by sharpening category boundaries. There is evidence of sharpening both of category boundary widths (Zlatin & Koenigsknecht, 1975) and difference limens (Aslin et al., 1981). The results also suggest that sharpening of a specifically linguistic nature occurs over and above any general refinement which may occur as a result of improvements in psychoacoustic acuity (Aslin et al., 1981).

Conclusions Regarding Development

Which Theory of Ontogenetic Development?

Unfortunately developmental research has only been conducted using a few speech contrasts and so conclusions must remain tentative. Nevertheless, it is clear that no single theory provides all the answers. Some maturational process or at least a nonspecific effect of experience seems to be involved in the refinement of acuity for speech contrasts. However, it appears that this is a *general* improvement in auditory acuity rather than an improvement specifically centered on speech perception (Aslin et al., 1981; Jusczyk et al., 1980; Pisoni, 1977).

Over and above this general improvement there is language-specific attunement of stop consonants evident in the differential *realignment* of category boundaries over cultures (Eimas et al., 1971; Lasky et al., 1975; Lisker & Abramson, 1964; Streeter, 1976b) and in the selective *sharpening* of phonemic category boundaries (Aslin et al., 1981; Zlatin & Koenigsknecht, 1975). There is evidence that the perception of fricative contrasts is *enhanced* or even *induced* by linguistic experience (Eilers & Minifie, 1975; Eilers et al., 1977; Holmberg et al., 1977). Finally, other fricatives (Trehub, 1976), liquids (Eimas, 1975; Miyawaki et al., 1975) and some stop consonants (Werker et al., 1981; Werker & Tees, 1983, 1984) appear to require specific linguistic experience for their *maintenance*. Once attenuated by lack of experience the inability to perceive liquid contrasts appears more pervasive and long-lasting than the inability to perceive fricatives (see Goto, 1971, and Trehub, 1976, respectively). For stop consonants, perception of unusual contrasts differing on place of articulation is attenuated early by lack of experience and these abilities are not regained (Werker et al., 1981; Werker & Tees, 1983, 1984). On the other hand, perception of a stop consonant contrast differing on voicing is attenuated by lack of experience some time between 7 months and 4 years but this ability is regained by 8-years-of-age. In the next section an attempt is made to incorporate these different findings into a general framework.

Psychoacoustic and Phonological Modes of Perception

Kuhl's (1978) theory regarding the evolution of language was outlined earlier. The basis of this theory is that language has been structured to capitalize upon natural categories which arise from the interaction of certain acoustic continua and the auditory system with which humans are equipped. If this is true then many speech contrasts should be discriminable at birth and the most discriminable should be those with a clear psychóacoustic basis. General developmental improvement should be due to increased psychoacoustic acuity as a result of maturation or psychoacoustic experience. Any specific improvements over and above such psychoacoustic improvements should be the result of the specific language environment. In this way psychoacoustic thresholds which function as category boundaries may be modified by linguistic experience. This view is similar to that put forward by Jusczyk (1981a, 1981b, 1984). He claims that there is no special speech mode of perception in infancy but rather that categorical perception has a psychophysical (psychoacoustic) basis. The basis of the categorical perception of speech then becomes more phonological as a function of linguistic experience.

If these two views are correct then contrasts along continua with clear psychoacoustically defined boundaries should be discriminated very well, if not categorically. To the extent that VOT is a major cue for discrimination of stop consonants (though see Pisoni, 1980) and that this is a purely acoustic cue based on the perception of asynchrony (Pisoni, 1977), infants' categorical discrimination of various stop consonants supports this view. In addition, according to Kuhl's evolutionary view those contrasts with a clear psychoacoustic basis should be those which are most universal across languages. Stop consonants fulfil this requirement whereas fricatives, for example, do not (Jakobson, 1968). As we have seen, some fricatives are not discriminated early in infancy.

Consider the following prediction based on the evidence on hand so far. At birth infants will clearly discriminate between contrasts with a clear psychoacoustic basis. In general these should be those contrasts which are universal over a wide range of languages. These we will call *robust* contrasts. Any development of the perception of these robust contrast will then be mainly due to attunement (realignment and sharpening) caused by specific linguistic experience, but specific linguistic experience will not be required for their maintenance. On the other hand, perception of contrasts with a less clear psychoacoustic basis, i.e., those which in general are not so universal over languages, will be more variable. These we will call *fragile* contrasts. Either these fragile contrasts will *not* be perceived at birth and will require induction or enhancement by specific experience, or they *will* be perceived at birth and will require ongoing specific experience for their maintenance.

What Sort of Experience is Necessary?

Aslin and Pisoni (1980b; Walley, Pisoni, & Aslin, 1981) claim that passive exposure to specific contrasts at a perceptual level is all that is required for the developments that occur in speech perception. On the other hand, Jusczyk (1981a, 1981b, 1984) suggests that experience only becomes effective, and therefore is only manifested in speech perception abilities, once the child begins to attach meaning to speech sounds in a communicative context. Thus, Jusczyk claims, that experience must be active and at a cognitive rather than perceptual level. Only then, Jusczyk claims, does the psychoacoustic mode for the perception of speech give way to a more phonological mode. This should begin when the child is actively engaged in language acquisition. The few developmental studies that have been conducted *within* the infancy period suggest that the view put forward by Aslin and Pisoni may be correct. For example, the study by Eilers et al. (1977) shows that the passive experience between 6 and 12 months enhances the perception of a fricative contrast which was not perceived previously. In addition, the research by Werker and Tees (1984; Werker et al., 1981) shows that if there is a lack of passive receptive experience between 6 and 12 months with stops differing in place of articulation, a previously perceived speech contrast is permanently lost. This evidence comes from contrasts which in the previous section we labeled as fragile and nonuniversal. The role of experience over development with the more robust universal contrasts is yet to be determined though there is some evidence that lack of experience attenuates perception of a certain voicing contrast specifically during the period of language acquisition (Werker et al., 1981; Werker & Tees, 1983). The results of the experiment we describe later also bear on this issue.

To date, few true developmental studies have been carried out with any contrasts; those that have been conducted have in the main compared only infants and adults. More developmental studies, specifically comparing infants, prelinguistic children, postlinguistic children, and adults are required so that a clear view of the role of experience can be gained. Furthermore, there are often other methodological problems involved. Some of these are discussed in the next section ahead of a description of our own developmental study.

METHODOLOGICAL ISSUES

In this section we first consider the problems involved in interpreting data from infant discrimination studies, and then two related issues—the nonequivalence of procedures used with infants and adults, and the lack of evidence for categorical identification in infancy.

Infant Discrimination Procedures

Three main discrimination methods are used in testing infants. Two of these involve habituation of a response—high amplitude sucking (HAS) or heart-rate (HR)—performed for an auditory reward, and subsequent dishabituation to a novel auditory reward. The third, the visually reinforced infant speech discrimination (VRISD) procedure, involves the visual reinforcement of a head-turn in response to the change of a background auditory stimulus.

Interpretation of Null Results.   There are two main problems with interpreting the results of infant auditory discrimination studies. The first of these specifically concerns the interpretation of discrimination data gained from the two habituation-dishabituation procedures. Eilers, Wilson, and Moore (1977) have noted that negative results obtained using these methods are ambiguous because of the dual role of the auditory signal as both discriminative stimulus and reinforcer. Failures to dishabituate to a novel sound may indicate either an inability to detect a change or that the change was detected but was not reinforcing or interesting. This ambiguity is absent in the VRISD method that Eilers and her coworkers use and advocate. In this procedure the failure of infants to turn their heads significantly more than chance when a target stimulus momentarily replaces a repeated background stimulus cannot be due to this change being discriminable but uninteresting to the infant. The operant head-turn response is under the control of independent visual reinforcement rather than the stimulus

sound. Provided the infant is under operant control of the reinforcer, any change in sound which is detected should result in an attempt by the infant to gain access to the visual reinforcement via a head-turn. Thus with the VRISD method, but not with the HAS or HR methods, a failure to respond indicates a failure to discriminate. An operant infant speech identification procedure which we have developed and will describe shortly is similar to the VRISD method in this regard.

Stimulus Bound Results.   Kuhl points out a second major problem in the interpretation of infant discrimination data. Discrimination procedures aimed at assessing the infant's ability to perceive a contrast commonly test this ability using only two tokens to exemplify that contrast. This leads to "stimulus bound" results, reflecting only the infant's ability to detect the difference between single exemplars of the categories involved (Kuhl, 1978). Jusczyk (1981a) and Kuhl (1978) have reviewed research indicating that the critical difference between categories is not encapsulated in a single token from each category. It is difficult to test more than one pair of tokens with procedures relying upon habituation. One way to do this would be to present a number of test tokens on the assumption that habituation to the original token remained constant. Another way would be to habituate the infant to a second habituation token (and maybe a third, etc.) and hope that the infant would remain attentive and not become habituated to the whole situation. It is somewhat easier to test discrimination with multiple tokens when no habituation is involved and the discriminative stimulus and the reinforcement event differ. As this is the case in the VRISD procedure it is admirably suited to multiple token tests and has been used in this way in a staircase adaptation of the procedure (Aslin et al., 1981). The same is the case for our infant speech identification procedure.

There are two other methodological problems which are not actually inherent in infant discrimination procedures themselves but which tend to diminish the value of results from studies using these procedures. The first is that methods for testing infant and adult discrimination differ grossly and therefore comparisons of results obtained for adults and infants are tenuous. The second is that the infant discrimination data are not complemented by infant identification data.

Infant and Adult Procedures

Our review of the ontogenetic development of speech perception demonstrated the crucial role played by infant-adult comparisons in theoretical formulations. Theories have been based on differences between adult and infant data obtained with different procedures and no attempts have been made to investigate their comparability (Trehub, 1979). Moreover, it has been found that the use of different discrimination methods even with adults can produce different results (Pisoni & Lazarus, 1974).

Aslin et al. (1981), Hillenbrand, Minifie, and Edwards (1979), Werker and Tees (1983, 1984; Werker et al., 1981), and Zlatin and Koenigsknecht (1975) are among the few who have included adults and either infants or children in the same test situation. It is notable that in none of these studies was habituation-dishabituation the common procedure; Hillenbrand et al. (1979) used the VRISD procedure; Aslin et al. (1981) used a staircase variation of the VRISD procedure; Werker and Tees (1983, 1984; Werker et al., 1981) used the VRISD procedure and a button-press variation for children and adults; and Zlatin and Koenigsknecht (1975) used an identification procedure adapted for children. Habituation procedures are not particularly apt for use with adults or children or even with infants older than about 6- to 8-months-of-age (Aslin et al., 1983; Eilers, 1980). Therefore, procedures in which both adults and infants respond to an auditory stimulus in order to be reinforced by a visual stimulus, e.g., the VRISD procedure and our infant speech identification procedure, are the most appropriate for comparison of infants and adults.[7]

The Necessity of Infant Identification Data

There are two main reasons why infant identification data is necessary. One involves maintaining a consistent definition of categorical perception based on both discrimination and identification functions. Use of just one of these does not constitute a true test of whether speech perception is categorical. The second reason is more an issue of function: it will be argued here that it is probable that different functions are involved in the processes of categorical discrimination and categorical identification.

The Definition of Categorical Speech Perception

Researchers generally acknowledge the need to investigate infant identification capacities. Few, however, elaborate on the need that would be satisfied by infant identification data (Aslin et al., 1977; Jusczyk, 1981b; Trehub, 1979; Walley et al., 1981). The simplest and most pragmatic reason is that there is a need to adopt a definition of categorical perception which is consistent across age. If we are to endorse (or even challenge) the generally accepted definition of categorical speech perception (Studdert-Kennedy et al., 1970) for infants then they must be properly tested for categorical perception. This requires that *both* discrimination and identification functions are obtained for infants.

A discrimination function alone can indicate areas of heightened ability but without a supporting identification function it cannot demonstrate an ability to categorize all tokens into two separate and distinct categories. For example, the

---

[7]It should be noted, however, that a limitation of both methods is that they cannot be used to test infants younger than about 6 months (Eilers, 1980).

assignment of exemplars to categories may be rather sloppy, such that the category crossover portion of the identification curve departs appreciably from the perpendicular. In such cases we would be loath to describe perception as clearly categorical, despite heightened discriminative ability around the boundary.

An identification function alone without any information on discriminative abilities can also lead to problems because it is not unknown for identification to be categorical even when within category discriminations are possible, for instance, in color categorization (Bornstein et al., 1976). Recent evidence suggests that under some conditions adults can discriminate between tokens drawn from a single category as defined by previous performance on an identification task or on a different discrimination task (Carney, Widin, & Viemeister, 1977; Hary & Massaro, 1982; Pisoni & Lazarus, 1974; Pisoni & Tash, 1974). In addition, discriminative ability for bilabial stops has been found to vary over a range of background VOT values (Aslin et al., 1981). This evidence suggests that the discrimination of speech sounds by adults is not limited purely by phonetic identity because if it were, the phonetic filter system should not enable the perception of acoustic differences within categories. Thus it is clear that both identification functions and discrimination functions are necessary for a complete description of categorical perception. This is no less a necessity with infants than adults.

Are Different Processes Involved in Discrimination and Identification?

It is possible that different neural or cognitive processes may be involved in discrimination and identification. Intuitively it would seem that discrimination is based on a single process, the perception of *any* difference between the particular tokens. Identification, on the other hand, would appear to involve first the abstraction of common bases for grouping sounds together, and then the comparison of each token with this abstraction. This would especially be the case if within-category discriminations are possible (Carney et al., 1977; Hary & Massaro, 1982; Pisoni & Lazarus, 1974; Pisoni & Tash, 1974). If different processes are involved in discrimination and identification it would be possible for infants to demonstrate a peak in discrimination at some point on the continuum without being able to set up categories and assign incoming sounds to these categories on the basis of this peak. For this reason it is important to obtain both discrimination and identification data from infants.

There are, however, at least two objections to this argument. The first is that it presents a rather lofty view of identification and that it is more likely to be the case that identification is based purely on psychoacoustic restraints such as the ability to perceive simultaneity and nonsimultaneity. If this were so then it could be argued that both discrimination and identification involve similar relatively automatic processes. On the other hand, it has been argued that, at least for adults, categorical perception of linguistically relevant dimensions, e.g., VOT, is not reducible to categorical perception of simple acoustic dimensions, e.g., TOT (Pisoni, 1980). Nevertheless, as set out earlier, it may be the case that this is not so for infants. It could be that infants *only* identify sounds on the basis of psychoacoustic differences and that the effect of linguistic experience is to build a superstructure of phonetic features on the basis of underlying psychoacoustic differences such that the phonetic features become functionally autonomous of their humble beginnings. In this case both discrimination and identification should have a strong and common psychoacoustic basis in infancy, while for adults identification (and perhaps discrimination to some extent) should have a more phonetic basis. Therefore, rather than providing an objection against the necessity for infant identification data, this adds a further reason to collect identification data both for speech and nonspeech continua, e.g., VOT and TOT, over development.

If such data could be collected in infancy, further issues in this vein could be investigated. For example, Eimas' feature extraction hypothesis (Eimas, 1975; Eimas, Cooper, & Corbit, 1973; Eimas & Corbit, 1973) could be investigated using an identification procedure in which infants were trained to respond differently to two bilabial stop tokens distinctly differing in voicing, e.g., 0 msec VOT /b/ and +70 msec VOT /p/, and then tested for generalized responses with alveolar tokens spanning the range of VOT values. In this way it could be determined if there is a phonetic voicing feature which generalises across speech sounds. On the basis of the above argument such a feature should be more evident in adults than infants.

The second possible objection against the view that discrimination and identification tasks involve different processes is that identification may be related to a general cognitive ability to form concepts rather than to any specific ability to categorize speech sounds. (This would be an especially potent criticism if infants were found to discriminate between sounds within the same category.) Thus, while infants may have categorical discrimination abilities, they may not show categorical identification if the latter relies upon cognitive and memorial abilities. If this were true categorical identification should only begin to emerge at about 6 to 7 months when infants begin forming concepts (Cohen & Strauss, 1979) or maybe later at about 10 months when prototypes begin to be abstracted (Strauss, 1979). Again it can be seen that this argument requires the collection of infant identification data for its resolution.

IDENTIFICATION IN INFANCY

The infant speech identification procedure which we will describe here overcomes problems set out in the previous section because, in addition to enabling identification data to be collected, it allows relatively unequivocal interpretation of negative results, allows multiple tokens to be presented to infants, and can be used to test infants, children and adults. In the experiment we describe, criticisms of earlier studies set out in the third section are overcome because we tested infants, 2-year-olds, 6-year-olds, and adults on both phonemic and nonphonemic contrasts.

Previous Attempts

There have been two previous attempts to condition bidirectional head-turns to speech sounds in infancy. Fodor, Garrett and Brill (1975) investigated 14- to 18-week-old infants' performance of anticipatory head-turns to sound sources to their left or right. All infants heard three sounds, /pi/, /ka/ and /pu/, which were played randomly from one of the two sound sources. For one group of infants, the shared phone group, visual reinforcement occurred only for responses to /pi/ or /pu/, while for another group of infants visual reinforcement occurred only for responses to /pi/ or /ka/. Their results suggest that infants were better at the shared phone task. However, conditioned head-turning, especially bidirectional, is notoriously difficult for infants younger than 5½ months (Aslin et al., 1983; Kuhl, 1983). Anticipatory head-turn hit rates for infants in Fodor's study were consistently less than 50% and only marginally greater than their false alarm rates (Aslin et al., 1983). Therefore caution should be exercised in interpreting these results or applying the testing procedure.

Aslin, Perey, Hennessy, and Pisoni (1977) were more directly interested in developing an infant identification procedure. They attempted to condition 5- to 6-month-old infants to turn their heads in one direction for an interesting visual reward when a synthetic speech sound from one adult category was presented and in the other direction when a sound from another adult category was presented. In the generalization tests it was planned to present sounds along the VOT continuum between the two training tokens to determine how infants identified these. Aslin et al. had only limited success; one infant performed quite well in training trials but nevertheless no generalization data could be gathered. When they changed their procedure so that the two responses required from infants were "head-turn" and "no head-turn" there was some overall improvement. However, this was mainly due to increased head-turns to the appropriate sound as it proved difficult for infants to indicate identification of the other sound by inhibiting a head-turn. Aslin et al. (1977) mention various aspects of their bidirectional head-turn procedure which may have detracted from its efficiency. One of these was that both sides of their display were visually identical. Thus there were no spatial localization cues to aid infants in making differential head-turns. Aslin et al. also note that their attempt to shape initial responses with sound localization cues and subsequent testing with sounds originating from the midline may have contributed to the inefficiency of their method.

The Infant Speech Identification (ISI) Procedure

Apparatus and Stimulus Sounds.   In building apparatus for our attempt to collect infant identification data we aimed to overcome these problems. Mothers sat on a chair facing the apparatus, infant on lap. The speaker through which sounds were presented was directly ahead of them. The apparatus consisted of a large three-part screen with the two outer panels hinged at 60° to the central panel. The left half of the apparatus was painted bright orange, and the right half painted bright blue. There were two reinforcement windows, one on each side. Each of these consisted of a square aperture covered by smoked plastic which could be illuminated to reveal a fluffy pink rabbit nodding and playing cymbals. Next to each aperture was a lamp which could be flashed on and off to shape infants' responses when appropriate. In the middle of the central screen there was a brightly colored cellophane mask illuminated from behind by a lamp which could be flashed on and off to attract infants' attention at the beginning of trials. The infants' behavior was monitored by means of a video system, the video camera being situated underneath the mask in the central panel.

The stimulus sounds were synthesized bilabial stop consonant plus vowel syllables,[8] ranging in VOT from −70 msec to +70 msec in 10 msec steps. Each token had an approximate duration of 300 msec. A stimulus block consisted of 10 tokens of the same VOT value each separated by 500 msec. Thus each stimulus block was about 8 sec in duration. Stimulus sounds were recorded on audiotape and presented via a Tandberg Crossfield series 9200XD tape recorder. Channels could be switched easily to present one of two different training tokens to infants. Generalization stimuli were recorded and presented on a second Tandberg tape recorder. Manipulation of lights, tape recorders, and reinforcers was centralized on an electronic integration unit.

Pilot Studies

In our initial attempt to develop an identification procedure, we used bilabial stops varying in VOT from −70 msec to +70 msec in 10 msec steps. We endeavored to train infants to make a head-turn to one side for one endpoint of the continuum (−70 msec) and to the other side for the other endpoint (+70 msec). Our intention was to train infants to a stringent criterion (6 consecutive correct responses) with these endpoint stimuli and then to test them on all fifteen 10-msec step VOT generalization stimuli interspersed with some reinforced endpoint trials. We had little success (1 of the first 12 infants reached criterion) until

[8]We are very grateful to J. E. Clark of Macquarie University, N.S.W., Australia and D. B. Pisoni of Indiana University, U.S.A. for their helpful advice and for providing synthesized speech sounds.

we adopted a less stringent criterion (3 consecutive correct responses) and incorporated into the procedure a return to training loop after each generalization test trial (Sinnot, Pisoni, & Aslin, 1983). We also found that we had to test infants slightly older than those tested by Aslin et al.—around 10 months compared with 5 to 6 months. These changes greatly improved the viability and success of the procedure and allowed us to run our first experiment.

The Main Experiment: Method

Infants were first given a laterality preference test to establish which side of the apparatus they preferred when both reinforcers occurred simultaneously. Initial training was then given on their *non*preferred side as a number of our earlier pilot subjects had shown a marked and persistent lateral preference. After training with random presentations of the two endpoint stimuli to a criterion of 3 consecutive correct responses (never all to the same stimulus), an infant was presented with an unreinforced trial in which a generalization test stimulus was presented. The direction of head-turn on this generalization trial was noted. Babies then returned to training until another three consecutive responses were made, and so on. In training trials an incorrect head-turn promptly resulted in the termination of the trial and of all stimulation, a correct head-turn promptly resulted in reinforcement, and if a response had not occurred by the fifth token (half way through a trial) the infant's response was shaped. Shaped trials were reinforced but were not counted as correct responses.

The procedure and apparatus were also adapted for children and adults. For children, a two-choice color-coded paddle-press response replaced the head-turn. For adults, two hand-held buttons replaced the paddles. The developmental nature of the study was explained to adults so that they could appreciate the rather inappropriate reinforcement by fluffy pink bunny rabbits. Side preference controls were not included for children or adults. Children (2-year-olds and 6-year-olds) and adults sat in age-appropriate chairs.

Eight groups of English language environment subjects were tested in a 2 × 4, contrast × age design. In the phonemic contrast groups the endpoint stimuli were a 0 msec VOT (voiced) bilabial stop plus vowel /ba/ and a +70 msec VOT (voiceless) bilabial stop plus vowel /pa/. The eight generalization stimuli were those between and including 0 msec to +70 msec in 10 msec steps. In the nonphonemic groups, endpoints were the same 0 msec VOT (voiced) /ba/ and a −70 msec VOT (prevoiced) bilabial stop vowel /-ba/. Generalization stimuli were those between and including 0 msec and −70 msec VOT in 10 msec steps. Infants between 9- and 11-months-of-age, 2-year-olds ranging between about 2½ up to 3 years, 6-year-olds ranging from 6 up to 7 years, and adults of 18+ years were tested.

For the generalization test data each subject was given a score on each of the eight generalization test stimuli. This was either '1', a response appropriate for a

TABLE 11.1

Response Details for Each of the Contrast X Age Groups

	Infants		2-year-olds		6-year-olds		Adults	
	Phonemic Contrast	Nonphonemic Contrast	Phonemic Contrast	Nonphonemic Contrast	Phonemic Contrast	Nonphonemic Contrast	Phonemic Contrast	Nonphonemic Contrast
Number of subjects tested	24	24	12	12	7	7	7	7
Number making at least one test response	20	10	11	12	7	7	7	7
Number making all 8 test responses	0	0	7	1	7	7	7	7
Total responses collected	47	12	65	34	56	56	56	56
Total responses possible	160	80	88	96	56	56	56	56

0 msec VOT endpoint stimulus /ba/ in both contrast groups, or '−1', a response appropriate for a +70 msec VOT endpoint stimulus /pa/ in the phonemic groups or for a −70 msec VOT endpoint stimulus /-ba/ in the nonphonemic groups. In addition, '0' was recorded if no response was made to a particular stimulus on the continuum. This could either be due to nonpresentation of the stimulus or to a null response when the stimulus was presented. As can be seen in Table 11.1, all 6-year-olds and adults responded to all generalization stimuli, but this was not the case for infants and 2-year-olds. Many of the 2-year-olds, especially in the phonemic group, responded to all eight stimuli. Although many infants came for three or more sessions none of them responded to all eight generalization stimuli, although in the phonemic group some infants had the necessary endurance to respond to all but 1 or 2 of the generalization tests. Nevertheless, the system of assigning zero scores allowed all subjects' data to be analyzed quantitatively.

In previous studies neither individual nor group identification curves have usually been subjected to quantitative analysis. However, we have developed a method whereby each subject's responses can be given two values: one which indicates their category boundary or crossover point and another which indicates the degree to which their identification function is sharply categorical. In this procedure each subject's set of eight values (1, 0, or −1) is separately multiplied by the coefficients of 7 perfectly categorical curves each with a boundary width of 10 msec, but with crossovers of 5, 15, 25, 35, 45, 55, or 65 msec VOT. (Those for the phonemic groups have a positive sign, those for the nonphonemic groups have a negative sign.) The crossover value for any individual's data is given by which of the seven ideal curves best fits that individual's data. Next, the categorical score for each individual is determined. This score indicates how well a particular individual's configuration of scores fits their best fit ideal categorical curve.[9] These values can then be subjected to the usual group statistical procedures.

Results

Let us first consider whether the procedure was effective. In Table 11.1 is shown the number of subjects tested, the number of subjects responding to at least one test stimulus, the number of subjects responding to all 8 test stimuli, the total number of responses obtained from subjects, and the total number of possible responses. As can be seen, seven adults and seven 6-year-olds were tested in each contrast group. All reached criterion and all gave all eight responses. One 2-year-old failed to reach criterion at least once and therefore no test stimuli were presented. Many of the remaining 2-year-olds, especially in the nonphonemic

[9]The assistance of K. Bird, R. G. Dickinson and T. Lewin in statistical matters is greatly appreciated.

group, were not presented with all eight stimuli due to fatigue. Chi-square analyses reveal that there is no significant difference between the proportion of 2-year-olds in the phonemic and nonphonemic group reaching criterion. However, a significantly greater proportion of possible responses were collected for the phonemic than for the nonphonemic group. This indicates that 2-year-olds in the nonphonemic group could differentiate between endpoint stimuli and therefore reach criterion but that it took them a relatively long time to do so.

For the infants it can be seen that performance is considerably better in the phonemic than the nonphonemic group. A significantly greater proportion of infants reached criterion in the phonemic group than the nonphonemic group and in the phonemic group a significantly greater proportion of possible responses were made. This indicates that infants found discrimination of the nonphonemic contrast especially difficult. Interestingly, the difference between infants in these two groups attests to the validity of our procedure; the procedure was *more* effective with the phonemic contrast.

Let us now consider the identification data graphed as they usually are in identification curves (see Fig. 11.1). Considering first the phonemic groups it appears that there may be some appropriate identification of generalization stimuli by infants. However, this identification could not be called categorical. Over age these phonemic curves seem to become appreciably more categorical, with the adult data similar to that collected by other methods. (We have also run adult subjects on a conventional two-choice identification procedure—one without bunny rabbits—and the results are indistinguishable from those collected in the ISI procedure.) All functions in the nonphonemic groups are less categorical than those in the phonemic groups. The infants' nonphonemic function appears to be rather random, the 2-year-olds', while variable, appears generally to be sloped in the appropriate direction, the 6-year-olds' responses appear to hover around chance, and the adults, while not deviating much from chance, show a slope in the appropriate direction.

These observations were supported by a 2×4 between-subjects analysis of variance of the categorical scores. Mean categorical scores are shown in Fig. 11.2. The analysis revealed a significant effect due to contrast group, indicating that subjects in the phonemic groups had functions that were more sharply categorical than those in the nonphonemic groups. There was also a significant linear trend of age, indicating that the curves become more categorical as a function of age. Of greatest importance however, were the significant interactions between contrast group and the linear age trend and between contrast group and the cubic age trend. These interactions indicate that for the phonemic contrast there is a linear improvement in boundary sharpness, i.e., functions become more categorical with age. On the other hand functions for the nonphonemic groups become more categorical between infancy and prelinguistic childhood (2 years) but drop to chance level by postlinguistic childhood (6 years). By

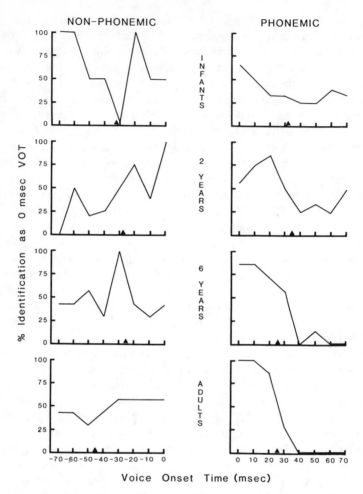

FIGURE 11.1. Identification curves for infants, 2-year-olds, 6-year-olds and adults for phonemic and non-phonemic bilabial VOT continua. The small arrow near the abscissa on each curve represents the mean crossover value. Details regarding the number of subjects tested and responses collected in each group are given in Table 11.1.

adulthood nonphonemic curves have regained their 2-year-old status. It is notable that just when the sharpness of the nonphonemic functions plummet, the main improvement in phonemic functions occurs.[10]

---

[10]It is possible that these results are artifactual and due in some way to the lack of a complete set of responses for many of the 2-year-olds. However, further analyses either omitting 2-year-olds without a complete set of responses, or omitting those with a complete set of responses led to essentially similar results.

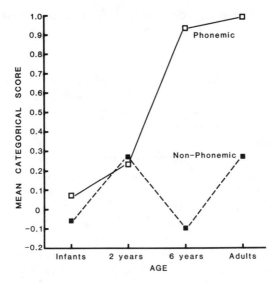

FIGURE 11.2.   Mean categorical scores for phonemic and nonphonemic contrasts at each age.

Category boundaries or crossovers were also calculated. Mean values for these are shown in Fig. 11.1 by the small arrow near the abscissa of each graph. These remain remarkably constant although there was a slight tendency for crossovers to become more negative for the nonphonemic contrast over age. Nevertheless, a 2 × 4 analysis of variance revealed no significant differences in absolute crossover values for contrast group, for age or for contrast × age interactions.

Implications

These results bear on a number of issues set out below.

The VOT Continuum—Negative and Positive Regions.   With the exception of 2-year-olds, subjects at all ages perceive the contrast in the positive region of the bilabial VOT continuum more clearly than the contrast in the negative region. As this is the case for the infants, who obviously have limited specific experience, it is possible that the prevoiced/voiced contrast is less salient perceptually than the voiced/voiceless contrast (Aslin et al., 1981). The difficulty we had in training infants to criterion in the nonphonemic condition supports this claim. Pisoni (1977) suggests that this is a psychoacoustic phenomenon related to a limitation on the processing of temporal order information, a suggestion consistent with the claim that infant speech perception is initially determined psychoacoustically. The relative prevalence of the voiced/voiceless compared with the prevoiced/voiced distinction in different languages (Jakobsen, 1968) suggests that the voiced/voiceless distinction may have been selected for in the evolution of languages (Kuhl, 1978).

The Role of Experience.   The analysis of the category crossover data shows that there is no change in category boundaries over age. This is consistent with evidence reviewed earlier that in English there is no significant realignment of category boundaries as a function of experience (Aslin et al., 1981; Lisker & Abramson, 1964).

With the exception of the 6-year-old nonphonemic data there is a general improvement in the sharpness of both phonemic and nonphonemic functions over age. This is likely to be due to refinement of acuity for speech contrasts (Aslin et al., 1981; Zlatin & Koenigsknecht, 1975). However, it could also be due to improvement in meeting the task demands over age, or general improvement in auditory acuity over age. To evaluate these two possibilities we are currently testing four more groups, one at each age, on an easily discriminable frequency continuum of harmonic tones.

The significant age by contrast group interactions show that there is also a role for specific linguistic experience. In their English language environment these children would be exposed to the voiced/voiceless contrast but not the prevoiced/voiced contrast. The continuing increase in sharpness of functions for the phonemic continuum, and the corresponding reduction in boundary width, is presumably due to such experience. Aslin, Pisoni, Hennessy, and Perey (1981) found that specific experience of the voiced/voiceless contrast by English listeners resulted in reduced VOT difference limens for this contrast, but not for the prevoiced/voiced contrast. As difference limens in discrimination studies are the correlates of boundary widths in identification studies, our results support those of Aslin et al. (1981). The results, in general, show that for the bilabial stop VOT continuum the effect of specific experience is to sharpen boundaries, i.e., attunement theory is supported. The results for the nonphonemic functions add support to attunement theory as there is no difference between boundary sharpness for 2-year-olds and adults; what little improvement there is between infancy and 2 years is common to both nonphonemic and phonemic contrasts and therefore probably best accounted for by general refinement of auditory ability.

The interesting point about the role of specific experience in this study is the age at which it becomes effective. Between 2 and 6 years, just when there is a large increase in the sharpness of phonemic identification functions, there is a large decrease (to chance level) in the sharpness of nonphonemic functions. It would not be parsimonious to attribute this reduction of ability to universal theory, i.e., to the attenuating effect of a specific lack of experience, because this would not explain the initial increase in sharpness from infancy to 2 years or the subsequent increase from 6 years to adulthood. This effect must then be related to language acquisition processes occurring between 2 and 6 years. It seems likely, therefore, that for these bilabial contrasts Jusczyk is correct in his claim that experience is only effective when infants begin to attach meaning to syllables, words, and phonemes, i.e., when language acquisition begins in earnest (Jusczyk, 1981a, 1981b, 1984). However, the results obtained here show that this active experience is a twin-edged blade: English language experience not only enhances perception of the phonemic bilabial contrast but also inhibits perception of the nonphonemic bilabial contrast. As these two opposite effects occur simultaneously, and as there is subsequent restricted improvement of ability for nonphonemic contrasts, this effect could possibly be an attentional one. This is supported by the studies by Werker et al. (1981) and Werker and Tees (1983). They also found a curvilinear trend for the discrimination of nonphonemic stop consonants differing in voicing. For the contrast between a voiceless aspirated and voiced breathy dental there appeared to be a complete loss of discriminative ability sometime between 7 months and 4 years as a function of lack of experience. However partial ability returned at 8 years and continued on to 12 years and adulthood. This evidence supports the notion that our pattern of results reflects some attentional effects rather than a complete albeit temporary loss of perceptual ability.

There are two possible attentional explanations of the curvilinear pattern of results over development for the nonphonemic contrast. It may simply reflect general refinement of contrast perception over age which is masked or interrupted by the lack of attention paid to nonphonemic contrasts during language acquisition. Alternatively, it may be that after the relatively mechanistic and psychoacoustically based perception of both phonemic and nonphonemic contrasts in infancy, active linguistic experience initially requires controlled attentional processes for the perception of contrasts which are meaningful in the language being acquired. These processes could then gradually become more automatic with age and experience (Schneider & Shiffrin, 1977). According to this view, the perception of phonemic contrasts would begin to involve controlled processes when language acquisition begins, around 2 years. Up to and including 6 years, as a result of their involvement in language acquisition, children would have little attentional capacity or resources available for nonphonemic contrasts. Older children and adults, however, should be able to process phonemic contrasts more automatically and therefore should have some attentional capacity or resources available for the perception of nonphonemic contrasts.

Turning to the nature of the linguistic experience, our results suggest that the relatively passive experience between infancy and two years had an equal and positive effect on both phonemic and nonphonemic contrasts but that the active experience between 2 and 6 years had an unequal effect. That is, there was no effect of specific linguistic experience until after 2-years-of-age. Recall that for the contrasts which we labeled fragile the presence or absence of specific linguistic experience affects perceptual ability before 12-months-of-age. This is of necessity mainly *passive* experience. Not so for the robust bilabials tested here: It seems that specific experience only affects their perception if it is *active* experience.

We can now restate and extend the theory which we put forward earlier. Robust contrasts are those which have a clear psychoacoustic basis and/or which are relatively universal across natural languages. Fragile contrasts are those with a less clear psychoacoustic basis and/or those which are relatively rare across natural languages. Fragile contrasts can be affected by passive linguistic experience and indeed require experience from birth for their maintenance, induction, or enhancement. Any modulation due to such experience or lack of experience is evident during the second half of the first year. Fragile contrasts lost during this period are difficult if not impossible to perceive later in life. Robust contrasts, on the other hand, are unaffected by specific passive experience. Only active experience can specifically modulate robust contrasts. Thus, any major differences in the perception of phonemic and nonphonemic robust contrasts can only occur once language acquisition begins. The *presence* of active experience sharpens and/or realigns robust category boundaries. The *absence* of active experience directs attention away from nonphonemic contrasts and perhaps broadens their boundary widths. However, as these robust but nonphonemic contrasts have a psychoacoustic basis, when language acquisition is largely complete, around 6 to 8 years, a return of perceptual ability is possible because less attention is then required for the perception of phonemic contrasts. Nevertheless, perceptual ability with these nonphonemic contrasts will probably always fall short of that with phonemic contrasts unless extensive training is provided.

These speculations make evolutionary sense. If a particular dimension is fragile due to a weak psychoacoustic basis, sensitivity to passive experience of a phonemic contrast from birth will be important to keep or make the contrast viable. On the other hand, if a dimension has a clear psychoacoustic basis and if particular contrasts along this continuum are relatively universal across languages, these contrasts should remain insensitive to the vagaries of early passive experience. Only repeated active experience should have functionally significant effects on the realignment and sharpening of these robust contrast boundaries. It remains for further research to investigate these possibilities. Nevertheless, the main finding of this study stands: Linguistic experience only has a specific effect on the identification of bilabial stops between the ages of about 2 and 6 years.

Further Research.   Our findings for bilabial stop consonants should be followed up with identification studies of other contrasts. In addition, studies of discriminative ability with this and other contrasts as a function of age need to be conducted. Studies by Aslin et al. (1981) suggest that *discrimination* of the nonphonemic /b/ versus /-b/ contrast by infants is possible. Our difficulty in training infants on the same contrast suggests that *identification* of this nonphonemic contrast is not possible until about 2 years. Thus, it is necessary to investigate infants' ability to discriminate but inability to identify contrasts.

Research is also required into the developmental course of robust and fragile contrasts. Given our hypotheses about the different ages when fragile and robust contrasts are susceptible to the effects of experience, developmental studies such as ours should be elaborated to test infants at various ages across their first year. Developmental studies such as those by Werker and her colleagues should be extended to include prelinguistic children. Such studies should cover a range of contrasts. A particular hypothesis to arise from research conducted so far is that the decline in discriminative ability for the /dʰ/ versus /tʰ/ contrast found between 7 months and 4 years (Werker et al., 1981; Werker & Tees, 1983) should only begin around the onset of language acquisition, i.e., around 2 or 3 years. A related but more difficult research question is to unconfound passive and active experience and the age of the child.

To date two nonphonemic voicing contrasts have been shown to have a curvilinear developmental course, /b/ versus /-b/ (see Fig. 11.2) and /dʰ/ versus /tʰ/ (Werker et al., 1981; Werker & Tees, 1983). Further research is required to investigate whether the ability to perceive other phonologically irrelevant contrasts is also lost during language acquisition only to be regained later. A likely contender would be the /ř/ versus /z/ contrast for which English-speaking adults have some ability despite it being phonologically irrelevant (Trehub, 1976). It should be the case that only the more robust contrasts should exhibit this curvilinear trend. In this regard some independent metric for the robust-fragile distinction is required in order to determine its psychological reality and heuristic value. This metric could incorporate the strength of the psychoacoustic basis of contrasts and their relative prevalence in natural languages.

Finally, it would be of interest to specify those particular aspects of language acquisition which modify the perception of phonemic and nonphonemic contrasts. If, as we suggest, apparent loss of perceptual ability has an attentional basis, then relevant training should produce improved perception (Werker & Tees, 1983). For example, children could be trained to perceive synchrony and asynchrony with zero versus negative TOT sounds. This may facilitate performance on prevoiced/voiced VOT contrasts.

Categorical Perception of Speech in Infancy?

Our results suggest that speech perception in infancy is not categorical but becomes increasingly so with linguistic experience. Therefore, on the basis of the identification data presented here and the discrimination data presented elsewhere, discrimination and identification functions for bilabial stops in infancy are not complementary. This is not to say that infants lack heightened discrimination around the adult category boundary. Indeed, many studies have shown just the opposite (Aslin et al., 1981; Eimas et al., 1971). Nor is it to say that there is no identification of bilabials in infancy—our data suggest that there is. Rather there is identification of bilabials in infancy but it is simply *not categorical*. Marrying this finding to the view that many of the speech contrasts used in languages take advantage of natural psycho-acoustically based categories (Kuhl, 1978), and the view that categorical perception moves from a psychoacoustic to a phonological basis over development (Jusczyk, 1981a, 1981b, 1984), it is possible that it is the addition of linguistic experience to the heightened discriminability around psychoacoustic thresholds present at birth that results in speech perception becoming more categorical. Finally, in conjunction with evidence from studies with adults (e.g., Carney et al., 1977) and variations in infants' difference limens as a function of VOT (Aslin et al., 1981), our results also raise the possibility that categorical perception of speech is not the all-or-none phenomenon it was once thought to be.

Evaluation of the ISI Method

The ISI procedure has proved to be a satisfactory research tool. We were able to use the method with minor adaptations for infants under 1 year, children of 2½ to 3 years, children of 6 to 7 years, and adults. Development of speech perception can be investigated in a task which is at least topologically similar over ages. In addition, the data obtained via this method for adults closely matched adult data collected in a control study by conventional means, indicating that it is tapping the same ability as the more usual identification or labeling method. By means of the maximized contrast method we have also been able to quantify just how categorical particular identification functions are and this quantification has revealed interesting results. Thus, the use of the ISI method has raised new issues in research into speech perception. In addition, it has also provided a procedure which may be used fruitfully to investigate other issues. Eimas (1975) lamented that a procedure was not available to investigate perceptual adaptation in infancy. Walley, Pisoni, and Aslin (1981) and Aslin, Pisoni and Jusczyk (1983) have claimed that in order to study the important issues of perceptual constancy and the categorization of speech, measures of generalization and perceptual similarity analogous to adult identification tasks are necessary. Such measures are now available.

However, this optimism should be tempered by considering the shortcomings of the method. First, the procedure is extremely time-consuming, especially for infants but also for 2-year-olds. It was not uncommon for an infant to attend three separate sessions of 15–40 minutes. And even then no infant and no infant's mother had the resilience or patience respectively to complete the series of eight generalization test trials. Such problems are not uncommon in testing infant speech perception but nevertheless need to be pointed out. Second, we tested infants with a mean age of approximately 10 months. Attempts to test infants much younger than this were unsuccessful. The youngest infant tested success-fully was around 9 months of age. This is particularly a problem when conclusions about experiential effects are being drawn.

SUMMARY AND CONCLUSIONS

In the second section a brief summary of Eimas' original research and other research since then showed that the categorical discrimination of speech in infancy can no longer be taken to imply a special innate mode of processing for speech by humans.

In the third section the development of speech perception was investigated. This revealed many possible experiential influences on speech perception but also that comprehensive developmental studies have not been performed for phonemic and nonphonemic contrasts or within and between cultures. Consideration of theories about the evolution of language systems and ontogenetic development converged on two views: first, that speech perception begins in infancy as a psychoacoustic phenomenon and ends in adulthood as a phonological phenomenon; and second, that different developmental processes may be involved for contrasts which differ on the degree to which they are universal and psychoacoustically based. This led us to consider whether the linguistic experience which results in developmental transition is passive perceptual experience at any time in development (Aslin & Pisoni, 1980b), or active cognitive experience when speech sounds start to take on differential meaning for the child (Jusczyk, 1981a, 1981b, 1984).

In the fourth section methodological issues were considered. It was argued that an infant identification procedure is required due to problems with some infant discrimination procedures, the lack of equivalence of procedures used with infants and adults and, more specifically, the possibility that speech perception in infancy is not truly categorical.

In the fifth section we presented our solution to these problems, the ISI procedure, which was used in an experiment aimed at resolving unanswered questions regarding the development of categorical identification from infancy through childhood to adulthood. The results of this experiment produced an unexpected effect: between 2 and 6 years a phonemic contrast came to be identified appreciably more categorically, while a similar but nonphonemic contrast ceased to be identified at all. This finding suggests that active experience with language directs the language learner's attention only to those contrasts which are meaningful. It is possible that this effect of active experience is specific to more robust psychoacoustically based and relatively universal contrasts. Further research is required on this period of development to investigate a number of issues: whether similar effects of experience are obtained for other contrasts; whether nonphonemic contrasts can be discriminated but not identified; whether selective attention to phonemic contrasts occurs for other continua; and whether childrens' attention can be redirected by short-term training. Together with other evidence obtained in the experiment, this specific 2- to 6-year-old effect also strengthens the view that infants initially identify speech contrasts but do so noncategorically and in a psychoacoustic mode. When language acquisition directs attention to phonemic contrasts, identification of those, and only those contrasts gradually becomes more categorical such that by adulthood speech is perceived in a phonological (and perhaps automatic) mode. Nevertheless, other evidence suggests that pure all-or-none categorical perception is probably a myth even for adults.

These results were obtained by the development of a procedure for testing identification of speech sounds by infants. While this ISI method has some drawbacks, these are not unknown in a similar discrimination method (the VRISD procedure). The future use of the ISI method should prove helpful in probing more deeply the processes involved in the development of speech perception.

ACKNOWLEDGMENT

Part of the research reported here was supported by grant A283159881 from the Australian Research Grants Scheme to D. K. Burnham and J. E. Clark. The assistance and cooperation of the Health Department of New South Wales, Baby Health Sisters, the Karitane Mothercraft Society and participating mothers and their babies is greatly appreciated. The manuscript benefited from comments and suggestions by S. Andrews and M. Taft. We wish to thank J. Ah Cann for her assistance in testing babies and drawing figures.

REFERENCES

Aslin, R. N. (1981). Experiential influences and sensitive periods in perceptual development: A unified model. In R. N. Aslin, J. R. Alberts, & M. R. Petersen (Eds.), *Development of perception: Psychobiological perspectives* (Vol. 2). Orlando, FL: Academic Press.

Aslin, R. N., Perey, A. J., Hennessy, B., & Pisoni, D. B. (1977, December). *Perceptual analysis of speech sounds by prelinguistic infants: A first report.* Paper presented at the 94th meeting of the Acoustical Society of America, Miami Beach, Florida.

Aslin, R. N., & Pisoni, D. B. (1980a). Effects of early linguistic experience on speech discrimination by infants: A critique of Eilers, Gavin and Wilson. *Child Development, 51,* 107–112.

Aslin, R. N., & Pisoni, D. B. (1980b). Some developmental processes in speech perception. In G. H. Yeni-Komshian, J. F. Kavanagh, & C. A. Ferguson (Eds.), *Child Phonology: Volume 2; Perception.* Orlando, FL: Academic Press.

Aslin, R. N., Pisoni, D. B., Hennessy, B., & Perey, A. J. (1981). Discrimination of VOT by human infants: New findings and implications for the effects of early experience. *Child Development, 52,* 1135–1145.

Aslin, R. N., Pisoni, D. B., & Jusczyk, P. W. (1983). Auditory development and speech perception in infancy. In M. M. Haith & J. J. Campos (Eds.), *Infancy and the biology of development.* Volume 2 of Carmichael's manual of child psychology, fourth edition (P. H. Mussen, series editor). New York: Wiley.

Bornstein, M. H., Kessen, W., & Weiskopf, S. (1976). Color vision and hue categorization in young human infants. *Journal of Experimental Psychology: Human Perception and Performance, 2,* 115–129.

Carney, A. E., Widin, G. P., & Viemeister, N. F. (1977). Noncategorical perception of stop consonants differing in VOT. *Journal of the Acoustical Society of America, 62,* 961–970.

Chomsky, N. (1965). *Aspects of the theory of syntax.* Cambridge, MA: MIT Press.

Cohen, L. B., & Strauss, M. S. (1979). Concept acquisition in the human infant. *Child Development, 50,* 419–424.

Cooper, W. E. (1979). *Speech perception and production: Studies in selective adaptation.* Norwood, NJ: Ablex.

Cutting, J. E. (1982). Plucks and bows are categorically perceived sometimes. *Perception and Psychophysics, 31,* 462–476.

Cutting, J. E., & Rosner, B. S. (1974). Categories and boundaries in speech and music. *Perception and Psychophysics, 16,* 564–570.

Eilers, R. E. (1980). Infant speech perception: History and mystery. In G. H. Yeni-Komshian, J. F. Kavanagh, & C. A. Ferguson (Eds.), *Child phonology. Volume 2; Perception.* Orlando, FL: Academic Press.

Eilers, R. E., Gavin, W., & Wilson, W. R. (1979). Linguistic experience and phonemic perception in infancy: A cross linguistic study. *Child Development, 50,* 14–18.

Eilers, R. E., Gavin, W., & Wilson, W. R. (1980). Effects of early linguistic experience on speech discrimination by infants: A reply. *Child Development, 51,* 113–117.

Eilers, R. E., & Minifie, F. D. (1975). Fricative discrimination in early infancy. *Journal of Speech and Hearing Research, 18,* 158–167.

Eilers, R. E., Wilson, W. R., & Moore, J. M. (1977). Development of changes in speech discrimination in infants. *Journal of Speech and Hearing Research, 20,* 766–780.

Eilers, R. E., Wilson, W. R., & Moore, J. M. (1979). Speech discrimination in the language-innocent and the language-wise: A study in the perception of voice onset time. *Journal of Child Language, 6,* 1–18.

Eimas, P. D. (1975). Auditory and phonetic coding of the cues for speech: Discrimination of the (r-l) distinction by young infants. *Perception and Psychophysics, 18,* 341–347.

Eimas, P. D. (1978). Developmental aspects of speech perception. In R. Held, H. Leibowitz, & H.-L. Teuber (Eds.), *Handbook of sensory physiology: Perception* (Vol. VIII). Berlin: Springer-Verlag.

Eimas, P. D., Cooper, W. E., & Corbit, J. D. (1973). Some properties of linguistic feature detectors. *Perception & Psychophysics, 13,* 247–252.

Eimas, P. D., & Corbit, J. (1973). Selective adaptation of linguistic feature detectors. *Cognitive Psychology, 4,* 99–109.

Eimas, P. D., Siqueland, E. R., Jusczyk, P., & Vigorito, J. (1971). Speech perception in infants. *Science, 171,* 303–306.

Fodor, J. A., Garrett, M. F., & Brill, S. L. (1975). Pi ka pu: The perception of speech sounds by prelinguistic infants. *Perception and Psychophysics, 18,* 74–78.

Goto, H. (1971). Auditory perception by normal Japanese adults of the sounds L and R. *Neuropsychologia 9,* 317.

Hary, J. M., & Massaro, D. W. (1982). Categorical results do not imply categorical perception. *Perception and Psychophysics, 32,* 409–418.

Hillenbrand, J., Minifie, F. D., & Edwards, T. J. (1979). Tempo of spectrum change as a cue in speech sound discrimination by infants. *Journal of Speech and Hearing Research, 22,* 147–165.

Hirsh, I. J. (1959). Auditory perception of temporal order. *Journal of the Acoustical Society of America, 31,* 759–767.

Holmberg, T. L., Morgan, K. A., & Kuhl, P. K. (1977, December). *Speech perception in early infancy: Discrimination of fricative consonants.* Paper presented at the 94th meeting of the Acoustical Society of America, Miami Beach.

Jakobson, R. (1968). *Child language, aphasia, and phonological universals.* The Hague: Mouton.

Jusczyk, P. W. (1981a). Infant speech perception: A critical appraisal. In P. D. Eimas & J. L. Miller (Eds.), *Perspectives on the study of speech.* Hillsdale, NJ: Lawrence Erlbaum Associates.

Jusczyk, P. W. (1981b). The processing of speech and nonspeech sounds by infants: Some implications. In R. N. Aslin, J. R. Alberts, & M. R. Petersen (Eds.), *Development of perception: Psychobiological perspectives.* (Vol. 1). Orlando, FL: Academic Press.

Jusczyk, P. W. (1984). On characterizing the development of speech perception. In J. Mehler & R. Fox (Eds.), *Neonate cognition: Beyond the blooming, buzzing confusion.* Hillsdale, NJ: Lawrence Erlbaum Associates.

Jusczyk, P. W., Pisoni, D. B., Walley, A., & Murray, J. (1980). Discrimination of relative onset time of two-component tones by infants. *Journal of the Acoustical Society of America, 67,* 262–270.

Jusczyk, P. W., Rosner, B. S., Cutting, J. E., Foard, G. F., & Smith, L. B. (1977). Categorical perception of nonspeech sounds by 2-month-old infants. *Perception and Psychophysics, 21,* 50–54.

Kuhl, P. K. (1978). Predispositions for the perception of speech-sound categories: A species-specific phenomenon? In F. D. Minifie, & L. L. Lloyd (Eds.), *Communicative and cognitive abilities: Early behavioral assessment.* Baltimore: University Park Press.

Kuhl, P. K., & Miller, J. D. (1975). Speech perception by the chinchilla: Voiced-voiceless distinction in alveolar plosive consonants. *Science, 190,* 69–72.

Kuhl, P. K., & Miller, J. D. (1978). Speech perception by the chinchilla: Identification functions for synthetic VOT stimuli. *Journal of the Acoustical Society of America, 63,* 905–917.

Kuhl, P. K., & Padden, D. M. (1982). Enhanced discriminability at the phonetic boundaries for the voicing feature in macaques. *Perception and Psychophysics, 32,* 542–550.

Kuhl, P. K., & Padden, D. M. (1983). Enhanced discriminability at the phonetic boundaries for the place feature in macaques. *Journal of the Acoustical Society of America, 73,* 1003–1010.

Lasky, R. E., Syrdal-Lasky, A., & Klein, R. E. (1975). VOT discrimination by 4- to 6-month-old infants from Spanish environments. *Journal of Experimental Child Psychology, 20,* 215–225.

Liberman, A. M. (1970). Some characteristics of perception in the speech mode. In D. A. Hamberg (Ed.), *Perception and its disorders: Proceedings of the Association for Research in Nervous and Mental Disorders.* Baltimore: Williams and Wilkins.

Liberman, A. M., Cooper, F. S., Shankweiler, D. P., & Studdert-Kennedy, M. (1967). Perception of the speech code. *Psychological Review, 74,* 431–461.

Liberman, A. M., Harris, K. S., Hoffman, H. S., & Griffith, B. C. (1957). The discrimination of speech sounds within and across phoneme boundaries. *Journal of Experimental Psychology, 54,* 358–368.

Liberman, A. M., Harris, K. S., Kinney, J. A., & Lane, H. (1961). The discrimination of relative onset-time of the components of certain speech and nonspeech patterns. *Journal of Experimental Psychology, 61,* 379–388.

Liberman, A. M., Ingemann, F., Lisker, L., DeLattre, P., & Cooper, F. S. (1959). Minimal rules for synthesising speech. *Journal of the Acoustical Society of America, 31,* 1490–1499.

Lisker, L., & Abramson, A. S. (1964). A cross-language study of voicing in initial stops: Acoustic measurements. *Word, 20,* 384–422.

Mattingly, I. G., Liberman, A. M., Syrdal, A. K., & Halwes, T. (1971). Discrimination in speech and non-speech modes. *Cognitive Psychology, 2,* 131–157.

Miyawaki, K., Strange, W., Verbrugge, R., Liberman, A., Jenkins, J. J., & Fujimura, O. (1975). An effect of linguistic experience: The discrimination of [r] and [l] by native speakers of Japanese and English. *Perception and Psychophysics, 18,* 331–340.

Morse, P. A. (1978). Infant speech perception: Origins, processes, and Alpha Centauri. In F. D. Minifie & L. L. Lloyd (Eds.), *Communicative and cognitive abilities: Early behavioral assessment.* Baltimore: University Park Press.

Morse, P. A., & Snowdon, C. T. (1975). An investigation of categorical speech discrimination by rhesus monkeys. *Perception and Psychophysics, 17,* 9–16.

Pisoni, D. B. (1977). Identification and discrimination of the relative onset time of two-component tones: Implications for voicing perception in stops. *Journal of the Acoustical Society of America, 61,* 1352–1361.

Pisoni, D. B. (1980). Adaptation of the relative onset time of two-component tones. *Perception and Psychophysics, 28,* 337–346.

Pisoni, D. B., & Lazarus, J. H. (1974). Categorical and noncategorical modes of speech perception along the voicing continuum. *Journal of the Acoustical Society of America, 55,* 328–333.

Pisoni, D. B., & Tash, J. (1974). Reaction times to comparisons within and across phonetic categories. *Perception and Psychophysics, 15,* 285–290.

Pisoni, D. B., & Tash, J. (1975). Auditory property detectors and processing place features in stop consonants. *Perception and Psychophysics, 18,* 401–408.

Remez, R. E. (1979). Adaptation of the category boundary between speech and non-speech: A case against feature detectors. *Cognitive Psychology, 11,* 38–57.

Rosen, S. M., & Howell, P. (1981). Plucks and bows are not categorically perceived. *Perception and Psychophysics, 30,* 156–168.

Schneider, W., & Shiffrin, R. M. (1977). Controlled and automatic human information processing: I. Detection, search and attention. *Psychological Review, 84,* 1–66.

Simon, H. J., & Studdert-Kennedy, M. (1978). Selective anchoring and adaptation of phonetic and nonphonetic continua. *Journal of the Acoustical Society of America, 64,* 1338–1357.

Sinnott, J. M., Pisoni, D. B., & Aslin, R. N. (1983). A comparison of pure tone auditory thresholds in human infants and adults. *Infant Behavior and Development, 6,* 3–17.

Stevens, K. N. (1972). The quantal nature of speech. In E. E. David, Jr. & P. B. Denes (Eds.), *Human communication: A unified view.* New York: McGraw-Hill.

Strauss, M. S. (1979). Abstraction of prototypical information by adults and 10-month-old infants. *Journal of Experimental Psychology: Human Learning and Memory, 5,* 618–632.

Streeter, L. A. (1976a). Kikuyu labial and apical stop discrimination. *Journal of Phonetics, 4,* 43–51.

Streeter, L. A. (1976b). Language perception of 2-month-old infants shows effects of both innate mechanisms and experience. *Nature, 259,* 39–41.

Studdert-Kennedy, M., Liberman, A. M., Harris, K. S., & Cooper, F. S. (1970). Theoretical notes: Motor theory of speech perception; A reply to Lane's critical review. *Psychological Review, 77,* 234–249.

Trehub, S. E. (1976). The discrimination of foreign speech contrasts by infants and adults. *Child Development, 47,* 466–472.

Trehub, S. E. (1979). Reflections on the development of speech perception. *Canadian Journal of Psychology, 33,* 368–381.

Walley, A. C., Pisoni, D. B., & Aslin, R. N. (1981). The role of early experience in the development of speech perception. In R. N. Aslin, J. Alberts, & M. J. Petersen (Eds.), *The development of perception: Psychobiological perspectives* (Vol. 1). Orlando, FL: Academic Press.

Werker, J. F., Gilbert, J. H. V., Humphrey, K., & Tees, R. C. (1981). Developmental aspects of cross-language speech perception. *Child Development, 52,* 349–355.

Werker, J. F., & Tees, R. C. (1983). Developmental changes across childhood in the perception of non-native speech sounds. *Canadian Journal of Psychology, 37,* 278–286.

Werker, J. F., & Tees, R. C. (1984). Cross-language speech perception: Evidence for perceptual reorganisation during the first year of life. *Infant Behavior and Development, 7,* 49–63.

Williams, L. (1977a). The perception of stop-consonant voicing by Spanish-English bilinguals. *Perception and Psychophysics, 21,* 289–297.

Williams, L. (1977b). Voicing contrasts in Spanish. *Journal of Phonetics, 5,* 169–184.

Zlatin, M. A., & Koenigsknecht, R. A. (1975). Development of the voicing contrast: Perception of stop consonants. *Journal of Speech and Hearing Research, 18,* 541–553.

V A CONCLUDING COMMENTARY

12 Perceptual Development in Infancy: Reflections on Some Central Issues

B. E. McKenzie
La Trobe University

R. H. Day
Monash University

In this final commentary we do not propose to summarize what has already been stated or to dwell further on issues already dealt with at length in the preceding chapters. Rather, we propose to highlight some emergent themes and to offer some speculations on the directions in which further research might usefully be developed.

We first discuss theoretical implications by way of two illustrations. The first relates to the debate on direct versus indirect perception and the second to the nature of representation of invisible objects. The value of research with very young subjects has long been recognized as contributing towards more general theories of mental representation. We conclude that there is still much gold to be won from this lode. The second theme concerns an increasing emphasis on process rather than product in perceptual development. Whereas earlier research sought to exhibit the competence of the young infant, the work described in the preceding chapters bears closely on the processes that underlie perceptual abilities and the limitations of these processes. Much recent research samples a single aspect of perceptual development and examines performance for different subjects at several ages. We suggest that a prime requirement for a fuller understanding of the processes involved is greater concentration on longitudinal studies over several aspects. There have been few attempts to develop more general models of perceptual development. A first step in the construction of such a model is the establishment of sequential relationships between different abilities. A second step in the validation of the model is to establish that treatment of a precursor ability has specific consequences for the later development of a target ability but not for another, i.e., for a control ability. There have been many cross-sectional analyses of separate capacities but few longitudinal studies whose aim is to establish sequential dependencies between these capacities. The third theme concerns individual differences, and particularly the use of habituation scores as predictors of concurrent and later cognitive status. It is now clear that habituation and familiarity measures are better predictors of later status than are standard infant psychometric tests. The kinds of processes underlying this continuity in development remain to be established.

THEORETICAL IMPLICATIONS

In Chapter 2 Crassini outlines some of the difficulties involved in the comparison of various theoretical approaches to perceptual development. Although his discussion concentrates largely on the classical philosophical positions that predate the scientific study of mind and behavior, the issues remain as relevant to current debates as they were to the early "baby biographers." We shall discuss two examples, the first concerning the effect of memory on the perception of object distance and the second, the nature of early notions about the properties of solid objects.

In studying the effectiveness of familiarity with the size of an object as a cue to its distance from the observer, Granrud, Haake, and Yonas (1985) conclude that "perception of distance from familiar size can only be a case of enrichment or indirect perception in which the perceiver uses knowledge stored in memory to extract information from otherwise uninformative visual input" (p.18). Indirect or constructivist theory (e.g., Rock, 1983) is contrasted with direct perception theory (Gibson, 1979). Processes that enrich sensory data are considered necessary in the former but in the latter no such mediation is required. For Gibson, veridical visual perception depends on the information contained in the optic array. Granrud and his coworkers found the familiar size of an object to be an effective cue for its distance that becomes operative at some time between 5 and 7 months. Infants were given 10 minutes experience with two objects differing in size and form. They were then presented with two equidistant objects of the same size, one identical to one of the familiar pair, the other matching the remaining one in form but now larger. It was predicted that the object of the smaller familiar size would be perceived as nearer and would therefore elicit more reaching than the other object. This prediction was confirmed for older but not younger infants. Knowledge of the physical size of a pair of different-sized objects induced 7-month-infants to reach preferentially for the apparently nearer of two same-sized objects. However this preference was evident only when infants were tested monocularly, and not when binocular information for actual distance was available. This latter finding is important since it implies that the differential behavior was based neither on generalization of a preference for the smaller and more graspable object nor on preference for a novel object. (One object was identical in all respects over familiarization and test trials, the other only in form.) Had either of these variables applied, there should have been a similar frequency of reaching in monocular and binocular conditions. Granrud et al. concluded therefore that greater reaching for the object of the smaller familiar size was attributable to its perceived apparent distance. That is to say, in accordance with constructivist theory, infants made use of knowledge stored in memory to enrich current visual input. Whether age effects are due to differences in memory or to the relative importance of the various cues for distance is not yet known.

In several respects the findings of this study are surprising. They imply that familiar size dominates or inhibits distance information arising from motion parallax. Regrettably, first trial responses were not treated separately in reporting the data. Only the results of infants who reached for a minimum of 6 trials were retained in the analyses. It might be expected that differential reaching would have declined over later trials where haptic and proprioceptive information about physical size and distance was available. Further, both shape and size constancy have been demonstrated at an earlier age than that of Granrud et al.'s subjects (see Chapters 4 and 5). Their results suggest that with prior visual-haptic experience and monocular testing, veridical perception of an object's physical size, i.e., size constancy, would no longer obtain. This is an important finding that warrants close investigation.

Whatever the outcome of additional investigations, our reason for selecting this particular work for discussion is to illustrate that the theoretical implications of whether or not there is enrichment or consructive processing of "otherwise uninformative visual input" is as pertinent today as it was to the ancients whose views are dealt with by Crassini. However, we have the advantage of more powerful weapons with which to attack the problem.

The second example of a recent study that has theoretical implications concerns early conceptions about the properties of objects. As Burnham (Chapter 7) has already indicated, there is vigorous debate about the Piagetian interpretation of infant responses to an object's disappearance. Burnham also evaluates critically the work of Bower (1974) in this respect. Baillargeon, Spelke, and Wasserman (1985), like Burnham, sought a method to investigate notions of object permanence that did not rely on manual search. They, too, used an habituation-dishabituation paradigm based on duration of looking at event sequences. Infants aged 5 months were first habituated to the back-and-forth movement of a screen through 180°. After habituation, a box was placed behind the screen so that it was interpolated in the path previously taken by the screen. Infants were then shown a possible and an impossible event. In the possible event the screen moved as before but stopped when it reached the box; in the impossible event it appeared to move through the space occupied by the box. (This event was presented by using two alleys containing identical screens and separated by a one-way mirror; the lighting was switched from one alley to another at critical times.) Infants looked longer at the impossible event sequence despite the fact that the screen moved in this sequence in a manner identical to its movement during habituation. A control experiment showed that there was no preference for the complete over the truncated movement. These results were interpreted to mean that infants appreciated that the box continued to exist while it was occluded by the screen. That is, even at 5-months-of-age it was recognized as having some permanence while out of sight. The results also imply knowledge that solid objects do not move through a space that is already occupied by another solid object. Spelke (in press) argues that infants have several basic conceptions about the nature of the physical world: objects exist continuously in time and space, they continue to exist from one point in time to another and from one place in space to another; they continue to exist when out of sight and can only move through unoccupied space; they tend to move on undeviating paths and begin to move only when contacted by other objects.

Although it has become evident that Piaget's timetable for the construction of notions of the physical world such as time, space, number, and causality need revision, it is not yet clear whether these notions are present at the very beginning, what their limitations are or how they are represented. It is very difficult to refer to such phenomena in other than conceptual terms. They suggest the existence of implicit automatic information acquisition processes rather than the protracted construction of representations of reality based on the detection of piece-meal characteristics of objects and events that gradually become coordinated. If the identification of objects and events is the primary task of the perceptual systems, the ability to make such identifications is simplified to the extent that they respond to higher rather than lower order elements.

PROCESS RATHER THAN OUTCOME ORIENTATION

A pervasive emphasis in preceding chapters is the attempt to specify the processes that may be involved in the different areas. It has been noted by Day (Chapter 4) that visual size constancy—the perception of the true physical size of an object at different distances—has been studied in early infancy using various experimental methods. Granrud (1986) has also found that infants as young as 4-months-of-age exhibit size constancy. In a series of experiments with 4- and 5-month-old infants he found binocular depth perception to be more veridical than monocular depth perception. Infants who were sensitive to binocular disparity perceived the relative distance of objects more accurately than those who were not. They reached more precisely for the nearer of two objects and this superiority was evident only under binocular viewing. Because accurate size perception depends on perceived distance and since Granrud had shown that infants sensitive to binocular disparity had more veridical distance perception, it was predicted that size constancy should be more evident in these infants than in those without such sensitivity. This prediction was supported. Development of disparity sensitivity was concomitant with enhancement in the perception of both distance and physical size of objects. Granrud notes that these findings provide unambiguous evidence of substantial developmental change in spatial perception between the ages of 4 and 5 months.

It is difficult to attribute this change to mechanisms unrelated to space perception since both the disparity-sensitive and the disparity-insensitive group were similar in accuracy of reaching and motivation to reach when tested monocularly. Thus, not only can infants begin to *detect* binocular disparity at around 4 months, they can also *use* this information to perceive the depth that is specified by it. The generality of this conclusion was supported using indices of visually-guided reaching to objects at different distances and dishabituation of looking to an object of novel size independent of its distance and the visual angle subtended by it. It would be of considerable interest to establish whether or not infants who are sensitive to binocular disparity are also advanced in tests of shape constancy.

Yonas and Granrud (1985) propose a developmental sequence in detection of various kinds of optical information for depth. An initial dependence on kinetic information produced by motion in light reaching the eyes is followed at around 4 months by sensitivity to binocular information and still later at around 5 to 7 months by sensitivity to pictorial depth cues such as interposition, shading and texture gradients. The question arises as to whether perception of the physical size and shape of objects varies with the kind of information that is made available. Granrud's findings (1986) suggest that the development of stereopsis adds significantly to the accuracy of spatial perception at least with respect to relative distance and physical size. It is conceivable that perception of these features on the basis of pictorial depth cues does not occur until later. To our knowledge there is as yet no data to confirm or reject this suggestion.

In the absence of surface and contour information, Börjesson and von Hofsten (1973) observed that adults viewing binocularly perceive translation in depth on the basis of retinal motion toward a common point. This principle of event perception seems also to obtain for 4-month-old infants (Kellman, von Hofsten, & Soares, 1985) with binocular viewing. When three points of light in a dark surround move in a frontoparallel plane toward and away from a central point, infants, like adults, perceive this concurrent motion as translation in depth. From the developmental sequence described earlier it could be predicted that this kind of event perception might be possible prior to the development of stereopsis.

The studies that have been described in this section have used a cross-sectional method. The sequence of detection of various depth cues is inferred from independent samples of infants of different ages. From such cross-sectional studies it is possible to establish that, in general a certain sequence obtains. Longitudinal studies provide a more direct and sensitive measure that allows us to conclude for each subject whether or not the sequence holds. In addition it is possible to establish that outcome X never occurs without the earlier occurrence of outcomes A and B. In order to ascertain that outcome A for example is functionally related to outcome X it would also need to be shown that it can be influenced by prior treatment of outcome A, and that this treatment has no effect on outcome Y (see above). By testing the one sample of subjects on several tests of perceptual abilities at different times, it would be possible to postulate functional dependences between them. Of course, the mere concomitance in appearance of new abilities does not establish their mutual interdependence. Nor does the earlier occurrence of a perceptual ability imply a functional relationship with a later one. However once a model is proposed on the basis of longitudinal results, sequential dependencies can be ascertained by experimental treatments. So far there have been few studies of this kind in the area of perceptual development. A program of such studies would go some way toward establishing whether such dependencies of later developing abilities on earlier ones is a feature of perceptual development. An answer to this question would clearly have important practical as well as theoretical implications.

INDIVIDUAL DIFFERENCES

It is only recently that the issue of differences between infants in response to environmental stimulation has received close attention. Measures of habituation, for example, have been shown to vary with such factors as prematurity (Caron & Caron, 1981), neurological status at birth (Lewis, Bartels, Campbell, & Goldberg, 1967) and maternal stimulation (Riksen-Walraven, 1978). With appropriate experimental control it can be shown that the process underlying habituation is not sensory adaptation, effector-fatigue or generalized decrement in arousal. Rather some active construction that reflects information processing is inferred and used to index perceptual discrimination, categorization, memory and concept formation. It is to be expected therefore that measures of habituation would correlate with other concurrent indices of information processing (e.g., rate of acquisition of an acquired association) and perhaps be predictive of later levels of intellectual functioning.

   With regard to concurrent measures the picture is complex. First the reliability of the measures needs to be established. Although there appears to be acceptable reliability of habituation indices within the one modality (Bornstein, 1985) indices derived from different modalities may show little correspondence. The habituation functions for visual fixation and heart rate, for example, may vary even when measured simultaneously to the same stimulus (McCall, 1979). These differential functions suggest the possibility that there is no single central mediating process (see Finlay & Ivinskis, Chapter 3). However, the measures of attention decrement and response recovery correlate moderately and their validity as an index of cognitive functioning is suggested by the association between them and a range of other cognitive skills (Bornstein & Sigman, 1986). It is also argued that decrement and recovery of attention "predict childhood cognitive competence more accurately than do traditional infant developmental tests . . . Whereas traditional infant tests account for between 0% and 8% of the variance in childhood intelligence (Median = 2%), at this time the attention measures account for between 8% and 59% (Median = 21%),'' (Bornstein & Sigman, 1986, p. 256). Whether this moderate continuity in cognitive development can be attributed to common underlying processes of a cognitive or motivational nature is not known.

In the study of perceptual discrimination of stimulus objects and events it has been observed that there are infants who show immediate spontaneous discrimination, those who do so only after some period of familiarization of habituation, and those who show no discrimination even after extensive exposure. Do these differences reflect a wider developmental difference in other areas, for example, in style of processing, in memory capacity, or in general intelligence? It may be profitable to analyze the performance of subgroups across a range of tasks and at different points in time in order to uncover the source of differences between subjects.

The significance of the kind of attention displayed towards objects has been emphasized in a recent report by Ruff (1986). She investigated exploratory manipulation in 6- to 12-months-old infants, and, like Berlyne (1970), distinguished between the intensive and selective aspects of attention. The intensity of attention was measured by Ruff as episodes when the infant, as judged by the experimenter, appeared to be concentrating on the object. These episodes of focused attention which Ruff called "examining" included looking at the object with an intent expression and simultaneous active manipulation of it. They constituted only 25% to 40% of the total duration of looking and clearly exclude casual or passive looking. The latency to examine and the duration of examining reflect different aspects of attention and are differentially related to other variables. Duration was not consistently related to age but decreased with familiarity and increased with novelty. Latency decreased with age but was relatively insensitive to familiarity-novelty. The strength of Ruff's studies lies in the "fine-grain" analysis of behavior. Her data suggest that what has frequently been treated as a unitary phenomenon may in fact consist of several separate processes. An implication of her findings is that there is much more to observe than merely duration of looking, the stock-in-trade of most habituation studies. Attention conceived of as examining, involving as it seems to do a number of components can not be easily accessed by so coarse a measure as duration of looking. What is clearly called for to capture fully the character of attention is a number of simultaneous measurements.

A CONCLUDING COMMENT

The three themes discussed above—theoretical implications, concern with processes, and individual differences—are by no means exhaustive. There are no doubt numerous others. The research reported in this collection of chapters while bearing on these unresolved issues has nevertheless settled, or gone some way toward settling, others. Together the findings indicate considerable progress. The themes we have raised in this last chapter may serve as pointers to where further research might profitably be directed and how that research might usefully be conducted. Our final comment is that while progress in the study of different areas of infant perception—spatial localization, form perception, auditory localization—has been gratifying, we seem still to be a long way from a more general theory to guide our enquiry. It is not too much to hope that reformulation of old concepts like attention and a vigorous pursuit of new methods—like Burnham's for infant identification of speech sounds—might lead more directly than hitherto to some general theoretical model. It is conceivable that this hope might be more quickly realized by a greater concentration on longitudinal than on cross-sectional experiments. The former stands more effectively to reveal inter relationships between the separate strands of infant perception to which the various studies reported here have been directed.

ACKNOWLEDGMENT

The thesis outlined in this section owes much to discussions with Professor Over. We gratefully acknowledge his contribution.

REFERENCES

Baillargeon, R., Spelke, E. S., & Wasserman, S. (1985). Object permanence in five-month-old infants. *Cognition, 20,* 191–208.

Berlyne, D. B. (1970). Attention as a problem in behavior theory. In D. I. Mostofsky (Ed.), *Attention: Contemporary theory and analysis.* New York: Appleton-Century-Crofts.

Börjesson, E., & Hofsten, C. von (1973). Visual perception of motion in depth: Application of a vector model to three-dot motion patterns. *Perception and Psychophysics, 13,* 169–179.

Bornstein, M. H. (1985). Habituation of attention as a measure of visual information processing in human infants: Summary, systemization, and synthesis. In G. Gottlieb & N. A. Krasnegor (Eds.), *Development of audition and vision during the first year of postnatal life: A methodological overview.* Norwood, NJ: Ablex.

Bornstein, M. H., & Sigman, M. D. (1986). Continuity in mental development from infancy. *Child Development, 57,* 251–274.

Bower, T. G. R. (1974). *Development in infancy.* San Francisco: Freeman.

Caron, A. J., & Caron, R. F. (1981) Processing of relational information as an index of infant risk. In S. L. Friedman & M. Sigman (Eds.), *Preterm birth and psychological development.* Orlando, FL: Academic Press.

Gibson, J. J. (1979) *The ecological approach to visual perception.* Boston: Houghton Mifflin.

Granrud, C. E. (1986). Binocular vision and spatial perception in 4- and 5-month-old infants. *Journal of Experimental Psychology: Human Perception and Performance, 12,* 36–49.

Granrud, C. E., Haake, R. J., & Yonas, A. (1985). Infants' sensitivity to familiar size: The effect of memory on spatial perception. *Perception and Psychophysics, 37,* 459–466.

Kellman, P. J., von Hofsten, C., & Soares, J. (1985, April). *Concurrent motion in infant event perception.* Paper presented at the Biennial Meeting of the Society for Research in Child Development, Toronto, Canada.

Lewis, M., Bartels, B., Campbell, H., & Goldberg, J. (1967). Individual differences in attention: The relationship between infants' condition at birth and attention distribution within the first year. *American Journal of Diseases of Children, 113,* 461–465.

McCall, R. B. (1979). Individual differences in the pattern of habituation at 5 and 10 months of age. *Developmental Psychology, 15,* 559–569.

Riksen-Walraven, J. M. (1978). Effects of caregiver behavior on habituation rate and self-efficacy in infants. *International Journal of Behavioral Development, 1,* 105–130.

Rock, I. (1983). *The logic of perception.* Cambridge, MA: MIT Press.

Ruff, H. A. (1986). Components of attention during infants' manipulative exploration. *Child Development, 57,* 105–114.

Spelke, E. S. (1985, November). *Object perception and the object concept in infancy.* Paper presented at the Minnesota Symposium on Child Development, Minneapolis.

Yonas, A., & Granrud, C. E. (1985). The development of the sensitivity to kinetic, binocular, and pictorial depth information in human infants. In D. Ingle, D. Lee, & M. Jeannerod (Eds.), *Brain mechanisms and spatial vision.* Dordrecht, Netherlands: Martinus Nijhoff.

Author Index

D

Dannemiller, J.L., 6, *15*, 74, *89*
Darwin, C., 37, 38, 39, 40, 41, 42, *44*, 143, *170*
David, E.E. Jnr., *275*
Day, R.H., 48, 58, *62, 63*, 67, 72, 73, 75, 78, 79–86, *89, 90*, 97, 98, 99, 100, 104, 106, 120, *123*, 125, 128, 130, 131, 134, 135, 136, 137, 138, 139, *141*, 143, 145–50, 152, 153, 156–62, 166–68, *169, 170, 171*, 202, 204, 205, 210, *217*, 282
De Boysson-Bardies, B., 14, *15*
De Casper, A.J., 12, *15*
De Lattre, P., 237, *274*
De Leon, J.L., 200, *216*
De Loache, J.S., 47, *62*, 84, 85, *88*, 98, 99, *123*, 135, *141*
Denes, P.B., *275*
Denis-Prinzhorn, M., 70, *89*
Denner, B., 200, *216*
Dennis, W., 26, 27, 31, 32, 34, 38, *44*
Descartes, R., 37
de Schonen, S., 79, *89*
de Witt, J., *233*
Dickinson, R.G., 146–48, 166, *169, 170*
Dobson, M.V., 48, *63*, 83, 86, *91*, 143, 145, *171*
Dobson, V., 4, *15*, 54, *62*
Dowling, K., 146, *170*
Doxsey, P.A., 131, 137, 138, 141
Drever, J., 76, *89*
Dumais, S.T., 54, *61*, 106, *123*
Durand, C., 14, *15*

E

Ebenholtz, S., 87, *91*
Edgren, R.D., 71, *89*
Edwards, T.J., 255, *273*
Eilers, R.E., 238, 240, 244, 245, 246, 247, 248, 251, 252, 253, 255, *273*
Eimas, P.D., 237, 240, 241, 246, 248, 251, 257, 269, 270, *273*
Endman, M., 10, *15*
Enright, M., 13, *16*
Epstein, W., 87, 88, *89*
Evans, D., 128, 133, 135, *140*
Ewert, J.P., 87, *89*, 157, *170*

F

Fagan, J.F., 8, *16*, 48, *62*, 73, *89*, 200, 208, 213, *216*
Fagan, J.W., 13, *16*, 202, *217*
Fantz, R.L., 13, *16*, 48, *62*, 73, 74, 80, *89, 90*, 99, *123*, 145, *170*, 199, *216*
Fearing F., 37, *44*
Fechner, G.T., 69, *89*
Fenson, L., 213, *216*
Ferguson, C.A., *272, 273*
Field, C.J., 190, 191, 192, *195*
Field, J., 79, *89, 90*, 99, 112, 113, 114, 116, *123*, 137, *141, 169, 170*, 180, 182, 184, 185, 186, *195, 197*
Field, T.M., 220, 222, 225, 226, *232, 233*
Fifer, W.P., 13, *15*
Finlay, D., 51, 53, 54, 56, 58, *62*, 152, *169, 170*, 284
Fisher-Fay, 183, 184, *196*
Flavell, J.H., *16*
Foard, G.F., 241, 242, *274*
Fodor, J.A., 258, *273*
Forbes, B., 180, 185, *196*
Forster, F.M., 188, *195*
Forsyth, G.A., 156, 162, 167, *170*
Fox, R., 106, *123*, 146, 166, *170, 274*
Fox-Kolenda, B.J., 189, 190, 191, *195*
Fraiberg, S., 189, 191, *195*
Freedman, D.A., 189, 190, 191, *195*
Freese, L.J., *15*
Friedman, M.P., *169, 197*
Friedman, S.L., *15*, 286
French, J., 54, *62*
Frye, D., 232, *233*
Fujimura, O., 246, 251, *274*

G

Gardner, H., 10, *17*, 220, *233*
Gardner, J., 220, *233*
Garino, E., 131, 132, 137, 139, *141*
Garrett, M.F., *17*, 258, *273*
Gatehouse, R.W., *196*
Gavin, W., 244–46, *273*
Gayl, I.E., 4, *16*
Gebauer, L., 157, *170*
Gelber, E.R., 213, *216*
Gesell, A., 79, *89*
Gibson, E.J., 4, 8, 9, *16*, 42, *44*, 58, *62*, 77,

Subject Index